Entrepreneurship in Ireland

Entrepreneurship in Ireland

Bernard O'Hara

Gill & Macmillan

Gill & Macmillan Ltd
Hume Avenue
Park West
Dublin 12
with associated companies throughout the world www.gillmacmillan.ie

978 07171 4976 6

Index compiled by Cover to Cover
Print origination in Ireland by TypeIT, Dublin
Printed by GraphyGems, Spain

The paper used in this book is made from the wood pulp of managed forests. For every tree felled, at least one tree is planted, thereby renewing natural resources.

Disclaimer
Statements in this book are made in good faith to provide general information on a range of business topics which are subject to constant change. They should not be regarded as comprehensive or for use without professional advice. Specific professional advice should be obtained at all times. Neither the publisher nor the author accepts any responsibility for any loss arising from any action taken or not taken by anyone using this material.

For my wife, Mary, and our family

CONTENTS

Appendices

LIST OF FIGURES

LIST OF TABLES

LIST OF ABBREVIATIONS

ABC	Activity-Based Costing
AEO	Authorised Economic Operator
AGM	Annual General Meeting
AIM	Alternative Investment Market (UK)
AMRF	Approved Minimum Retirement Fund
AMTs	Advanced Manufacturing Technologies
APR	Annualised Percentage Rate (of interest)
ARD	Annual Return Date
ARF	Approved Retirement Fund
AVC	Additional Voluntary Contribution
BCG	Boston Consulting Group
BES	Business Expansion Scheme
BIC	Bank Identifier Code
BIC	Business Innovation Centre
BPR	Business Process Re-engineering
BRIC	Brazil, Russia, India, China
CA	Companies Acts
CAD	Computer-Aided Design
CAM	Computer-Aided Manufacturing
CAT	Capital Acquisitions Tax
CEBs	County Enterprise Boards
CIM	Computer Integrated Manufacturing
CIP	Competitiveness and Innovation Programme
CRO	Companies Registration Office
CSETs	Centres for Science, Engineering and Technology
CSO	Central Statistics Office
CTM	Community Trade Mark
CV	Curriculum Vitae
DPP	Director of Public Prosecutions
EAT	Employment Appeals Tribunal
EC	European Community
ECB	European Central Bank
EEA	European Economic Area
EEC	European Economic Community

EGM	Extraordinary General Meeting
EIC	European Information Centres
EIF	European Investment Fund
EMS	European Monetary System
EPA	Environmental Protection Agency
ERG	Existence-Related Growth
EU	European Union
FDI	Foreign Direct Investment
FMS	Flexible Manufacturing System
FRS	Financial Reporting Standard
GATT	General Agreement on Tariffs and Trade
GDP	Gross Domestic Product (the value of all goods and services produced in a country's economy during a specific period)
GNP	Gross National Product (the value of all goods and services produced in a country's economy during a specific period which is retained there after deducting the value of net payments overseas, especially, in the case of Ireland, profit repatriation by multinational corporations)
GPA	Government Procurement Agreement
HEA	Higher Education Authority
HETAC	Higher Education Training Awards Council
HPSU	High Potential Start-Up
HRB	Health Research Board
HRM	Human Resource Management
HSA	Health and Safety Authority
IBAN	International Bank Account Number
IBEC	Irish Business and Employers Confederation
ICSTI	Irish Council for Science, Technology and Innovation
ICT	Information and Communications Technology
ICTU	Irish Congress of Trade Unions
IDA	Industrial Development Authority
IEX	Irish Enterprise Exchange
IFSC	Irish Financial Services Centre
IPO	Initial Public Offering
IPPC	Integration Pollution Prevention Control
IRCHSS	Irish Research Council for Humanities and Social Sciences
IRCSET	Irish Research Council for Science, Engineering and Technology
ISO	International Standards Organisation
JIT	Just in Time
JLC	Joint Labour Committee

KPIs	Key Performance Indicators
LRC	Labour Relations Commission
MBI	Management Buy-In
MEBO	Management Employee Buy-Out
MBO	Management by Objectives
MBO	Management Buy-Out
MEAT	Most Economically Advantageous Tender
MRP	Materials Requirements Planning
NAMA	National Asset Management Agency
NASDAQ	National Association of Securities Dealers Automated Quotation (USA)
NCA	National Consumer Agency
NCB	National City Brokers
NDP	National Development Plan
NERA	National Employment Rights Authority
NESC	National Economic and Social Council
NQAI	National Qualifications Authority of Ireland
NSAI	National Standards Authority of Ireland
NSS	National Spatial Strategy
ODCE	Office of the Director of Corporate Enforcement
ODI	Outward Direct Investment
OECD	Organisation for Economic Co-operation and Development
OJEU	Official Journal of the European Union
OPS	Occupational Pension Scheme
OPT	Optimised Production Technology
PAYE	Pay As You Earn
P/E	Price/Earnings (ratio)
PEST	Political-legal, Economic, Socio-cultural and Technological
PIN	Prior Information Notice
PLC	Public Limited Company
PPPs	Public Private Partnerships
PPSN	Personal Public Service Number
PRSA	Personal Retirement Savings Account
PR	Public Relations
PRSI	Pay Related Social Insurance
PRTLI	Programme for Research in Third-Level Institutions
P/V	Profit/Volume (ratio)
R&D	Research and Development
RAC	Retirement Annuity Contract
ROCE	Return on Capital Employed

ROS	Revenue Online Service
S	Section (of an Act)
SART	Self Administered Retirement Trust
SCS	Seed Capital Scheme
SEO	Search Engine Optimisation
SFI	Science Foundation Ireland
SI	Statutory Instrument
SMART	Specific, Measurable, Attainable, Realistic, Time-bound
SMEs	Small and Medium Enterprises
SRCs	Strategic Research Clusters
SRCOP	Standard Rate Cut-Off Point
SWOT	Strengths, Weaknesses, Opportunities, Threats
TQM	Total Quality Management
WCM	World-Class Manufacturing
WTO	World Trade Organisation
UK	United Kingdom
USA	United States of America
USC	Universal Social Charge
USP	Unique Selling Proposition
VAT	Value Added Tax
VIES	VAT Information Exchange System
VRT	Vehicle Registration Tax

Foreword

Entrepreneurship will be a key component of future economic growth. Entrepreneurs and the new business start-ups that they create are now widely recognised as a major engine of economic and social development in our economy. While the obvious benefits of new jobs and wealth creation are clear to see, entrepreneurs also play a pivotal role in the effective operation of the market economy. They act as a catalyst for the commercialisation of research, new technologies and ideas, creating new industries and markets. They drive increased competition within and across borders as new companies enter the marketplace and force existing players to become more efficient and productive. They deliver new innovative products, services and customer solutions to growing world markets. Ultimately, the rewards and benefits extend not just to the entrepreneur and the economy, but to the end customers who receive a better choice, quality, service and price.

Ireland has a strong culture of entrepreneurship and we rank highly in international comparisons in terms of new start-ups per capita. Ireland is an ideal location to start and grow a business. The World Bank's *Doing Business 2010* report rates Ireland as the easiest place in the European Union (EU) to start a business and as having the most business-friendly tax regime of any country in Europe or the Americas. Ireland is now widely recognised as a pro-business environment, with a range of supports and policies in place to drive new business start-ups and assist entrepreneurs on their journey from idea generation to company growth. This book provides a comprehensive guide to the start-up environment in Ireland and introduces entrepreneurs to the range of State supports available locally and nationally.

Enterprise Ireland welcomes this publication as a valuable resource for all students of entrepreneurship (regardless of their academic discipline) and prospective entrepreneurs. It is also a practical reference book for entrepreneurs and start-up managers that are currently in the process of planning and setting up their new business ventures.

While entrepreneurs have the essential characteristics needed to start and grow a business – drive, commitment, determination and vision – these characteristics alone are not enough to guarantee success. Effective market research, business planning and the ability to manage the implementation of your business plan are all fundamental requirements for new business success. If you 'fail to plan you plan to fail'. This book allows entrepreneurs to understand, plan and manage all key aspects of starting a business and will no doubt assist, guide and motivate future generations of innovative entrepreneurs.

Frank Ryan
CEO, Enterprise Ireland
www.enterprise-ireland.com

Introduction

Ireland is developing rapidly as an entrepreneurial society. More Irish people are now starting and managing their own businesses. With amazing ingenuity, these businesses are introducing new products and services, adopting modern technologies, developing export markets and creating new jobs. In recent years the big success story has been the huge growth in the export of services, especially general business, financial and computing services. Irish entrepreneurs are now seen as desirable role models, modern patriots and wealth creators, attitudes which are supported and nurtured by society and its institutions. The Irish State is now making a huge investment in research and development in an effort to create a knowledge economy, with the objective of successfully commercialising new intellectual capital. In this context, Ireland still needs more entrepreneurship at all levels; an increasing number of start-ups, fewer failures; and the development of a large number of innovative businesses with the capacity to develop scale and trade in international markets.

An entrepreneur requires four sets of skills: technical, entrepreneurial, personal and managerial. Technical knowledge and experience of the targeted business sector are very important for success in any enterprise. Entrepreneurial skills encompass the ability to develop an enterprise to exploit a perceived market opportunity by organising the necessary resources, undertaking the risks involved and providing value for customers with the objective of long-term gain. Leadership, interpersonal, communications and negotiation skills are important personal attributes. Managerial skills are also required.

This book provides an introduction to the enterprise environment in Ireland in Chapter 1 as well as a review of current policies focused on research, development and innovation in a 'smart economy'. In Chapter 2 entrepreneurship is explained and possible sources of business ideas are explored as well as the main intellectual property rights. Chapter 3 considers the various types of business organisation in Ireland as well as their diverse legal, financial, taxation, auditing and administrative obligations. In Chapter 4 the importance of marketing and its main elements are considered. Sources of finance, working capital, cash management, costing and pricing, financial statements and published accounts are explored in Chapter 5. Chapter 6 addresses the taxation obligations of small and medium-sized enterprises. Operations management as well as quality, new product development, insurance and legal issues relating to goods and services are considered in Chapter 7. Human resource management and relevant employment law are explained in Chapter 8. Chapter 9 deals with the various stages of business growth, insolvency and exit strategies. The final chapter is on general management and the main elements involved in the process.

This book provides an introduction to the enterprise environment in Ireland, possible business opportunities and a synthesis of the main managerial issues which arise in running a small or medium-sized enterprise. This is not a book about 'how to do it'. There is no such book! Managing any business involves a wide range of knowledge, skills, competence and experience which each manager has to be able to apply in the current and expected economic, technological and social environment having regard to his/her enterprise, circumstances and opportunities. An entrepreneur has to be able to synthesise and evaluate various theories and techniques as well as a wide range of economic forecasts to position his/her business for a complex, uncertain and changing environment. This is not a simple process.

Having started Enterprise Development as a subject in Galway-Mayo Institute of Technology in 1984 and teaching on it over the years as well as on short programmes for businesspeople, I have found that many students express the need for a book on entrepreneurship with a strong applied orientation in the Irish context. It is hoped that this book will be helpful in this regard and provide an *opéritif* for the more specialised publications on each topic, some of which are listed in the References and Bibliography at the end of the book. Many entrepreneurs are now starting and managing private limited companies and, as a result, this topic receives considerable space in this book.

I would like to thank the following colleagues for comments on various chapters: Carmel Brennen, Delma Carey, Jerry Casey, Larry Elwood, Joseph Farrell, Marie Finnegan, Clodagh Geraghty, John Kennedy, Hugh McBride, Patricia McCann, Tony McDonogh, Marie Murphy, Michelle McNicholas, Ivan McPhillips, Shane Moran, Peadar O'Dowd, Edel O'Connor and, in particular, John Hynes. I would also like to sincerely thank Mary Kennedy for all her help, and the staff of the library of Galway-Mayo Institute of Technology. I alone am responsible for any errors in the book. My sincere thanks to Marion O'Brien, Aoife O'Kelly and the staff of Gill & Macmillan for all their help, as well as Kristin Jensen. Finally, I would like to thank my wife, Mary, and all our family for their understanding, help and support while this book was being written.

Bernard O'Hara

Chapter 1

Enterprise environment

Give a person a fish and he/she has food for a day; teach a person to fish and he/she has food for life.

ADAPTED FROM AN ANCIENT CHINESE PROVERB

Learning objectives

- To trace the development of enterprise in Ireland from protectionism to recent times
- To consider the important role of small and medium enterprises
- To explore possible future business opportunities, especially arising from investment in the knowledge economy
- To consider future skills needs and regional development in the context of the National Spatial Strategy
- To know the State organisations that support Irish enterprise.

This chapter is structured as follows:

1.1 Introduction

Enterprise is essential for the economic, social and cultural development of all nations. The United States of America (USA) is regarded as a very enterprising society, where the growth of small businesses is the prime motivator of economic development. Enterprise development and innovation are part of the fabric of that society, reinforced by educational, economic, social and political institutions as well as the media. Attitudes are conditioned by the big American dream; that anyone, regardless of background, can make it in business and where failure is seen as a learning experience. Entrepreneurship is espoused early as a possible career choice and constantly acclaimed by society. Stories of famous American inventors such as Benjamin Franklin and Thomas Edison as well as great entrepreneurs such as Andrew Carnegie, Henry Ford, Bill Gates, Steve Jobs and many others appear in children's books.

Ireland is developing rapidly as an entrepreneurial society. More people are now starting and managing their own businesses and Irish people are the most enterprising in the European Union (Global Entrepreneurship Monitor, 2010). This resurgence in entrepreneurial spirit is a most welcome development. With amazing ingenuity, these businesses are introducing new products and services, adopting modern technologies, developing export markets and creating new jobs. In Ireland, entrepreneurs are now seen as desirable role models, modern patriots, wealth creators and job creators, attitudes which are supported and nurtured by society and its institutions. While most people associate enterprise with starting and managing one's own business, it is not confined to that. Enterprise and innovation are also important in established businesses, in all kinds of social and cultural organisations and in the public sector. It is clear from the literature that a favourable environment – political, social, economic and educational – is essential for the promotion of entrepreneurship (Cannon, 1991; Timmons, 1999). Attitudes, opportunities and rewards for successful enterprise are all important considerations. Entrepreneurs are influenced by the value system of their society. The enterprise environment is dynamic, with potential for policy-makers to influence change for the benefit of present and future generations. As Shakespeare wrote:

> Men at some time are masters of their fates;
> The fault, dear Brutus, is not in our stars,
> But in ourselves, that we are underlings.
>
> JULIUS CAESAR (1599), ACT 1, SCENE 2

The main objectives of Irish industrial policy are the development of indigenous enterprises, especially those with export potential; investment in and commercialisation of research and development; the attraction of inward investment; the creation of a competitive economy; and balanced regional development (National Development Plan, 2007–2013). Ireland wants more business start-ups, more survivals, more high-growth organisations, innovation from new and existing businesses, high productivity and growth in exports. This chapter sets the context for entrepreneurship in Ireland.

1.2 Economic development

This section briefly traces the development of the Irish economy from the era of protectionism to recent times under the following headings:

a)   Protectionism
b)   Free trade
c)   Investment in education
d)   Industrial economy
e)   The Celtic Tiger
f)   Recession and reorientation.

a)   Protectionism

During and following the Great Famine in Ireland from 1845 to 1849, emigration took place on a massive scale. In the early twentieth century, an employment culture developed which cherished a safe, permanent, pensionable job in the public sector and sheltered private sector services like banking and the professions. Work in wealth-producing activities such as industry, agriculture, fisheries, horticulture, forestry and international services was not held in high esteem. The successful person was often the subject of envy and the prevailing attitudes were hostile to business. In this environment, many of Ireland's most entrepreneurial young people left its shores for countries which provided them with opportunities to earn their livelihoods. The society that emerged during the 1950s was one of economic stagnation, continual balance of payments crises, rising unemployment, massive emigration and a declining population. Inertia, apathy, cynicism and a general mood of despondency prevailed. The country had a small, insular manufacturing sector, catering almost exclusively for the home market, most of which was established behind the high tariff barriers imposed under the protectionist policy followed after 1932. Agriculture, then the dominant form of economic activity in the country and dependent on the British market alone for exports, was unable to generate income growth or halt the decline in employment (O'Hagan and Newman, 2008). The motive behind protectionism was to create a strong indigenous industrial base (similar to the approach taken by other economies), but it failed, leaving an anaemic, uncompetitive economy which retarded economic growth and enterprise. An open economy is now seen as a major driver of enterprise and this had been stifled.

b)   Free trade

Dramatic changes in economic policy and performance followed the publication of a White Paper, *Programme for Economic Expansion*, on 12 November 1958. Now referred to as the *First Programme for Economic Expansion*, it was based on a celebrated report, *Economic Development*, prepared chiefly by T. K. Whitaker, Secretary of the Department of Finance. It became a milestone in Irish economic development. Its main strategies were the creation of economic growth by developing an export-orientated manufacturing sector in Ireland, changing industrial policy from protectionism to free trade, attracting foreign investment and the promotion of indigenous enterprise with various tax concessions, grants and subsidies. It was a seminal plan and marked the start of the modern industrialisation of Ireland. A number of development bodies had been established: the Industrial Development Authority (IDA) in 1949 to foster industrial development, Córas Trachtála in 1952 to promote exports, Gaeltarra Éireann (now Údarás na Gaeltachta) in 1958 to support employment creation in the Gaeltacht areas and the Shannon Free Airport Development Company in 1959 to promote development in that region. In a remarkable change of policy, most sections of the Control of Manufactures Acts 1932–1934 (legislation restricting foreign ownership of manufacturing companies) were replaced by the Industrial Development (Encouragement of External Investment) Act 1958, which introduced a range of incentives to be used to promote Ireland as a location for industrial development. The 1932–1934 Acts were completely repealed in 1964; thereafter, there were no restrictions on foreign ownership of industry in Ireland or on the repatriation of profits. Various tax concessions and generous grants to promote industrial development were introduced in the 1950s and early 1960s.

Economic growth exceeded all expectations during the period of the *First Programme for Economic Expansion* (1959–63). Confidence grew and Ireland formally applied for membership of the European Economic Community (EEC) as it was then called, now the European Union (EU), in 1962, but the application was withdrawn when President de Gaulle of France vetoed the United Kingdom's application in 1963. The *Second Programme for Economic Expansion*, covering the period 1964 to 1970, set a target growth rate of 4.2 per cent per annum, but dissatisfaction with progress led to the abandonment of the programme in 1968. A third programme, *Economic and Social Development*, 1969–72, ran its course. Tariffs were reduced unilaterally in 1963 and 1964, while the Anglo–Irish Free Trade Agreement was signed in 1965 and Ireland joined the General Agreement on Tariffs and Trade (GATT) in 1967. Over 500 new manufacturing industries, most of them export led, were established in Ireland during the 1960s, and they made a big contribution to the growth of the economy. These activities spawned several indigenous enterprises. Employment in manufacturing increased, emigration fell and the standard of living started to rise, with improvements in infrastructure, education, social conditions and healthcare. Protectionism gradually gave way to free trade, culminating in Ireland's membership of the EEC on 1 January 1973 (O'Hagan and Newman, 2008).

c)   Investment in education

The highly influential report *Investment in Education*, published in two volumes in 1965 and 1966, recommended expansion and investment in education at all levels. Free post-primary education was introduced in 1967, a significant decision in the subsequent development of the country. Investment in education at all levels increased, especially at third level, with expansion in the existing universities, the opening of a network of regional technical colleges (now institutes of technology) in the 1970s and the establishment of the National Institute of Higher Education in Limerick in 1972 and another in Dublin in 1980 (both became universities in 1989). Investment in education was a major objective of public policy, aided by European Union funds. This investment in human resources created a national competitive advantage for the country and led to unprecedented growth towards the end of the twentieth century.

d)   Industrial economy

The country changed quickly from an agricultural economy to an industrial one from the 1970s. In 1979 Ireland broke the link with sterling which had existed since 1826 and joined the European Monetary System (EMS) in an effort to reduce inflation (Haughton, 2008). Employment grew during the 1970s with numerous multinational companies established in the State. Because of heavy dependence on foreign firms, slow growth in indigenous industries, the cost of industrial development and the changing international climate, the Government asked the National Economic and Social Council (NESC) to carry out a fundamental review of industrial policy in December 1979, with a major part of the review undertaken by the Telesis Consulting Group. The Telesis report, with NESC comments, was published in October 1982 (NESC, no. 64). It recommended *inter alia* that priority should be given to the development of internationally traded indigenous industry, a more systematic programme for developing linkages between indigenous and foreign-owned firms, a reduction in grants offered to foreign firms and positive discrimination in favour of projects with 'desirable characteristics' such as key business functions located in Ireland, stand-alone projects and those with significant potential for linkages.

Ireland's economic performance during the early 1980s was poor, with no growth, balance of payments crises, high inflation, excessive Government spending and a large national debt. Profligate expenditure during the late 1970s and early 1980s led to continuous annual current budget deficits. Increased taxation and high interest rates further depressed demand and exacerbated the recession. Manufacturing employment declined, unemployment increased to 17 per cent of the labour force by 1987 and emigration was high. The national economic crisis called for a major reform of fiscal policy, which took root in 1987. Major cutbacks took place in State spending and a social partnership agreement between the Government, employers and trade unions provided tax reductions in return for wage moderation. Restoration of the public finances created an environment for macroeconomic stability and facilitated investment. There was a big increase in inward investment, especially from the United States, and EU Structural Funds to prepare Ireland for the single market were used constructively to aid State investment in infrastructure and education. Considerable improvement took place between 1987 and 1991, with economic growth averaging 4.7 per cent per year. Employment started to increase from 1989 and State finances were gradually brought under control.

The report of the Industrial Policy Review Group in 1992 (*A Time for Change: Industrial Policy in the 1990s*, the 'Culliton Report') supported the development of an export-orientated indigenous enterprise sector, with a spirit of self-reliance and a determination to take charge of our own economic future, and recommended lowering the cost and improving the quality of public utilities as well as reforming the taxation system. It also advised that policy should focus on all aspects of competitiveness, productivity and reforming the State agencies supporting industrial development. In 1993, Forfás was established as the State body with responsibility for policy advice on the development of enterprise, trade, science, technology and innovation, with IDA Ireland responsible for attracting inward investment to Ireland and Enterprise Ireland for promoting indigenous enterprises. While policy shifted towards the promotion of indigenous businesses, the attraction of foreign direct investment continued. New inward investment created numerous new enterprises, not only in low-cost assembly work but also in high-technology, knowledge-intensive operations.

e) The Celtic Tiger

Difficult international conditions slowed employment growth in the early 1990s, but from 1994 to 2002 there was a period of unprecedented growth. The performance of the Irish economy during the last decade of the twentieth century was astonishing by previous standards. By the dawn of the new millennium the country had achieved sustained and significant growth in output, exports and employment creation. Between 1989 and 1998, the total at work increased by 408,400 from 1,113,200 to 1,521,600, an increase of 36.7 per cent (Central Statistics Office, Quarterly National Household Surveys). Unemployment was reduced rapidly after 1994, despite an increase of about 3 per cent per year in the labour force arising from a natural increase, rising female participation and net inward migration. The unemployment rate fell from 15 per cent in 1993 to just under 5 per cent early in 2000. This increase in employment and drop in unemployment coincided with unprecedented levels of economic growth, with gross national product (GNP) growth averaging 7.5 per cent from 1994 to 1999 (CSO). The country approached full employment for the first time since independence and scarcity of labour became a problem in many sectors. This growth created buoyancy in State revenue, which led to healthy budget surpluses and facilitated major reductions in taxation over a number of years, giving those at work increased disposable incomes. Extra resources were also provided for education, healthcare and social welfare. In terms of living standards, the country had converged to the European Union norm, with gross national product per capita at about 95 per cent of the EU average, compared with less than 70 per cent in 1987. The world saw Ireland as the 'Celtic Tiger', a popular misnomer for Ireland's long-delayed economic development (Haughton, 2008; MacSharry *et al.*, 2000).

This transformation in the Irish economy came from the confluence of a number of factors: membership of the European Union, macroeconomic factors, fiscal policy, labour supply, high productivity and social partnership. Membership of the European Union was a major factor, opening access to new markets and reducing the country's bilateral dependence on the United Kingdom. Devaluation in 1993 resulted in significant gains in price competitiveness. The main macroeconomic reasons were a growth in global trade, favourable exchange rates up to 2000, low interest rates, attraction of foreign direct investment (FDI) and a big expansion in indigenous enterprises, many of which developed export markets (Haughton, 2008). This pro-enterprise environment was enhanced by prudent fiscal policies from 1987, which reformed public finances and introduced low corporate, personal and other taxes. Favourable demographics characterised by a high birth rate created a supply of skilled labour in the 1990s, and this led to an increase in employment without a corresponding increase in wages as demand for labour went up. This made the Irish economy particularly competitive in the 1990s and productivity increased considerably. Social partnership agreements from 1987 led to wage moderation, which, with lower personal taxes, led to higher take-home pay in real terms. Ireland enjoyed Objective 1 status for Structural Funds, which led to considerable investment with Irish matching funds in human resource development, various infrastructural projects and aid to the enterprise sector. More efforts were made to increase competition, extend customer choice, promote innovation and efficiency as well as deregulation in some enterprises. Ireland joined the single European currency when it was launched in 1999 (euro notes and coins were introduced in January 2002). These developments created an environment where business could flourish.

While all this was very impressive, it ignored the dual economies operating in Ireland: a dynamic, high-technology, high-growth, export-led multinational sector and a slower-growing, less export-orientated indigenous sector. By the year 2000 there were about 1,100 multinational companies operating in Ireland, especially from the US, employing over 124,000 staff in manufacturing, chiefly in electronics, information and communications technology (ICT), pharmaceuticals and healthcare, engineering and international financial services. The indigenous sector grew rapidly in the 1990s but not at the same rate as the multinational sector. According to Forfás surveys in 2003, there were 297,549 employed in companies supported by enterprise agencies, IDA Ireland, Enterprise Ireland, Shannon Development and Údarás na Gaeltachta (see Table 1.1).

There was a big increase in the country's manufacturing base and exports up to 2002 as well as a rapid expansion in internationally traded services. Employment growth led to the end of involuntary emigration and increased disposable incomes, and additional State revenue enabled social services to be improved. According to the Quarterly National Household Survey of the Central Statistics Office, there were 1,930,042 in the Irish workforce in 2006: 822,808 women and 1,107,234 men. Employment in the construction sector peaked at 284,600, or 14.7 per cent of total employment, by the end of 2006. There were 2.139 million in the workplace by the end of 2007, but much of the increase over the previous years came from part-time jobs. About 1.4 million of that figure worked in the services sector, or approximately two out of every three people at work. The Irish economy evolved quickly from agricultural dominance, to industry, to services. By the end of 2007 there were 334,700 foreign nationals at work in Ireland (Quarterly National Household Survey, 2008). According to census figures, the population of the State was 4.339 million in April 2007, compared with 3.626 million in 1996. While many indigenous enterprises developed export markets over the years, some began to extend their activities in overseas markets with outward direct investment (ODI) and by 2004, Irish investment outflow exceeded inflow for the first time. This trend is likely to continue (Forfás, 2007a).

Table 1.1: Agency-supported firms in manufacturing and internationally traded services, 2003

	Total	Indigenous	Foreign-owned
Number of firms	8,663	7,390	1,273
Number of full-time employees	297,549	147,895	149,654
Average number of employees per firm	34	20	118
Sales (€ mn) (2002)	99,341	23,588	75,753
Direct expenditure in the economy (payroll, procurement of Irish raw materials and services) (€ mn) (2002)	34,170	16,677	17,493
Exports (€ mn) (2002)	78,803	8,785	70,018

Source: Forfás Surveys 2003, published in the Enterprise Strategy Group report, *Ahead of the Curve* (2004)

f)   Recession and reorientation

Price increases from 1999 and full employment led to wage inflation outside the national agreements and benchmarking awards in the public sector in 2001. This wage inflation, combined with the appreciation of the euro against sterling and the US dollar, led to a big decline in price competitiveness. Exports from manufacturing and employment in that sector fell. An independent central bank could have increased interest rates to curtail inflation, but by then Irish monetary policy was determined by the European Central Bank (ECB), which aggravated the Irish situation by reducing interest rates and fuelling the property bubble. The EU Stability and Growth Pact was devised to keep the finances of countries in the euro under control by ensuring that any Government deficit did not exceed 3 per cent of gross domestic product (GDP) and that national debt did not exceed 6 per cent. As a member of the euro zone, the option of devaluation to restore competitiveness was not available. From 2002 to 2007, growth in the Irish economy came from a booming construction sector and consumer spending, fuelled by cheap credit, reckless bank lending and 'light touch' regulation, with no regard to ethical considerations (Cooper, 2010; Ross, 2010). This was exacerbated by excessive Government expenditure, financed by unsustainable property-based taxation revenue and big consumer spending. In 2008 economic growth came to an abrupt halt due to the confluence of a number of factors, including the collapse of the sub-prime housing market in the USA during 2007 and the closure of Wall Street's Lehman Brothers in September 2008, which led to a global banking and credit crisis as inter-bank lending dried up, as well as the crumbling of the Irish housing and personal credit bubbles. This resulted in a swift and deep recession, with negative growth in Ireland, a huge reduction in State revenue, a big increase in unemployment, increased taxation, increased payments in welfare and a large deficit, breaching the EU Stability and Growth norms. The Government had to guarantee deposits and most of the debts in six Irish financial institutions on 30 September 2008 and later provide capital to keep the banks in existence. The National Asset Management Agency (NAMA) was established to take over most of the toxic debts of the Irish banks in an initiative designed to facilitate their recapitalisation and enable them to resume responsible lending. Pay was reduced in many private-sector organisations and across all of the public sector from January 2010, as levies on pay were imposed. The key fundamentals that had to be addressed were the banking crisis, the fiscal deficit, competitiveness, the maintenance and generation of employment opportunities as well as the creation of an environment for sustainable economic development. On 28 November 2010, it was announced that Ireland had agreed an €85 billion credit facility with the European Union, the European Central Bank and the International Monetary Fund (with €17.5 billion to be provided by the State) to avoid borrowing in the bond market for three years.

Ireland learned an expensive lesson: that it could not rely on sectors driven by domestic demand, such as construction, wholesale and retail operations and locally traded services, to generate economic growth and employment. Sustainable growth depends on the export of competitive goods and services. The Government has to create the conditions to ensure that the cost of doing business in Ireland is competitive for the enterprise sector. It is expected that increased economic activity will generate additional State revenue to reduce part of the fiscal deficit, with the remaining structural part to be addressed by cost reductions and increased taxation (ESRI, 2009). The Government's economic recovery report, *Building Ireland's Smart Economy* (2008), states:

> Future economic growth will depend on re-orientating the economy towards exporting goods and services. To achieve this we need to stimulate the growth of enterprise, take advantage of the significant potential from the development of the green economy, reduce the relative cost of doing business, continue investing in both labour and productive infrastructure, increase competition across the economy, attract high value added employment, guide the construction sector to a more sustainable growth path and address issues such as the cost and security of energy supply.

1.3 Role of small and medium enterprises (SMEs)

While the future attraction and retention of foreign direct investment will be important for Ireland, as will the development of large indigenous enterprises, a key aspect of industrial policy is the development of small and medium enterprises (Table 1.2).

Table 1.2: Classification of small and medium enterprises

Enterprise category	Headcount	Turnover	or Balance sheet total
Medium	< 250	≤ €50 million	≤ €43 million
Small	< 50	≤ €10 million	≤ €10 million
Micro	< 10	≤ €2 million	≤ €2 million

Source: European Commission (2008)

- A medium enterprise is defined by the European Commission as an enterprise which has fewer than 250 employees and either an annual turnover not exceeding €50 million or a balance sheet total not exceeding €43 million.
- A small enterprise is an enterprise which has fewer than 50 employees and either an annual turnover not exceeding €10 million or a balance sheet total not exceeding €10 million.
- An SME ceases to qualify as such if a large enterprise owns more than 25 per cent of its shares.
- A micro-enterprise is one with fewer than 10 employees and either an annual turnover not exceeding €2 million or a balance sheet total not exceeding €2 million.

By 2005, with a workforce of just over 1.9 million in the country, approximately 350,000 people were employed in the public sector, 109,000 in farming and the balance in the enterprise sector. According to the report of the Small Business Forum, *Small Business Is Big Business* (2006), there were over a quarter of a million small businesses in Ireland in 2005, employing fewer than 50 people each (Table 1.3).

Table 1.3: Number of enterprises by level of employment (2005)

Business size	50+ employees	20–49 employees	10–19 employees	2–9 employees	1 employee	Total
Number of businesses	7,000	4,000	6,000	85,000	131,000	233,000
Per cent	3.0	1.7	2.6	36.5	56.2	100
Number of employees	675,000	138,000	111,000	397,000	131,000	1,452,000
Per cent	46.5	9.5	7.7	27.3	9.0	100

Source: Report of the Small Business Forum (2006), *Small Business Is Big Business* (CSO data, March–May 2005)

There were 7,000 businesses with over 50 employees in each and a total of 675,000 people. Over half of those employed in the enterprise sector worked in small businesses (about 777,000 people). There were 131,000 businesses employing just one person each, mainly professional people and self-employed tradespeople; 85,000 employing between two and nine people; and 6,000 with 10 to 19 employees. Small businesses operated in all sectors of the Irish economy, with construction, the largest, employing about a quarter of the total. The other main sectors were wholesale and retail, business services, manufacturing industry, transport, communications, finance, education, health and other services.

Small businesses are dispersed around the country and supply a huge range of local services as well as contributing to the economic, social and cultural life of the local population. Small businesses are able to give excellent customised service and value, with many deciding to remain small and trade locally. However, many of these are now experiencing intense competition from bigger organisations and international competitors in retailing, professional services, hotels, restaurants, entertainment and other services. The internet has brought new competition and opportunities to many sectors. Small businesses have to maximise their efficiency, quality and productivity to survive. The small business sector has become an incubating ground for many enterprises with the ambition to grow and develop export markets. Enterprise Ireland is working closely with those businesses and many are very successful. These are enterprises with the potential to build technological capability, to innovate with research and development and to support the creation of high-value products and services. Many small and medium-sized businesses are now very innovative in the production and export of high value-added products in sectors such as software, medical devices, engineering, food and biotechnology.

The Report of the Small Business Forum (2006) recommended that the Government should adopt a national entrepreneurship policy focused on increasing the number of start-ups and especially increasing the number aspiring to high growth. This includes enhancing the culture to support entrepreneurship. In addition, the report identified a number of issues that need to be addressed if the small business sector is to realise its full potential, as shown below.

a)   Issues that face growing businesses
- Difficulty in accessing finance, especially for the service sectors with few capital assets that do not qualify for support from the enterprise development agencies, as well as cash flow difficulties arising from long delays in payment
- Weak management capability
- Lack of innovation, both technological and non-technological
- Under-exploitation of information and communications technology.

b)   Issues that face all small businesses

- Burdensome and costly compliance regulations in relation to tax, employment, accounts, companies, licences, statistics and trade-related issues
- Rising local authority charges, including a development charge towards the cost of local infrastructure, such as roads, water supply and sewerage
- Poor access to information and advice
- Inadequate infrastructure, including broadband connectivity, transport, energy (including cost) and waste management.

c)   Issues that face start-ups

- Lack of a systematic approach to entrepreneurship.

1.4 Future business opportunities for Ireland

The Enterprise Strategy Group report, *Ahead of the Curve: Ireland's Place in the Global Economy* (2004), stated that:

> the nature of global trade is changing, and future economic development will be strongly influenced by:
> - The shift towards services as a major driver of gross domestic product (GDP) growth,
> - The increasing role of knowledge as a driver of economic development and an influencer of new products.

The report (p. 42) identified opportunities for indigenous enterprises and inward investment in internationally traded services across a range of sectors and activities, especially with regard to advances in technology and the new corporate tax rate of 12.5 per cent on all trading activities. The sectors considered to offer opportunities were education for international students; finance; healthcare; tourism; aviation; construction; engineering; environmental, professional, consultancy, agricultural and bloodstock services; and creative and maritime services. The report recommended promoting Ireland as a location for European headquarters of multinational companies, franchising, intellectual property, sales and marketing, shared and outsourced business processes, supply chain management and various services delivered electronically.

The Enterprise Strategy Group saw high-value manufacturing remaining a fundamental component of Ireland's enterprise environment. Their report stated that for organisations in Ireland to develop future market opportunities, they must complement their existing production and operational strengths with new capabilities:

- Developing expertise in international markets to promote sales growth

- Building technological and applied research and development (R&D) capability to support the development of high-value products and services.

The activities with potential are those where Ireland has or can develop competitive advantage, differentiation and critical mass, sourced by natural resources, research and clusters of companies with specific expertise. The report identified the following as sectors which could offer opportunities for further development (p. 45): agri-food, pharmaceuticals and biotechnology, information and communications technology, medical technologies and consumer goods with strategic use of design and high margins. The development of other productive activities such as marine and forest resources and alternative energies is also important. To compete and grow, Irish industry has to be creative, innovative, flexible and adaptable, with the capacity to develop scale and international markets in niche segments.

Locally traded services do not receive the attention they deserve despite the increasing number employed in these activities. The size and growth of employment in sheltered services is influenced by the productivity of wealth-creating, export-orientated enterprises in the country and by net disposable incomes. However, the competitiveness of wealth-creating activities in the market sector is influenced by the quality and price of services from the sheltered sector (those activities which do not, or cannot by their nature, compete in the international marketplace) and by the taxable base to support public services. The Enterprise Strategy Group report (2004) stated: 'through the promotion of competition and innovation, locally-traded services will contribute effectively to the future growth of enterprise'. The adoption of new technologies, innovation and customisation can create new opportunities for locally traded services, many of which have potential for internationalisation.

One of the success stories of the Irish economy in recent years has been the big growth in the export of services. Internationally traded services are now the main drivers of economic growth, accounting for 43 per cent of exports in 2007. These include services relating to general business activities; financial services; computing, especially software; tourism and travel. Services, both domestic and international, are now a huge part of the Irish economy. Employment in services is expected to increase significantly, especially those with the potential to trade at international level. It is predicted that market services will account for 70 per cent of Irish exports by 2025 (Fitzgerald *et al.*, 2008). There are many services where Ireland can provide a competitive advantage in international markets, based on knowledge, differentiation, low rate of corporate taxation, unique heritage, worldwide diaspora and good interpersonal skills. Many companies have the potential to add service components to their business products. A new research and development grant scheme is now available for private companies, administered jointly by Enterprise Ireland and IDA Ireland, with services eligible for the first time.

The Enterprise Strategy Group report (2004) recommended that industrial policy should focus on niche activities for development where Ireland is world class. It identified five areas which, if fully developed, could provide Ireland with competitive advantages: expertise in international markets; expertise in technology with product and service development; world-class skills, education and training; favourable taxation policies; and effective and agile Government response to the needs of enterprise. It listed four prerequisites for the development of the competitive advantages listed above: cost competitiveness, physical and communications infrastructure, innovation and entrepreneurship, and management capability. The report recommended dismantling the legislative shelters that restrict competition, prioritising investment in the National Spatial Strategy-designated gateways and hubs and re-energising the recommendations of the strategic management initiative for the *Delivery of Better Government* (1996). The entrepreneurial potential of immigrants is also huge with regard to their enormous contribution in the United States (*Innovation*, November 2007).

1.5 Knowledge economy

As traditional manufacturing declines, most advanced economies are interested in what are called 'sunrise industries' – knowledge-based, market-driven, high-technology enterprises. One of the major objectives of current Irish industrial policy is the creation of a knowledge economy based on research, development, innovation and commercialisation.

Research is creative work undertaken in a systematic manner to generate new knowledge. Future innovative developments in products and services will come from the generation and use of new knowledge. Francis Bacon once observed that 'knowledge is power' and Benjamin Franklin, one of the founding fathers of the United States, made a prescient comment in *Poor Richard* that 'an investment in knowledge pays the best dividends'.

Development means utilising the knowledge that comes from research. Innovation is the process of adapting new ideas to add value commercially and requires the capacity to access and use the available knowledge. This requires different skills from those of research. Innovation is influenced by talent for accessing the global pool of knowledge in a specific topic, connectivity, networks, absorptive capacity, experimentation and flexibility. Successful innovation involves adapting existing knowledge to specific needs, preferably based on some unique competitive advantage to ensure long-term sustainability. Businesspeople have to realise that catching up is far more difficult than staying ahead.

Commercialisation is the process of bringing products and services to the marketplace. As global competition increases and with some low-level activities transferring to lower-cost economies, Ireland has to find new sources of competitive advantage. The objective is that this will happen with the generation and commercialisation of new knowledge. Ireland is now part of a rapidly changing global village with numerous sources of new knowledge, where the challenge is to integrate the discovery and commercialisation of new knowledge for the benefit of society.

In 1999 the *Technology Foresight Ireland* report (ICSTI, 1999) recommended that investment in science should be substantially increased, which led to the establishment of the Programme for Research in Third-Level Institutions (PRTLI) and Science Foundation Ireland (SFI). With a generous donation from Atlantic Philanthropies (a US philanthropic body controlled by an Irish-American, Chuck Feeney) and State funding, the Programme for Research in Third-Level Institutions was established in 1998 by the Higher Education Authority (HEA) to enable the universities and institutes of technology to develop research infrastructures and programmes. It supports research in science, technology, engineering and social sciences, including business and law. Science Foundation Ireland was established in 2001 to finance research in two key disciplines: information communications technology and biotechnology. It also has a research frontiers programme for mathematics, science and engineering. Research funds were provided for PRTLI, SFI, Teagasc, the Marine Institute, Enterprise Ireland, the Environmental Protection Agency (EPA), the Health Research Board (HRB) and other organisations. Two research councils were established to promote research in third-level institutions: the Irish Research Council for Science, Engineering and Technology (IRCSET) and the Irish Research Council for Humanities and Social Sciences (IRCHSS). A number of Centres for Science, Engineering and Technology (CSETs) and Strategic Research Clusters (SRCs) were established with SFI funding to promote collaboration between higher education and industry. Under the Seventh EU Framework Programme for Research and Technological Development (FP7), a budget of over €50 billion was provided to promote European Union leadership in the global knowledge economy, with a big emphasis on collaboration.

The research vision for the country was expressed as follows in *Building Ireland's Knowledge Economy* (Forfás, 2004a):

> Ireland by 2010 will be internationally renowned for the excellence
> of its research and be at the forefront in generating and using new
> knowledge for economic and social progress, within an innovation-
> driven culture.

According to this 2004 report, about one-third of both foreign and indigenous enterprises in Ireland were active in research and development in 2001. Expenditure on research and development at 1.4 per cent of GNP was under the EU average of 1.9 per cent, 2.7 per cent in the US and 3.1 per cent in Japan. Businesses were advised to recognise the value of research and innovation, both of which were seen as essential for survival and sustainability. The State would like to see far more enterprises active in research and development. A government report, *Strategy for Science, Technology and Innovation 2006–2013* (Government Publications, 2007b), identified the need for increased numbers with research qualifications, to double the number of PhD graduates (from a base of 647 in 2003), with a significant increase in research capacity, as well as investment in fourth-level education and the public research system. The State committed €8.2 billion for investment in research under the *National Development Plan 2007–2013* (NDP) and in the *Strategy for Science, Technology and Innovation 2006–2013*. This investment was spread across a number of programme areas to create world-class research in science, technology and innovation. The research is focused on core competences in specific technologies where Ireland has expertise and advantages: food processing, computers, electronics, pharmaceuticals, biopharmaceuticals, life science, energy, marine, geosciences, medical device engineering and the environment. The European Union's Lisbon Strategy 2000–2010 set an objective of establishing the most competitive and dynamic knowledge-based economy in the world. It agreed a target of 3 per cent of GDP for gross expenditure on R&D by 2010. Ireland's target was 2.5 per cent of GNP by 2010, with two-thirds of this to come from the private sector (Forfás, 2004a).

According to the report *Building Ireland's Knowledge Economy*:

> sustained investment in R&D is an essential foundation to maintain the competitiveness of the enterprise base and to develop Ireland as a knowledge based society, so as to increase productivity growth, provide a source of opportunity in new growth areas and to develop a base for creating knowledge driven competitive advantage across sectors of the economy.

The objective of this huge investment in research, which represents a paradigm shift in State policy, is to turn it into commercial value for the Irish economy. Taxpayers will expect a return for this investment. It is essential that research and development in higher education are aligned with the business sector to root this talent base in Ireland and provide a vital link in the innovatory process, as well as making the country more attractive for foreign direct investment. Problem-solving and developing new ways of undertaking activities are an integral part of the process. There is also enormous potential for the application of new knowledge and technologies in services. Inventions, innovation and commercialisation originate from many sources and this diversity has to be respected and supported. The educational experiences from first to fourth levels, as well as the economic, social and cultural environment, are important factors. A culture of exploration, experimentation, creativity, critical thinking and innovation has to be fostered at all levels of education as well as in business and society. A knowledge-based society requires lifelong learning, wide diffusion of knowledge, exploration and innovation. Bradley and Kennelly (2008) see huge potential for future competitiveness in 'a marriage of capability, creativity, innovation, culture, identity and sense of place'. According to the Government's report, *Building Ireland's Smart Economy* (2008), a key feature of its approach is

> building the innovation or 'ideas' component of the economy through the utilisation of human capital – the knowledge, skills and creativity of people – and its ability and effectiveness in translating ideas into valuable processes, products and services. A second important aspect is the greening of the economy and the development of green enterprise.

This policy has research, innovation and commercialisation at its core, which the report states 'will be the successful formula for the next phase of the development of the Irish economy'. The smart economy is not only about research and new products, it is chiefly about innovation in every aspect of a business. It is dependent on smart people with good business ideas, innovation and enterprise. Ireland wants people that can respond to this challenge in the spirit enunciated by President John F. Kennedy in his inaugural address on 20 January 1961: 'Ask not what your country can do for you – ask rather what you can do for your country.'

The report of the Innovation Taskforce, *Innovation Ireland* (2010), listed six principles as fundamental to creating an ecosystem in which each element, and each interaction, supports innovation across the economy and society. These are:

1. The entrepreneur and enterprise must be at the centre of our efforts.
2. Establishing, attracting, growing and transforming enterprises must be the focus of a coherent national effort.
3. Availability of smart capital is crucial for starting, growing and transforming enterprises.
4. An education system which fosters independent thinking, creativity and innovation is vital to achieving the smart economy.
5. The State should actively accelerate success by encouraging flagship projects and by prioritising the provision of excellent infrastructure.
6. We must sharpen the focus of our national research system to target areas of potential strategic and economic advantage for Ireland.

It is expected that a strong knowledge-based economy together with innovation in the traditional production sectors, based on natural resources and competitive advantage, and growth in internationally traded services will provide the resources to make continuous improvements in infrastructure and public services as well as the creation of a society based on social cohesion and a good quality of life.

Irish aspirations are in line with EU policy as outlined in the *Europe 2020* strategy (European Commission, 2010). This strategy has three mutually reinforcing priorities:

- Smart growth: Developing an economy based on knowledge and innovation.
- Sustainable growth: Promoting a more resource-efficient, greener and more competitive economy.
- Inclusive growth: Fostering a high-employment economy delivering social and territorial cohesion.

Technology transfer

Technology transfer has been defined as:

> a formal transferring of new inventions, creations, discoveries, innovations, processes and the like which result from scientific research conducted at public research organisations to a commercial environment.

This definition came from the *National Code of Practice for Managing and Commercialising Intellectual Property from Public–Private Collaborative Research* (ACSTI, 2005), which was published to help develop clear policies for all parties in the technology transfer process. In the past Ireland's base in high technology came from external licences, but in the future, it is hoped that some will originate from the transfer of knowledge generated in the country. The terms of knowledge transfer agreements have to be reasonable to ensure commercialisation. Forfás (2004a) stated:

> The production of primary research information is not the end but the beginning of a process that continues until the usefulness of that information is realised. The commercialisation of research and knowledge for Ireland's economic benefit through intellectual property management and technology transfer needs to be a priority for all higher education and public research institutions and it is essential that institutes establish strong capabilities in this regard.

In the past the emphasis in research was on discoveries and getting published in learned journals, but now there is also a strong commitment to commercialisation. Commercialisation in this context is the use of intellectual property to bring new products and services to the marketplace though one's own business or by licensing agreements with other organisations. The new knowledge created has to be used for the benefit of society, to enhance competitiveness, to promote growth, employment and living standards as well as improve the quality of life in terms of health and the environment. Maximising the returns from investment in research is crucial to Ireland's economic, social and cultural progress. With support from Enterprise Ireland, technology transfer offices were established at some higher education institutions to promote patents, licences, technology transfer and the establishment of spin-off companies. It is expected that regional alliances and industrial clusters will develop to share resources, expertise, training, transnational networks and to leverage economies of scale (Cunningham and Harvey, 2006). The objective is to establish knowledge-intensive clusters of enterprises.

Enterprise Ireland has various funding programmes in place to facilitate research and development as well as commercialisation of new technologies, for example innovation vouchers, proof of concept (to explore commercial potential), technology development (more focused market-driven approach), commercialisation plans (to increase commercial value) and innovation partnerships (collaboration between business and higher education to find solutions to problems). The patent fund provides financial aid for higher education institutions to protect intellectual property. Enterprise Ireland also has a growth fund to help small and medium enterprises to increase competitiveness through business innovation.

Business incubation centres

The concept of business incubation centres originated in the United States and from the 1980s many were established on the campuses of universities, which resulted in numerous spin-off high-technology companies. In Ireland, Enterprise Ireland has funded the establishment of business incubation centres at all higher education institutions and some in collaboration with community groups, known as Community Enterprise Centres, to facilitate the formation of viable, sustainable enterprises with the potential to develop export markets. These centres provide dedicated high-quality, fully serviced office space at reduced rent for aspiring entrepreneurs to develop their projects for commercialisation during a specific period, after which they are expected to leave and secure their own facilities. The business incubation centres provide technologically advanced telephone, internet and broadband services as well as access to a wide range of support services, business mentoring and networking opportunities. According to the Enterprise Strategy Group (2004), educational institutions have a third role after education and research: the promotion of enterprise. They state:

> The exploitation of knowledge and commercialisation of research
> must become embedded in the culture and infrastructure of the
> higher education system. This requires continued emphasis on new

> campus company start-ups, a pro-innovation culture of intellectual property protection and exploitation, programmes in entrepreneurship, consulting services, information services, new forms of graduate development programmes and greater links between higher education institutions and private enterprise.

Several successful companies have emerged from third-level campus incubation centres, including Baltimore Technologies, Trinitect, Q Set and Andor Technology, but the best-known company became Iona Technologies, a software company which was successfully floated on the NASDAQ stock exchange in 1997 and at its peak had a market capitalisation of over €1.5 billion. Founded by three academics from Trinity College, Dublin – Dr Chris Horn, Annrai O'Toole and Dr Seán Baker – it operated as a campus company from 1991 to 1993 and originated from a European Union-funded information technology research programme known as ESPRIT. Iona Technologies became one of the first campus companies in Ireland to commercialise their research. It was sold in June 2008 to an American software group for €103.8 million. (*Irish Times*, 2008).

1.6 Future skills needs

In a knowledge economy it is the learner who will inherit the future. Prior to the start of the recession in 2008 there were predictions that the country would need a big increase in the size of its workforce and that considerable upskilling was required.

Tomorrow's Skills: Towards a National Skills Strategy, the report of the Expert Group on Future Skills Needs (2007), stated that the Irish economy would be likely to require 950,000 extra workers between 2006 and 2020. These were expected to come from the school leaving cohort (640,000), through increased participation and inward migration (310,000). The Group's vision for Ireland by 2020 is a 'well-educated and highly skilled population contributing optimally to a competitive, innovation-driven, knowledge-based, participative and inclusive society'. The Expert Group concluded that if Ireland is to realise its vision of a new knowledge economy which can compete in international markets, the following educational objectives had to be achieved by 2020:

- That 500,000 in the workforce progress by at least one level on the national framework of qualifications established by the National Qualifications Authority of Ireland (NQAI) (Figure 1.1)
- That 48 per cent of the labour force have qualifications at levels 6 to 10
- That 45 per cent have qualifications at levels 4 and 5
- That the remaining 7 per cent should have qualifications at levels 1 to 3
- That the retention rate at Leaving Certificate should reach 90 per cent
- That the progression rate to third-level should increase from 55 per cent to 72 per cent.

Figure 1.1: The national framework of qualifications

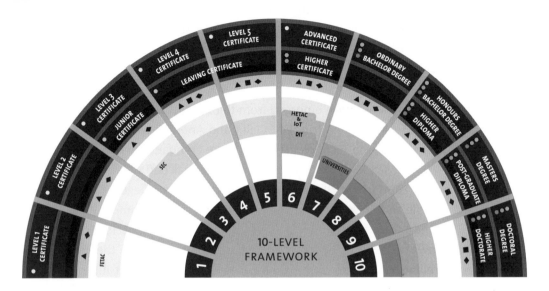

AWARDING BODIES

    FETAC - Further Education and Training Awards Council
    SEC - State Examinations Commission *(Department of Education & Skills)*
    HETAC - Higher Education and Training Awards Council
    IoT - Institutes of Technology *(make their own awards at specified levels under Delegated Authority from HETAC)*
    DIT - Dublin Institute of Technology
    Universities

AWARDS IN THE FRAMEWORK

There are four types of award in the National Framework of Qualifications:

● **Major Awards:** are the principal class of awards made at a level

▲ **Minor Awards:** are for partial completion of the outcomes for a Major Award
■ **Supplemental Awards:** are for learning that is additional to a Major Award
◆ **Special Purpose Awards:** are for relatively narrow or purpose-specific achievement

Source: National Qualifications Authority of Ireland

Figure 1.1 illustrates the 10 levels in the national framework of qualifications and shows the various awarding bodies whose awards are included in the framework. Most HETAC qualifications in Institutes of Technology are now awarded by each one under delegated authority granted in accordance with section 29 of the Qualifications (Education and Training) Act 1999. The unexpected economic developments of 2008 changed the Expert Group's projections and the eventual situation will depend on the depth and length of the recession.

1.7 National Spatial Strategy

The State is committed to balanced regional development. The first major report on regional planning in Ireland was the controversial Buchanan Report in 1968, which recommended the establishment of a small number of growth centres. This was far from popular and led to the publication of IDA Regional Industrial Plans in 1973 which supported the dispersal of economic development. The first industrial estates were established in Galway and Waterford in the early 1970s, and others followed in Dublin, Limerick and Cork. As these centres developed and rural areas declined, there were demands for better balanced development which, it was accepted, would not be achieved by market forces alone. Diseconomies arose from the huge growth in and around Dublin with inflated house prices, energy costs, long commuting times and a big deterioration in the quality of life. A National Spatial Strategy (NSS) was launched in 2001 to promote more balanced regional economic, social and physical development, to be achieved through 'engines of growth' known as gateways and hubs. Gateways are strategic locations with a critical mass of population, economic base, support services and infrastructure which have the capacity to promote development throughout their surrounding regions. The nine gateways selected were Dublin, Cork, Limerick, Shannon, Galway, Waterford, Dundalk and Sligo. In addition, Letterkenny/Derry and Athlone/Tullamore/Mullingar were designated 'linked gateways' to work together to promote regional development in these areas.

Hubs are designed to support the role of gateways and the development of smaller towns as well as the surrounding rural areas. The hubs named were Cavan, Ennis, Kilkenny, Mallow, Monaghan, Tuam and Wexford. In addition, Ballina/Castlebar and Tralee/Killarney were designated 'linked hubs' to work together to develop their areas. In the following decade little was done to support the diversified spatial strategy. An increasing population is expected to result in more urbanisation, high-rise buildings and considerable investment in the supporting infrastructure, with density dividends, which requires good long-term spatial planning (Coleman, 2007). It is envisaged that SMEs will make a major contribution to balanced regional development in the country, especially with the use of modern communications technologies.

1.8 State support for Irish enterprise

The functions of the main State organisations and other bodies which provide support and assistance for Irish business are outlined below, with the year of the organisation's establishment shown in brackets. They are classified as follows:

a)   Industrial/commercial support and assistance
b)   Education and training
c)   Research
d)   Community development
e)   Others.

a)   Industrial/commercial support and assistance

- **Forfás** (1993) is the State agency responsible for policy advice on the development of enterprise, trade, science, technology and innovation in Ireland as well as advising and co-ordinating IDA Ireland, Enterprise Ireland and Science Foundation Ireland in respect of their functions. (www.forfás.ie) The Advisory Council for Science, Technology and Innovation (2005) operates under the aegis of Forfás. It provides advice and develops policies on science, technology and innovation. (www.sciencecouncil.ie)

- **IDA Ireland** (1993) is responsible for attracting inward investment to Ireland in manufacturing and internationally traded services as well as promoting the expansion of existing operations located here. (www.idaireland.com)

- The mission of **Enterprise Ireland** (1998) is 'to accelerate the development of world-class Irish companies to achieve strong positions in global markets resulting in increased national and regional prosperity'. It assists companies engaged in manufacturing and internationally traded services employing 10 or more and new enterprises with growth potential. It is particularly interested in start-up businesses with high potential. A high-potential start-up company (HPSU) is defined by Enterprise Ireland as one which:
  - has a product or service based on technological innovation
  - is likely to achieve significant growth in three years (sales of €1m per annum and employment greater than 10)
  - has projected sales with a big export orientation
  - is ideally led by an experienced management team with technical and commercial competencies.

  Enterprise Ireland can provide various types of funding: grants, repayable grants, equity, redeemable preference shares, research and development finance and innovation grants. (www.enterprise-ireland.com)

- **Shannon Development / Shannon Free Airport Development Co. Ltd** (1959) is a regional development agency in the mid-west region with special responsibility for managing the Shannon Free Zone, promoting tourism and other key strategic projects like the E-towns initiative, Shannon Broadband Ltd and Knowledge Network Locations. (www.shannondevelopment.ie)

- **Údarás na Gaeltachta** (1980) is a regional development body responsible for the promotion of economic, social and cultural development of the Gaeltacht regions so as to encourage the preservation and promotion of the Irish language. Údarás-supported projects include industrial, tourism, aquaculture, audio-visual activities, natural resource-based enterprises and community development initiatives. (www.udaras.ie)

- **City and County Enterprise Boards** (1993) are the first point of contact for start-up and micro-enterprises with fewer than 10 employees. They can provide a feasibility study, employment and capital grants. There are a total of 35 City and County Enterprise Boards and they are key elements of State strategy to generate more balanced regional development.

- **Bord Iascaigh Mhara** (Irish Sea Fisheries Board, 1952) has responsibility for the development of the sea fish industry, aquaculture and the diversification of the coastal economy so as to enhance employment and income. (www.bim.ie)

- **Business Innovative Centres** (BICs, 1988) were established in Dublin, Cork, Limerick and Galway to provide support for innovative start-up and early-stage enterprises in the medium to high-technology sector. Supports include training, feasibility studies, incubation assistance, business planning and access to a network of contacts. They have a seed capital fund and also manage the business angels programme on behalf of Enterprise Ireland and InterTrade Ireland.

- **An Bord Bia** (Irish Food Board, 1994) aims to work in partnership with industry in the promotion of Irish food, drink and horticulture nationally and internationally. (www.bordbia.ie)

- **Fáilte Ireland**, established in 2003 from the merger of Bord Fáilte Éireann and CERT, is the national tourism development authority. Working with the industry, it provides strategic and practical support to develop and sustain Ireland as a high-quality competitive tourist destination. (www.failteireland.ie)

- **Tourism Ireland**, established under the framework of the Belfast Agreement of Good Friday 1998, is responsible for marketing the island of Ireland as a premier tourist destination. It is jointly funded by the two governments and is accountable to the North/South Ministerial Council. (www.tourismireland.com/corporate).

b) Education and training

- **Educational institutions** (universities and institutions of technology).
- **FÁS** (Foras Áiseanna Saothair, the State Training and Employment Authority, 1988) provides a wide range of training and employment programmes to all sectors of industry and commerce, an employment recruitment service, an advisory service to industry and various community development programmes. It is also responsible for the national trades' apprenticeship scheme, the One Step Up and Reaching into the Workforce initiatives for upskilling staff. (www.fas.ie)
- **HEAnet** is Ireland's national education and research network, providing internet services to staff and students in Irish universities, institutes of technology and other educational and research bodies. It provides connectivity to other networks in Ireland and around the world. (www.heanet.ie)
- The **National Centre for Partnership and Performance** was established in 2001 to lead and support change and innovation in the Irish workplace. (www.ncpp.ie)
- **Skillnets** (1999) is an industry-led body that organises and provides support for learning networks of small and medium-sized enterprises.

c) Research

- **Higher educational institutions** (universities and institutions of technology).
- **Science Foundation Ireland** (SFI) was established in 2001 to manage an investment

fund to support basic research likely to generate new knowledge, state-of-the-art technologies and competitive enterprises in strategic fields relevant to Ireland's industrial and economic development, especially biotechnology and information and communications technology. It was given responsibility for investing €1.4 billion during the lifetime of the *National Development Plan 2007–2013*. (www.sfi.ie)

- The **Embark Initiative** forms a portfolio of research-funding programmes operated by the Irish Research Council for Science, Engineering and Technology (IRCSET). These programmes support the education of researchers and the development of their early careers. The emphasis is on innovative, original and exploratory research to promote Ireland's growth, development and competitiveness. (www.embark.ie)

- The **Health Research Board** promotes and supports research on health matters in Ireland. (www.hrb.ie)

- The **Irish Research Council for the Humanities and Social Sciences** (IRCHSS) was established in 2000 to promote research in the humanities and social sciences in the third-level sector. (www.irchss.ie)

- The **Marine Institute** promotes research and development in the marine sector. (www.marine.ie)

- **Teagasc** (1988) provides an integrated research, advisory and training service for agriculture, the food industry and rural development. (www.teagasc.ie)

- The **Higher Education Authority** (HEA) was established in 1971 to further the development of higher education in Ireland.

- The role of the **Environmental Protection Agency** (EPA) is to protect the environment. It regulates the licensing and control of large-scale waste and industrial activities to ensure that they do no harm to the environment nor endanger human health. It also sponsors research on various environmental issues. (www.epa.ie).

d)   Community development

- The **Western Development Commission** was established in 1999 under the Western Development Commission Act 1998 to foster integrated economic and social development in seven counties, all of Connacht as well as Clare and Donegal. It prepares policy documents, promotes strategic initiatives in various sectors and operates the Western Development Commission Investment Fund, which can provide equity and loan capital for projects deemed to be commercially viable. (www.wdc.ie)

- **Area partnership Companies** (1990) were established to counteract disadvantage in certain areas of long-term unemployment, poverty and social exclusion. They give grants for approved projects. Community development in this context refers to a process through which local community life is enhanced by a wide variety of activities focused on anti-exclusion measures and capacity building.

- **LEADER** companies (1991) originated with an EU initiative to promote integrated rural development. Their mission is to facilitate new approaches for integrated sustainable rural development. They provide public funding for the implementation of multi-sectoral plans to develop specified areas. All companies operate as autonomous bodies in accordance with their agreement with the Department of Community, Equality and Gaeltacht Affairs. (www.irishleadernetwork.org)

e) Others

- **InterTrade Ireland** (1999) is a cross-border body established under the Belfast Agreement to increase the number and value of all-Ireland trade and business networks. (www.intertradeireland.com)
- The **Arts Council** is responsible for developing the arts in Ireland. It provides grants to artists, arts organisations and other groups to promote the arts. It also provides advice and information on the arts to the Government as well as to a wide range of individuals and organisations. (www.artscouncil.ie)
- The **Irish Film Board** (Bord Scannán na hÉireann) has a responsibility to develop and support the Irish film industry as well as promote Ireland as a location for international film and television production. (www.filmboard.ie)
- The **Competition Authority**'s role is to enforce competition law, adjudicate on mergers and promote competition in general for the benefit of consumers. (www.tca.ie)
- The **Crafts Council of Ireland** (1976) is the national design and development organisation for the craft industry in Ireland. (www.ccoi.ie)
- The **Digital Hub Development Agency** was established to create an international digital enterprise area in Dublin. (www.thedigitalhub.com)
- The **National Competitiveness Council** (1997) reports on key issues relating to competitiveness in the Irish economy and makes recommendations for improvements. (www.competitiveness.ie)

Other organisations supporting entrepreneurs

- **Chambers Ireland** represents the interests of all Chambers of Commerce operating in Ireland. (www.chambers.ie)
- The **Small Firms Association** (SFA) is an independent association within the Irish Business and Employers Confederation representing and supporting small businesses. (www.sfa.ie)
- The **Irish Small and Medium Enterprises Association** (ISME) represents and supports small and medium-sized enterprises. (www.isme.ie)
- **Plato Ireland Ltd** provides support for SMEs exploring growth and expansion.

1.9 Summary

Enterprise is essential for the economic, social and cultural development of any nation. Ireland is developing rapidly as an enterprising society. The main objectives of Irish industrial policy are the development of indigenous enterprises, especially those with export potential, investment in and commercialisation of research and development, attraction of inward investment, the maintenance of a competitive economy and balanced regional development.

The Irish economy has evolved from protectionism to free trade, the industrial economy, the Celtic Tiger, to the recent recession. The small and medium-sized enterprise sector is crucial to continued progress. One of the major objectives of current Irish industrial policy is the creation of a knowledge economy based on research, development, innovation and commercialisation. There is now considerable investment in research through State bodies and the private sector. The new knowledge created must be used for the benefit of society, to enhance competitiveness and to promote growth, employment and living standards. The links in this process are research, development, technology transfer and commercialisation.

To cater for the expected growth of the economy, the report of the Expert Group on Future Skills Needs (2007) recommended a big increase in the workforce and ambitious targets for upskilling, but their projections have to be adjusted in light of the depth and length of the recession which started in 2008. It is State policy that there should be balanced regional development in the country, supported by the National Spatial Strategy.

Questions

1. Discuss the main developments in the Irish economy since 2000.
2. What recommendations would you make for the promotion of small and medium enterprises?
3. What do you understand by the knowledge economy?
4. Explain what is meant by technology transfer.
5. Using the internet, establish the current assistance available for those seeking to establish an internationally traded service in Ireland.

Chapter 2

Business opportunities

Other people see things and say why?
But I dream of things that never were and say why not?

GEORGE BERNARD SHAW

Learning objectives

- To consider some definitions of an entrepreneur
- To outline some personality traits of entrepreneurs
- To explore various sources of business ideas
- To explain various intellectual property rights, including copyright, patent, trade marks and design
- To comprehend various criteria for assessing business ideas
- To outline the contents of a feasibility study and a business plan.

In this chapter the following topics are addressed:
2.1 Entrepreneurship
2.2 Sources of business ideas
2.3 Protecting intellectual property
2.4 Assessing business ideas
2.5 Feasibility study
2.6 Business plan
2.7 Summary

2.1 Entrepreneurship

This section looks at the following:
a) Definitions of an entrepreneur
b) Personality traits.

a) Definitions of an entrepreneur

- 'A person who sets up a business or businesses, taking on financial risks in the hope of profit' (*Concise Oxford Dictionary*).

- 'A person who always searches for change, responds to it, and exploits it as an opportunity' (Drucker, 1985).
- 'An entrepreneur is someone who perceives an opportunity and creates an organisation to pursue it' (Bygrave, 1994).
- 'An entrepreneur is one who creates, manages, and assumes the risk of a new venture' (Cunningham and Lischeron, 1991).
- 'An entrepreneur is one who creates a new business in the face of risk and uncertainty for the purpose of achieving profit and growth by identifying opportunities and assembling the necessary resources to capitalise on them' (Zimmerer and Scarborough, 2002).
- 'A person who habitually creates and innovates to build something of recognised value around perceived opportunities' (Bolton and Thompson, 2005).
- 'A individual who orchestrates, operates and assumes risks for a business venture' (Central Statistics Office, 2007).
- A person who 'buys at a certain price and sells at an uncertain price' (Cantillon, 1755).

In a review of the literature, five key elements feature prominently:
- The ability to identify and exploit a business opportunity
- The human creative effort of developing a business or building something of value
- A willingness to undertake risk
- Competence to organise the necessary resources to respond to the opportunity
- The chance of profit or loss.

An entrepreneur can be defined as a person who develops an enterprise, or adds value, with a chance of profit or loss, in response to a perceived market opportunity by organising the necessary resources, undertaking the risk involved and providing a product or service of value to customers. Entrepreneurship is the process of developing an enterprise to exploit a market opportunity by organising the required resources, managing risk and providing value for customers with the objective of long-term gain. When entrepreneurial behaviour takes place inside existing organisations, it is known as intrapreneurship or corporate entrepreneurship. Creativity, innovation and entrepreneurship are essential for the survival of established businesses. Contrary to general belief, most new businesses, products and services are developed by existing enterprises, with a far lower failure rate than for start-up projects (Sathe, 2003). There are also social entrepreneurs who add value in non-profit-making organisations by adopting new ideas and innovating. An excellent example of social entrepreneurship was the vision, planning and organisation of the Special Olympics World Summer Games in Ireland and the spectacular opening ceremony in Croke Park on 21 June 2003, with Mayo-born Mary

Davis as chief executive officer and Denis O'Brien as chairperson of the organising committee (Connolly and McGing, 2005). There are also entrepreneurial people in every occupation, profession, community, sporting and cultural group, as well as in public sector organisations.

b)   Personality traits

There is a vast literature on the psychological and personality traits of entrepreneurs which attempts to understand what motivates them (for example, McClelland, 1987; Mitton, 1989; O'Farrell, 1986; Vesper, 1995). The most widely quoted psychological theory is the one developed by David McClelland in his book *The Achieving Society* (1961), where he claims that entrepreneurs have a high need for achievement. Other studies (especially Rotter, 1966) suggest that entrepreneurs have a high internal locus of control and a big desire to be their own boss and control their own destiny. In an Irish study by O'Connor and Lyons (1983), the common personality traits identified were a need for independence, control of their own fate, need for achievement, feedback on performance, strong sense of responsibility, self-confidence, positive self-image and calculated risk-taking. Money did not feature high on the list. Each prospective entrepreneur has to consider if he/she has the desired qualities. There is no definite set of personality and behaviour traits applicable to all successful entrepreneurs. The traits listed in Table 2.1 could apply to people who achieve success in any walk of life. Entrepreneurs require good managerial, interpersonal, communication, negotiation and problem-solving skills as well as technical competence in the activity.

There is also a vast literature on the social background of entrepreneurs. Some are pushed into entrepreneurship by family background, unemployment, frustration in their existing career or other reasons, but many are attracted by the challenge and need to control their own destiny. Many entrepreneurs are the first-born in families, while some have role models in parents who were in business (O'Farrell, 1986). Studies of the educational background of entrepreneurs show a variety of levels. However, most successful entrepreneurs have prior work experience in the targeted business sectors (Timmons, 1994). Hisrich and Peters (1998) emphasise the importance of prior technical knowledge of the specific business sector as well as general managerial experience. O'Farrell (1986) identifies three types of entrepreneurs in an Irish study: the graduate (engineering or business with a big emphasis on added value), the opportunist (a person developing a business based on his/her experience in a variety of jobs) and the craftsperson (generally based on an apprenticeship or technical background).

Successful entrepreneurs are able to turn setbacks and failures into learning experiences, to adapt, change and move in new directions. Walt Disney went bankrupt on three occasions before successfully launching the Disney Corporation and Henry Ford failed twice before becoming a famous car manufacturer (Lambing and Kuehl, 2007).

Table 2:1: Traits of an entrepreneur

Customer focus	Ability to identify and exploit market opportunities
	Constant assessment of customer needs
	Commitment to attracting and retaining satisfied customers
Organising ability	Good planner
	Good organiser of all the required resources
	Proactive in change management and innovation
	Good time manager
	Focused on goals and objectives
Leadership	Vision
	Self-starter
	Initiative
	Inspirational and able to empower others
	Reliable
	Goal-orientated
	Good networker
	Positive 'can do' approach
Confidence	Self-belief
	Self-confidence
	Self-reliance
Motivation	Determination to succeed despite adversity or obstacles
	Good interpersonal skills
	Team builder
	Good motivator of staff
	High achiever
	Focused on results, high productivity and continuous improvement
Risk-taking	Calculated risk-taker
	Sense of responsibility to all stakeholders
Creativity	Open mind
	Willing and able to learn quickly
	Lateral thinker
	Ability to adapt to change and listen to feedback
	Innovator
	Flexible
	Creative thinker
Commitment	Doer
	Total passion and commitment to the business
	Willpower
	Perseverance
	Able to work under pressure
	Willingness to make personal sacrifices for the business
	Energetic
	Good health
	Control over all the key aspects of the business
	Capacity for hard work
	Determination

Denis O'Brien, who developed enterprises in private radio broadcasting, telecommunications and mobile telephones in Ireland and abroad, was unsuccessful in his first business
venture, a shopping channel on Sky television (Creaton, 2010; O'Gorman and Cunningham,
2007). Thomas Edison, who said that genius was '1 per cent inspiration and 99 per cent
perspiration', failed on numerous occasions and managed in the process to become a
famous inventor with over one thousand patents, the most ever for one individual. Edison
also had the ability to apply and commercialise new ideas, including the incandescent light
bulb in 1879 (Bolton and Thompson, 2005). There are very few successful entrepreneurs
that did not experience setbacks at some stage of their careers.

Successful entrepreneurs come from a wide variety of backgrounds with varying
talents, educational experiences, career paths, motives and aspirations. They are all special
people. They have the ideas, the organising ability, the willingness to take risks and a passion
to make their businesses succeed. They generally have a strong work ethic and are zealous
about their dreams, their products or their services and have the ability to transmit that
enthusiasm to others. Those people make huge investments in finance, reputation and
personal time. With a big responsibility to all stakeholders, most new entrepreneurs wonder
in the early stages how they can meet their payroll and other costs when they fall due. The
rewards for success can be high, but the price of failure is also costly. The financial risks
involved include little or no income during the early stage, the possibility of losing the entire
investment and, unless trading in a limited company, unlimited liability for business debts.
Having identified the opportunities and the appropriate timing, most new entrepreneurs
have a vision of what they would like to accomplish, a 'can-do' approach, high confidence
in their own abilities and the leadership skills necessary to organise the required resources.

A Forfás study, *Entrepreneurship in Ireland* (2002), identified the following as
important factors for entrepreneurs:

> a family background in business, possession of relevant skills and
> knowledge, a strong interest in business, access to formal and
> informal supports, ability to access finance and to develop or buy
> in necessary complementary skills and experience, possession of a
> marketable idea and a willingness to work hard.

It takes some time to see if new entrepreneurs have the required commercial competence and
sagacious decision-making skills to turn their dreams into sustainable enterprises. Some new
entrepreneurs have external coaches or mentors during the early stage of their businesses.

2.2 Sources of business ideas

In considering sources of business ideas it is important to remember the words of Albert
Einstein: 'Imagination is more important than knowledge.' The vast majority of new

businesses originate from simple ideas that can come from anywhere. A business is established to create a product or service of value to customers at a profit for the owner(s). Aspiring entrepreneurs have to identify needs or expected requirements in the marketplace which are not being served and decide that they can do so at a profit. These entrepreneurs endeavour to establish competitive advantage by satisfying the needs of potential customers better, faster, cheaper or in a more convenient manner than existing suppliers. According to Timmons (1994), most entrepreneurs use their prior technical and business experience of an industry and market sector to establish their businesses. Knowledge of the targeted market sector, with its own unique features relating to the changing needs of customers, trade practices in the supply and distribution channels as well as a network of contacts, is very important for any aspiring entrepreneur seeking a gap in a market and a business opportunity (Vesper, 1995). People with good knowledge of a market sector are able to identify new needs of customers and how these can be developed into opportunities for new businesses. New entrepreneurs have to get the quality of their products or services right first time, meet and, if possible, exceed the expectations of customers and survive in the market sector regardless of the trade practices operating there as well as in the supply and distribution channels. There are numerous sources of business ideas. Just consider all the new products and services that became available in the last 20 years by entrepreneurial creativity – that rate of innovation will accelerate in the future.

The main sources of business ideas include the following:

a) Creativity and innovation
b) Replicating an existing business idea
c) Personal skills, experience, hobbies
d) Tourism, leisure, arts, culture, entertainment, services
e) Local resources and/or needs
f) Import substitution
g) Future needs arising from change
h) Market gap analysis
i) Licensing
j) Franchising
k) Purchasing an existing business
l) Management buy-out (MBO)
m) Research and development

a) Creativity and innovation

According to the British philosopher John Stuart Mill, 'all good things which exist are the fruits of originality'. In business, this involves creativity and innovation. Creativity is conceptualising and developing something that does not exist or a new way of doing something. It is thinking about things that never were and asking why not? It is the process of associating known information with new combinations. Roberts (2004) states that:

> Creativity involves originality, imaging new things, seeing new patterns and connections. Yet, as important as this originality is, it is not enough. For the point is not just to come up with something new, but instead something distinctive that works.

Creative minds are alert to new ideas, new technologies, new applications, new products, new services and new ways of doing things. The interaction of people from different backgrounds, with varying educational and work experiences as well as ethnic origins, can contribute to creativity. According to de Bono (1973), 'creative thinking is not a talent; it is a skill that can be learnt'. He also recommends lateral thinking, breaking away from 'fixed ideas and fixed channels of thought in order to find new and better routes' (1973, 1978). In other words, he recommends 'thinking outside the box'. Creativity, or a new discovery, is rarely an Archimedes 'Eureka' moment. It requires huge commitment, passion, self-confidence and perseverance in a supporting environment. According to Nickerson (1998):

> Students need to believe that creativity is determined by motivation and effort to a significant degree. They need to understand that creative products are seldom produced without intent and effort, that there is considerable evidence to support the belief that most people have potential they never realise and that persistent effort to develop that potential is likely to be successful . . . Students need to know too that . . . truly outstanding creative works in science and art have often taken many years – sometimes the better part of a lifetime – to produce . . . They need to understand that if one really wants to be creative in a substantial way, one must be prepared to work at it.

Innovation is defined in the *Strategy for Science, Technology and Innovation* (Government Publications, 2007b) as 'doing new things, or doing old things in new ways'. It is the successful application of new ideas for the benefit of the organisation and consumers. It is defined by Lordan and Cooney (2002) as 'a process whereby new ideas are put into practical use to add value commercially'. An innovation has to create value for the business and its customers, which is influenced by three key factors: utility, price and cost. Innovation originates with creative ideas or experimentation. According to the Enterprise Strategy Group (2004):

Innovation requires a particular mindset that involves curiosity, creativity and problem-solving, the ability to continually question established ways of doing things and the ability to apply knowledge, insights and intuition to change them.

Innovation can originate anywhere and with anyone – consumer complaints about the poor quality of a product or service, suppliers, competitors, all categories of staff, the general public – and it is not confined to research and development. The majority of business innovations are not technological. Innovation can involve change to existing products or services, sources of supply, processes, markets, management practices or customer service. It can be a very simple idea. The application of new technologies to existing practices has huge innovation potential, and the World Wide Web has uniquely changed the way commerce is conducted. Schumpeter (1950) refers to the process of 'creative destruction', where there is a constant search for something new which destroys the old, but most innovation is incremental in nature. According to Schumpeter, the most important competitive weapon is not lower prices but new ideas. Entrepreneurs are regarded as more innovative than the managers of small businesses. Innovators do not like structured situations and prefer flexibility to solve problems as well as responsible risk-taking. The culture of an organisation has to support innovation, generating new ideas, challenging existing practices and experimenting, and must empower staff at all levels to think about new business opportunities. Innovation is not dependent on new knowledge creation but on the capacity to access and adopt the available knowledge on a global scale. Rather than relying on internal ideas only, Chesbrough (2006) supports open innovation, where a business leverages internal and external sources. Open innovation inspires a business to find the best business model, whether that originates from an internal source or from an external one. The new challenge for entrepreneurs is to be able to convert research findings, whenever they originate, into products and services that satisfy the needs of customers at a profit.

Drucker (1985) identified seven sources of innovation:

- Unexpected success, failure or an outside event (for example, recent interest in the environment)
- Incongruity between reality as it actually is and what it is assumed or ought to be (for example, expansion of e-commerce)
- Process need (security software for e-commerce)
- Industry and market changes (use of the internet)
- Demographic changes (immigration to Ireland)
- Changes in perception, mood and meaning (interest in organic foods)
- New knowledge, both scientific and non-scientific (application of new knowledge).

According to Drucker, innovation is not achieved by inspiration or special moments but by hard work, and the experience gained from failures can be part of the process. Change is always a catalyst for innovation. Drucker states that innovation is 'the specific tool of entrepreneurs, the means by which they exploit change as an opportunity for a different business or a different service'. Charles Handy in *The Empty Raincoat* (1995) argues that the old certainties are gone and that change and turbulence are about us. This rapid pace of change, with new needs to provide better experiences for customers, is creating new business opportunities. Small businesses can respond quickly in a customised, flexible manner to cater for the changing preferences of customers in a market segment. Innovation has huge potential in existing businesses that constantly seek to improve their processes, products, services, marketing and management in response to change in the external environment. The business landscape is littered with the ruins of once successful enterprises that did not innovate and change. Most Irish businesses are open to new ideas and new developments and are willing to break the mould by taking moderate risks in pursuit of innovation. These businesses expect creativity and innovation from staff, with many stimulating new ideas in suggestion schemes and brainstorming sessions. Innovative organisations seek to consistently outperform their competitors by responding to the new needs of their customers. Successful businesses are constantly innovating. The personal computer, the mobile telephone and the internet have revolutionised the business environment, with enormous future potential for innovation. The Enterprise Strategy Group (2004) suggests that Ireland could develop a co-ordinated policy for organisational innovation with regard to its positive experience with social partnership. Enterprise Ireland is endeavouring to get indigenous organisations to engage in research and development, to innovate and to commercialise new knowledge. The potential for innovation in all kinds of services is enormous, especially with the application of new technologies.

b)   Replicating an existing business idea

A prospective entrepreneur could consider replicating an existing business idea and developing a new business, often in a niche area. The vast majority of new businesses take this route, especially in relation to all kinds of services. Ideas which are successful in other countries and other areas within this country are widely adopted. These business ideas can originate from travel, experience, journals and the media. However, the success of a product or service in one country or location is no guarantee that it will succeed elsewhere. This is where local knowledge and market research are important.

The idea for Ryanair was replicated from a very successful no-frills, low-fares airline, Southwest Airlines in the United States. Tony Ryan, then chief executive of Guinness Peat Aviation, saw the potential for a similar airline in Ireland. He started Ryanair in 1985 and, after heavy losses in the early years, was advised to close it down by his personal financial adviser, Michael O'Leary. Tony Ryan believed in his dream and rejected the advice. Michael

O'Leary took over the management of Ryanair in 1993 and developed it into the most successful low-fares airline in Europe (Creaton, 2005; Ruddock, 2007).

c)   Personal skills, experiences, hobbies

Many successful businesses are established using a person's own skills, knowledge, expertise, networks and experience, including domestic knowledge. This is an important source of business ideas and the one most likely to succeed. Most local services are developed using personal skills and experiences.

Numerous Irish people have used their personal skills and experiences from the construction industry to develop very successful organisations at home and abroad. Dermot Desmond knew the financial services business when he founded National City Brokers (NCB) in 1981. He sold a 56 per cent stake to Ulster Bank in 1994 and developed many other internationally traded services as well as pioneering the development of the very successful Irish Financial Services Centre (IFSC) in Dublin (Rogan, 2007). After leaving school at a young age, Freda Hayes worked with her father in a thatched cottage in Blarney, County Cork, selling souvenirs to visitors. As the business prospered, her father, Christy Kelleher, purchased the Mahony Mills in Blarney in 1975 for a knitwear factory. Freda became chief executive on the retirement of her father and over the following 14 years expanded the company to a turnover of €30 million and a workforce of over 350. She became one of the most respected entrepreneurs in the country. Disagreement with family members about future direction led to their purchasing her shareholding and she ceased all involvement with the company. She re-entered the business world by acquiring the House of James retail chain and later Meadows & Byrne (Garavan, Ó Cinnéide et al., Vol. 2, 1997).

After her experience in the Great Southern Hotel in Galway serving American visitors, Mary Bennett, the first woman elected President of Galway Chamber (of Commerce and Industry) in 1985 and later of Chambers Ireland in 1988, established her own successful retail store, selling the best of Irish and European merchandise to visitors and locals as well as developing a mail order service, exporting all around the world. That business became what is now Treasure Chest in Galway. Following her father's sudden death, Carol Moffett became managing director of Moffett Engineering in County Monaghan at the age of 19. She developed the two-person family business into a very successful exporting company (Kenny, 1993). Evelyn O'Toole, an environmental science graduate from Sligo Institute of Technology, started Complete Laboratory Solutions (CLS), a scientific contract laboratory, at Rosmuck in 1994. By 2008, it was employing over 40 graduates. Mayo-born Dr Seán Rowland, a former national teacher, shocked the educational establishment in Ireland in 2000 when he established Hibernia College, an online college offering innovative, accredited and blended learning programmes at postgraduate level. By 2009 Hibernia College was serving students in 26 countries.

Some small businesses were started by former employees of multinational and indigenous organisations as specialised suppliers to their former employers. While such provenance has obvious advantages in facilitating the establishment of a business, it is a dangerous long-term strategy to be dependent on one or a few customers. As these businesses gained experience from such linkages, they expanded to serve a wider range of customers and some developed export markets. There is a large number of people employed in these organisations today, with excellent technical and commercial experience, who could become very successful entrepreneurs if they were to perceive the pull factor as attractive, rather than wait for a push factor like downsizing or closure. All public organisations, State departments, the health service, schools, colleges and local authorities purchase a considerable volume of materials and services annually. Again, careful market research and compliance with the special procurement requirements can identify huge opportunities for entrepreneurial creativity based on personal skills and experience.

Many people have turned their hobbies and leisure activities into successful businesses. Bill Gates, co-founder of Microsoft, and Steve Jobs, co-founder of Apple Computers, dropped out of college and turned their teenage hobbies of playing with computers into vast corporations. Michael Dell started Dell Computers from his dormitory room at the University of Texas. Henry Ford dreamed of making a car which most people could afford and developed a prototype for the first one at his garage in Detroit. Numerous singers and musicians have turned their hobbies into successful professional careers.

d)   Tourism, leisure, arts, culture, entertainment, services

There are many business opportunities in the changing tourism, hospitality, leisure, arts, culture and entertainment sectors. Tourist, hospitality and leisure projects include the provision of accommodation of all types, transportation, catering, entertainment and gifts as well as the provision of a wide range of activity and cultural holidays. Many successful hotels in Ireland originated as bed and breakfast operations in homes to supplement family incomes.

There are numerous success stories of cultural entrepreneurs in the arts and entertainment sectors which owe their origin to creativity and initiative. Instead of adopting a homogenised mass culture, Irish people have achieved global cultural renown on an massive scale for a small nation. Irish music, song, dance, film, literature and drama have achieved worldwide recognition. One has only to think of musicians such as U2, the Cranberries and Westlife; singers such as Enya, Sinéad O'Connor and Mary Black; the dance phenomenon of *Riverdance*; filmmakers Neil Jordan and Jim Sheridan; actors such as Liam Neeson, Brendan Gleeson and Gabriel Byrne; Nobel laureate Seamus Heaney, Maeve

Binchy, Sebastian Barry, William Trevor, Colm Tóibín, Anne Enright, Roddy Doyle, Celia Ahern, Marian Keyes and many others in literature and great playwrights such as Brian Friel, Martin McDonagh and Tom Murphy. There are also great developments in the visual arts. The staging of *Riverdance* during the interval in the 1994 Eurovision Song Contest stunned audiences in Ireland and across Europe. From there, Moya Doherty and John Colgan expanded their independent production company, Tyrone Productions, and brought Irish dancing to the international stage (Garavan *et al.*, 1997). *Riverdance* also turned Michael Flatley into a very successful artistic entrepreneur. Margaret Nelson started Capital Radio, which was named FM 104 in 1992, and it soon became the leading independent commercial station in Dublin. It was taken over in 2008 by UTV for €52 million.

Most employment growth in the future will be in internationally traded services as well as personal services such as finance, insurance, education, healthcare, tourism, professional, consultancy, environmental, marketing and software. With the roll-out of broadband technologies and increasing commuting times, more people are deciding to work from home as self-employed professionals. The potential for the application of new technologies to knowledge-based services is enormous, especially with regard to the new rate of 12.5 per cent corporate tax on traded services. There are huge opportunities in other countries for the development of services from Ireland, including design and construction in Saudi Arabia, China and India. It is also expected that more public services in Ireland and in other countries will be outsourced.

e)   Local resources and/or needs

Many businesses are established around local resources such as materials, facilities, amenities and skills. Frustration with existing products and services can provide business ideas. Gaps in the existing supply of goods and services required locally can identify needs for small businesses, for example, catering, crèche facilities, healthcare, repairs, hair salons and similar operations. Food production offers huge possibilities, especially products based on good diet.

A local need for an air service from Connemara to the Aran Islands inspired Galway entrepreneur Pádraig Ó Ceidigh to acquire Aer Arann in 1994, which he developed into a regional airline. Seán Quinn started selling a local resource, sand and gravel, from his family's farm in Derrylin, County Fermanagh, in 1973 and went on to establish the Quinn Group and a global business empire with interests in cement, concrete and insulation products, as well as container glass, hotels, pubs, golf courses, general insurance and medical insurance. By 2007 he was Ireland's richest person, though by 2010 his empire was in serious trouble because of his investment in Anglo-Irish Bank. One of the simplest ideas was developed by Geoffrey Read, who decided to sell bottled spring water and established Ballygowan Spring Water Company Ltd in 1981 at Newcastle West, County Limerick. He quickly developed it into a very successful business with high export content (Garavan *et al.*, 1997). Brian and Eamonn Fallon heard their sister complain one day at dinner that she could not find rented accommodation in Dublin. Their response was the establishment of a property website, www.daft.ie, which made these two Dublin-born entrepreneurs into millionaires (Cooney, 2007). They started the business with no external funding.

A local need for a fast food outlet in Ballinasloe, County Galway inspired Pat McDonagh to set up his first business there in 1978: a small-scale take-away. This humble beginning laid the foundation for the Supermac's chain of restaurants around the country (Garavan *et al.*, 1997). The desire to feed calves more quickly inspired John Concannon of Tuam to develop a plastic feeding system for cattle in 1987 from a farm workshop and establish JFC Manufacturing Co. Ltd. By 2006, the company was selling innovative quality plastic products to a variety of sectors, including agriculture, construction, healthcare, recycling, chemical and marine in over 30 countries. The company invested heavily in research and development (O'Gorman and Cunningham, 2007). Frustration experienced by tourists at the limited opening times of banks influenced Brian McCarthy to establish the Foreign Exchange Company of Ireland in Killorglin, County Kerry, in 1981. It became Fexco and diversified into a variety of financial services, including global payments, outsourcing, travel and leisure, consumer financial transfers and administering prize bonds on behalf of the National Treasury Management Agency (Rogan, 2007). Eugene Murtagh founded a small engineering business in a shed on his parents' farm in Kingscourt, County Cavan in the late 1960s, which became the Kingspan Group in 1972, providing insulated roof and wall cladding systems for the local construction industry. The adoption of new technologies and continuous innovation enabled the company to grow and maintain a competitive advantage as it expanded into a range of related activities. By 2008 it had a turnover in excess of €1.8 billion, with 43 manufacturing plants in 20 countries, employing over 6,500 people. In 1989, John Flaherty established what became C and T Manufacturing at Ballybane, Galway, as a specialist company focused on import substitution in the supply of tool-making services to multinational companies operating in Ireland. It became a global supplier to the sheet metal industry with operations in several countries, including China, employing 984 people by 2008. In that year John Flaherty was named Ernst & Young Entrepreneur of the Year. New local needs like security and crime prevention also offer new opportunities.

f)   Import substitution

A study of a list of imported products and services can provide ideas for business opportunities. This source inspired Seán Hannick to establish Killala Precision Components Ltd in 1981, which later developed exports to several countries.

g)   Future needs arising from change

Changes in the economic, social, technological and legal environment are always fertile sources of new business ideas. Modern information and communications technology is fostering change, innovation and new business opportunities, including the whole area of internet shopping. New legislation often creates new needs, for example new regulations on health and safety resulted in a number of people starting consultancy practices. Deregulation in telecommunications and air transport created new customers, new businesses and additional employment, with companies like Ryanair, O_2 and FM 104. It is expected that environmental concerns will generate huge business opportunities in the future.

h)   Market gap analysis

Market gap analysis involves a careful consideration of the competitive strategies followed by existing suppliers to a market in an effort to identify a business opportunity. There are numerous business opportunities ranging from small niche markets to the possibility of building global businesses. In 1977 Loughrea veterinary surgeon Michael Burke identified a gap in the market for generic pharmaceuticals for veterinary practices and started what became the Chanelle Group. By 2004 the group was doing business in over 80 countries, providing human and animal pharmaceuticals.

i)   Licensing

If a business is not prepared to invest in its own research and development, it can acquire new technology by licensing. Licensing is a legal agreement whereby an organisation, known as the licensor, transfers its technological expertise or the right to sell its patented product to another organisation, known as the licensee, in return for an upfront fee and/or a royalty based on sales. The upfront payment, a contribution towards the research, development and commercialisation costs of the licensor, is based on the uniqueness of the product, the level of technology and the quality of patent protection. Royalty rates normally vary from 2 to 7 per cent of net sales (excluding taxes, freight, discounts) but can be higher in specific cases. The rate is influenced by the level of technology, potential profitability, selling and distribution costs. The licensor does not become involved in the management of the affairs of the licensee's business. Many organisations find it more advantageous to license a new product rather than developing one internally or carrying out their own research and development. Licensing reduces the risks and costs involved in new product development while gaining access to the expertise of another organisation. However, there are some risks involved in licensing, especially inability to control the licensee and exposure to possible product liability. A comprehensive licensing contract, incorporating all possible areas for disagreement, is essential. The following are the main provisions of a licensing contract: participating parties, the technology being licensed, territories covered, exclusive or non-exclusive, downpayment and royalties, improvements, infringements, duration, reviews, alterations, termination, accounts and the law applicable to the agreement. This requires careful negotiation of all aspects of the agreement, which should benefit both parties. Such a symbiotic relationship requires frankness, trust, compatibility and a good knowledge of the business culture experienced by the other party.

j)   Franchising

A franchise is a right to operate a business given by the owner of a trade mark (the franchisor) allowing the user (franchisee) to market a product or service under the franchisor's name in a specified geographical area. It involves a transfer of the technical knowledge required to establish a business quickly with an existing and successful brand. Back-up guidance, training, support and advertising are provided by the franchisor, all of which reduce the risk involved. The theory behind a franchise is that by adopting a product or service which is already a market success, the chances of initiating a successful business are much better than starting with a new idea. However, it is advisable for a person considering a franchise to undertake market research on a sample of existing franchises and their customers as well as potential consumers in the new geographical area and the competition. A franchise can fail just like any other business venture, so it is essential to take prudent precautions in assessing a proposal. Franchising is advantageous to the franchisor in that it facilitates sales and increased income in a new area with little capital outlay and low risk, and to the franchisee in gaining quick access to a proven business concept, a recognised business name and existing brand loyalty. However, some caution is required. Just because a product succeeds in one market is no guarantee that it will succeed in a new market because of different cultural norms. Costs include an initial fee, a franchise package fee (based on the package of support provided), a management service fee (a regular payment for the ongoing franchise rights and services provided by the franchisor, which can vary from 0 per cent up to 10 per cent of turnover) and an advertising levy (a contribution of about 3 per cent of turnover to a central fund which is used for advertising the franchise). Instead of a management service fee, some franchisors require their franchisees to purchase supplies (at an appropriate mark-up) exclusively from them or from a nominated supplier who pays a commission for the agreement. Consequently, a franchisor has a vested interest in ensuring that the franchisee's business is a success. In addition to these fees, a franchisee, has to provide the premises, equipment, fixtures, fittings and the working capital required. In selecting a franchise the following are important considerations: track record of the franchisor, the profitability of current franchises, possible market opportunities, competition, the costs involved and the package of support provided. The viability of the franchise has to be assessed with regard to the industry, market sector, market opportunities, changes on the horizon, projected sales, total costs (capital and revenue) and expected return on investment after paying all fees. A franchise contract has to be drafted carefully, covering all possible areas of disagreement, including prospective territory, fees, obligations, right to sell, transfer as an inheritance, renewal or termination of the agreement, as well as providing benefits to both parties. Legal advice should be obtained on any franchise proposal before the contract is finalised. An operating manual specifying the way all aspects of the franchise should be conducted by both parties is usually prepared. Some well-known franchises in Ireland include Supermac's, McDonald's, Burger King, the Body Shop, Bewleys, Sherry FitzGerald and car retailers. Anita Roddick started the Body Shop in 1976 as a one-woman cottage business based on natural ingredients and developed it into a successful global franchise company, selling it in 2006 for €957 million (*Irish Times*, 11 September 2007, p. 13). The success rate of franchises is high.

k)   Purchasing an existing business

A person or organisation can purchase an existing business as a going concern or acquire just the name and goodwill. Purchasing an existing business can expedite market entry and reduce the risks of failure as there is already an established customer base. Considerations like location, premises (with the benefit of a surveyor's report), equipment, track record, markets, customer base, turnover, costs, other assets, earnings, cash flow, staffing and reputation are all carefully assessed. The purchase price is negotiated with regard to the tangible business assets and the goodwill (usually a multiple of the net profit figure). As future earnings are worth less than the same figure received today, their present value can be determined using discounted future cash flows (with the aid of present value tables). In some cases it is cheaper to buy an existing business than to start a new one. A loss-making organisation can sometimes be acquired at a bargain price if new management believe they can turn it into a viable enterprise. It is important to explore the reason for selling in all cases as well as the reaction of customers to the owner's departure. Many small businesses are built around the personalities and reputations of the owners.

l)   Management buy-out (MBO)

A management buy-out involves the acquisition of a business or a majority shareholding by its managers. It usually involves high borrowing because of the inability of the new owners to put up substantial equity capital. Consequently, the management team is required to prepare a comprehensive proposal (in effect a business plan) seeking funds for the initiative. The proposal must show that the business is capable of generating sufficient profits and cash flow to finance loan repayment commitments and provide adequate working capital. The plan covers the following issues *inter alia*:

- History of the business
- Its existing markets and customers

- Accounts for the past three years
- Production facilities
- Staffing, strengths and weaknesses
- Industry and market analysis
- Valuation of properties, plant, equipment and other assets
- Projected accounts and cash flow statements for up to three years
- Management team, names, qualifications, experience and competence in all the key functional areas
- The objectives of the sellers and purchasers
- Assurance that the new organisation can operate completely without the former owners
- A statement about how the selling price is decided.

Seller-motivated buy-outs arise for many reasons: lack of strategic fit (where the activity is not part of redefined objectives), disappointing performance, need to raise finance for other acquisitions and in a family-owned business a wish to reward management for past performance and loyalty. The selling price is a matter for negotiation between the parties, but is influenced by earnings potential, customer base and valuation of all assets. Any management buy-out involves complex financial, legal, taxation and managerial issues, with good professional advice essential before finalising an agreement. Other options are a management buy-in (MBI), the purchase of a business by a team of external managers, and a management–employee buy-out (MEBO), the purchase by existing managers and employees.

m)   Research and development

Research and development are fertile sources of new business ideas, but the big challenge is successful commercialisation. Developing new products requires ambitious, competent entrepreneurs and the necessary resources. High-technology enterprises are usually developed by management teams with complementary technological and managerial talents. Innovations can be patented and, if commercially successful, the financial returns can be high. As Ireland develops from a low-cost producer to a diversified knowledge-based economy, its future competitive advantage has to be based on investment in research and development, with various initiatives underway at present, as outlined in Chapter 1. A good Irish example is Creganna, which was founded in Galway in 1980 by Ian Quinn as an engineering company, but by 2009 it had evolved to become a world leader in research and development in medical device technology. By then it had a staff of 800 with plants in Galway, Minnesota and Singapore.

Many high-technology internet companies originated from research and development. Several high-technology businesses in the Silicon Valley of California originated in Stanford University, especially after the start of the internet in the early 1990s. Two of the best-known early internet companies were Google and Yahoo. Google, founded in 1998 at Stanford University by two young impecunious computer science graduates, Larry Page and Sergey Brin, operating out of a garage, became the world's most popular internet search engine in five years. Yahoo, which became the best-known provider of internet portals helping people find what they want, was founded by two Stanford students, Jerry Yang and David Filo. By 1999 it had 1,600 employees and was valued at $44 billion (Bolton and Thompson, 2005). Amazon, founded in 1994 by an electrical engineering and computer science graduate from Princeton, Jeff Bezos, became the largest bookstore in the world, pioneering the selling of books on the internet. eBay, founded in 1995 by Pierre Omidyar, became a very successful online auction house within a few years of Meg Whitman becoming its CEO in 1998 and later a virtual fixed price marketplace. It has no supply or inventory costs as goods sold are supplied direct from sellers to buyers (Bolton and Thompson, 2005). Peter Thiel invented PayPal, a global electronic payments system, in Stanford University. Facebook, which quickly became a very successful social networking website, was founded by Harvard students Chris Hughes and Mark Zuckerberg in 2004. In one of the most amazing Irish stories of the internet age, two Limerick brothers aged 16 and 18, Patrick (Young Scientist of the Year in 2005) and John Collison, developed software that allows heavy users of eBay to manage the inventory more efficiently, and formed a company, Auctomatic, in 2007, with capital of €15,000. After taking on two British partners they sold their business to a Canadian company in 2008 for a price believed to be in excess of €3.2 million. The Irish State is expecting that its large investment in research and development will yield similar results in the future. The convergence of different technologies is creating numerous new business opportunities. The production of primary research is not now seen as the end but the start of a process which is focused on commercialisation through intellectual property management and technology transfer.

2.3 Protecting intellectual property

Intellectual property can result from a person's creativity, ingenuity and inventiveness. This property can be protected and turned into profitable assets for several years. The main intellectual property rights are:

a)   Copyright
b)   Patent
c)   Trade mark
d)   Registered design.

a)   Copyright

Copyright is the exclusive property right of the author of a book or other original literary, dramatic, musical or artistic work (including architecture, engravings, photographs), sound recordings, films, television broadcasts, cable programmes, performances, computer programs or original databases to publish that work or make copies of it, broadcast it or perform it in public. The relevant legislation is the Copyright and Related Rights Act 2000 as amended in 2007. Copyright vests in the author of a literary work, the producer of sound recordings, the producer and principal director in a film and in a broadcast by the person making it. The author (composer, etc.) does not have to claim copyright. It is her/his property from the time the work comes into existence, unless it was produced in the course of a person's employment, where copyright vests in the employer. In commissioned work, copyright remains with the author unless it is specifically assigned to another party (see Chaper 2). There is no registration system for copyright. Copyright is not infringed if the holder gives permission for performance, use or publication or where the use of a reasonable extract is fully acknowledged. Copyright is assignable under the provisions of a specific contract. Artwork, wording and photographs used to identify and differentiate a product or service in the marketplace are also protected by copyright law. The term of protection for literary, dramatic, musical and artistic work is the lifetime of the author and 70 years thereafter; for cinematograph films, it is 70 years after the death of the last of the following: principal director, author of the screenplay, author of the dialogue or composer of the music. In respect of other protected work such as sound recordings, broadcasts and cable programmes, the period is generally 50 years (Chapter 3 of the 2000 Act). A 25-year term is granted to a person who publishes for the first time a work on which copyright has expired (s 34). Certain databases are protected for 15 years, but any substantial change to the contents could lead to an extended period (s 325). A database comprises 'a collection of independent works, data or other material arranged in a systematic or methodical manner'. Section 322 (2) of the Copyright and Related Rights Act (2000) provides that:

> Where a database is made by an employee in the course of employment, his or her employer shall be regarded as the maker of the database, subject to any agreement between them.

Copyright exists in an original database, one which by reason of the selection or arrangement of its contents involves original intellectual creation by the author.

The copyright protection is extended on a reciprocal basis to works first published in countries which are parties to the Berne Universal Copyright or the Rome conventions on the subject. The Universal Copyright Convention accepts work first published in Ireland as complying with certain required formalities if all copies from the first publication bear the symbol of the letter c in a circle: ©. It should contain the name of the copyright proprietor and year of first publication and is usually inserted on the back of the title page of a book. Copyright is in general not infringed where use of a work amounts to 'fair dealing', which can arise for the purposes of research, private study, criticism, review as well as certain use by libraries, archives and museums, with full attribution. An organisation or society representing various copyright owners can be registered under the Act as a licensing body authorised to negotiate and grant licenses either as owner, or exclusive licensee of a copyright, or as an agent of a number of copyright owners. These licensed organisations are regulated by the Controller of Patents, Designs and Trade Marks. The author of copyright work has 'moral' rights: a paternity right (the right to be identified as the author of a work) and an 'integrity right' (the right to object to the work being used in a way that distorts or mutilates the work in a derogatory way). A photographer has the copyright of a photograph, but where one is commissioned for private use, the photographer cannot make it available to the public without the permission of the person who commissioned it.

The publisher of every book (or any other publication covered by the legislation) first published in the State is required to send a copy within one month of publication, at his/her own expense and without request, to each of the following libraries:

- National Library of Ireland
- Trinity College Dublin
- National University of Ireland, Cork, Dublin, Galway, Maynooth
- University of Limerick
- British Library
- Dublin City University.

A publisher is also required, if a request is made within 12 months of publication, to deliver four copies to the following address:

Irish Copyright Agency,
C/o The Library,
Trinity College,
Dublin 2.

These copies are for the Bodleian Library, Oxford; University Library, Cambridge; the National Library of Scotland; and the National Library of Wales (s 198).

b)   Patent

A patent is a property right granted by the State for a limited period giving its owner the exclusive right to make, sell or use an invention. If the inventor is an employee who developed the invention during the course of his employment, the property right belongs to the employer. It is advisable that ownership of such rights is covered in a contract of employment. The normal maximum length of a patent in Ireland is 20 years, but it is possible to obtain a short-term one for 10 years. Annual renewal fees are payable to keep a patent in force. The law on the subject is contained in the Patents Act 1992 and related rules. Before an invention can be patented it must satisfy three criteria: it must be new at the date of application, involve some inventive ingenuity and be capable of industrial application (see Chapter 2). New in this context means that it is not part of the existing state of the art anywhere in the world. An invention has to be protected before it is disclosed in public, otherwise a patent will not be registered. Patented inventions range from developments in high technology to mundane improvements in ordinary gadgets. The following do not qualify for the grant of a patent: a discovery, scientific theory or mathematical method, an aesthetic creation, methods of medical and veterinary treatments, plant and animal varieties or biological processes for their production and inventions which are contrary to public order or morality (Patents Office, 1998a). An application for a patent is made on the prescribed form to the Patents Office, accompanied by a request for the grant of a patent, a description and specification of the invention, with 'claims' defining the scope and protection for the invention, together with drawings and an abstract of the information and the appropriate fee. It is usually a two-stage process: an application for a provisional patent (an inexpensive and simple procedure which gives protection for one year and establishes prior claim to the invention) and a request for a full patent (a more detailed and expensive procedure which, if granted, establishes property rights for 20 years in the State). Most inventors employ a patent agent to undertake this work. A successful application for a patent is published in the *Patents Office Journal* after the expiry of a period of 18 months from the filing date. A patented invention can be sold partially or outright or licensed in return for negotiated royalties. There is an obligation to notify the Patents Office of such transfers.

A patent granted in Ireland is not effective in other countries. However, it is now possible under the 1977 European Patent Convention to make a single application to the Patents Office in Ireland or to the European Patent Office seeking a European patent, which, if granted, is effective in those countries which are members of the European Patent Organisation. A European patent designating Ireland has the same effect as if it were a full patent granted in the State. This procedure is expensive for small enterprises because of document translation requirements. Most countries are members of a system that enables an application in one country to be submitted within 12 months in other countries based on the initial application (claiming 'priority'). This means that the European patent application is back-dated to the time of the first application and is assessed against the public knowledge at that time.

There is no such thing as a worldwide patent, but the Patent Co-operation Treaty of 1970 (which was ratified by Ireland in 1992) provides a procedure whereby a single international application in one of the contracting states can obtain designation in up to 115 countries. This system is administered by the International Bureau of the World Intellectual Property Organisation in Geneva.

c)   Trade mark

A trade mark is any name, sign or symbol capable of being represented graphically and used in the normal course of trade to distinguish the goods and services of a business from those of its competitors and thus create market identity and brand loyalty. It can be a word, name (including a personal name), logo, letter(s), brand, design, device, label, numerals, the shape of goods or their packaging or a combination of these things. Registration of a trade mark at the Patents Office (Government Buildings, Hebron Road, Kilkenny) gives its owner the exclusive right to use it. However, some trade marks cannot be registered, for example words which are in regular use, words which are identical or confusingly similar to others or initials in the form of capital letters (Patents Office, 1998b). To be effective, a trade mark must be distinctive rather than descriptive. In addition to creating a unique exclusive identity for a business, a trade mark can be a very effective marketing device. It can also be franchised or used to sell other products or services (collateral product merchandising). Registration of a trade mark is initially for a period of 10 years and thereafter it can be renewed indefinitely if in commercial use. The relevant legislation is contained in the Trade Marks Act 1996 (and rules: SI No. 199). The Controller of Patents, Designs and Trade Marks has the discretion to accept or refuse an application as well as allowing it subject to any amendment deemed appropriate. When a trade mark is accepted it is published in the *Patents Office Journal*. It is not entered in the register until after the expiration of a three-month period allowed for any opposition to registration and payment of the appropriate fee. Under what is called the Nice Agreement for the Registration of Marks, goods are grouped into 34 classes and services into eight. Under Council Regulation (EC) No. 40/90 of 20 December 1993, it is possible to make an application for a community trade mark (CTM) covering all states of the EU in a single transaction in the host country, or directly to the Office for Harmonisation in the Internal Market (OHIM) in Alicante, Spain, in contrast with separate applications and fees hitherto.

d)   Registered design

Designs, including features like distinctive packaging, can be registered and protected under the Industrial Designs Act 2001. A design can be registered for the appearance of the whole or part of a product resulting from its features, in particular, the lines, contours, colours, shape, texture or materials relating to the product itself or its ornamentation. Registration can be sought for any industrial or handicraft item, packaging or graphic symbols. A design must be new and have special character. An application for registration is made by the owner, generally the author. When registered, protection is given for five years, but it is renewable up to a total of 25 years. A registered design can be licensed or transferred. Since 6 March 2002 a European Registered Design Right can be obtained for all EU member countries. There is also the European Unregistered Design Right, which can be obtained for three years.

2.4 Assessing business ideas

Business ideas are very common. However, it takes more than good ideas to create viable businesses. Ideas have to be screened and assessed to see if they have commercial potential and that the business has the capability to produce the required quality and quantity. Timmons (1994) states that 'opportunities are created, or built, using ideas and entrepreneurial creativity'. The four key criteria used in a preliminary assessment of business ideas are:

a)   Market opportunity
b)   Competent entrepreneur
c)   Adequate resources
d)   Profit potential.

a)   Market opportunity

Finding a possible business idea, following a search or some chance occurrence, is the first step in the process of initiating a new business. The next stage is trying to establish if there is a market opportunity for the idea. Any good business idea has to be based on customers' needs and the aggregation of those has to be sufficient to justify further consideration of the idea. Many needs exist in society which are experienced by too few potential consumers or by people without the purchasing power to satisfy them to create a commercially viable business. The potential of a selected market has to be attractive for an entrepreneur. What is a market? A market can be defined as the aggregation of individuals or organisations with a need for a product or service who have the purchasing power, willingness and authority to make that purchase and the overall potential to make its provision commercially viable. A person can easily identify a gap in a market, but is there a market in the gap? The essential question is: can the new business attract and retain sufficient customers to create a viable enterprise? A business is established by attracting and retaining a critical mass of satisfied customers at a profit. Otherwise, there is no business opportunity there. This requires market research to ascertain if there is a potential market, preferably a growth one with little risk; its possible size; a profile of likely buyers; and the trade practices in the targeted sector.

The business idea does not have to be unique, but it has to have an appeal to attract sufficient customers, with some new attraction such as utility, style, convenience, accessibility or price. A good question to ask is: why should people buy this new product or service? What potential attraction has it over existing products or services? Customers buy benefits, good feelings, solutions to problems and what they perceive to be value for money in terms of their expectations. Opening the first restaurant in a small town is not a unique business idea, but it may have an appeal to sufficient customers to create a successful business. Customers must perceive that the new business can offer them better value than existing providers. This is the challenge for a new business idea. It is important to identify possible customers and try to estimate demand. A survey of potential customers could be useful at this early stage, and if the findings are positive, more detailed market research can be carried out. The market size, possible share, structure, growth rate, competition and barriers to entry are all important considerations. The potential market for the new product or service must be measurable, accessible, with demand big enough to yield a good return on investment and lead to repeat business which is sustainable regardless of the reaction of competitors. Timing is also important for many reasons: existing market needs, competition, availability of a specific grant and many other considerations. A window of opportunity can exist for a time and then disappear. This window of opportunity should be opening up and not in the process of closing (Bygrave, 1994). A preliminary assessment of the possible market is made to see if there is a business opportunity which offers a realistic commercial return over many years.

Most small and medium-sized enterprises (SMEs) are unable to meet the needs of a big market for a standard product because of limited resources and their inability to supply the quantity required on a regular basis or compete on costs with large organisations with economies of scale. Consequently, many SMEs identify a market niche for specialty products which they have the capability and resources to provide. This is a sensible strategy for most SMEs. If successful, they can then develop other markets.

### b)	Competent entrepreneur

It takes a competent entrepreneur to identify a business opportunity based on customers' needs and organise the required resources to create a viable enterprise. Such a person has to have entrepreneurial skills, technical knowledge related to the proposed business and management skills as well as a good knowledge of the business sector in question. The most important qualities are the ability to perceive an opportunity, the courage to undertake the risk involved, the competence to organise all the necessary resources and the energy to pursue the dream. Ideally, the entrepreneur should have an appropriate qualification in the activity and experience in the same or a similar business. There are examples of people who have started successful businesses without relevant experience, but they are few and far between. Several researchers have noted that the most successful entrepreneurs have gained a number of years' experience in the same or similar industry prior to their start-up (Hisrich and Peters, 1995; Timmons, 1994; Vesper, 1995). Starting a business is not the best time for learning on the job; it could be a traumatic and expensive experience. Defective work and/or inadequate service can cause irreparable harm to the reputation and image of a new business. In addition to the entrepreneurial and technical skills required, the promoter has to have a wide range of managerial competence covering all the key functional activities: marketing, production, finance and personnel. Any deficiencies must be identified and addressed and there must be planning for continuous development. Managerial experience in a similar business is invaluable. If the entrepreneur has no experience in the business, he/she can get some before starting or seek partners and/or management staff with the experience. If the entrepreneur wants to develop a growth business, he/she has to recruit a management team with strengths and proven performance in all the main functional activities.

c) Adequate resources

A person needs some personal resources or access to private funds to start a business. No institution will finance an entire project. The more capital a promoter can put up, the easier it is to raise extra finance, but the resources of most new entrepreneurs are limited. Many also like to keep their investment low in an effort to reduce the risk involved. Consequently, limited resources have to be used frugally, for example low ownership of fixed assets by leasing premises and equipment, purchasing used machinery and operating a low-overhead enterprise with some work subcontracted out. The available capital is used to leverage the required finance from grants (where applicable), family members, investors and banks.

d) Profit potential

Entrepreneurs do not start businesses for philanthropic reasons. The chief motives include a desire to work for themselves, have control over their activities as far as possible, and of course the attraction of profits. Entrepreneurs realise that it is difficult to become wealthy working for someone else and potential profit is the big attraction. They seek a far greater return on their investment than that available from other sources. An entrepreneur assesses the profit potential of a business before starting, and the key financial criteria include estimated sales, volume and revenue, gross margin, fixed costs, net profit and cash flow. A quick calculation based on these measures gives a good indication of profitability:

(Gross margin x Sales volume) – Fixed costs = Net profit.

A business has to earn profit to survive as well as rewarding the promoter(s) for the extra effort and risk-taking involved. This profit must be earned after paying a reasonable salary to the entrepreneur (some take a low figure for the first two or three years) and to any family members involved in the project. If a person leaves secure employment to start a business, he/she expects a salary in excess of what could be earned as an employee. The gross margin, cost structure, net profit/sales, return on capital employed, return on net worth and length of time to break even are all important considerations. Cash flow is also of vital importance, especially the length of time required before it leads to a surplus and the ability to meet repayments on borrowings. Profits earned after paying a salary to the promoter can be ploughed back into a business to help finance expansion, with the expectation of making and realising a good capital gain at some future date, or paid out as dividends, or a combination of both.

2.5 Feasibility study

Whether a person proceeds with a business idea which appears to have good commercial prospects depends on many factors, including alternative career prospects, age, family obligations, the views of friends contacts, advisers, role models, the state of the economy, available resources, self-belief and self-reliance. Networks of possible customers and suppliers are also important factors. Other considerations include the long hours of work required, good health, high energy level, ability to work under pressure, anxiety about foregoing a regular income in the short term at least, risk to all or some personal savings, security for borrowings and the support of spouse and family where applicable, as well as obligations to staff, customers, suppliers and the general public. A number of people have a vested interest in the success of every business.

If the prospective entrepreneur plans to proceed with the idea, he/she may prepare a feasibility study and/or a business plan. A feasibility study is a report on all the key elements required to develop a possible business opportunity into a commercially viable enterprise. It enables a promoter to research, collect, collate and assess the information required before deciding if a possible business opportunity is worth progressing further. The contents of a feasibility study are shown in Appendix 1. Feasibility study grants may be available from relevant State organisations. If the results appear promising and identified problems can be overcome, a business plan is then prepared. Although many successful businesses are established without feasibility studies or business plans, they are very useful for new entrepreneurs.

2.6 Business plan

A business plan is an integrated programme of all the key elements of an enterprise designed to show its commercial viability and how this can be achieved in the target market. The preparation of a business plan forces an entrepreneur to think through all aspects of the proposed enterprise. While the document can contain the excitement and enthusiasm of the promoter(s) for an enterprise, it is not designed to impress grant and funding agencies, but to establish specific achievable goals and the means by which they are to be attained. It is then a planning aid to be used to guide a business over two to three years, against which actual performance can be measured. The chief objectives of a business plan are establishing the viability of a project, convincing potential investors of its profitability, showing how this can be achieved and providing a yardstick to measure performance. Many business plans are just aspirations, based more on fantasy than reality, which make them worthless.

The usual format of a business plan is as follows:

- Cover page
- Promoter(s)
- Type of business organisation
- Business opportunity
- Executive summary
- Product or service proposed and its unique selling proposition
- Industry and competitor analysis
- Strategic analysis
- Marketing information (target market sector, size, market research undertaken, profile of potential customers, competitive position, source of competitive advantage, marketing plan)
- Operational plan, location, facilities, rents, operations
- Human resources, especially particulars of the management team
- Finance required, funding sources, profitability
- Critical risks
- Start-up schedule
- Appendices
  - Market research data
  - Projected accounts and cash flow forecasts for three to five years
  - Break-even analysis.

It is important that all assumptions are clearly stated. In assessing any business plan, the assumptions on which it is based are first considered, and if these are unrealistic, the plan itself is meaningless. It is advisable for a promoter to prepare his/her own business plan as far as possible, with whatever help is required from other people. Regardless of how well it is prepared and how carefully all assumptions are made, no business plan turns out exactly as envisaged. This outcome does not make the effort futile; the methodology involved forces an entrepreneur to research, assess and evaluate all the main elements involved in the creation of a successful business before undertaking the project. This invaluable process provides a framework for undertaking the venture.

Appendix 2 outlines the main features of a comprehensive business plan. In practice, most are not as detailed as the one outlined here. The plan is preceded by a cover page which contains the name, address and contact details of the promoter(s). This is followed by a table of contents with the page numbers of the main headings.

The first section gives details of the promoter(s), the type of business organisation (sole trader, company or other) and a brief introduction to the business and its products or services. Section 2 is an executive summary (the last section to be written), giving the gist of the entire proposal and stating how it is proposed to exploit the opportunity. If this section fails to impress potential lenders or investors, they may not waste time reading the remainder! Section 3 includes a description of the product or service, its unique features and competitive advantage. This is followed in Section 4 by an industrial and competitor analysis to assess the attractiveness of the targeted market. Section 5 incorporates a strategic analysis with core competence, SWOT analysis and the business strategy adopted (cost leadership, differentiation and focus strategy; see Chapter 4). In Section 6 there is an analysis of the target market segment, size, trends, customer profiles, research findings, possible market share and a marketing plan. Section 7 includes location of the business and a description of the premises, with production schedule requirements listed and costed as well as quality assurance plans and any specific legal obligations. Section 8 provides information on the management team, the overall competence of which is vital to the success of any enterprise, as well as specific staffing requirements and the organisational structure. This is followed in Section 9 by a financial plan outlining the investment required and sources of funds as well as profitability, liquidity and break-even indicators. Section 10 states the critical assumptions and risks inherent in the project, with scenario and sensitivity analysis of some key variables, what action will be taken if specific targets are not reached and any contingency plans. The last section contains a project plan and critical path of the start-up schedule. It is usual to provide supplementary information in appendices, such as market research data, projected accounts, balance sheets and cash flow forecasts for three to five years as well as costing/pricing data, break-even analysis and audited accounts for the past three years if applicable. If the business plan shows a satisfactory outcome with good profit potential and all the necessary resources can be obtained, the promoter(s) continues preparation for the launch of the enterprise. In 2009, many businesses had to change their business plans to survival plans from three to six months to cater for the new reality.

2.7 Summary

An entrepreneur can be defined as a person who develops a business with a chance of profit or loss in response to a perceived market opportunity by organising the necessary resources, undertaking the risk involved and providing a product or service of value to customers. Successful entrepreneurs come from a wide variety of backgrounds with varying talents, educational experiences, career paths, motives and aspirations. Most new businesses and products are developed by existing enterprises, with a far lower failure rate than for start-up projects.

The vast majority of new businesses originate with simple business ideas that can come from anywhere, but the application of new technologies has enormous potential. The main sources include personal skills, interests, hobbies and experiences, local needs, replication, innovation, licensing, franchising, purchasing an existing business, management buy-out and research and development.

Intellectual property can result from a person's creativity, ingenuity and inventiveness. This property can be protected and turned into profitable assets for a number of years. The main intellectual property rights are copyright, patents, trade marks and registered designs.

A business is established to create a product or service of value to customers at a profit for the owner(s). Four key criteria are used in the preliminary assessment of a business idea: possible size of the market opportunity, the competence of the entrepreneur, the available resources and the profit potential.

An aspiring entrepreneur usually prepares a feasibility study (a report on all the key elements required to develop a possible business opportunity into a commercially viable enterprise). If the feasibility study is positive, a business plan is prepared, which is an integrated programme of all the key elements of an enterprise designed to show its viability and how that can be achieved in the target market.

Questions

1. Discuss the traits of an entrepreneur.
2. Explain what you understand by the following.
   a) Creativity
   b) Innovation
   c) Patent
   d) Trade mark
   e) Feasibility study
   f) Business plan
3. Compare and contrast licensing and franchising.
4. Write a profile of an entrepreneur of your choice.
5. Discuss how you would assess business ideas.

Business plan project
Many students are asked to prepare a business plan for a new enterprise during a course on entrepreneurship. Table 2.2 lists the essential features and where useful material can be found in this book.

Table 2.2: Business plan project

Essential features	Useful chapters in this book
1. Finding a business idea	Chapter 2 (2.2; 2.3; 2.4)
2. Researching target markets	Chapter 4 (4.3, e)
3. Type of business organisation	Chapter 3
4. Marketing: • Market research findings in the target market segment • Competitor analysis • Business strategy • Competitive advantage • Marketing strategy	Chapter 4 (4.3; 4.4; 4.5; 4.6; 4.7; 4.8)
5. Operations	Chapter 7
6. Human resources	Chapter 8
7. Finance: • Investment required • Working capital • Sources of finance • Costing and pricing • Projected accounts • Cash flow statements	Chapter 5 5.1 5.3 5.2 5.4 Appendix 2 5.3
8. Taxation	Chapter 6
9. Start-up	Chapter 9 (9.2)
10. General guidance	Chapter 2.6, Appendix 2

Chapter 3

Business organisations

Anyone who has never made a mistake has never tried anything new.

ALBERT EINSTEIN

Learning objectives

*   To understand the issues which are important when considering the type of legal structure to establish for a new business
*   To explore the diverse legal, financial, taxation, auditing and administrative obligations for each type of legal entity.

The chapter is structured as follows:
3.1   Introduction
3.2   Sole trader
3.3   Partnership
3.4   Company
3.5   Co-operative society
3.6   Summary

3.1 Introduction

One of the first decisions to be made by a person starting his/her own business is to decide on the type of business organisation to establish. The forms of business organisation in the private sector in Ireland are sole trader, partnership, company and co-operative society. Each type of organisation has its own advantages and disadvantages, a different management structure and diverse legal, financial, taxation, auditing and administrative obligations. In addition, there are many branches of foreign companies operating in Ireland. There are no restrictions on foreign ownership of any business organisation in Ireland or on the repatriation of profits. Business organisations can also form joint ventures to undertake specific projects. A joint venture involves an agreement whereby organisations remain independent but establish a new body jointly owned by the partners. The new body is managed in accordance with an agreement between the participating organisations.

3.2 Sole trader

A sole trader, or sole proprietor, is a person who fully owns his/her own business, receiving all income and profits, but with responsibility for all liabilities. There is no limit to the number of employees a sole trader may have. Most farmers, shopkeepers, publicans, self-employed tradespeople and providers of various services such as hairdressers, photographers, doctors, dentists, accountants, solicitors and barristers operate as sole traders. It is the most common type of business organisation in Ireland, representing about 70 per cent of small businesses (Small Business Forum, 2006).

a)   Formalities

There are no formalities to be complied with when starting business as a sole trader, with three exceptions:

- Where a specific qualification is obligatory
- Where a licence is required
- Where the person intends to trade under a name other than his/her own.

These exceptions apply also to partnerships and companies. Specific qualifications are required before a person can provide certain services: solicitors, barristers, accountants, doctors, dentists, pharmacists and some others. There may also be specific registration requirements and obligations imposed by professional bodies. Certain services require a licence before a person can start in business: publicans, auctioneers, petrol retailers, moneylenders, pawnbrokers and many others. Every individual with a place of business in the State and carrying on business under a name which does not consist of his/her true last name, without any addition other than his/her true first names or the initials thereof, is obliged to register the name with the Registry of Business Names, Companies Registration Office, as required by the Registration of Business Names Act 1963. In addition to it being a legal requirement, registration of business names is required by some State agencies and banks and to have a presence on the internet. Registration involves the completion of a simple form giving the business name, date of adoption, place of business, nature of the activity and the name, address and nationality of the proprietor. It is obligatory for these particulars to be furnished to the Registrar of Business Names within one month of the date of adoption of the business name. If the Registrar is satisfied with the information submitted, a certificate of registration is issued which must be displayed by the sole trader in a conspicuous position in the principal place of the business and every branch office. All documents used by the sole trader to solicit business, such as catalogues, circulars, business cards and stationery on which the business name appears, must state the true first and last names and any former names of the proprietor and his/her nationality if not Irish. The Minister for Enterprise, Trade and Innovation has discretion to refuse the registration of any name which is undesirable, but such a decision can be appealed to the High Court. It is important to ensure that the business name adopted does not make the user liable for the infringement of a trade mark (by using a similar one) or to an action for passing off (attempting to mislead the public by using a name similar to another business), because a person must not take unfair advantage of the reputation and goodwill already established by another organisation. The Register of Business Names is available for inspection at the Registry of Business Names upon the payment of a small fee. Any changes which occur in particulars already furnished are required to be registered on a special form with the Registrar of Business Names. The Registrar is to be notified within three months when a person ceases to trade under a particular business name.

b)   Organisational structure

The chief advantages of the sole trader type of organisation are the ease with which it can be established, managed and terminated. There are few regulations to be complied with when compared to companies. However, in some cases there are special requirements for particular businesses, especially those producing and storing food, and promoters must comply with any specific legal obligations applicable to their businesses. A sole trader is obliged to keep proper books and records (which should be separate from his/her personal affairs) and to prepare accounts for income tax purposes, but is not required to publish the accounts or to have them audited. All the profit after tax belongs to the owner. The proprietor must register as an employer if he/she employs staff. He/she must register for Value Added Tax (VAT) if liable and submit annual income tax returns in accordance with the regulations for self-assessment. A sole trader is not obliged to register the details of any loans secured by mortgages. If a sole trader wants to go out of business, all he/she has to do is pay all the creditors in full and cease trading.

The chief disadvantage of this type of organisation is that the owner has unlimited liability for debts. A sole trader is liable for business debts to the extent of his/her business and private assets. Even a matrimonial home may have to be sold to pay debts if both spouses consent to its mortgage for a business loan, which is not a wise decision. As a consequence it is important that as many risks as possible are covered by insurance. A sole trader does not qualify for the 12.5 per cent rate of corporate tax, a benefit confined to limited companies and co-operative societies (see Chapter 6). There is generally a limit to the amount of finance a sole trader can raise because of the extent of his/her own capital, the security that can be provided and the risk inherent in lending a large sum of money to one person. This type of business structure does not enjoy continuity of existence; the death of the sole proprietor means the dissolution of that particular organisation, leading in many cases to succession and inheritance problems unless prudent arrangements are made. The sole trader can transfer the business by conveyance to a successor or a purchaser during his/her lifetime or leave it to a successor under a will. It is common for such a will to include a provision whereby the beneficiary has to compensate other members of the family before he/she can acquire the business. Nevertheless, the sole trader is a very simple and convenient type of organisation for a small business where there is perceived to be little risk.

3.3 Partnership

A partnership is 'an association of persons, excluding an incorporated company, carrying on a business in common, with a view to profit' (s 1, Partnership Act 1890). A partnership requires at least two members; the maximum is 10 for a banking business and 20 for any other business, except for accountants and solicitors where there is no restriction and some other specific exceptions (Limited Partnership Act 1907 and s 13 Companies (Amendment) Act 1982). According to the Small Business Forum (2006), 12 per cent of small businesses in Ireland in 2005 were partnerships. Persons who have entered into a partnership are collectively called a firm. Every firm within the State carrying on business under a name which does not consist of the true last names of all the partners is obliged to register the name with the Registrar of Business Names. The main law relating to partnerships can be found in the Partnership Act 1890, the Limited Partnerships Act 1907 (as amended) and case law.

a)   Formation

The essence of a partnership is an agreement between the partners. A partnership can be constituted by a contract expressed as a deed, by a written agreement, by a verbal agreement or inferred from facts or circumstances. A partnership agreement can be inferred from the behaviour of two or more persons where they are in business together sharing profits. A verbal agreement is not recommended because of the difficulty of proving its provisions in the event of a dispute. Partners can draw up a written agreement specifying all aspects of the agreement. The recommended procedure is to get a solicitor to prepare a deed of partnership covering all aspects of an agreement between the partners, with special attention to issues which usually cause disputes. A deed of partnership contains the following provisions *inter alia*:

- Name of firm, name and address of each partner, type of partner involved
- Date of commencement
- Duration
- Purpose of the business and its location
- Amount of capital to be subscribed by each, and interest thereon, if any
- Duties of each partner and the extent of his/her powers and authority
- Interest to be paid on loans by partners to the firm and whether balances in the partners' current accounts are to be charged or credited with interest and, if so, at what rate
- Drawings and interest chargeable, if any

- The salary of each partner and how it is to be increased thereafter, together with details of what expenses are payable
- The obligation to keep proper books and records, the preparation of final accounts, an obligation to have them audited and the accessibility of all documents to partners
- How profits and losses are to be shared
- Management of the partnership
- The procedure for admitting new partners and dealing with resignations, retirements and deaths
- The method of calculating goodwill in the case of the death or retirement of a partner
- The procedure for selling a partnership interest
- The procedure to be followed in the event of a dispute arising between the partners and the procedure by which the agreement can be changed.

b) Dispute

Where a dispute arises about the interests of partners in partnership property or their rights and duties, it is resolved, where possible, by reference to the agreement, express or implied. If the dispute cannot be settled by reference to the partnership agreement, it is resolved in accordance with section 24 of the Partnership Act 1890.

- All the partners are entitled to share equally in the capital and profits of the business and must contribute equally towards the losses, whether of capital or otherwise, sustained by the firm (on the surface this may appear fair, but it does not take into account such matters as the amount of capital contributed by each partner or the amount of work done by each and other relevant facts).
- The firm must indemnify every partner in respect of payments made and personal liabilities incurred by him/her in the ordinary and proper conduct of the business.
- A partner is entitled to interest at the rate of 5 per cent per annum on any loan to the partnership from the date of payment.
- A partner is not entitled, before the ascertainment of profits, to interest on the capital subscribed by him/her.
- Every partner may take part in the management of the partnership business.
- No partner shall be entitled to remuneration for acting in the partnership business.
- No person may be introduced as a partner without the consent of all existing partners.
- Any difference arising as to ordinary matters connected with the agreement may be decided by a majority of the partners.
- The partnership books are to be kept at the place of business of the partnership (or the principal place, if there is more than one), and every partner may, when he/she thinks fit, have access to and the right to inspect and copy any of them.

It is important to realise that the provisions of section 24 apply only where the agreement is silent on a particular point.

c) Types of partnership

There are two types of partnership: a general partnership and a limited partnership. A general partnership is one where each partner contributes an agreed amount to the firm and becomes its agent with unlimited liability. There are different types of general partners: active, sleeping and quasi. An active partner has capital in the firm and participates in its management. A sleeping, or dormant, partner is one with capital in the firm who takes no active part in its management. A quasi partner is one with capital in the firm but who has retired and left his/her money in the partnership, receiving income, varying with the profits, or a person who holds himself/herself out as a partner or allows himself/herself to be represented as such. Active, sleeping and quasi partners have unlimited liability for the debts of the firm. General partnerships in Ireland are chiefly in family businesses and the professions. Professional firms take out indemnity insurance to limit or cover their exposure to unlimited liability.

A limited partnership consists of one or more persons called general partners who are liable for all debts and obligations of the firm, and of one or more persons called limited partners, who at the time of entering into such a firm contribute thereto a sum or sums as capital or property valued at a stated amount and who are not liable for the debts or obligations of the firm beyond the amount so contributed. A body corporate may be a limited partner. This form of partnership is regulated by the Limited Partnerships Act 1907 (as amended). All limited partnerships must be registered with the Registrar of Companies. A limited partner is prohibited from taking part in the management of the firm and has no power to bind it in any agreement. If a limited partner takes part in the management of a partnership, he/she becomes liable for all the debts and obligations of the firm incurred while acting in that capacity. Limited partnerships are rare in Ireland.

d) Management

A partnership commences from the date partners start a business in common with a view to profit. The agreement to start can be expressed or implied. A partnership is managed in accordance with the agreement between the partners. In the absence of an agreement, each partner is entitled to participate in the management of the firm. Each partner is an agent of the firm and of the other partners for the purpose of the business of the partnership. A partner's authority may be limited, but he/she can still bind the firm if a third party is not aware of that fact. The firm is also bound by acts done within the scope of a partner's apparent or ostensible authority (acts normally done in a business of that nature). The rights and duties of partners may be varied with the consent of the partners, and such consent may be either express or inferred from a course of dealing. A majority of partners cannot expel a partner unless a power to do so has been conferred by the express agreement between them. There is a fiduciary duty on each partner to act in the utmost good faith with his/her own fellow partners. Partners are bound to render true accounts and full information of all things affecting the firm to any partner or his/her legal representative. Every partner must account to the firm for any personal benefit derived without the consent of the other partners from any transaction concerning the partnership or from any use of partnership property or business connection. The firm must keep proper books and records, and most partnership agreements require the accounts to be audited. There is no legal obligation on a partnership to have its accounts audited or to publish them unless the limited members are companies. A partnership is not a separate legal entity, and each partner is assessed for income tax on his/her share of the profit as a self-employed person (see Chapter 6).

e) Dissolution of a partnership

Subject to any agreement between the partners, a partnership is dissolved in the following circumstances:

- If entered into for a fixed term, by the expiration of that term
- If entered into for a single adventure or undertaking, by the termination of that adventure or undertaking
- If entered into for an undefined time (a partnership at will), by any partner giving notice to the other or others of his/her intention to dissolve the partnership
- By the death or bankruptcy of any partner
- By the happening of any event which makes it unlawful for the business of the firm to be carried on or for the members of the firm to carry on in partnership (Partnership Act 1890).

A partnership can also be dissolved by the court on the grounds of insanity or incapacity of a partner, misconduct, a breach of the partnership agreement, where the business can only be carried on at a loss and whenever circumstances have arisen which, in the opinion of the court, render it just and equitable that the partnership is dissolved (s 32 and s 35 of the Partnership Act 1890).

On dissolution, all partnership assets are sold. Accounts are prepared and the available finance is distributed in accordance with the agreement, or in its absence or silence under section 44 of the Partnership Act 1890. It provides, subject to any agreement, that the following rules shall be observed:

- Losses, including deficiencies of capital, are to be paid first out of profits, next out of capital and lastly, if necessary, by the partners individually in the proportion in which they are entitled to share profits.
- The assets of the firm including the sums, if any, contributed by the partners to make

up losses or deficiencies of capital are to be applied in the following manner and order:

- In paying the debts and liabilities of the firm to persons who are not partners therein
- In paying to each partner what is due from the firm in respect of any advances
- In paying to each partner what is due from the firm in respect of capital
- The ultimate residue, if any, is to be divided among the partners in the proportion in which the profits are divisible.

f) Advantages and disadvantages of a partnership

A partnership enables a number of people to form an association by sharing their talents and capital contributions in a business venture with a view to profit. It is an easy and inexpensive type of organisation to establish. A partnership has access to more finance than an individual sole trader and it does not have to register the particulars of any loans secured by mortgages. The big disadvantage of a partnership is that general partners have unlimited liability for debts. Each partner is jointly liable for all the debts of the firm. A partnership is not a legal entity. Partnerships have a reputation for instability and often have to be dissolved over petty disputes, a factor which restricts their ability to raise a large amount of finance. Other disadvantages include divided authority, lack of continuity and difficulty in disposing of a partnership interest.

3.4 Company

A company is a legal entity created by the association of a number of individuals to carry on a business or an undertaking in common and registered under the Companies Acts 1963–2009. When a company is registered it is said to be 'incorporated', which means that it becomes a legal entity separate from its owners, who are known as members or shareholders.

A company has three unique characteristics:

- Separate legal entity
- Perpetual succession
- Limited liability of members in limited companies.

Separate legal entity

A company is a separate legal entity in law regardless of the control its owners have over the management. As a legal entity a company can own property, make contracts, sue or be sued and has all the powers necessary to carry out its objectives. The concept of a company as a separate legal entity was exemplified in the leading English case *Salomon v. Salomon & Co. Ltd* (1897 AC 22). Salomon formed a limited company to take over his sole proprietorship business. The only shareholders were Salomon, his wife and their five children. In exchange for his business, the company gave Salomon 20,000 fully paid-up £1 shares and debentures (loan capital) of £10,000, secured by a charge on the company's assets. Salomon obviously then had complete control over the business, as he had prior to incorporation. Shortly afterwards, the company was put into liquidation with insufficient funds to repay all secured and unsecured creditors. The liquidator argued that the whole affair was contrary to the true intent of company law, that it was a sham, that the company was an agent, trustee or nominee of Salomon who remained the real proprietor of the business, and that as a result the unsecured creditors should be paid out of the liquidation proceeds before Salomon's secured charge. The Court of Appeal agreed, but on appeal, the House of Lords held that there was no fraud involved and that the company was a legal entity separate from Salomon. Consequently, Salomon was entitled to the payment of his secured loan in priority to the unsecured creditors. The debts were owed by the company as a separate legal entity and not by the shareholders (Ellis, 2003; Forde and Kennedy, 2007).

As a general principle, the separate legal entity of a company is respected, but there are circumstances where, in the interest of justice, it can be ignored. This is referred to as 'lifting the corporate veil', where the courts will look at the members behind the corporate legal entity. This is done where fraud is involved and for other reasons authorised by law. The separate legal status of a company has to be fully respected by its owners in all its activities. This means that the company has to keep its own books and records, which are separate in every respect from those of the owners. It also means that owners cannot take company income or property for their own use or pay personal debts out of its funds.

Perpetual succession

Perpetual succession means that a company continues its existence regardless of changes in ownership. The death, bankruptcy or incapacity of any member does not affect the existence of a company. Ownership is represented by shares, which are transferable, and the withdrawal of any member does not affect the future of a company. A company continues in existence despite changes in ownership until it is duly wound up.

Limited liability of members in limited companies

One of the chief advantages of a limited company is the limited liability of its members. Liability is limited to the par value of each share held, or in respect of companies limited by guarantee, the amount of the guarantee. If a person owns 10 €1 shares in a company limited by shares which are fully paid up, he/she has no further liability for the debts of the company. If, however, only fifty cent is paid on each share, the shareholder could, and would, be asked to pay the balance of the share price (fifty cent more per share) if required. When paid, that would be the total extent of a shareholder's liability for the business debts. A limited company is fully liable for all its debts. If it is unable to pay its debts, it could be wound up. It is the shareholders who have limited liability, not the company. There are a number of exceptions to this principle of limited liability: where fraud is involved, where authorised by statute and where personal guarantees are given.

The privilege of limited liability does not give shareholders and directors a licence to defraud a company and its creditors with impunity. Where members are convicted of fraud with intent to defraud a company's creditors, the courts can, in the interest of justice, make them personally liable for some or all of the debts. The Companies Acts have a number of provisions which allow the courts to make members of a company liable for the debts of the company. If, in the course of winding up a company, it appears that any business was carried on with intent to defraud creditors, or for any fraudulent purpose (known as fraudulent trading), the High Court may, if it thinks proper to do so, declare that any persons who were knowingly parties to it shall be personally responsible for all or any of the debts or other liabilities of the company. Because of limited liability it is common practice for financial institutions to require directors to sign personal guarantees for loans given to a company. If a director signs a personal guarantee for a loan to a company, he/she thereby undertakes to repay that loan with accrued interest and costs out of his/her private assets if the company defaults. Preferably, a personal guarantee should not be given, as it circumvents limited liability; a guarantor should be fully aware of all its implications and receive legal advice before signing any such agreement.

Types of companies

In general, companies can be classified as:

i) Limited (with the liability of members limited) and
ii) Unlimited (with no limit to the liability of members).

They can be private (when certain conditions are satisfied) or public. Any company which is not a private company is a public one.

i) Limited companies

A limited company is one where the liability of its members is limited to the amount, if any, unpaid on the shares respectively held by them. The Small Business Forum (2006) stated that about 18 per cent of small businesses in Ireland in 2005 operated as limited companies.

There are five types of limited companies:

- A private company limited by shares
- A public limited company
- A company limited by guarantee not having a share capital
- A company limited by guarantee having a share capital
- A single-member private limited company.

A private company limited by shares is one with a share capital which, by its articles of association, restricts the right to transfer its shares, limits the number of members (owners) to 99 and prohibits any invitation to the public to subscribe for any shares or debentures of the company (s 33 CA 1963 as amended). It is unable to seek a stock exchange quotation. Since the enactment of the Companies (Amendment) Act 1986, all limited companies are obliged to file annual accounts with the Registrar of Companies, but less information is required in respect of those classified as small or medium-sized private limited companies (see Chapter 5). The vast majority of companies registered in Ireland, including Irish subsidiaries of foreign corporations, are private limited companies. A private company must have at least two directors.

A public limited company (PLC) is one with at least seven members and a minimum allotted share capital of €38,100, at least 25 per cent of which is fully paid up before the company commences business or exercises any borrowing powers, and has no restriction on the right to transfer its shares. Such shares are generally freely transferable and there is no limit to the number of members. Subject to complying with the appropriate regulations, a public limited company can seek a stock exchange quotation. A quoted company (also called a listed company) is a public limited company with its shares traded on the stock exchange. A public limited company cannot commence business until it obtains a trading certificate from the Registrar of Companies. It is obliged to file a full set of accounts annually with the Registrar of Companies.

A company limited by guarantee and not having a share capital is a public one with a minimum of seven members where liability is limited to the amount they undertake to contribute in the event of its being wound up. Usually, this is a nominal amount, generally €1 each (the minimum figure). This type of company is used by non-profit organisations such as charitable organisations, some sporting bodies, proprietary clubs, voluntary bodies, community centres, professional and trade associations.

A company limited by guarantee having a share capital is a private one where liability is limited to the amount its members undertake to contribute to the assets in the event of its being wound up in addition to the amount, if any, unpaid on the shares held by them. The number of its members cannot exceed 99.

Since 1 October 1994, a sole person can form or become a **single-member private limited company** (European Communities – Single Private Limited Companies Regulations 1994, SI No. 275 of 1994). The regulations provide, subject to certain modifications, that all the provisions of the Companies Acts applicable to private companies limited by shares apply also to single-member companies. However, the sole member can dispense with holding general meetings, but must prepare and file the appropriate accounts and returns. Single-member companies require at least two directors and a secretary. A guarantee company having a share capital can also be incorporated with one member.

ii) Unlimited company

An unlimited company is one where there is no limit to the liability of its members. This means, in effect, that shareholders can be sued by creditors if the company fails to honour all its liabilities. A private unlimited company has to have a minimum of two shareholders and a public one must have seven. An unlimited company does not have to publish its accounts.

b) Forming a private company limited by shares

Any two or more persons associated for any lawful purpose may, by subscribing their names to a memorandum of association and complying with the requirements of the Companies Acts, form a private company limited by shares. No company will be registered with a name which is undesirable. This can occur where the proposed name is identical or confusingly similar to a name already registered or with a well-known international company, common trade mark or a name regarded as deceptive or misleading. The proposed name can be checked on the website of the Companies Registration Office. The name can also be checked on the Patents Office website if it is planned to register it as a trade mark. The following documents must be prepared and submitted to the Registrar of Companies:

i)   Memorandum of association
ii)   Articles of association
iii)   Form A1 duly completed.

i) Memorandum of association

The memorandum of association is the constitution of a company (the form of which is set out in Table B of the first schedule of the 1963 Companies Act). It must include the following:

- The name of the company with 'Limited' or 'Teoranta' as the last word in its name in the case of a private company (the name clause)
- The objects of the company (the objects clause)
- A statement that the liability of its members is limited (the limited liability clause)
- The amount of share capital with which the company proposes to be registered and the division thereof into shares of a fixed amount (the capital clause)
- A request to the Register of Companies to incorporate the company (the association clause).

Other clauses can be included at the discretion of the promoters. The memorandum must contain the names, addresses and descriptions (occupations) of all the subscribers. No subscriber to the memorandum may take less than one share and each subscriber must write opposite his/her name the number of shares he/she takes. The memorandum of association must be printed, dated, bear a stamp as if it were a deed and be signed by each subscriber in the presence of at least one witness, who must attest the signature. The members of a company are those who have subscribed to the memorandum of association and others who have agreed to become members, with their names recorded on the register of members.

ii)   Articles of association

Articles of association are rules drawn up to govern the internal management of a company, regulating the relationship between it and its shareholders. They cover, *inter alia*, such matters as the issue and transfer of shares; the rights attaching to shares; meetings of directors and shareholders; voting rights; the appointment, removal, duties and powers of directors and secretary; the use of the company seal; accounts; audit and winding up. A private company limited by shares may adopt a model set of articles contained in Table A, Part 1 of the first schedule to the 1963 Companies Act. Any Table A article not excluded or modified is deemed to apply. A private company is prohibited from making any invitation to the public to subscribe for any shares or debentures of the company. The articles of a private company place a restriction on the right to transfer its shares, for example by allowing a transfer only at the discretion of the directors. The articles of a company can be altered or added to by special resolution of shareholders at a general meeting (one carried by a majority of 75 per cent), subject to the Companies Acts and the memorandum of association. To be valid, the articles of association have to be printed, numbered, stamped, signed by each person who has signed the memorandum and witnessed. It is common for small businesses operating as private companies to have a shareholders' agreement in place to cover issues which could cause disagreement between them. Such an agreement could include the following:

- Remuneration entitlements of directors and key employees
- Rights to dividends and return of capital
- Procedures for transferring or selling shares
- Any other matter likely to cause disagreement.

iii)   Form A1

Form A1 must be fully completed when making an application to incorporate a company. It requires the name of the company, the address of its registered office, details of its secretary and directors, their consent to act, the subscribers and details of their shares. Form A1 also incorporates a statutory declaration that the requirements of the Companies Acts have been compiled with and a declaration that the purpose, or one of the purposes, for which the company is being formed is the carrying on by it of an activity in the State. The activity has to be classified by code in accordance with the system used for economic activities in the EU. The document has to state the place(s) in the State where it is proposed to carry on the activity and where the central administration of the company will be located. This statutory declaration must be signed by either a solicitor who is forming the company, or a director or secretary in the presence of either a commissioner of oaths, a notary public, a solicitor or a peace commissioner and dated, which must not predate the dates of other signatures on the form and other documentation (s 42(a) Companies (Amendment) No. 2 Act 1992). A company is required to have at least one of its directors resident in a member state of the European Economic Area (all EU states as well as Norway, Iceland and Liechtenstein), otherwise a bond in the prescribed form is required (s 44(8) Companies (Amendment) Act 1999).

All the above documents duly completed together with the appropriate fee are sent to the Registrar of Companies seeking registration of a company. If the proposed name is acceptable and all documents are in order, the company is registered and a certificate of incorporation issued. It is thereby entitled to commence business as a private limited company. (For up-to-date information on registering any type of company, see www.cro.ie).

The effect of registration is stated in the Companies Act 1963, s 18(2):

> From the date of incorporation mentioned in the certificate of incorporation, the subscribers of the Memorandum, together with such other persons as may from time to time become members of the company, shall be a body corporate with the name contained in the Memorandum, capable forthwith of exercising all the functions of an incorporated company, and having perpetual succession and a common seal.

Publicity

Every Irish company must have a registered office in the State, with its address submitted to the Registrar of Companies with the documents registering the company and any change of location notified within 14 days. Every company must paint or affix its name in a conspicuous position on the outside of every office or place in which it carries on business (s 114 CA 1963). The company name must be recorded on business letters and order forms, together with the names of all directors (last names and first names or initials), nationality if not Irish, the place of registration, the registered number and the address of its registered office. If a company is in the process of being wound up, this fact has to be stated (s 303 CA 1963). All this information must be displayed on the company's website and in all electronic communications such as emails.

Shares

A simple definition of a share is that it is the individual portion of a company's capital owned by a shareholder. This does not mean that the shareholder owns any part of the assets of the company, but owns the company together with the other shareholders. Each shareholder is in a variable contract, under which the company may, provided it uses the proper procedure, vary any of its terms. Share capital listed in the memorandum of association of a company is known as 'the authorised' or 'nominal' capital. It is the maximum amount of share capital a company can issue without changing the capital clause of its memorandum. The total value of the shares issued and allotted is called 'the issued share capital'. The amount paid up, called 'the paid-up capital', is part of the equity (shareholders' funds) of a company; uncalled capital is treated as a contingent asset in a note attached to the accounts.

There are different types of shares but the two chief types are ordinary and preference. Ordinary shares are those which do not carry a right to a fixed rate of dividend, rank last in a winding-up situation, but participate in the profits after other shareholders are paid and usually carry voting rights. Ordinary shareholders are the real owners of a company. The value of ordinary shares depends on the success of a company but the nominal figure remains the same. It is up to the annual general meeting of a company to declare a dividend out of profits on a recommendation of the directors. A preference share (preferred stock) is one which gives preferential rights to its holder, usually the payment of a fixed rate of dividend out of distributable profits annually, and a right to have the capital repaid in priority to other shareholders in the event of liquidation. The holders of preference shares usually do not have voting rights.

Every shareholder is furnished with a share certificate. A limited company with a share capital must make a return to the Registrar of Companies within one month of allotting any shares, stating the number and nominal amount of the shares comprised in the allotment, the names, addresses and occupations of the allottees and the amount, if any, paid or due and payable on each share. Every company must keep a register of members. The equitable title to shares transfers to the purchaser following a sale. When the transfer is registered by the company the purchaser becomes a member, replacing the seller in respect of these shares. The transfer does not affect the company in any other way.

Debentures

A debenture is a document which acknowledges the existence of a debt. As such, a debenture is not a loan but a document providing evidence for a loan. A debenture has specific terms relating to interest, capital repayment, security and is redeemable on a certain date. It is usually issued for seven to 20 years. Unlike shareholders, debenture holders are not members of the company; they are creditors. The borrowing powers of directors are usually stated in the memorandum of association. A debenture or other loan may be secured, where the lender is given certain rights in the event of default, or unsecured, where the provider ranks with unpaid suppliers of goods and services in liquidation. Security is usually provided by a mortgage on property, a fixed charge on a specific asset (which ensures that it cannot be sold without the consent of the lender) or a floating charge over present and future assets of a class such as stocks or debtors or all current and future assets in a company. A floating charge does not attach to any assets on creation, but floats over them, thus enabling the company to give good title to the assets in the course of its trade, but it crystallises (attaches to specific assets) when a certain specified event occurs, such as the appointment of a receiver. A debenture holder is given a prescribed rate of interest which must be paid regardless of the profitability of a company. If a company defaults in its payments to the lender, the debenture instrument gives the lender a number of rights; the most important is usually the right to appoint a receiver to the company. A company is obliged to register certain charges with the Registrar of Companies within 21 days of their creation.

Board of directors

While shareholders are the legal owners of a company, they delegate its management to a board of directors. Every company must have at least two directors. The following are prohibited from being directors of companies: undischarged bankrupts, a body corporate, the auditor of the company or a person convicted on indictment of any offence in connection with the promotion, formation or management of a company, or any offence involving fraud or dishonesty whether in connection with a company or not. A person is not permitted to be a director of more than 25 companies at any particular time.

The first directors are now named in the registration documents and are deemed to be appointed when the company is incorporated. Procedures for the appointment, retirement and removal of directors are contained in the articles of association. A director may be removed by an ordinary resolution (one carried by a simple majority). Extended notice (28 days) of such a resolution is required and a copy of it must be sent to the director in question, who is entitled to be heard in his/her own defence at the meeting. If permitted by the articles, a private company can appoint a named director for life. The removal of such a director would require the alteration of the articles by passing a special resolution (a majority of three-quarters) and then passing an ordinary resolution dismissing the director. Even though a director may be removed from office in accordance with company law, he/she may still be entitled to damages for breach of any employment or service contract.

A director does not have to own shares in a company unless required to do so by the articles. The articles usually authorise a company to pay directors for their services and the reimbursement of expenses duly incurred. Details of directors' emoluments must be disclosed in the financial accounts of a company laid before each annual general meeting. The aggregate amount of directors' and past directors' pensions, any payments in respect of loss of office and particulars of any loans to directors must also be disclosed. A company is prohibited from making tax-free payments to directors and any payments to directors for loss of office, or on retirement, must be approved by a general meeting. A person in accordance with whose directions or instructions the directors of a company are accustomed to act (excluding advice given in a professional capacity) is known as a 'shadow director'. Under section 27 of the Companies Act 1990, such a person is treated for certain purposes as a director of the company.

Functions of a board of directors

A board of directors is responsible for compliance with all relevant obligations under the Companies Acts. These include, *inter alia*, the following:

- To maintain proper books and records
- To prepare annual financial statements and a directors' report
- To have an annual audit (unless exempt, see Chapter 5)
- To maintain all the required registers
- To hold general meetings, extraordinary general meetings as required and directors' meetings
- To file an annual report and other documents with the Registrar of Companies
- Co-operation with a receiver, liquidator or examiner.

A board of directors is responsible for ensuring that all legal and compliance obligations are observed, the appointment of a chief executive or managing director and other key staff, authorising capital expenditure, strategic planning, monitoring progress against plans and for taking corrective action when required. It has a big role in profit planning, the review of progress and ensuring that the company is not engaged in reckless trading, thereby placing creditors at risk. The board also decides on dividend policy and makes a recommendation thereon to the annual general meeting. A board of directors does not get involved in operational matters unless they are critical.

A board of directors has a responsibility to shareholders, staff, customers and the general public. Directors are obliged to perform their duties in accordance with company law and the memorandum and articles of association of their company, using whatever skills, knowledge, expertise and experience they possess. A director could be held liable for negligence in the performance of his/her duties. The procedures for convening board meetings, general meetings, the quorum at such meetings, the election of a chairperson of the board and the conduct of such meetings are all outlined in the articles. Minutes of all meetings must be kept. A director who is in any way interested in a contract or proposed contract with the company is obliged to declare the nature of the interest at a meeting of directors. A copy of every such declaration is required to be entered within three days in a book kept for that purpose, which should be available for inspection without charge at its registered office by any director, secretary, auditor or member of the company. All directors are in a fiduciary position in relation to the company (one of utmost good faith). Every action by a director acting in that capacity must be carried out in good faith for the benefit of the company.

A board of directors can be composed of full-time (executive) and part-time (non-executive) directors. Full-time directors are involved in the daily management of a company. Part-time directors can be a big asset to any board, bringing objectivity, fresh ideas and wide experience as well as complementary expertise and knowledge to board discussions. They have an important role in improving the performance of a board and the quality of decisions made.

Managing director

A managing director is appointed by the board of directors for such a period and on such terms as deemed appropriate. Article 112 of Table A of the 1963 Companies Act states that:

> the directors may entrust to and confer upon a managing director any of the powers exercisable by them upon such terms and conditions and with such restrictions as they think fit, and either collaterally with or to the exclusion of their own powers, and may from time to time revoke, withdraw, alter or vary all or any of such powers.

A managing director is both an office holder (a director) and an employee (manager) and will have a contract of employment specifying the conditions and terms of his/her employment. A managing director is responsible for ensuring that the objectives and goals specified in the strategic plan approved by the board of directors are attained. The managing director is obliged to make regular reports to the board on company performance and seek approval for strategic issues. He/she is responsible for the recruitment, training and motivation of staff as well as all aspects of the management of the company in accordance with the policies and plans approved by the board of directors.

Secretary

Every company must have a secretary, who may be one of the directors. The duties of a company secretary are onerous and, in addition to general office administration, include the convening of all meetings, keeping minutes, implementation of board decisions by notifying the appropriate people, ensuring that the company complies with relevant legislation and its own registered documents, keeping the various registers and ensuring that company stationery complies with all legal requirements as well as making an annual return and various other statutory returns to the Registrar of Companies.

A company is obliged to keep the following registers:

- Register of members
- Register of directors and secretaries

- Register of directors' and secretaries' interests
- Directors' service contracts (s 50 CA 1990)
- Register of applications and allotments of shares
- Register of transfers
- Register of debenture holders and charges
- Register of contracts for the purchase of own shares
- Register of interests of persons in its shares (applies to public limited companies only)
- Minute books of general meetings, board meetings and sub-committee meetings.

A change in a company address has to be notified to the Companies Registration Office (CRO) within 14 days on Form B2. Any change of a director or secretary has to be notified on Form B10 within 14 days. Special resolutions and certain other resolutions passed by the company have to be registered within 15 days of their passing.

General meetings

There are two types of general meeting: the annual general meeting (AGM) and an extraordinary general meeting (EGM). Every company is obliged to hold an annual general meeting in each calendar year, except the first one, which must take place within 18 months of incorporation. Not more than 15 months can elapse between one AGM and the next. The directors of a company are obliged to present a profit and loss account, a balance sheet (made up to a date not more than nine months before the annual return date), the auditors' report (unless exempt, see later under Audit in Chapter 5) and the directors' report to each AGM. A meeting of directors must approve the audited accounts for signature by two directors, fix a date for the AGM and authorise the secretary to convene it. Every company is expected to have a number of meetings each year, but it must hold a minimum of two per year: a meeting of directors to approve the accounts for signature and an annual general meeting of all members.

The usual agenda for an AGM is as follows:
- Minutes of the last AGM
- Consideration of the accounts, auditors' report and directors' report
- Declaration of a dividend
- Election of directors in place of those retiring
- Reappointment of the auditor and his/her remuneration.

Any other matter is deemed to be special business. The quorum, length of notice and conduct of the meeting are regulated by the articles. A copy of the profit and loss account, balance sheet, auditors' report and directors' report must be sent to every member of the company and every debenture holder. The minimum notice required for AGMs of all companies is 21 days, not less than seven days for any other meeting where the company is a private company or an unlimited company, and 14 days for the rest. If less than 21 days' notice is given, all shareholders and the auditors must consent in writing to the meeting's being held at short notice. In the case of any general meeting at which a special resolution is to be proposed, 21 days' notice is required. A company is required to receive a special notice of 28 days where resolutions are tabled other than by the directors either to dismiss a director or to appoint a new auditor, or not reappoint the existing person. The company is then obliged to give notice of the motion to members.

An extraordinary general meeting can be convened by directors or when requisitioned by members holding not less than 10 per cent of the paid-up capital with voting rights, or in the case of a company without share capital, one-tenth of members with voting rights. Section 40 of the Companies (Amendment) Act 1983 makes it obligatory for the directors of all companies with a share capital to convene an EGM where the net assets (total assets less total liabilities) of the company are half or less of the company's called-up share capital, for the purpose of considering what measures, if any, should be taken to deal with the situation. Auditors are required to state whether in their opinion there existed at the balance sheet date a situation which would require the convening of an EGM under section 40.

Annual return

An annual return signed by a director and secretary must be sent to the Companies Registration Office at least once a year (s 125 CA 1963 and s 59 Company Law Enforcement Act 2001). The return has to be made up to the company's annual return date (ARD) and filed within 28 days thereafter.

Dividends

In general the payment of dividends is regulated in the memorandum and articles of association of a company, but can only be paid out of profits. A company does not have to distribute all or any of its profits in a particular year. The articles of most trading companies provide that dividends are declared by general meetings, but cannot exceed the amount recommended by the directors. Directors are usually given permission to pay interim dividends out of profits. If an interim dividend is paid, the one paid after the AGM is known as the 'final dividend'.

Advantages and disadvantages of a limited company

The advantages of a limited company are many:
* It is a separate legal entity from its members
* The liability of members for company debts is limited
* It has perpetual succession

- Ownership is represented by shares which are transferable without affecting the existence of the company
- It is easier to raise capital for companies than for other business organisations
- A company can qualify for the reduced rate of corporation tax on trading profits, which is far lower than the marginal personal tax rate (see Chapter 6).

A company has a number of disadvantages:
- It is subject to a wide range of regulations, controls and obligations
- There is a cost involved in registering a company
- A company must appoint an auditor (unless exempted) and an annual return, accounts and various documents have to be filed with the Registrar of Companies
- Breaches of the Companies Acts can lead to heavy penalties.

3.5 Co-operative society

A co-operative society is a legal entity created by the association of at least seven persons and registered under the Industrial and Provident Societies Acts 1893–2005. It is formed as a jointly owned and democratically controlled organisation to serve the needs of its members and not for profit, a feature which distinguishes it from other types of business organisation. It is not a common type of business organisation. Co-operatives are based on the principles of self-help, self-responsibility, democracy, equity and solidarity. A co-operative society, or to give it its correct legal name, an industrial and provident society, is defined as:

> a society for carrying on any industries, businesses, or trades
> specified in or authorised by its rules, whether wholesale or retail,
> and including dealings of any description with land. (s 4 Industrial
> and Provident Societies Act 1893)

On registration it becomes a body corporate with perpetual succession, a common seal and the liability of members is limited. As a separate legal entity it can sue or be sued. Membership is voluntary and open to anyone willing to accept the responsibilities of membership, without any social, political, racial or religious discrimination. Shares purchased are transferable but not withdrawable. They may be refunded in certain circumstances at the discretion of the committee of management.

Co-operative societies are democratic organisations with strict adherence to the principle of 'one person, one vote'. For this reason an individual shareholding is limited to €7,618 except for agriculture or fishing societies, where the limit is €126,974. Where a registered society is a member of another society it can have a holding in excess of these limits in that society. These limits can be altered by the relevant minister. The holders of share capital receive a limited rate of interest, if any, as specified in the rules of the co-operative. The surplus of a society, after providing for development and the provision of common services, may be distributed among members. Some provision is supposed to be made by the society for the education of its members, officers, employees and the community it serves in the principles and techniques of co-operation. The emphasis in co-operative societies is on providing a service to members rather than profits and dividends. There are now different types of co-operatives in existence: producer, consumer, housing, worker, credit, industrial, marketing and community development. They are common in the agribusiness sector, especially multipurpose dairies and livestock marts, but have made little impact in other sectors except group water schemes. Some former co-operatives have become public limited companies.

a)   Formation

The first step in the formation of a co-operative society is to call a public meeting of people in a locality with similar needs to discuss how these needs can be met by self-help. If the meeting decides that these needs can be addressed by their own leadership and initiative through a co-operative society, a steering committee is usually appointed to investigate the matter fully and report back to a second meeting. The steering committee then researches all aspects of the proposed project and reports back to the second meeting, often with help from a representative of a national co-operative body and a person who has undertaken a similar project in a neighbouring locality. If the meeting is happy with the report and the answers to questions raised, it makes a decision to form a co-operative society, decides the membership subscription and appoints a new steering committee to prepare the necessary documents for registration of a co-operative society. A co-operative society can be formed and registered by any group of seven or more persons by completing Form A and submitting it, duly signed by the seven members (and the secretary if not one of the seven), with two copies of the proposed rules of the society (also duly signed) and the appropriate fee to the Registrar of Friendly Societies. The people who sign the application are called special members and they act as a committee of management until the first statutory general meeting. No society can be registered under a name identical with any other existing organisation. The name must include the words 'society' and 'limited'.

The most important document is the rule book, which is analogous to the memorandum and articles of association of a company. The rule book covers the following matters *inter alia*:

* Name, objectives and address of the registered office of the society
* Terms of admission of members, including any society or company
* Mode of holding meetings, right of voting and of making, altering or rescinding rules
* The appointment and removal of a committee of management, managers or other officers as well as their respective powers and remuneration

- Determination of the amount of interest in the shares of the society which any member other than a registered society may hold
- The registration and transfer of shares
- The keeping of proper books and records
- The appointment of auditors
- Determination of whether and how members may withdraw from the society and provision for the claims of the representatives of deceased members
- Mode of application of profits
- Provision for the custody and use of the seal of the society
- Borrowing powers
- Annual return.

When the Registrar of Friendly Societies has examined and approved the application with the proposed rules and name, a certificate of registration is issued and the society thereby becomes a corporation with the liability of its members limited. The special members admit applicants to membership of the co-operative and issue them with share certificates. The first statutory general meeting of all members is convened as soon as possible after registration. The steering committee renders an account of its stewardship to date, answers all questions raised and resigns. This general meeting then elects the first committee of management in accordance with its rules (in most cases the members of the steering committee and a few others) and appoints auditors. The new committee of management will normally hold office until the next AGM. A copy of the certificate of registration and rules, when bound together, form the rule book of the society and must be made available to members for a small fee. Rules may be amended by a majority of two-thirds of the members present and voting at a special general meeting of members called for that purpose. Any amendment to a rule is not valid until it is registered. Every society is obliged to paint or affix its name outside every office or place where its business is carried on.

b)   Management

Any co-operative society, to be successful, must satisfy an economic need, be managed by a competent committee, receive the enthusiastic support of its members and keep them fully and regularly informed of developments. The committee of management of a co-operative society is elected by the members of the society at the first general meeting and subsequently at every AGM. In order to ensure continuity of management, the rule book generally stipulates that only a certain proportion of the committee of management retires each year, but they may offer themselves for re-election subject to being otherwise eligible under the rules (a term limit may be specified in the rules). Large agricultural co-operatives organise their membership into electoral regions so as to give fair representation to each. A committee of management approves the goals of a society in accordance with its rules, agrees detailed plans to achieve these goals, monitors performance against plans on a regular basis and takes corrective action as necessary. It also appoints the chief executive, monitors his/her performance, approves the staff structure and numbers, decides on membership in accordance with the rules, approves all major decisions such as capital investment, decides on the distribution of surpluses, ensures that all legal obligations are adhered to and renders an account of its stewardship to each AGM of members. A committee elects its own chairperson. The chief executive and his/her staff are responsible for the implementation of the policies and plans agreed by the committee of management. A committee must ensure that proper books and records of all transactions are kept in accordance with legal and accounting requirements. Co-operative societies are liable for corporation tax.

The accounts must be audited to a year end between 1 September and 31 January and presented to the AGM. An annual return of the receipts, expenditure, funds and effects of the society as audited, accompanied by a copy of the auditors' report, must be filed with the Registrar of Friendly Societies not later than 31 March. A copy of the last balance sheet together with the auditors' report must be displayed in a conspicuous place at the registered office of the society. Once every three years a triennial return, showing the shareholding of each person in the society, must be sent to the Registrar. This special return is in addition to the annual return for the year in question.

3.6 Summary

One of the first decisions to be made by a person starting a business is to decide the type of business organisation to establish. The choice is between a sole trader, a partnership or a company, or a co-operative society can be established to serve the needs of members. Each type of organisation has its own advantages and disadvantages as well as different legal, financial, taxation, auditing and administrative obligations.

The sole trader is a simple type of organisation and by far the most common in Ireland. Its chief advantages are the ease with which it can be established, managed and terminated. Its chief disadvantage is that the owner has unlimited liability for business debts. A partnership is adopted by some family businesses and professional practices. It is an easy and inexpensive type of organisation to establish. Its big disadvantage is that general partners have unlimited liability for business debts.

A company is a legal entity separate from its members, with perpetual succession and limited liability for members of a limited company. Ownership is represented by shares, which are transferable. It is easier for a company to raise finance than for another type of business organisation and it qualifies for the reduced rate of corporation tax on trading profits. A company has to comply with a wide range of regulations, controls and obligations.

A co-operative society is generally established to serve the needs of members rather than for profit. It is to be found chiefly in the agribusiness sector and in group water schemes.

Questions

1. Explain each of the following.
    *   Separate legal entity
    *   Personal guarantee
    *   A company limited by guarantee not having a share capital
    *   Co-operative society
2. Consider the issues which would influence a person to operate as a private company limited by shares rather than as a sole trader.
3. Describe the steps involved in the registration of a private company limited by shares.
4. Discuss the roles of the following in the management of a company.
    a) Board of directors
    b) Managing director
    c) Secretary
    d) Annual general meeting and extraordinary general meeting
5. Discuss the considerations that arise in the establishment of a partnership.

Chapter 4

Marketing

A customer is the most important person ever in this office . . .
A customer is not dependent on us; we are dependent on him.
A customer is not an interruption of our work . . . he is the purpose of it.
We are not doing him a favour by serving him; he is doing us a favour by
giving us the opportunity to do so.

NOTICE DISPLAYED AROUND THE OFFICES OF L. L. BEAN INC., USA (KOTLER, 2003)

Learning objectives

- To examine the concept of marketing and its important role in any organisation
- To explore the main elements of the marketing planning process
- To understand the steps involved in the preparation of a marketing plan
- To introduce the reader to international marketing.

This chapter is structured as follows:

4.1 Introduction to marketing

According to Drucker (1983), 'The aim of marketing is to make selling superfluous. The aim is to know and understand the customer so well that the product or service . . . sells itself.' Marketing has been defined by Kotler and Armstrong (2008) as:

> the process by which companies create value for customers and build strong customer relationships in order to capture value from customers in return.

No business can exist without customers. Marketing is concerned with attracting, retaining and satisfying customers at a profit. The modern approach to marketing is to provide benefits and value for customers as well as developing profitable relationships with them. Customers are always interested in value for money. Value is a combination of quality, service and price (Kotler and Armstrong, 2008). The basic concept of marketing involves providing customers with what they want, rather than what you think they want. Sometimes this is a difficult concept for a young entrepreneur to comprehend, especially one who thinks that he/she has just the product or service required by the marketplace. Most new products fail because their promoters adopt a product-led approach rather than a marketing-orientated one. Marketing accepts that the customer, not the producer, is king and acts accordingly. Businesses with a marketing orientation listen to existing and potential customers and are responsive to continuous change through innovation and the development of new market offerings to maintain a competitive advantage. A business has to devise a marketing strategy by selecting its target market, the customers' needs it plans to serve, the product or service to be provided, the price to be charged, how it will communicate with its customers and develop long-term profitable relationships with them.

4.2 Elements of marketing management

Marketing management covers four main activities: market analysis, target marketing, marketing mix and marketing planning and control, as illustrated in Table 4.1. All these activities have to be managed and integrated in order to engage in successful marketing.

Table 4.1: Elements of marketing management

Market analysis	Target marketing	Marketing mix	Marketing planning
Customer analysis	Market segmentation	Product	Marketing plan
Market measurement	Target market selection	Price	Implementation
Competitor analysis	Market positioning	Place	Control
Company capability	Market entry and timing	Promotion	
Market research and information		(Additional for services:	
		People	
		Physical evidence	
		Process)	

4.3 Market analysis

The marketing process has to establish the target market for a proposed product or service by undertaking the following research:

a)   Customer analysis
b)   Market measurement
c)   Competitor analysis
d)   Company capability
e)   Market research and information.

a)   Customer analysis

The main purpose of customer analysis is to identify needs which are not being served at present. What do these customers want? What are they really seeking? Can any trends in customers' motivation or behaviour be identified? Customer analysis focuses on customer needs, on understanding who buys what, when, where, how and why. The successful marketing person has to understand what influences a consumer, from recognition of a need for a product or service to purchase. Different considerations apply in five types of markets: consumer (individuals and households purchasing for personal consumption), producer (individuals and organisations purchasing for production purposes), reseller (individuals and organisations purchasing for resale), Government (purchases by Government departments) and international (all the foregoing types outside the State) (Kotler, 2003; Murray and O'Driscoll, 1999).

Consumers buy products and services to satisfy a variety of needs, all of which are influenced by economic, social, cultural and personal experiences. Customers form expectations about products and services which influence the purchase decision, and they buy perceived benefits and value. A marketeer has to understand what a buyer is really seeking in the purchase of a product or service. After establishing what the consumer buys and why, the next question is who does the buying. The decision-making unit can be an individual or group of individuals. Various personal and family characteristics influence the buying role, for example, culture, social norms of society and stage in the family life cycle. Finally, the buying behaviour of consumers varies depending on the type of product: some are purchased on impulse, others on a routine basis after limited consideration, or after extensive thought as the case may be. The influence of brand loyalty and habitual purchasing habits makes it difficult for a new product or service provider to be considered and requires effective, focused marketing.

With regard to the producer market, a business-to-business market, the buyers are more interested in profit rather than satisfaction and usually involve a number of people in the process. While the technological aspects and quality of the products are important, producers also have regard to the needs of their business customers and understand their specific requirements. Trade shows are very common in business-to-business marketing.

The reseller market can vary considerably from one to another and requires careful research before entering. For some products there are many decisions to be made; for example, in the purchase of a motor car, consideration has to be given to product make, type, brand, vendor, timing and method of payment. After purchase and use, the buyer evaluates the product to ensure that the right decision was made. Here, depending on the nature of the product, a good after-sales service can promote customer loyalty and generate favourable comment between prospective buyers (Kotler, 2003).

With regard to the Government market, special considerations apply with the emphasis on competitive procurement. It behoves an interested supplier to carefully research this huge market, especially the procedures involved (see Appendix 3 on public procurement).

Businesspeople are constantly trying to find out what customers want so that they can satisfy their needs. This can be done by talking, listening, researching relevant publications or conducting surveys. Producers have to know not only the needs of customers, but also those that arise along the channels of distribution, another factor sometimes ignored by new entrepreneurs. If a producer proposes to sell through wholesalers and/or retailers, it is important to talk with a representative number at an early stage. These people will not carry out any research for producers, but they can provide invaluable insights into many practicalities of the trade. As many new products have to compete for shelf space, they must have some attraction and value for both intermediaries and consumers, unless it is proposed to sell direct to customers. Quality products in good demand, with an acceptable profit margin and credit terms, presented in well-designed packaging with bar codes so that they can be scanned electronically at checkouts, together with low storage and handling costs as well as good supporting promotional activities, are just some of the considerations taken into account by retailers. Any marketeer has to carefully study the buying process and influences relating to his/her product or service before starting to prepare a marketing plan. He/she has to understand potential customers' perceptions of the company and its product or service as well as its marketing communications (Rogan, 2007).

b)   Market measurement

An entrepreneur wants to know if there is a demand for the proposed new product or service, if the price is right, the possible sales figure, a profile of potential customers and the possible reaction of competitors. Every business sector has its own peculiar features, so it is essential to research it carefully, talking with members, suppliers, customers and sales representatives.

Any entrepreneur requires a measure of current and future market size for a product or service. This information is essential for any economic assessment of a business proposal, not only for a new business, but also for an established one. The trend in a market is also important; is it growing, stable or declining? Market share (company sales related to market size) is a very important measure of performance. Measuring market size is not an easy process and various procedures are employed. In some cases, market information can be obtained from trade associations and market research reports or can be calculated from various statistics or primary data. Considerable information can be gathered from internal company records, published accounts, marketing literature and the internet as well as from sales staff and people in the trade. Useful publications include the census of population, the Household Budget Survey, trade publications for specific industries and a wide range of information available on computer databases. Forecasts of sales are established on the basis of a survey, test marketing and personal experience. The first involves carrying out a survey of the opinions of buyers, sales staff and experts in the field. A forecast can also be based on a test market of potential buyers and previous experience from an analysis of past sales records. Sensitivity analysis, using a computer spreadsheet with a range of estimates from the most optimistic to the most pessimistic, is widely used. The method used depends on the purpose as well as the availability and reliability of data.

c)   Competitor analysis

A new market entrant can increase the size of the market by generating sales to new customers, attract customers from existing suppliers or a combination of both. Attracting existing customers means providing a better-quality product or service, or a cheaper one, for the long term. This requires good competitor analysis. It involves identifying possible competitors in the target market and understanding their marketing strategies as well as assessing their strengths and weaknesses. Every new entrepreneur enters a specific industry and business sector with its own unique competitive environment over which there is little or no control. The business sector choice is a major decision and one which has huge implications for the success of any enterprise. The ideal situation is entry to a growing market with low risk (O'Gorman and Cunningham, 2007). Once an enterprise has targeted a business sector, it then conducts a competitor analysis to identify possible opportunities for itself.

New growth industries offer an opportunity to make high profits. As the industry matures, the high profits attract new entrants, thus increasing the competition. When the industry reaches the mature stage, intense competition usually leads to a shakeout of the weaker companies. If entry to a market is easy and cheap, new enterprises will be attracted if they can compete cost-effectively with established suppliers. Existing suppliers like to see high barriers to entry, for example cost, lead time, protection of a patent or restricted access to supplies or distribution channels (Kotler, 2003). According to Porter (1980, 1985), there are five forces shaping the degree of competition in an industry:

- The degree of rivalry among existing competitors
- The threat of new entrants
- The bargaining power of customers/buyers
- The bargaining power of suppliers
- The threat of substitute products or services.

If a business is faced by a few powerful customers (buyers) with whom it must trade to get the business, prices will be forced down. Similarly, a few powerful suppliers of a product or service can exert enormous influence on prices. If there are several suppliers, competition will ensure that supply prices are not excessive. The threat of substitutes for any product can limit an industry's profit potential. An analysis of Porter's Five Forces Model enables an enterprise to understand the competitive environment in which it operates. He suggests that a business should enter a growth industry where there are many suppliers and customers but limited competition.

An enterprise must understand the marketing activities of its competitors and use that information to establish a unique place for its product or service, thereby creating a differential advantage in an effort to win market share and long-term profitability. Table 4.2 illustrates a model which could be used in the analysis of competitors.

Table 4.2: Competitor analysis model

1.	List present and potential competitors
2.	Establish the strategies and competitive position of each
3.	Establish their objectives
4.	Establish their strengths and weaknesses
5.	Establish their pattern of competitive activities and reaction behaviour
6.	Establish their resource base
7.	Establish their key competitive advantages
8.	Establish their key competitive vulnerabilities
9.	Identify possible opportunities

Source: Adapted from Murray and O'Driscoll (1999)

The objective is to consider the products and services offered in the target market by competitors and identify their marketing strategies in relation to distribution, price and marketing communications. The first step is to determine the existing and potential competition. Existing competitors can be identified quickly from talking with people in the business as well as to relevant industry and trade organisations. Establishing the potential competition is far more difficult, but every effort has to be made to scan the horizon as far as possible, especially if entry is easy and cheap. Once competitors are identified, their strategies and competitive positions have to be established in respect of each market segment. This analysis may identify segments which are well served and others which could offer opportunities. The third step involves an identification of the objectives of each competitor, which can be acquired from reported information or inferred from past and present behaviour. Business and trade exhibitions, websites, sales literature and annual reports are all invaluable sources of information on competitors. Strengths and weaknesses of each competitor are identified. The pattern of competitive activities followed by competitors is then identified and the way they react to change, thus facilitating predictions for the future. It is important to know something about the human, financial, marketing and technological resources of each competitor that could be used to defend their positions. The key competitive advantages and vulnerabilities of each competitor are identified, which provides useful information for marketeers. This analysis of competitors may identify opportunities for an enterprise to obtain a competitive advantage in the target market.

Competitive advantage

Competitive advantage is the ability to deliver a product or service in one or more ways which competitors are unable to match. Sources of competitive advantage include size (with economies of scale), brand identity, quality, price, service, technology, knowledge, resources, location, convenience and innovation. The objective is to deliver superior customer value and satisfaction leading to repeat business and sustainable competitive advantage. A competitive advantage differentiates a product or service from that of competitors and establishes a unique selling proposition (USP), which gives a business a wonderful promotional opportunity. It has to be maintained by continuous innovation in a changing environment.

According to Porter (1980, 1985), there are three generic strategies for creating and sustaining competitive advantage: low cost, differentiation and focus strategy. A cost-leadership strategy seeks to achieve the lowest cost of production in the industry and compete on price, with no better example than Ryanair. This strategy depends on mass production, use of the latest technologies, high productivity, favourable access to raw materials, economies of scale, bargaining power with suppliers and low-cost operations. It is a dangerous strategy for a small firm which is unable to secure economies of scale, bargaining power with suppliers and low operating costs. The second type, differentiation, involves supplying a unique product or service for which consumers are prepared to pay a higher price. There are many sources of differentiation, for example design, quality, reliability, performance, custom-made products, technology, after-sales service, reduced lead time, good supplier and channel linkages as well as customer service. Differentiation can provide an immediate competitive edge, but competitors can quickly follow, unless it emanates from a number of sources or is protected by a patent. With a focus strategy, an organisation concentrates on one or more segments or niches of the market and does not try to serve the entire market with one product. A focus strategy is based on a superior understanding of the specific needs of customers in a target market and uses that information to provide a better service than competitors. As a result the organisation achieves either differentiation by serving the needs of customers in the niche market better than competitors, or at a lower price, or both. A focused differentiation strategy is generally followed by small businesses. The industry, sector and segment selected as well as the competitive strategy adopted are crucial managerial decisions which have major influences on the development of any business (O'Gorman and Cunningham, 2007).

d) Company capability

It is important to assess the capability of the existing or proposed business to determine if it is able to satisfy the needs identified in the target market in an efficient and competitive manner with regard to quantity, quality, price and cost. This involves an assessment of the strengths and weaknesses of the current market position (where applicable) and the core competence required. The capability must be evaluated for the industry, segment and competitive environment in which it is to be deployed. Murray and O'Driscoll (1999) suggest a four-stage evaluation process for an existing business, as shown in Figure 4.1.

Figure 4.1: Process for evaluating company capability

Source: Murray and O'Driscoll (1999)

The first step involves measuring the existing performance of the company under two main criteria: how well the target customers' needs are satisfied at present and its competitive performance measured by market share and profitability. This performance is then evaluated in relation to the competition and other suitable norms. Good or bad performance is traced to the company's resources at the diagnosis stage. The final stage is identification of strengths and weaknesses. The three main elements in any marketing strategy – customers, competitors and capability – are combined in a SWOT analysis of strengths (S), weaknesses (W), opportunities (O) and threats (T). Core competence has to be linked to the opportunities identified in the target market. Competitive advantage is created by producing a distinctive product or service for a niche market, identified after a careful analysis of the business sector concerned, the market segment targeted and the competition and established on the core strengths of the enterprise. These core strengths can be based on skills, knowledge, technologies and customer service. Sustaining the advantage involves constant monitoring of the external and internal environment, flexibility, agility and continuous innovation. The ability to respond in a fast and flexible manner to meet the specific needs of customers is a major asset for any business.

e)   Market research and information

Every business, and not just those at the start-up stage, requires a good and continuous flow of marketing information to help managers make better decisions. This information incorporates consumers, competitors, company capacity, suppliers and the changing political, legal, economic, social, cultural and technological environment. With experience, managers of companies are able to identify what information is required, what sources to use and how data should be analysed and communicated to the people making marketing decisions. A good marketing information system provides the data required to ensure that the changing needs of customers are met. Marketing information can be gathered from five main sources:

- Internal accounting records
- Sales and marketing staff
- Publications
- Marketing intelligence
- Market research.

Internal accounting records

Internal accounting records are an invaluable, easily accessible and free source of essential market information. With the use of computer spreadsheets, invoices can be analysed quickly in any detail required. A ranking of customers from largest to smallest can easily be obtained, as well as average sales per customer, average period of credit taken, seasonality in sales, geographical breakdown, sales by market segment, salesperson, customer group and trends compared with previous years. When marketing personnel analyse such information they are often surprised to find that up to 80 per cent of sales (and hopefully profits) are coming from 20 per cent of customers, following the pareto principle. If this is happening, do the key customers deserve special attention?

Sales and marketing staff

Invaluable marketing information can be gathered daily by staff that are properly trained to listen, record and report it in a regular and systematic manner. This information could include customers' perception of the product, service, company and staff; why they are purchasing from a particular organisation; why they are purchasing from competitors; the changes they require; and how the existing supplier could provide a better service. Complaints from customers should be recorded and assessed. Future demand could be forecast on a customer basis if appropriate information is collected, assessed and used. With modern scanning technology it is possible to collect accurate information on the sale of all products in retail outlets.

Publications

Considerable marketing information can be gathered from relevant publications, various Government reports, import and export statistics, the Central Statistics Office, State agencies, chambers of commerce, other relevant business organisations, books, newspapers, trade publications, trade directories, Kompass directories, libraries, European Information Centres (EICs), Thom's Directory and the internet.

Marketing intelligence

Marketing intelligence sources provide information about developments in the commercial environment relevant to a company. These developments include socio-political changes, economic, monetary and fiscal changes, initiatives by competitors, changes in customers' tastes and new technology. The sources used include newspapers, journals, periodicals, trade magazines, radio, television, internet, Eurostat (EU statistics), the published reports of competitors, customers, suppliers, distributors, business contacts and experts in the field as well as trade fairs, exhibitions, trade meetings and conferences. This information should be gathered in a systematic manner, analysed and presented on a regular basis to those making marketing decisions.

Market research

It is not always possible to obtain all the marketing information required from the above sources. As a result it may be necessary to carry out some specific market research (Chisnall, 1992; Domegan and Fleming, 2007; Rogan, 2007). Market research can be defined as the systematic process of gathering, recording, analysing, interpreting and presenting data for the purpose of making marketing decisions. Before conducting any form of market research, a person has to decide what information is required and where it can be sourced. It may be possible to provide the information required from internal records or from secondary sources, for example using data from various publications or linking relevant information from the census of population with the Household Budget Survey. If secondary data is not available it may be necessary to conduct a survey to obtain primary information. Before starting a survey it is necessary to clarify a number of issues:

- What information is required?
- Why is this information needed?
- Who can supply the information?
- What is the best way to obtain this information?
- What level of accuracy is required?
- What resources are available for the survey?
- What is the cost of the proposed methodology?

Data can be collected by observation, surveys and experiments (Domegan and Fleming, 2007). In observational research, information is gathered by observing the target group.

Survey research involves asking people questions about knowledge, attitude and buying preferences. A person can use a variety of techniques in a survey: postal survey, telephone survey, personal interview, focus groups or online. Questionnaires have to be carefully designed and pre-tested before use. In a postal survey, questionnaires are sent by post to the target group, who are asked to complete and return them to the sender. The response rate is usually quite low, which can distort the findings. A telephone survey involves conversations with the target group, which is a useful procedure, but there is a limit to the number of questions that can be asked. Personal interviews are widely used in market research and can be very effective, but they can be time consuming and costly, depending on the number involved. A personal interview can be used for an in-depth exploration of various qualitative issues relating to marketing. A focus group involves bringing a number of people together (six to 10 at a time) and conducting a discussion about the matters under research. It provides an opportunity to learn what people think about a product or service and why. This is a very useful and cost-effective technique.

Regardless of which technique is used, it may not be possible to survey everyone in the target audience because of its size and cost. As a result a sample has to be chosen, which can be by random selection (where each member of the target group has an equal chance of being chosen), stratified random sampling (random sample of particular sub-groups), quota sampling (a quota from specific groups) or representative sampling (selection in proportion to each sub-group). The size of the sample depends on the accuracy required and the resources available. Experimental research is used for gathering information on cause-and-effect relationships, for example test marketing.

Figure 4.2: Market research process

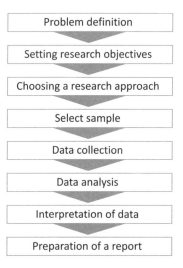

Source: Adapted from Murray and O'Driscoll (1999)

The market research process is expected to be objective, which requires adherence to the steps outlined in Figure 4.2. The first step involves a clear statement about the marketing problem to be researched. This is followed by clearly stating the research objectives. Market research may have one of three objectives: exploratory research is designed to gather preliminary information to help define a problem; descriptive research is undertaken to describe things such as the attitudes of consumers; while causal research is conducted to test cause-and-effect relationships. Specific research objectives must be agreed. The next step involves a consideration of the various techniques that could be used, their suitability and cost with regard to the target audience. Data can be gathered from secondary sources (material already collected by others for some other reason), and these are generally consulted before any primary research is undertaken. Then the most appropriate way to find the required information is identified. If the target audience is too large to survey fully, a sample has to be selected, usually on a representative basis, which has to be carefully established. The next decision involves how, where, when and from whom the data will be collected. Some primary sources to be researched include existing customers, suppliers and competitors in the target market as well as new offerings at relevant trade fairs.

There are two broad types of research: quantitative and qualitative. The former involves collecting and analysing numerical data and answering a question like 'how many?' Qualitative research involves collecting and reflecting on perceptions so as to gain an understanding of various activities and addresses questions like 'why?' or 'how?' When collected the data is analysed under appropriate headings and transformed into meaningful information for interpretation. Most large surveys are now designed to facilitate computer analysis and there are several relevant packages on the market. The final stage involves the preparation of a report, with the information presented in a clear and concise format for the intended users. This final report contains a title page, a table of contents, a statement relating to the objectives of the study, a summary of the research, findings, conclusions and recommendations.

Regular marketing information has to be collected, stored in an accessible manner, updated, extracted when required, analysed and evaluated. Nowadays, this information is kept on a computer database. This up-to-date market information is available to aid managerial decision-making on a continuous basis. It is an invaluable resource designed to reduce the uncertainty and risk inherent in all business planning.

4.4 Target marketing

Every market is made up of various segments consisting of consumers with different needs, purchasing power, buying habits and responses to promotions. What often appears to be one mass market actually consists of many smaller, more homogenous segments, each with a unique set of characteristics (Kotler, 2003). No single marketing approach will appeal to all consumers. Each segment is a separate potential target market and may require a specific marketing programme to establish a competitive advantage and build a loyal customer base. Some delimitation of a mass market is also required because it would be impossible for an SME to service it with scarce resources. Target marketing involves four activities:

a)   Market segmentation
b)   Target market selection
c)   Market positioning
d)   Market entry and timing.

a)   Market segmentation

Market segmentation is the process of identifying groups of consumers in a market with specific needs and expectations. A company has to decide what criteria should be used to segment a market. The most common criteria used in a consumer market are geographic (country, county, urban, rural), demographic (age, gender, occupation, income, stage in family life cycle) and psychographic variables (customer preferences) (Kotler, 2003; Kotler and Armstrong, 2008). Each segment or niche identified may require a separate product and/or marketing promotion tailored to its specific requirements. After establishing the profile of customers in each target segment, an evaluation of commercial attractiveness is carried out.

Having evaluated the various segments, a company can decide to pursue one of three options (Kotler, 2003): a niche strategy (going for one market segment), a multiple niche strategy (serving two or more segments with different products and marketing programmes) or a mass-market strategy (addressing the total market with one product and marketing programme). No option is superior to the others; the decision depends on the market, product and company resources. However, most SMEs with limited resources find it advantageous to adopt a niche market approach. They can establish a close relationship with consumers, enabling them to cater for specific needs and gain a competitive advantage over larger and less flexible businesses. Once a company succeeds in a segment and earns a reputation for quality, service and reliability, it is easier to enter new segments. The ultimate in market segmentation is 'customised marketing', or 'one-to-one' marketing.

b)   Target market selection

A business has to decide what market it should serve. After considering segmentation options, the next decision is target market selection – the act of selecting one or more segments for commercial development (Kotler and Armstrong, 2008). Before a business enters a market it usually has a good understanding of the competitive structure of the industry or business area concerned. It has to understand the marketing operations of competitors at present and identify segments which are not well served. However, poor service alone is not a criterion for entry; the possible business opportunity has to be large enough to justify a separate marketing programme. A commercially attractive market segment has considerable unsatisfied needs, little competition and potential for growth. A business needs the capability and resources required to service the target market segment selected.

c) Market positioning

The next stage is market positioning, defined by Kotler and Armstrong (2008) as:

> arranging for a product to occupy a clear, distinctive, and desirable place relative to competing products in the minds of target consumers.

This involves the adoption of a specific competitive position in a market segment after a careful evaluation of customers' requirements, preferences and their perceptions of competing products. Market positioning locates a product in relation to customer needs and the anticipated competition. Promoting one product benefit creates a unique selling point. The key to establishing competitive advantage is product differentiation, which addresses the question of why customers should buy your product or service rather than that of competitors. Market positioning is designed to create the desired perception and image for a product or service to reinforce its competitive advantage. Positioning is supported by appropriate promotion stressing its unique image, benefits and value. The market segment chosen need not be permanent. It can be reviewed and altered with changes in the environment, leading to continuous innovation, development and the creation of new opportunities for greater profit.

d) Market entry and timing

Once market positioning is decided, the next question is how to enter the target segment. Basically, a business can enter a market by internal development, acquisition or collaboration jointly with another company to exploit a new business opportunity. Timing strategy involves careful assessment of the correct time to enter a market.

4.5 Marketing mix

Marketing mix refers to a set of key components used in the implementation of a marketing plan. McCarthy (1978) classified these marketing components as 'the four Ps'. This concept says that buyers are influenced by variables relating to:

a)   Product
b)   Place (distribution channels)
c)   Price
d)   Promotion.

a)   Product

A product is anything that can be offered for sale that might satisfy a need or a want. The big challenge for any new product is its ability to satisfy these needs and wants better than its competition and at a profit. Each product can be considered on three main levels (Kotler, 2003): the core product (the actual item or service being offered for sale), the tangible product (design, features, quality, brand name and packaging) and the augmented product (various services like warranty, service, maintenance and items which exceed customers' expectations). Products can be classified into three groups according to their durability – durable, non-durable and services – each of which requires a unique marketing approach. A product can consist of a number of lines of various shapes, sizes and contents, depending on specific demand (Kotler, 2003). Services have four main unique features: intangibility (they cannot be seen, felt, tasted or verified prior to use), variability (with quality depending on who provides them), perishability (cannot be stored) and inseparability (cannot be separated from their provider). The impression created by staff in the provision of a service is of vital importance. The marketing of services is evolving as a specialised activity to cater for its unique features (Glynn and Barnes, 1995; Lovelock, 1999). It is important to remember that customers buy products for the psychological benefits they provide as well as their physical and service utilities. Other important issues include branding, logo, packaging, labelling, customer service and product life cycle (Kotler, 2003).

Branding is an important marketing issue in relation to a product or service. A brand is a name, term, sign, symbol or design or any combination of these which is used to identify and differentiate the product of one producer from those of competitors because of the expected benefits derived from its purchase, with the objective of attracting and retaining customers (Kotler and Armstrong, 2008). A business has to decide its brand policy – whether to sell products under its own name, a distributor's name – or whether it should develop an individual brand. A successful business brand can facilitate sales when customers look for that brand instead of just the product type. As the power of distributors increases, more are using their own brands, for example the major supermarkets. This development has major advantages for retailers in attracting and retaining customer loyalty, but it has created problems for many producers who like to market their own brands (Rogan, 2007). The creation of a successful brand name gives a producer advantages in the distribution chain. If customers ask for a specific brand, intermediaries respond by carrying it, otherwise they would just stock the product type from whatever source they choose. A brand has to be carefully chosen to reflect the market positioning of the business and the target audience, and complement its logo with the objective of promoting a competitive edge. Brand identity is designed to create visual recognition, represent the expected benefits, provide differentiation and establish customer loyalty. It should convey a simple, consistent, unique and strong message of the expected benefits to be derived from its purchase. The brand should be consistently displayed on all promotional material.

A logo is an emblem or device used as a symbol of an organisation in display material. It is a unique visual symbol devised to promote an organisation and its product or services. Once agreed, it should appear beside the business name on the front of premises, on all letterheads, printed material, signage, vehicles and the business website in a consistent manner. Sometimes a tag line is displayed to describe what the business does or to sell the benefits of using a product or service, for example 'making your life healthier'.

Packaging, designing and producing a suitable container or wrapper can play a big role in the marketing of some products. In many cases retailers demand convenient packaging before carrying a new product, a factor some SMEs discover to their surprise. Well-designed packaging can provide convenience for customers, promotional opportunities for producers and quick service for retailers. A business has to develop a packaging concept for some products and test it to ensure that the desired objectives are achieved before adopting it for use (Kotler and Armstrong, 2008).

Many products require labelling for identification, description, promotion and in some cases to comply with relevant legislation. A business is sometimes required to provide customer services in relation to the sale of certain products. It has to decide what services to offer and how they will be provided, for example maintenance services and warranties.

Product life cycle

Every new product enters a life cycle, with changing threats and opportunities, of four stages: introduction, growth, maturity and decline (Kotler, 2003; Kotler and Armstrong, 2008). The introductory stage for a product is a period of slow growth, as it takes time for customers to know about its existence, and it may take longer to stimulate them to consider purchasing it. If it is a unique product it may be possible to charge a premium price to cover the heavy promotional costs involved in this stage, as many firms incur potentially disastrous losses during the introductory stage of a product. If successful the product moves to the growth stage, increasing sales and profits, when a business tries to improve quality and enter new market segments. Competitors are attracted if prospects look good. At some point, sales growth will slow down and reach a plateau as the product enters the maturity stage. This slow-down in growth can lead to overcapacity in the market, intensified competition and more expenditure on promotion to maintain market share, when businesses seek innovative ways to maintain their position. Most products in the marketplace are at the maturity stage of their life cycles. Eventually a product enters the decline stage, with continuous deterioration in sales and profits. The decline can be rapid or slow; skilful marketing can delay but not reverse the ultimate decline and dropping of a product (Kotler and Armstrong, 2008). The characteristic profit trend of a product is similar to its sales profile throughout its life cycle.

Knowledge of the product life cycle is important in deciding on marketing strategy. However, it is difficult to determine exactly when one stage ends and the next begins, as the length of the cycle varies from product to product. Most growth-orientated businesses develop a product mix (offering a number of products for sale). In a multi-product firm, each product in the portfolio has to be marketed with regard to its stage in the life cycle. Each product is regularly appraised with regard to sales growth, market share and profitability. This assessment can lead to pruning, where necessary, and new product development so as to develop a stable business not dependent on one product or market.

Consumer adoption process

The consumer adoption process focuses on the way individuals react from first hearing about a new product until they purchase it. They go through a number of stages: awareness, interest, evaluation, trial, adoption or rejection (Rogers, 2003). People vary considerably in the time span required for the above stages. According to Rogers, a minority react quickly with immediate purchase (innovators), others are slower but purchase early (early adoptors), followed by a larger group (early majority), leading to a slow decline (late majority) and finally those who require considerable convincing before purchase (laggards). Acceptance of any new product takes time. The process is represented by a near-normal distribution curve when plotted over the time span of the entire process. Knowledge of the adoption process helps to target limited marketing resources on potential innovators and early adoptors if they can be easily identified. Businesses try to influence customers by creating awareness and interest by effective communications.

b) Place

Selecting where and how to distribute a product is one of the most demanding decisions facing any organisation. The method adopted can vary from direct selling to final customers, to using one, two or more intermediaries. The one chosen, known as the marketing or distribution channel, affects every other marketing mix decision and involves a commitment for some period of time. In some cases it is not easy to attract intermediaries where their expected return is low. The internet is a new channel with the potential to transform every business. There is a big shift underway from the marketplace to marketspace: trading on the internet.

Channel selection is made after careful consideration of many factors: alternatives available, the requirements of intermediaries, customer behaviour and preferences, product characteristics, the outlets used by competitors and the potential for a symbiotic relationship. Each alternative is evaluated in relation to potential sales, costs, control, future adaptability and flexibility. Distribution channels are experiencing continuous change, as exemplified in retailing over recent years; consequently, the freedom to adapt to new conditions has to be preserved. A target channel has to be selected and terms agreed. The selected channel has to be managed effectively, motivated and regularly evaluated against criteria agreed at the start. This evaluation can lead to revision, with members dropped or added, to cope with changing needs.

All the major activities involved in physical distribution, such as order processing, warehousing, inventories and transportation, has to be carefully planned within a unified framework designed to minimise costs, optimise efficiency and provide the desired level of customer service. Physical distribution provides many opportunities for organisations to innovate in an effort to establish differential advantage.

c)   Price

Businesses establish prices to maximise sales and profits. Pricing is influenced by many factors: uniqueness of the product or service, entry costs, stage in the product life cycle and competition in the market. It is an important decision and influences customers' perception of value. There are two main approaches used in pricing products and services: one based on costs and the other on demand.

In a cost-orientated approach a business plans that each sale recoups the variable cost of sales as well as an arbitrary contribution to overheads based on expected sales and a satisfactory profit. Demand-orientated approaches consider the elasticity of demand at various prices, that is, the sensitivity with which customers respond to price changes. Keen demand is likely to result in high prices and weak demand in low prices. A common form of this approach is price discrimination – charging different prices for the same product at different times or at different locations – a feature widely used in the tourism industry to reflect seasonality in the business and special-event pricing. Prices are often established by adopting 'the going rate', a procedure widely used when selling a homogenous product in a highly competitive market. The discounts expected by intermediaries, where applicable, also have to be taken into account in pricing decisions. Sealed-bid pricing, where organisations compete for orders or jobs on the basis of sealed bids, is another method used.

Pricing is a very important consideration for the launch of a new product. Market entry price strategy is either a 'penetration approach', opting for a low price to capture a large market share, the strategy pursued by low-cost airlines; or a 'skimming approach', where the organisation takes advantage of some unique feature and goes for a high price.

When an organisation plans to charge a premium price it has to consider the reaction of customers and competitors. In respect of a differentiated product, customers base their buying decisions on a number of factors, such as quality, service and reliability; price is one important consideration. (Costing and pricing are covered in more detail in Chapter 5.)

d) Promotion

Before customers can purchase a product or service, they must be aware of its existence. An organisation has to communicate with its present and potential purchasers as well as other interested parties, and that is the function of its communications mix (all the methods available to an organisation to achieve this objective). However, communications has to reinforce the image and message the business wants to convey regarding to its market segment and positioning. All four Ps of the marketing mix has to be consistent.

The steps involved in devising an effective marketing communications strategy are outlined in Table 4.3.

Table 4.3: Marketing communication strategy

1.	Identification of the target audience
2.	Determination of specific objectives
3.	Design of message
4.	Choice of media
5.	Establishment of total promotion budget
6.	Implementation of communications mix selected
7.	Measurement of results
8.	Evaluation of results

Source: Adapted from Kotler (2003) and Murray and O'Driscoll (1999)

The first step involves identifying the target audience from the customer analysis, competitive position, market segment and positioning already established. Once the target audience is identified, the next stage is the determination of specific objectives. The usual objectives desired are purchase, high satisfaction rating and favourable comment. In designing a communications message, an organisation has to consider what to say (content), how to say it (structure), message format (sound or print illustration) and who should say it (source) (Kotler and Armstrong, 2008). Ideally, a message is designed to attract attention, generate interest and lead to the desired action. The next stage is selecting the appropriate media to reach the target audience and involves the use of several elements of the communications mix. In deciding on the mix, an organisation has to consider the advantages and costs of each element. This is followed by the establishment of a promotions budget and its allocation to the different media selected. The promotions programme is then implemented, followed by a measurement of the results achieved and finally an evaluation of the entire programme. This approach can be applied to each element of the promotions mix. When a programme is badly implemented, money spent on promotion may be wasted because of poor planning and lack of clarity in the objectives sought.

Elements of the communications mix

Businesses have to communicate the benefits of their products and services to their customers and in many cases 'non-customers'. They use methods such as advertising, sales promotions, public relations, personal selling and direct marketing (Table 4.4). They have to identify their target audience and the most effective means of communicating with them. The big emphasis is on communicating the benefits of a product or service (Rogan, 2007).

Table 4.4: Marketing communications mix

Advertising	Sales promotions	Public relations	Personal selling	Direct marketing
Advertisements on:	Gifts	Press releases	Sales presentations	Direct mailing
• National radio	Competitions	Photographs	Trade fairs	Telemarketing
• Local radio	Exhibits	Speeches	Samples	Fax mail
• Television	Demonstrations	Announcements		Email
• National and local	Special offers	Annual reports		Internet
newspapers	Samples	Sponsorship		Website
• Magazines	Trade shows			Mobile
• Trade journals	In-house displays			telephone
• *Golden Pages*	Good customer			Digital
Packaging	service			marketing
Brochures	Reduced-price			
Flyers	offers			
Business cards				
Good letterhead				
stationery				
Directories				
Display signs				
Attractive logos				
Name on premises				

Advertising is any form of communicating information about a product or service to target markets by means of written or spoken words or visual material. It can involve simple and cheap procedures such as the use of business cards, brochures, flyers, good stationery and logos as well as the display of the business name on premises and vehicles. Networking at various business and social events and distributing business cards is an effective way of establishing contacts and following up on leads. Advertising generally refers to paid promotion in various media. Advertising is expensive and has to be repeated to have an impact. The choice of media has to be carefully made with regard to desired objectives, costs, the target audience, the message to be communicated and how to express it. An advertisement has to be designed to capture attention, to generate interest in the product or service, to offer something of value, to create a desire to purchase and to provide a procedure whereby the potential purchaser can respond (Kotler, 2003). It should contain a good attractive headline which arouses interest, a photograph or illustration to capture attention, a description of the product or service offered, emphasising benefits to the consumer, and a convenient way to respond. It should be as creative as possible, but not misleading. An entry in the *Golden Pages* is quite cheap, with wide circulation and is convenient to use.

Sales promotions consist of a diverse range of incentives designed to encourage product trial in an effort to stimulate sales. Incentives offered to potential customers could include free samples, coupons, special offers, competitions, special display features and help with merchandising. Special promotions are widely used when introducing a new product or service to the market and at the maturity stage of a life cycle.

Public relations (PR) involves a variety of procedures designed to promote the image of a business and its product(s) or service. Favourable publicity about a business and/or its products or services can be obtained using press releases, news items, speeches, special events, public service activities and sponsorship. Brochures, annual reports and magazines are all used in the process. Most organisations have many opportunities for good PR, but it requires initiative, planning and co-operation with the media. A publishable press release has to have a newsworthy appeal, for example the appointment of new key staff, an increase in employment or sponsorship of some sporting, social or cultural activity. It has to be written to interest readers or listeners as the case may be, with a headline that will attract attention. The gist of the story has to be in the first two or three sentences, with the remainder consisting of supplementary information. The print media like photographs. A press release (average length 200 words) should state the name, address, telephone number, email address and job title of the sender from whom additional information can be had if required.

Personal selling involves company personnel selling direct to intermediaries or final consumers. It can be very effective, especially where product knowledge is required for technical equipment. Organising a sales force requires decisions about objectives, strategy, structure, number and compensation package (Kotler, 2003). The objectives can include searching for leads, providing information about a product or service, selling, servicing customers' requirements, especially with technical advice and assistance, gathering information and in many cases accounts collection. Selling involves five steps: preparation with good product knowledge based on customers' needs, overcoming objections by stressing benefits, presentation, closing the sale and follow-up communications to establish a long-term business relationship. Managing a sales force involves a number of elements: recruitment and selection; training in selling techniques; briefing on the organisation's product, policies and customer focus; as well as supervision, motivation and evaluation of individual and group performance (Kotler, 2003). The big emphasis in personal selling is now on developing and maintaining good long-term customer relationships so as to attract repeat business and positive recommendations by customers to other potential customers. A good salesperson has the ability to listen and to ask relevant questions, with feedback providing valuable information that can be used to supply a better product or service.

Direct marketing is an interactive procedure where businesses communicate directly with customers in an effort to generate sales. Many organisations sell direct to customers, while others use direct marketing to supplement other distribution channels. It includes direct mail, catalogues, telemarketing (using the telephone to secure orders), email and the internet (McGoey, 1998). Direct mail can be sent to potential purchasers by email where they have given permission, or sent 'cold' by post or delivered to homes. A mailshot generally includes some incentive to reply, such as a discount if purchased before a specific date or inclusion in a draw.

We now have instantaneous worldwide communication with the internet, which is essential for almost all businesses. Most have their own websites. A well-designed website which is updated regularly is a wonderful way to market a business on the world stage, but it needs to catch the attention of a visitor and has to be easy to navigate. A website has to be promoted on- and offline. Online promotion seeks prominent visibility on the major search engines such as Google and Yahoo. An important aspect of this promotion is search engine optimisation (SEO), improving visibility on these engines using portals and links. A portal is an online site for general or specific information; some are free and others have to be paid for. A link is an online connection to the website. Businesses try to have many links to their websites. The offline promotion of a website involves recording its address on all published material. By going online, businesses are able to interact on a personal basis with customers and many are finding it very effective in generating new sales and increased profits. We now have e-commerce – buying and selling by electronic means, chiefly the internet, which includes e-marketing – electronic marketing promotion and e-procurement – the buying side of the process. E-business involves the electronic use of the intranet (an internal network), the extranet (connection with suppliers and distributors) and the internet (worldwide computer network) to conduct business (Kotler and Armstrong, 2008). Mobile telephones and text messaging are now also widely used in marketing communications. Digital marketing includes social networking such as Facebook and LinkedIn, micro-blogs like Twitter and numerous new mechanisms.

4.6 Services marketing

Special considerations arise in respect of the marketing mix for services. Services have four major characteristics which affect marketing strategies:
- Intangibility

- Inseparability
- Variability
- Perishability (Kotler, 2003).

Unlike physical products, services are intangible and cannot be seen, felt or examined prior to purchase. As a result, potential customers will seek evidence of the service from the place of its provision, from staff and the communications of the provider as well as from others with experience of it. A service provider has to promote the benefits of the service. Inseparability refers to the fact that a service is produced and consumed at the same time. As a result, the potential consumer is interested in who provides the service and the quality to be expected. This can give rise to variability in the standard of provision. Many purchasers, based on experience, may seek a specific provider, even within the same business. Perishability means that services cannot be stored. Demand for many services has peaks and valleys, and strategies have to be devised to provide a better match between supply and demand.

In addition to the traditional four Ps of the marketing mix – product/service, place, price and promotion – Booms and Bitner (1981) suggest three others in respect of services: people, physical evidence and process. Because services are provided by people, the recruitment, training and motivation of good, competent and customer-focused staff can provide a big competitive advantage for providers. Providers can demonstrate quality by the physical evidence they provide in satisfying the needs of their customers. They can use different processes in response to the needs and expectations of specific groups of customers, for example self-service facilities in a restaurant or table service. According to Kotler (2003), service providers face three main tasks in marketing:

- Innovative offerings
- Managing service quality to meet and exceed customer expectations
- Managing productivity.

Berry and Parasuraman (1991) found five determinants of service quality:
- Reliability
- Responsiveness
- Assurance
- Empathy
- Tangibles, such as physical facilities, equipment, staff and promotional material.

An important aspect of the process is seeking feedback from customers and satisfactorily resolving any complaints. Product support services offer providers a big opportunity for competitive advantage, but they have to be focused on the specific needs of their customers (Kotler, 2003).

4.7 Customer service

People are very important in the provision of any service or product and in good customer service. Good marketing practice begins with fostering the right attitudes in staff. Marketing is everyone's job in an organisation, from the telephonist to the chief executive. Everyone is there to serve customers in one form or another. Customers are the most important people in any business; in effect, they are its paymasters. A culture of customer service permeates all marketing-orientated businesses. Staff are carefully recruited and trained, with positive customer attitudes inculcated. Competent, well-trained, satisfied and motivated staff are great ambassadors for any business. Employees have to believe in the product or service being provided and the manner in which it is promoted. This focus on staff, known as internal marketing, is essential for the creation of a customer-conscious culture in a business. A successful business is developed by increasing the number of its satisfied customers, thereby ensuring that they return and recommend it to others. The best marketing people listen to their customers and avail of all possible opportunities to receive feedback (Quinn, 2006). What makes customers happy? What annoys them? Ringing your own organisation, visiting your own website or randomly speaking with customers can be very enlightening for any manager. Customers have to be facilitated in every way possible and treated with the utmost respect.

Feargal Quinn purchased his first shop in 1965 and developed it into Superquinn, which owned 19 supermarkets and had more than 4,200 staff when it was sold in 2005 at an estimated price of €450 million (Rogan, 2007). His competitive advantage was good customer service. Keeping close to the customer was one of the eight characteristics identified by Peters and Waterman (1982) in their study of America's best-run companies at that time. All these companies learned from their customers and implemented their recommendations where possible. Their staff were driven by a deep commitment to customer service. In their book, *A Passion for Excellence*, Peters and Austin (1986) described a number of ways in which excellent companies maintain their commitment to customer service: constantly listening to customers, measuring of customer satisfaction on a regular basis and providing a complaint response mechanism.

Successful organisations use a variety of customer listening procedures, ranging from the simple to the elaborate. In one procedure, senior management spend a large portion of their time talking with customers. Another major source of information is regular customer surveys, ranging from interviews with random customers, focus group sessions (group discussions with a number of customers) to more formal surveys with representative samples. It is important for a business to have a mechanism in place for gathering, examining and rectifying the causes of any customer complaints. Complaints cannot be ignored, as they provide useful feedback. A dissatisfied customer can be lost and may express critical views on a product or service to others, which can cause considerable harm to the reputation of a business. Customer-focused businesses welcome complaints, consider them and take appropriate corrective actions. The criticism of customers can be more important than praise. According to Feargal Quinn (2006):

> The real value in listening to customers comes from discovering what they don't like, what hasn't worked, what needs to be changed, what the other guy is doing better. The real value is in hearing all the things you don't want to hear.

Another useful survey question is to ask customers of competitors why they do not buy from you. Such feedback from customers and others keeps businesses and their staff focused on changing needs and tastes. This approach applied to customers, suppliers and distributors develops what is called 'relationship marketing', a process of fostering good, solid, long-term business relationships with the objective of attracting repeat business. It is far easier and cheaper to retain customers than to attract new ones.

4.8 Marketing planning

Knowledge and a keen appreciation of the various elements of the process are required for the preparation of a marketing plan. In preparing a marketing plan, its author has to reflect on the various elements involved and devise a realistic plan with regard to the expected economic environment and the capacity of the business. A marketing plan identifies market choice (industry, sector, segment) and specifies how a business will compete in its targeted market with regard to its competitive advantage. Competitive advantage is based on a differentiated product or service with special features which provides the desired benefits and value for customers. This becomes its unique selling proposition and is the foundation of a good marketing plan. Table 4.5 shows the contents of a marketing plan.

Table 4.5: Contents of a marketing plan

1. Executive summary
2. Table of contents
3. Market analysis of the current situation
4. SWOT analysis – identification of market opportunities
5. Marketing objectives
6. Marketing strategies to be adopted to achieve objectives
7. Marketing budget – allocation
8. Action programmes to implement the plan
9. Organisation and implementation
10. Monitoring and control

Market analysis involves using good recent marketing information and research to identify the exact requirements of existing and potential customers in the target market, a measurement of market size, a competitor analysis and a realistic assessment of company capability. The general macroeconomic environment is also assessed. Where applicable, the current marketing position of the company is examined in relation to segment(s) served, size, market share, prices, margins, distribution and promotion policies. The pattern of competitors' behaviour is assessed in relation to each of these activities as well as their strengths and weaknesses. In a SWOT analysis, the strengths (S) and weaknesses (W) of the organisation's performance are examined as well as the opportunities (O) and threats (T) in the external environment. The purpose of this assessment is to identify market opportunities which can be met by company competence and capability. Arising from this analysis, the organisation considers the main issues facing it and decides on its target market and competitive strategy. It then establishes its marketing and financial objectives in terms of market share, sales volume and profits. Under marketing strategies, the company states how its objectives will be achieved in relation to the market segment(s) targeted, differentiation, positioning and entry strategy for a new organisation as well as choosing the appropriate marketing mix, product, price, distribution and promotion, all of which have to be mutually supportive. The key issues to be addressed in a marketing plan after a careful study of all relevant information are the following:

- Market choice (industry, sector, segment)
- Planning for competitive advantage
- Market positioning
- An effective promotions programme.

From this, a supporting budget is prepared, showing costs and financial allocations to the various components. If the plan is financially acceptable, the next stage is developing action programmes and deadlines for each element of the marketing plan. This is followed by the organisation and implementation of the plan. A good marketing plan facilitates selling and various special promotions which have to be undertaken in every business. The final stage states how the marketing plan is to be monitored and controlled. It is also advisable to include a contingency plan, detailing what will happen if there are specific deviations from the targets set.

Marketing performance is usually monitored on a weekly and monthly basis against targets. The main measures used are sales volume and value, market share, marketing expense to sales ratio, distributor performance and customer attitude tracking. If underperformance is detected, corrective action is required by motivating the sales force (if applicable), cutting production, changing prices or other appropriate action. Periodically a profitability audit is carried out by product, segment, territory, channel or salesperson so as to facilitate good decision-making. It is common to carry out a comprehensive periodic marketing audit of all related functions to examine if a business is pursuing its best marketing opportunities and doing so in an effective manner.

4.9 International marketing

Irish enterprises are being encouraged to internationalise their activities where possible. The number of SMEs engaged in international marketing is increasing, but it is still seen as an area of major weakness in Irish businesses (Enterprise Strategy Group, 2004). It is not an easy process because of different political, legal, economic, social and cultural considerations in each market as well as language, currency (in some cases) and other specific requirements (Bradley, 1991; De Búrca *et al.*, 2004; Ghauri and Cateora, 2006). However, the prospects of profitable sales opportunities abroad provide the incentives required for many companies. In most cases an Irish SME has to export to achieve growth. A company has to have the managerial competence and capacity required for exporting as well as adequate financial resources. Enterprise Ireland is now giving special attention to SMEs with the ambition and potential to develop export sales.

Table 4.6: Export market entry strategy

1.	Setting goals and objectives
2.	Screening potential markets
3.	Deciding which market to enter
4.	Deciding how to enter the target market
5.	Marketing plan for the target country
6.	Implementation
7.	Market monitoring, evaluation and control

Before deciding to engage in export marketing, a company usually prepares a plan, starting with its goals and objectives as well as deciding whether it will market in one or more countries (Table 4.6). Most SMEs start with one niche export market and develop from their own experience. The second step involves screening a number of countries as potential markets. The criteria used are the nature of the product and each country in terms of proximity, political stability, level of economic and social development, income levels, culture, traditions and trading reputation. Some are then selected for further market analysis, which involves research on industry structure, market size, growth potential, export and import regulations, existing and expected competition, market segments served, customer needs, relevant laws and trade practices, especially in relation to distribution channels and terms of payment. Other issues include adaptation of the product or service for the target market, packaging, labelling, quality, quantity, health and safety regulations, trade regulations, currency (our two major trading partners, the UK and the USA, have other currencies), transportation, handling, storage, delivery, servicing, language, documentation, possible prices, related costs, method of payment and the promotions mix. Any business with significant currency exposure has to consider hedging the risk with good advice. International trade shows specific to the sector and trade missions provide useful market information. After a careful assessment of the targeted markets, they are ranked in relation to profit potential, competitive advantage and risk. Usually one market is selected for development initially, based on the expected rate of return on the investment and level of risk involved. This is usually a market where the exporter can develop a profitable niche based on some competitive advantage. The costs of entering an export market can be high and good market research is essential.

An exporter is advised to apply for Authorised Economic Operator (AEO) status from the Revenue Commissioners to facilitate international trading. Authorised Economic Operator status is an EU supply chain security certification awarded to exporters that satisfy the required specified standards for security and customs compliance. From 1 January 2008, organisations trading in Europe were required to be AEO-certified if they wished to avoid delays in shipments and increased inspections as well as difficulties trading with the USA and other countries outside the EU. AEO-certified organisations are given priority treatment at customs with fewer checks and controls than non-AEO businesses.

The next consideration is deciding how to enter a market: exporting, a joint venture or direct investment. Exporting can be done indirectly or directly. Indirect exporting is more common and involves fewer risks for a beginner. The selling is done through a domestic-based importer/distributor (who buys the product and sells it abroad on his/her own account), a domestic-based export agent (who seeks foreign buyers for a commission) or through a co-operative organisation (which sells on behalf of a number of producers). An agent sends all orders received to the exporter. The goods are then supplied and invoices sent to the customers. When payment is received the agent is paid the agreed commission, which is included in the cost of the goods. Distributors and agents have to be carefully selected. Direct exporting can be carried out by the company itself by supplying export customers directly, by its own sales staff based in the importing country or through a foreign branch or subsidiary. A joint venture involves an agreement between the exporting company and an organisation in another state to establish production and marketing facilities in that country. This can be done with licensing by contracting production to a local firm or establishing a new jointly owned venture. Direct investment involves establishing production facilities in the target market. Central to the market entry strategy is the distribution channel to be used for the targeted consumers.

The next stage involves the preparation of a marketing plan for the specific target market covering segmentation, positioning, entry, timing and a promotions mix adapted to local conditions. This requires considerable local knowledge and research. The marketing plan is then implemented and controlled in relation to the targets set. Export records have to be classified, with each product receiving a tariff code number, and the relevant information supplied to the Central Statistics Office.

An exporting company usually establishes a special department or section to organise and service exports. Results obtained are carefully monitored and evaluated. The experience gained is used to revise the marketing plan for the target market and in many cases to develop other export markets. The big challenge for Irish SMEs is the development of export markets.

4.10 Summary

No business can exist without customers. Marketing is concerned with attracting, retaining and satisfying customers at a profit. The modern approach to marketing is providing benefits and value for customers as well as developing profitable long-term relationships with them.

Marketing management consists of market analysis, target marketing, marketing mix, market planning and control. Customer analysis tries to establish who buys what, when, where, how and why in a target market. It incorporates market measurement, competitor analysis, linking the core competence of a business to market opportunities and market research. Target marketing involves segmentation, selecting a target market, positioning, market entry and timing strategies.

Marketing mix addresses the four Ps: product, place, price and promotion, all of which influence potential buyers. Marketing planning focuses on market choice (industry, sector, segment), competitive advantage in the target market, market positioning and developing an effective promotions programme, all of which have to be mutually supportive. Marketing is everyone's job in an organisation, from the telephonist to the chief executive. A marketing-orientated organisation inculcates a culture of good customer service. Listening to customers and non-customers as well as dealing with customer complaints provide useful feedback.

As services are intangible, inseparable, variable and perishable, they pose different challenges and require specific strategies. Service marketing incorporates three additional Ps: people, physical evidence and process. Service providers face three main tasks in marketing: differentiating and innovating in their offerings, managing service quality to meet and exceed customer expectations, and managing productivity.

International marketing is seen as a major weakness in Irish businesses. It is not an easy process for many reasons and requires careful research. Enterprise Ireland is now giving special attention to SMEs with the ambition and potential to develop export sales. Entry strategy to an export market can involve direct exports from a company or selling through domestic-based importers/distributors, an agent or a co-operative organisation. Other options are establishing a joint venture with an organisation in another country or direct investment in the target market. The big challenge for Irish SMEs is the development of export markets.

Questions

1. Explain what you understand by a marketing-orientated organisation.
2. Discuss the main elements of marketing management.
3. Describe how you would carry out market research on specific questions relating to a business proposal.
4. Consider the marketing communications mix used by an organisation with which you are familiar.
5. Discuss the steps involved in the preparation of a marketing plan.

Chapter 5

Finance

Annual income twenty pounds,
Annual expenditure, nineteen, nineteen six, result happiness.
Annual income twenty pounds,
Annual expenditure twenty pounds ought and six, result misery.

Mr Micawber in David Copperfield by Charles Dickens

Learning objectives

- To explore the key characteristics of the various sources of finance – short term, medium term and long term – for a business in Ireland
- To appreciate the importance of working capital and cash management in a business and the processes involved
- To comprehend the basic principles of costing and pricing
- To understand the obligation to keep proper books and records and the knowledge to analyse accounts
- To appreciate the legal obligations of companies in relation to the publication of accounts, the annual general meeting and the annual return

The chapter is structured as follows:

5.1 Introduction to finance
5.2 Sources of finance
5.3 Working capital and cash management
5.4 Costing and pricing
5.5 Accounting records
5.6 Financial statements and their interpretation
5.7 Published accounts
5.8 Summary

5.1 Introduction to finance

Charles Dickens (1812–70) fully understood how important it was for annual income to exceed expenditure; otherwise the result was misery, as he knew only too well from the bitter experience of his own family (his father had been imprisoned for failure to pay his debts). This is also the core principle of business finance. Every business has to be managed to ensure that income exceeds expenditure after the initial start-up period. Most small businesses are started with limited financial resources provided by the entrepreneurs, borrowings and, if eligible, grants. There are other sources available for certain enterprises depending on eligibility. New enterprises endeavour to get operational quickly. While the financial objective is to earn profits as soon as possible, it takes time to establish a loyal customer base and a commercially profitable business. A business is expected to earn a gross profit (sales less cost of sales) on trading which is sufficient to cover all overheads and provide a satisfactory salary for the entrepreneur as well as reasonable profit. It takes some time for a new business to reach this situation, which varies in length depending on the nature of the business, but the quicker the better.

First of all it is important to understand what is meant by fixed assets, current assets, current liabilities and net worth. Fixed assets are those with an expected useful life of greater than one year used in a business for the purpose of trading and not intended for resale. They can include tangible assets such as land, buildings, plant, equipment and motor vehicles or intangible items such as goodwill, patents and trade marks. All fixed assets are valued at historical cost unless otherwise stated. Freehold land is not depreciated; it appreciates in value over time and is regularly revalued to reflect market value. The difference is treated as a capital reserve in accounts. Current assets include cash and those assets which can be converted into cash easily within a short period, for example inventories (stocks) and debtors (the total money owed to the business by debtors). Inventories are valued at cost or net realisable value, if less. Liabilities (debts payable by a business) are classified as current and long term. Current liabilities are debts which must be paid within a few months at most, for example trade creditors (the total money owed by the business to trade creditors), current taxation and accrued expenses. Long-term liabilities are debts payable in more than 12 months, for example term loans. There could also be a contingent liability, one which may arise in certain circumstances, for example possible compensation payable out of a legal action against the business. Net worth (total assets less all liabilities) represents the owners' equity in a business. In a limited company it is the total of issued share capital, reserves and accumulated profits.

The distinction between capital and revenue expenditure is very important in finance. Capital expenditure is money spent in acquiring or augmenting fixed assets, which are used for trading and not for resale over the medium to long term, for example land, buildings and machinery. Money spent in the acquisition of fixed assets is not treated as an expense in accounts. Such purchases are debited to the appropriate fixed asset account and a portion of the cost of assets which lose value over time, due to use and lapse of time, is written off each year as a depreciation charge. Capital purchases are usually financed by medium- or long-term finance and have to be planned carefully (see below).

Revenue expenditure is money spent on the day-to-day running of a business, for example purchases for resale, salaries, repairs, commercial rates and general expenses. All expenses of a revenue nature are charged as costs in the accounts of the period to which they relate. A business has to generate sufficient cash from operations to pay for revenue expenditure. In a start-up situation finance has to be obtained to cover the costs of start-up as well as ongoing business expenses as they fall due for a period. After this initial period revenue expenditure is expected to come from cash inflow (allowing for any cyclical requirements). This initial period of negative cash flow is often called 'the valley of death' and some organisations do not survive it. It is important to have sufficient cash to survive this period which is often exacerbated by slow payments from debtors and suppliers demanding immediate payment because of the business's lack of track record. After this initial difficult period any successful business has to be profitable and generate a positive cash flow. In a business start-up an entrepreneur has to estimate the amount of finance required for the acquisition of fixed assets, the costs of the start-up and working capital and decide on the most appropriate sources.

5.2 Sources of finance

A businessperson rarely has all the finance required to start a business and is dependent on external sources. He/she tries to raise the necessary finance from a number of sources at the lowest possible cost, the least risk and preferably without affecting control of the business (Kennedy *et al.*, 1995). In a start-up situation the entrepreneur tries to keep the ownership of fixed assets to a minimum and operate with as few overheads as possible. The amount of finance required depends on the nature of the business; a service business requires far less than a manufacturing one. A new entrepreneur has to estimate the finance required for the purchase of fixed assets, start-up costs and working capital. The biggest problems in securing finance for a new business are risk, lack of track record and usually a shortage of securities. County Enterprise Boards can provide some financial supports for small businesses. Enterprise Ireland provides a variety of financial packages for high-potential start-up companies involved in manufacturing and internationally traded services. It can take up to a maximum of 10 per cent of ordinary share capital in a qualifying venture and if necessary provide extra capital in the form of repayable preference shares. State funding has to be matched by private investors, promoters, friends or a venture capital fund. It is very common for the promoters of new enterprises to underestimate the amount of finance required for their establishment and operational requirements. Under-capitalisation can result in cash flow problems which, if not quickly rectified, can result in liquidation.

Business finance consists of equity (owners' funds) and debt (borrowed funds). Sources of finance are generally divided into three categories:

a)   Short term
b)   Medium term
c)   Long term.

a)   Short-term sources of finance

Short-term sources of finance refer to a period of less than one year and are used for working capital needs. Permanent working capital needs have to be financed by long-term finance. The chief sources of short-term finance include the following:

*   Trade creditors
*   Accrued expenses
*   Deferred taxation
*   Bank overdraft
*   Inventory financing
*   Factoring
*   Accounts receivable loans
*   Bills of exchange
*   Business credit card.

Trade creditors

Trade credit is a spontaneous source of short-term finance for most businesses. There is a big temptation for all businesses to delay payments and 'lean on the trade'. Most financial controllers try to stretch the credit period as far as possible without affecting credit ratings. If a discount is offered there is a cost involved in not paying promptly. A discount of 2 per cent if paid in 10 days, or the full price within 30 days (20 days later), has an annualised cost of 36.5 per cent (2 per cent x 365/20). Trade credit may not be a source of finance for a new business, as many suppliers of new customers demand payment in advance or on delivery and only allow credit when a satisfactory trading record is established.

Accrued expenses

Accrued expenses such as electricity charges, telephone cost, wages and salaries, which arise spontaneously in all businesses, are usually paid in arrears and represent a free short-term source of finance.

Deferred taxation

Deferred taxation liabilities such as PAYE and PRSI deductions from wages and salaries, Value Added Tax (VAT), income tax and corporation tax are free sources of finance until remitted to the Collector-General. If these taxes are not paid by the due date, interest is charged (which is not allowable for tax purposes).

Bank overdraft

An overdraft is a short-term overdrawing of a current account with the prior agreement of a bank manager. The interest rate is variable and changes in line with the general market rates. An overdraft is a convenient, cheap and flexible source of finance for a short period; there is a requirement for the account to be in credit for at least 30 days in a year. A bank overdraft is intended to meet a temporary shortage of funds and not the permanent financing requirements of a business. A bank overdraft is always repayable on demand. There is usually an upper limit to an overdraft facility and it is generally, but not always, given without security. Additional charges are usually incurred if the authorised overdraft limit is exceeded. Finance can be raised by short-term loans for a year or two in respect of specific purchases. An overdraft used to finance specific assets that generate enough cash to repay the borrowing is known as a self-liquidating loan. Such loans can be interest only or amortised. In the former, only the interest is paid during the life of the loan and the principal at the maturity date (this is called a bullet repayment). With amortised loans a portion of the principal is paid with the appropriate interest in each instalment on the repayment schedule. Short-term loans are generally secured (Power *et al.*, 2005).

Inventory financing

A business can raise short-term funds on the security of inventory in one of three ways: a chattel mortgage, a trust receipt or a warehouse receipt. A chattel mortgage gives the lending institution a mortgage over an itemised list of stock owned by the borrower, usually slow-moving items of high value. This stock can only be sold with the lender's permission. A trust receipt is an instrument acknowledging that the borrower holds specific items of listed stock in trust for the lender. As listed goods are sold the appropriate funds are remitted to the lender. Under a warehouse receipt the inventory is under the control of the lender. In a terminal warehousing agreement the inventory is kept at the lender's premises and when an item is sold it is released to a purchaser when the lender is paid. In field warehousing the inventory is stored on the borrower's premises under the control of a third party. When an item is paid for the lender authorises its release to the purchaser. The cost of this type of finance is high and the third party also has to be paid (Power *et al.*, 2005).

Factoring

Factoring is a procedure whereby a business can sell some or all of its trade debts to a company specialising in this activity and receive regular payments or a lump sum to about 75 per cent of the value of outstanding debtors. The factoring company undertakes the collection process on behalf of the organisation for an agreed discount. Factoring can be done with recourse, where the business itself carries the risk of bad debts, or without recourse, where the factoring company carries the risk. The outstanding balance of the total credit figure is remitted to the borrower when debtors pay in full, less the costs, interest and fees charged for the loans advanced. The use of credit cards involves factoring debts. The seller receives the amount due promptly, less the agreed fee, and the buyer usually gets 30 days to clear the account. If the factoring company bears the risk of bad debts, it will charge extra for the service. Factoring is not cheap and it can affect the image of a business.

Accounts receivable loans

Accounts receivable (debtors) can be used as a source of short-term finance by pledging them as collateral. The business collects the debts and repays the loan as per the agreement. A development of accounts receivable financing is invoice discounting, where a lender will advance up to 80 per cent of the face value of approved invoices. A business submits certain invoices to the lender for consideration and, if deemed acceptable, approval is given. When invoices are paid a borrower passes the proceeds to a lender in accordance with their contract. The lender keeps the amount advanced, plus interest on that figure, and remits whatever is left back to the borrower. Invoice discounting has become an important source of debtor finance.

Bills of exchange

A bill of exchange is defined as:

> an unconditional order in writing addressed by one person to another, signed by the person giving it, requiring the person to whom it is addressed to pay on demand or at an agreed future time a certain sum of money to, or to the order of, a specified person or to bearer. (Bills of Exchange Act 1882)

It is a contract under which a buyer accepts a legal agreement by writing 'accepted' across the bill and signing it, undertaking to pay the specified amount on a stated future date, usually 30, 60, 90 or 180 days later. The seller can either hold the bill to maturity or sell it to a bank at a discount for immediate cash. Bills of exchange are now rarely used in domestic trade but are common in international trade.

Business credit card

A business credit card can be used to pay for certain expenses such as travel, accommodation and online transactions. It is very cheap and convenient for purchases up to the agreed threshold, when cleared within the time limit.

b) Medium-term sources of finance

Medium-term sources of finance, from one to five years, are used for the purchase of assets which lose their value due to lapse of time and/or usage over a few years, such as machinery, equipment and vehicles. The medium-term sources of finance are:

- Leasing
- Hire purchase
- Term loans (Kennedy *et al.*, 1995).

Leasing

Leasing is a procedure whereby a person, called a lessor, purchases an asset and supplies it on lease to a person called a lessee on specific terms. There are two chief types of leasing: operational and financial. Operational leasing takes place when a person leases a specific asset from a business engaged in that activity for an agreed period, on agreed terms. A lessee secures use of an asset without any capital investment and does not have to worry about obsolescence or a change in technology. Financial leasing is a tax-based procedure whereby a business can persuade a business specialising in this activity to purchase a required asset and lease it on special terms. The lessor can write off the cost of such assets for tax purposes in accordance with the current writing-down provisions against its income from the trade of leasing, and the lessee can claim for the lease payments against taxation.

Hire purchase

In a hire-purchase agreement a person obtains possession and use of an asset, but not immediate ownership, and pays for it by regular instalments over a specified period. Ownership does not pass until the final instalment is paid. Hire purchase is a very expensive source of finance because the interest charged is a flat rate on the selling price for the full period of the agreement. In other words, no credit is allowed for repayments. It is important to know the true rate of interest charged on any loan, that is, the actual rate charged on the daily balance outstanding. A simple formula for calculating the approximate true rate of interest is:

$$\frac{\text{Quoted flat rate x 2 x Number of instalments}}{\text{Number of instalments} + 1}$$

It is now obligatory for all lenders to disclose the true rate of interest charged, known as the annual percentage rate (APR). This is defined in the Consumer Credit Act 1995 as being 'the total cost of credit to the consumer, expressed as an annual percentage of the amount of credit granted'.

In an instalment credit sale agreement, ownership of an asset passes immediately to the purchaser, who pays for it by regular instalments over an agreed period, but the interest rate charged is high. Under the Consumer Credit Act 1995, a hire purchase or instalment credit sale agreement must be in writing and specify *inter alia* the cash price, the price charged, the rate of interest and the annual percentage rate applicable.

Term loans

The most common sources of external finance for Irish businesses are bank loans. Many banks offer special rates and supports. There are two main types of loan: secured and unsecured. The former is given on the security of one or more assets of the borrower, while there is no security required for the latter. A term loan is one negotiated between a borrower and a financial institution for a period of from one to seven years or longer, with an agreed repayment schedule. Such a loan is usually granted after careful consideration of a detailed submission from the borrower. The rate of interest is variable, but payable only on the outstanding balance. It is important to determine the annualised percentage rate charged on the loan. The rate can be fixed for a period if required, but it can be expensive to change if the need arises. Some term loans have provisions for 'rest periods' at the start, when only the interest is payable. An arrangement fee is generally charged prior to draw-down to cover the administrative costs involved.

A person or organisation seeking a term loan of any duration is generally required to make a written submission to a financial institution. The following information is required:

- The legal entity requiring the loan and an outline of the origin and development of the business to date
- Management team: full particulars of the senior management team
- Amount of the loan
- Purpose of the loan
- Duration
- Financial accounts: audited accounts for the previous three years
- Projected accounts and cash flow forecasts for the next three to five years
- Assumptions made in the projected accounts
- Repayment schedule showing how it is proposed to repay the loan
- Securities offered as collateral for the loan
- A business plan.

A term loan agreement is embodied in a contract covering all or most of the following depending on the figure involved: amount of the loan, duration, terms, purpose, repayment schedule, interest, security, fees, share option scheme if applicable, restrictive covenants dealing with future borrowings, minimum working capital, salaries, directors' fees, dividends and provisions for dealing with default in repayments. All the terms of a loan agreement are negotiable to some extent. Banks are not in the risk business and will seek as much security as possible. They are far more cautious in their lending since 2008.

It is not advisable to give a personal guarantee, but if there is no alternative, legal advice should be obtained.

The European Investment Fund (EIF), a subsidiary of the European Investment Bank, provides venture capital for SMEs and a range of partial-loan guarantee schemes, working through banks and other intermediaries. The European Investment Bank has provided finance to Irish banks for lending to SMEs. Finance is also available through the Competitiveness and Innovation Programme (CIP) of the European Union.

Criteria used in assessing a loan application

'I must be cruel only to be kind', wrote William Shakespeare in *Hamlet* (Act 3, Scene 4). The same adage can often be used by lenders when assessing applications for loans. In some cases they can perform a better service for prospective borrowers by refusing loans than by granting them. Such refusals can provide the incentives for prospective borrowers to make more realistic evaluations of their plans. The most important criterion in assessing an application for a loan is the ability of the prospective borrower to repay the loan and appropriate interest. A loan is not made on the basis of security alone; a security is a protection of last resort. Start-up enterprises are very difficult to assess and statistically they have a high failure rate. Borrowers and lenders have a responsibility to ensure that any investment financed by borrowed funds is viable, profitable and capable of generating enough surplus cash to cover the loan repayments.

Applications for loans are assessed within the framework of six Cs:

- Character – establishing the legal status of the borrower as well as the character and track record of the promoter(s) involved.
- Conditions – an assessment of the industry, sector and segment where the business is operating and its opportunities.
- Competence – an assessment of the capabilities of management.
- Capital – the amount of equity contributed by the promoter(s) and a review of the existing and proposed capital structure.
- Capacity – the ability of the borrower to repay the loan and interest based on an assessment of the projected accounts and cash flow forecasts as well as the assumptions made in their preparation.
- Collateral – the security the borrower is prepared to offer. The types of security most acceptable include mortgages on land and buildings, fixed and/or floating charges on other assets, chattel liens (in respect of plant and equipment), personal guarantees, stocks and shares as well as life assurance policies.

A borrower has to convince the lender that the business can generate sufficient surplus cash to repay the loan and interest as well as leaving a margin of safety for unforeseen circumstances. Under the Consumer Credit Act 1995, any loan agreement must be in writing and signed by both parties. A borrower is often required to submit regular financial reports to the lender during the period of the loan. Generally most small businesses are able to obtain bank loans and overdraft facilities up to a specific amount. All banks have special deals for new business start-ups. However, the retail banks perceive new and growing companies as high risk and usually require security in the form of assets and personal guarantees. Small businesses in the services sector experience difficulty in securing loans because many have few capital assets and they are not eligible for any support from the enterprise development agencies (Small Business Forum, 2006).

c) Long-term sources of finance

Long-term sources of finance are used to fund long-term investments in land, premises, plant and equipment as well as the permanent working capital required by a business. As a business grows, more permanent working capital is required. The chief long-term sources of finance for a business are as follows:

- Owners' capital
- Retained profits
- Grants
- Preference shares
- Sale and leaseback
- Debt financing (Kennedy *et al.*, 1995).

Owners' capital

The owners of a business are required to make some financial contribution to its funding. Such finance, known as equity capital, provides permanent funds for the business, with an opportunity for the owner(s) to earn high profits if the business prospers and the risk of losing some or all of the investment if it does not succeed. Creditors like to see a business with a good equity base because it provides a cushion against losses and increases creditworthiness. Equity capital is generally classified in the financial literature into four categories: seed capital, venture capital, development capital and ongoing equity capital (Kennedy *et al.*, 1995). Seed capital, the finance required to plan and establish the feasibility of a business, is the first to be spent, carries the highest risk and is the most difficult to raise. Venture capital is the finance required for the start and early development of a business to purchase assets and provide for working capital. As the failure rate of new enterprises is high, a big portion of seed and venture capital is lost, a factor which makes such finance difficult to raise. Most high-technology companies depend on venture capital. Development capital is the finance required for growth and expansion. Ongoing equity capital is required to maintain a reasonable equity base as the business expands.

In a company, the owners invest in ordinary shares which are not repayable at a certain date but qualify for dividends out of profits and rank last in a winding-up situation.

Payment of dividends to ordinary shareholders depends on profits and is at the discretion of the directors. Holders of ordinary shares have voting rights, so they at least in theory control a company. If a company succeeds the value of such shares rises and this profit is realised when the shares are sold. Ordinary shareholders have what are called pre-emption rights: the right to purchase any new shares in proportion to their existing holding. This right enables them to maintain control and prevent dilution of their wealth.

Owners' funds come from personal savings, family members, private investors (business angels) or friends, or private borrowings. Personal savings, family members and friends are obvious sources. A 'business angel' is a wealthy individual, often a retired business owner or executive, who invests capital in a business start-up and may also act as a mentor. The Business Angel Partnership, sponsored by Enterprise Ireland, InterTrade Ireland and the Business Innovation Centres, provides a framework for this process in Ireland. This source of funds can provide an investor with access to a start-up company with good growth potential, while the company can avail of the vast business experience and networks of the investor. Start-up companies are pre-screened for eligibility. Potential investors are contacted. A meeting is arranged between an interested investor and the company, but it is up to both parties to reach an agreement about the specific terms. An individual can borrow money to invest in ordinary shares in a company. Subject to certain conditions, an individual could claim interest relief on money borrowed to acquire ordinary shares in or lend to a 'qualifying company' (generally a non-quoted trading or holding company). The investor had to have a 'material interest' in the company (own or control more than 5 per cent of the ordinary share capital) and be employed as a full-time or part-time director or employee. This relief could not be claimed on interest paid on loans taken out to purchase shares under the Business Expansion Scheme or the Seed Capital Scheme. This incentive is to be phased out from 2011.

If the funds invested by the owners are insufficient to give a reasonable equity base, the owners can consider investing more of their own funds, introducing new members or raising finance from financial institutions or from venture capitalists in return for an equity stake in respect of companies with good growth potential. The introduction of new members could dilute control for existing owners if they do not take up their proportionate share, as ordinary shares are usually not redeemable and share in all future profits and dividends of the company. However, possessing a 60 per cent share in a successful company may be far better than owning 100 per cent of a small, weak one. The provision of venture capital by financial institutions in Ireland dates back to the 1970s and in general is confined to enterprises with good management teams and high growth potential. A venture capitalist takes a minority equity stake in a company, often up to 40 per cent. There is no interest charge involved as the venture capitalist is interested in a capital gain. Any applicant for venture capital is required to submit a comprehensive plan to one of the institutions involved in this type of finance. The venture capitalist will seek one or more seats on the board of directors and may even seek a say in the appointment of some members of the management team as well as insisting on an exit mechanism for the investment, for example a promise to bring the company to the stock exchange. Venture capital is an expensive source of finance but it is often the only one for a high-technology company with good growth potential. A venture capitalist is interested in projected growth in turnover, profits and value as well as an ambitious, competent management team.

There are three special sources of equity finance for certain companies:

- Business Expansion Scheme (BES)/Employment and Investment Incentive Scheme
- Seed Capital Scheme (SCS)
- Initial public offering (IPO)/Employment and Investment Incentive Scheme

Business Expansion Scheme (BES)

The 1984 Finance Act introduced a special tax incentive known as the Business Expansion Scheme to encourage individuals to subscribe for new ordinary shares in certain manufacturing and service companies. It was renewed to 31 December 2013. A 'qualifying taxpayer' could invest up to a maximum of €150,000 per annum in new ordinary shares issued in a 'qualifying company' engaged in a 'qualifying trade' and write the investment off against tax at his/her marginal rate. The 'qualifying company' had to be incorporated and tax resident in Ireland as well as qualifying as a micro, small or medium-sized enterprise under EU regulations and located in an 'assisted area'. An 'assisted area' includes all of the country except Dublin, Kildare, Meath and Wicklow and, since 1 January 2009, Cork City and County (excluding the docklands). A medium-sized enterprise located elsewhere in Ireland may qualify in respect of seed or start-up capital only. Under one of the EU conditions of approval, other State aids may be reduced, with a few exceptions (Duffy, 2008). 'Qualifying trades' include manufacturing, certain computer services, film production, specific tourism undertakings, commercial research and development activities and certain internationally traded services provided they are approved for grant aid, as well as certain recycling activities. The maximum amount which could be raised by a company under this scheme is €2 million, subject to a maximum of €1.5 million to be raised in a 12-month period. The shares must be held for a minimum of five years, otherwise the relief is claimed back. There are restrictions on this and other reliefs for individuals with income in excess of a specified figure (see www.revenue.ie).

There were two ways to invest: through a qualifying company or a BES fund. The tax incentive was very attractive for investors and a qualifying company, but most external investors wanted an exit mechanism to be put in place after the five years. One mechanism was a put-and-call option which allowed company promoters to buy out investors at a specific price. One big success story was the Kerry company, Stockbyte, established by Jerry Kennelly with some BES finance and sold in 2006 to Getty Images for more than €100 million.

It was announced in the 2011 Budget that the BES was to be replaced by a new Employment and Investment Incentive Scheme linked to employee numbers. Under the new scheme, a business can raise €10 million in funding and is to be subject to a simpler certification process than its predecessor.

Seed Capital Scheme (SCS)

A Seed Capital Scheme was introduced in 1995 to help people who leave employment (or are unemployed) to start their own businesses. An individual who satisfies certain conditions may obtain a refund of tax paid in the previous six years for investment in new ordinary shares in a new company which is engaged in a BES-type activity or approved research and development activities. The maximum relief granted to an individual for any year is €100,000 and the funding ceiling for a qualifying company is €2 million. The SCS applies until 31 December 2013. To qualify for the relief the individual must be a full-time employee or full-time director in the new company and derive at least 75 per cent of his/her total income from Schedule E (PAYE) sources and not own more than 15 per cent of the ordinary share capital of another company, with limited exceptions (Martyn and Reck, 2010).

Initial Public Offering (IPO)

An initial public offering is where a privately owned company goes public for the first time and sells shares. This route could enable an organisation to raise a large amount of equity and also provide a mechanism for owners to sell their shares if they wish. If successful, a public offering can create considerable wealth for the owners because it capitalises earnings at a multiple (price-earnings ratio). It can be a costly process if shares are priced too low. If they are too high, they may not attract buyers. There are also big costs and risks in going public, with good professional advice essential. The Irish Enterprise Exchange (IEX) was launched in 2005 to enable small and medium-sized companies to access public markets. Now called the Enterprise Securities Market, an applicant company has to have a minimum capitalisation of €5 million, but no trading record is required and there is no requirement for the public to hold a minimum number of shares. Irish developing companies can use other markets like the Alternative Investment Market (AIM) in Britain and the NASDAQ in New York. Obtaining a listing offers an opportunity to raise funds and provide an exit route for those that wish to realise value. There are a number of ways of raising equity finance by selling shares:

- A public offering
- A private placement or a placement through the stock exchange to a single investor or group of investors
- Through a rights issue of shares in proportion to existing holdings (where new shares are offered to existing shareholders at a discount)

- A plan for employees (Lucey, 1996; Power *et al.*, 2005).

Retained profits

Profits earned in a business can be paid out to the owners as dividends or retained to finance future needs. Retained profits are an important source of finance for most businesses and, as part of the equity, they do not affect control.

In a company, the directors make a recommendation on dividends to each annual general meeting. They can recommend that all, part or none of the profits be paid in dividends. Dividends can only be paid out of profits or reserves of undistributed profits. A public company may be vulnerable to a takeover bid if retained profits create a situation where the asset value per share greatly exceeds its price.

Grants

A grant is free money given to an eligible enterprise by a State agency to stimulate development. Some or all of a grant is repayable if the business does not survive for a specific period. An enterprise is required to submit a business plan to the State agency when applying for a grant. Generally, grants are now only given for manufacturing activities and internationally traded services. However, City and County Enterprise Boards can offer a variety of grants and other supports to aid start-ups and job creation in small businesses with fewer than 10 employees.

Preference shares

A company can raise capital by issuing preference shares, which give their holders the right to a fixed rate of dividend out of profits every year and the right to repayment of their capital in priority to other shareholders in a liquidation. Preference shareholders rarely have voting rights and thus have no control over a company. Preference shares are a flexible source of finance in so far as the dividend does not have to be paid every year and are permanent loans treated as shares without any charge over company assets. Preference shares are cumulative, unless the contrary is stated, which means that dividends not paid accumulate and arrears are paid out of subsequent profits before paying dividends to ordinary shareholders.

Redeemable preference shares are redeemable on a specific date. Enterprise Ireland can take cumulative convertible redeemable preference shares in high-potential start-up companies, which can also be provided by friends and business angels. These are 'soft loans' with fixed redemption dates unless they are converted into equity. Cumulative redeemable preference shares have a first claim on dividends out of profits and no voting rights until they are converted. Such preference shares from Enterprise Ireland can be converted into a maximum of 10 per cent of the equity capital and are redeemable after five years unless they are converted. A company using such finance has to sign an agreement containing covenants (promises), warranties (binding obligations) and restricted transactions (things which cannot be done without the permission of Enterprise Ireland).

Sale and leaseback

A business does not have to own the premises where its activities are carried on; it can lease them. A company can even lease premises from one of its shareholders. When starting a business a promoter can consider leasing a premises rather than seeking immediate ownership and use the available finance for working capital.

If a business owns a building it can be sold to an investor, such as a financial institution, and its use obtained by a long-term lease on terms advantageous to both parties. A leasing contract usually contains renewal options and provision for regular rent revisions. The benefit of any capital appreciation accrues fully to the lessor.

Debt financing

Finance can also be obtained as long-term debt. Debt is borrowed money which does not affect the control or ownership of a business, with interest charged deductible against taxation. Borrowing for capital investment in land, premises, plant and machinery is generally considered acceptable provided the business is able to earn a greater return than its cost on operations and generate sufficient net cash flow to meet scheduled repayments, as well as having regard to possible increases in the interest rate charged. The interest charged can be variable or fixed, but there may be additional charges if a borrower wants to clear or move from a fixed-rate loan. Debt is usually raised on the basis of a security, known as collateral, and failure to honour repayments can have serious consequences.

A debenture is a document acknowledging the existence of a long-term loan, with a specific maturity date, interest charge, repayment schedule and other provisions. Section 2(1) of the 1963 Companies Act states that a debenture 'includes debenture stock, bonds, and any securities of a company whether constituting a charge on the assets of the company or not'. (A bond is a long-term loan with specific interest charges, repayment schedule and maturity date.) A debenture is usually structured as a balloon loan, with only the interest payable on a regular basis and the principal at maturity (Lucey, 1996). It is usually secured with a fixed charge on specific assets and/or a floating charge over current assets. If a company defaults in its payment, the debenture instrument gives the lender the right to appoint a receiver to the company.

5.3 Working capital and cash management

Working capital is the funds invested in the short-term assets of a business – in effect, the excess of current assets over current liabilities. It is generally called net working capital; gross working capital is the total capital invested in current assets. Working capital is financed by some short-term funds, but adequate long-term capital is essential. Different business activities have different working capital needs. The working capital cycle, or cash conversion cycle, is the length of time it takes for the initial cash outflow for goods and services to be realised in payment for sales. Each element of working capital – purchases, production cycle, credit sales – has its own life and liquidity characteristics. Many businesses make inadequate provisions for their working capital requirements. Adequate working capital is necessary on a permanent basis in every business and any increase in sales requires extra working capital. There are also seasonal and cyclical requirements for additional working capital (Lucey, 1996).

Overtrading involves increasing sales beyond the limit of existing financial resources – a precarious practice. If a business is overtrading, extra finance has to be provided or they must slow down the rate of growth to a level that can be sustained within existing resources. A business which is liquid (sufficient working capital) but not profitable can survive in the short term; in the long term, a business has to be profitable and liquid. Working capital management involves control of the following:

a)   Inventory
b)   Debtors
c)   Creditors
d)   Cash.

a)   Management of inventory

Inventory represents a big investment for many businesses. In a manufacturing organisation there are usually stocks of raw materials, work in progress and finished goods. The importance of effective inventory control cannot be overemphasised, with the objective to keep levels as low as possible without affecting production or sales. Supply chain management, with the application of new technologies and just-in-time supplies, has led to a considerable reduction in stock. Laser scanning systems which automatically record each item at the point of sale are now widely used in sales outlets. They simultaneously adjust stock levels, thus facilitating reordering. Demand-based management, where a business only manufactures a product after receipt of order and can meet the customer's expectations, keeps investment in working capital to a minimum.

b)   Management of debtors

Much business takes place electronically with credit or charge cards, but granting credit is an issue for many enterprises. The management of debtors, or accounts receivable, involves the control of credit sales and balancing the gains derived from giving credit to customers with its associated costs. It is concerned with increasing sales at planned margins and being paid within the agreed period. A decision to give credit is a marketing one, influenced by trade practice in a sector and the nature of the business. This desire to increase sales has to be evaluated with regard to the extra profit generated after taking the additional costs and possible bad debts into consideration. In financial terms trade credit given is an interest-free loan to a customer. As a result, a cash business has numerous advantages over one which gives credit. The total investment in debtors is influenced by the volume of credit sales, the period allowed and the effectiveness of follow-up procedures. There are a number of costs involved in giving trade credit:

- The cost of the money invested in debtors
- The cost of any discounts offered
- The cost of bad debts
- The administrative cost.

The money used to give credit has either a real cost (interest paid on borrowed funds) or an opportunity cost (income foregone on the money used to give free credit to customers). Many businesses are obliged to use overdrafts and term loans to give trade credit.

Some businesses offer discounts to encourage prompt payments, but the cost involved can be high. Terms of '2/10 net 30' (2 per cent discount if paid within 10 days, otherwise the full amount is payable in 30 days) is an annual rate of 36.5 per cent. Every business which gives credit has to decide whether it should allow discounts, and if so, on what terms. If the decision is to offer discounts, it has to consider the cost of various rates in relation to the speed-up in payment achieved and the cost of finance.

One of the objectives of credit management is to prevent bad debts, or at least to keep them as low as possible. Any firm which gives credit has some bad debts. The longer an account is outstanding, the greater the probability of a bad debt arising. The loss involved in a bad debt depends on the contribution margin (gross profit) in the selling price; the higher the contribution margin, the lower the loss involved. In any bad debt the marginal cost (the variable cost of producing one unit) and the contribution margin are lost. Table 5.1 shows the additional sales required to offset a loss arising from bad debts at different contribution margins (gross profit/sales).

Table 5.1: Additional sales required to offset bad debts

Actual bad debt	Contribution margin					
	10%	15%	20%	25%	33⅓%	50%
€	€	€	€	€	€	€
1,000	10,000	6,667	5,000	4,000	3,000	2,000
2,000	20,000	13,333	10,000	8,000	6,000	4,000
3,000	30,000	20,000	15,000	12,000	9,000	6,000

The administrative cost involved in giving credit includes staff, accommodation, postage, telephone, printing, stationery and debt collection expenses. In some cases a personal visit is required to secure payment. All the costs involved in giving credit come out of the sales margin and can quickly turn a profitable sale into a loss-making one.

Credit policy

Every firm that gives credit has to determine its policy on the following:

i)   Credit assessment
ii)   Length of credit
iii)   Interest to be charged
iv)   Retention of title
v)   Procedures.

Credit assessment

Most organisations set limits below which they will not open new credit accounts because of the costs involved. Before a business opens a new credit account it tries to establish creditworthiness. The customer is asked to fill a credit application form giving full details about his/her organisation and the name of the person who authorises payments (useful information to have on file). This information can be supplemented with an assessment by marketing staff, as well as analysing published accounts, requesting a bank reference, two or three trade references, information from other credit managers or seeking a credit agency's report if deemed necessary. Ultimately, the decision to give credit to any customer is a matter of personal judgement after evaluating the available information.

Length of credit

A business has to decide the length of credit to allow as well as the limit for each customer, which is recorded on a ledger. A new account is carefully monitored until a satisfactory trading relationship develops. Any change in a customer's credit rating is recorded on the ledger. A customer's ledger is an invaluable source of credit information: it can flag the first sign of liquidity problems arising. Other warning signs include the issuing of post-dated cheques and frequent requests for copies of invoices and statements as well as payments on account. Because of the amount and length of time involved in some transactions, interim, or stage payments, retainers or deposits are included in contracts of sale.

Interest to be charged

Each firm has to decide if it should charge compound interest on overdue accounts. Ireland implemented the European Communities (Late Payment in Commercial Transactions) Regulations 2002 to address the problem of late payments in both the public and private sectors. The Prompt Payment of Accounts Act 1997 applied only to the public sector. Under the 2002 regulations, payment for the supply of goods or services is to be made within 30 days of receipt of invoice, unless the day is otherwise agreed by contract. Suppliers who are not paid on time are entitled to payment of interest on the amount outstanding at a rate of 7 per cent above the European Central Bank rate. Some large organisations apply unfair contractual payment terms to small businesses. According to the Small Business Forum (2006),

> Small businesses that supply goods and services to large organisations are often compelled to accept long delays in payment, either because of unreasonable contract terms, or because they are afraid to pursue on-time payment for fear of losing business.

Retention of title

A retention of title clause in a contract of sale is designed to prevent ownership of goods supplied on credit passing from the supplier to the customer until they are paid for. For a retention of title clause to be valid it has to be incorporated into the terms of the sale which are accepted by the purchaser prior to completion of the contract. If the purchaser does not pay for the goods, the seller can recover them. Goods over which title is retained belong to the seller until payment is received. It is a factor which lenders now consider when assessing the security value of inventory.

Procedures

A business has to decide the procedures to be followed in respect of invoices, statements and 'chasing up' payments. It is important to ensure that a credit sale leads to the issue of an invoice as soon as possible, containing the order number, full particulars of the goods supplied and the credit terms, with the details promptly recorded on the debtors' ledger. It is important to ensure that the invoice contains no error, which could be used by the customer as an excuse to delay payment. Many businesses receive payments by electronic transfer or direct debit. It is advisable to have the business's international bank account number (IBAN) and bank identifier code (BIC) on all invoices to customers outside the State to facilitate quick payment. Every effort is made to obtain payment as soon as possible within the credit period. A statement is sent out to a credit customer at the end of each month showing the balance outstanding. If a credit customer does not comply with the credit terms, the sales department is notified to refuse supply of new credit orders until the account is cleared or approval given. Some organisations find that a salesperson calling regularly on the customer is the best way to get quick payment. Each organisation has to decide how it will chase overdue debts, which can involve legal action. The average collection period is calculated regularly and carefully monitored. A useful procedure used to control debtors is the preparation of an 'ageing schedule', showing the amount and percentage of the total outstanding for various periods of time. The final stage is to consider taking legal action for the outstanding debt and even obtaining a judgement. Some organisations also insure their credit sales. Debtors should remember the adage of Benjamin Franklin: 'Creditors have better memories than debtors!'

c) Management of creditors

Creditors are an integral part of working capital and careful management can help the cash position. The management of creditors, or accounts payable, is the inverse of the procedure involved for debtors. In general, businesses try to stretch credit as far as possible without affecting credit ratings or incurring costs, as well as taking discounts if offered. The management of creditors also involves control of purchases, ordering supplies as required or on a just-in-time basis and establishing sale-or-return agreements for stock, if applicable. It is important to have good relationships with suppliers as well as proper procedures in place for recording receipts and initiating the payment process.

d) Management of cash

The management of cash involves planning the finances of an organisation to achieve maximum cash availability, liquidity and good interest income on surplus funds. The following principles are common in the management of cash:
- Income is collected as soon as possible, preferably with sales, and every effort is made to speed up payments from credit customers
- Receipts not paid by electronic transfer are lodged promptly for security and income reasons
- Payments are stretched as far as possible without affecting credit ratings
- Cash which is surplus to immediate requirements is invested in interest-earning investments with regard to yield, risk and ease of withdrawal.

Working capital requirements

A very simple, but approximate, way to calculate working capital requirements is to calculate the cash required to support an extra euro's worth of sales for an existing business. The following relationships are established from the last set of final accounts, stocks to sales, debtors to sales and creditors to purchases, as shown in Table 5.2.

The last accounts for this business showed that stocks were 20 per cent of sales and debtors 25 per cent (both uses of funds) and creditors (a source of funds) were 20 per cent of purchases. The difference, 25 per cent, tells us that for every euro of sales, 25 cent is required for working capital. This procedure assumes that the above relationships remain approximately the same during the following year. If it is planned to increase sales next year by, say, €10,000, an extra €2,500 is required for working capital.

Table 5.2: Calculating working capital per euro of sales

(a) Use of short-term funds		%
Stocks/sales		0.20
Debtors/sales		0.25
		0.45
(b) Source of short-term funds		
Creditors/purchases		(0.20)
		0.25

Cash management

Cash management is concerned with optimising the amount of cash available to a business to ensure that it has sufficient funds to meet payments as they fall due and investing any surplus. Good cash management is essential in any business and, like a household, it must have more cash coming in than going out in payments. In other words, cash inflow must exceed cash outflow. The survival of a business depends on its ability to generate enough cash both in amount and in time to meet all its financial obligations.

Liquidity and solvency

Liquidity means the availability of cash with which a business can meet all its short-term debts as they fall due. A business is insolvent if it is unable to pay its debts. A business can be illiquid (with insufficient cash to pay its immediate debts) and still be solvent. A business is solvent when total assets exceed total liabilities and it has the ability to meet its financial obligations with cash, near cash (assets which can be quickly converted into cash) and/or credit. The ability to generate sufficient cash to meet debts depends on the condition of assets in relation to cash, access to credit and the time allowed. A solvent business could be forced into liquidation if it is unable to pay its debts as they fall due for payment. This is why liquidity is so important in business management. Some businesses plan a 'cash cushion' of a minimum balance over and above budgeted needs, a feature very common in US companies.

Cash flow forecast

A cash flow forecast, or cash budget, is by far the most widely used procedure for forecasting cash requirements. It shows, over periods varying from a week, a month, a year or longer, the expected cash inflows and outflows of a business. Possible deficiencies and surpluses are indicated. Management can use this information for planning purposes, arranging borrowing facilities for the deficiencies and investing surpluses. The accuracy of a cash flow forecast depends on the assumptions upon which it is based, in particular the sales projection and its pattern over the period. A cash flow forecast is more comprehensive than a working capital calculation. The former includes all cash movements into and out of a business, making no distinction between capital or revenue expenditure, while the latter covers the working capital elements of stocks, debtors and creditors only.

The preparation of a cash flow forecast involves four steps:

i) Forecasting all cash inflows and their timing

ii) Forecasting all cash outflows and their timing

iii) Calculating the cash surplus or deficit for each period

iv) Adding or subtracting the surplus or deficit for each period to/from the cash balance at the start to get the cumulative cash position at the end (see Table 5.3).

This predicted cash position assists in forecasting overdraft requirements at specific periods and identifying when surplus funds can be invested.

i) Preparation of a cash inflow forecast starts with the estimated sales for each month, or other period as appropriate, divided between cash and credit sales. Cash sales are recorded in the month they are expected. After establishing the timing of receipts from credit sales, the actual cash inflow is recorded for the appropriate month. Any other receipts are recorded in the actual months they are expected.

ii) A cash outflow statement is then prepared, showing the actual payments expected to be made each month. A production schedule is prepared for a manufacturing business, from which the raw materials purchases figures are determined. Raw materials purchased are recorded in the months the actual payments are expected to be made with regard to the credit terms allowed. All other costs and expenses like wages and salaries, including employer's PRSI contributions, rent, rates, light, heat, power, postage, stationery, interest charges, selling costs, VAT and other expenses are budgeted and the actual payments are recorded in the months the outflows are expected to take place. Expenditure of a capital nature, for example the purchase of fixed assets and the repayments of loans, is recorded in the actual months payments are expected to be made.

iii) The total cash outflow is subtracted from the aggregate of the inflow for each month to give the surplus or deficit for that period.

iv) The opening balance at the start of each month is added to the cash surplus or deficit for that period to give the cumulative position at the end, which is the starting figure for the following period.

All assumptions made in the preparation of any budget are stated. Only cash flows are recorded; an accounting adjustment such as depreciation, which does not involve a cash flow, is not included. An example of a cash flow forecast is shown in Table 5.3.

Table 5.3: Cash flow forecast for year ended 30 June year X

The following information was extracted from the records of ABC Co. Ltd, a retail organisation, in December Year X, for the preparation of a cash flow forecast in respect of the first six months of the following calendar year.

1. Sales are expected to average €48,400 in January and February and €60,500 per month thereafter, with 50% of sales for cash and the balance payable one month later. No discount is allowed.

2. A term loan of €5,000 is expected in March.

3. Purchases for stock per month are expected to be delivered at a rate of €24,200 in January and €30,250 each month thereafter until June. The normal period of credit is one month and no discount is received. Stocks are purchased one month before the expected sales; the purchases in December are expected to be sold in January, and so on.

4. The sales and purchases figures above include VAT at 21%. The company uses the cash received system for VAT. A sum of €6,000 is to be paid to the Collector-General in January in respect of the previous November/December taxable period, €7,350 in March in respect of the January/February period and €9,450 in May for March/April (ignore VAT on the purchase of equipment).

5. Salaries, including employer's PRSI contribution, amount to €3,000 per week and there are five pay weeks in January and April.

6. Maintenance to premises is expected to average €1,000 per month, payable monthly.

7. Selling costs are budgeted at €2,000 per month, payable a month in arrears.

8. Administration costs are expected to average €3,000 per month, payable monthly.

9. A sum of €10,000 is to be paid for equipment in May and the same figure in June.

10. A sum of €10,000 is payable in respect of corporation tax in March and €3,000 for commercial rates in June.

11. The depreciation charge applicable to the period is €10,000.

12. The following balances are expected at the end of the preceding December:

Debtors	€24,200 (to be received in January)
Creditors for purchases	€24,200 (payable in January)
VAT	€ 6,000 (payable in January)
Selling expenses	€ 2,000 (payable in January)
Bank balance	€ 4,000

Cash flow forecast for the period 1 January to 30 June year X

		See note	Jan €	Feb €	March €	April €	May €	June €
	Cash inflow							
	Cash sales	1	24,200	24,200	30,250	30,250	30,250	30,250
	Credit sales	2	24,200	24,200	24,200	30,250	30,250	30,250
	Grant	3			5,000			
	Other income	4						
a)	Total cash inflow	5	48,400	48,400	59,450	60,500	60,500	60,500
	Cash outflow							
	Purchases	6	24,200	24,200	30,250	30,250	30,250	30,250
	VAT	7	6,000		7,350		9,450	

Table 5.3 (continued)

	Salaries	8	15,000	12,000	12,000	15,000	12,000	12,000
	Maintenance	9	1,000	1,000	1,000	1,000	1,000	1,000
	Selling	10	2,000	2,000	2,000	2,000	2,000	2,000
	Administration	11	3,000	3,000	3,000	3,000	3,000	3,000
	Equipment	12					10,000	10,000
	Taxation	13			10,000			
	Rates	14						3,000
	Other expenses	15						
b)	Total cash outflow	16	(51,200)	(42,200)	(65,600)	(51,250)	(67,700)	61,250
	Net cash flow (a – b)	17	(2,800)	6,200	(6,150)	9,250	(7,200)	(750)
	Add opening balance	18	4,000	1,200	7,400	1,250	10,500	3,300
	Cumulative cash balance	19	1,200	7,400	1,250	10,500	3,300	2,550

Explanatory notes:

(1) 50% of sales each month is for cash.

(2) The balance of the sales figure for each month is payable in the following one. We are told that €24,200 is to be received in January in respect of December sales.

(3) A term loan of €5,000 is expected to be received in March.

(4) Any other income is recorded here.

(5) These figures are the total inflows for each month.

(6) The purchases for each month are payable in the following one. A sum of €24,200 is payable in January in respect of purchases during December.

(7) Value Added Tax (see Chapter 6). The figures are provided but the relevant calculations are as follows adopting the cash received basis of accounting for VAT:

	Jan/Feb	March/April	May/June
Taxable period	€	€	€
Sales = cash received (including VAT)	96,800	114,950	121,000
Sales excluding VAT, €96,800 x $^{100}/_{121}$	80,000	95,000	100,000
a) VAT on sales (21% of €80,000, etc.)	16,800	19,950	21,000
Actual purchases including VAT	54,450	60,500	60,500
(€24,200 + €30,250, etc.)			
Purchases excluding VAT, €54,450 x $^{100}/_{121}$	45,000	50,000	50,000
b) VAT paid on purchases (21% of €45,000, etc.)	9,450	10,500	10,500
c) VAT payable to Collector-General			
(a – b)	7,350	9,450	10,500
Payable	March	May	July

(8) There are five paydays in January and April, hence €15,000 in each of these months and €12,000 in each of the rest.

(9) Maintenance costs are payable monthly.

(10) Selling expenses are payable a month in arrears, €2,000 is payable in January in respect of December.

Table 5.3 (continued)

(11) Administration costs are payable monthly.

(12) Equipment is to be purchased in May and June. We are not told when payment is made, so it is assumed that it will take place at the time of purchase.

(13) Corporation tax of €10,000 is payable in March.

(14) Commercial rates of €3,000 are due in June.

(15) Other expenses are recorded here if applicable.

(16) This is the total of the outflow in respect of each month.

(17) This line is the difference between the cash inflow and outflow for each month. Brackets indicate an excess of outflow over inflow.

(18) The opening cash position at the start of each month is the closing figure for the preceding one.

(19) The aggregate of the net cash flow for each month and the opening figure is the cumulative cash balance at the end.

Note: Depreciation is not a cash flow.

Inflation

Inflation – the loss in the purchasing power of money due to increases in the prices of goods and services – has serious consequences for cash management. In an inflationary period, additional working capital is required to finance even the same volume of activity and to replace fixed assets. In normal circumstances with no inflation, the depreciation charged in the accounts each year is usually sufficient to replace a fixed asset at the end of its useful life. In inflationary times, the accumulated depreciation charge is not sufficient to replace a fixed asset because the annual figure is based on historical cost and not its expected replacement price. In such conditions it is essential to earn and retain sufficient profits to finance ongoing activities.

Lifeblood

Cash flow forecasts enable management to ensure that there is sufficient cash available at the right time, at the lowest cost possible, to meet commitments as they fall due. Deviations from the cash forecast require prompt action. This can involve postponing capital expenditure, accelerating cash inflows with price reductions through a clearance sale, liquidating unproductive assets or rescheduling debts.

Cash flow forecasts can be prepared very easily on a computer spreadsheet. Sensitivity analysis is often used in forecasting cash requirements by evaluating the key assumptions in relation to the most optimistic, the most pessimistic and the most likely outcome. It is recommended practice to provide for a minimum cash balance as a contingency plan for an emergency. Special payments such as capital expenditure, taxation, dividends and repayment of loans require careful cash planning. The maintenance of planned profit margins is very important for the generation of sufficient cash to meet requirements. Cash is the lifeblood of any business and consequently good cash flow forecasting is essential, not only for growth, but for survival.

5.4 Costing and pricing

Pricing is one of the most important functions for the management of any business. The general objectives of any pricing policy are recovery of full costs, attainment of a satisfactory profit and value for consumers. The optimal selling price is one at which marginal cost equals marginal revenue, the point at which profits are maximised, but in practice most small businesses seek a satisfactory return with regard to their planned target, competition and the general economic situation. Costs are classified as fixed and variable. Fixed costs are those that remain the same at different levels of activity in the short term and variable costs are those that increase or decrease in direct proportion to changes in activity levels. Every sale has to recover its variable cost and make a contribution to fixed costs and to profit. Costs alone do not determine the selling price of a product or service; in a market economy, price is determined by supply and demand. The initial selling price of a new product depends on two key factors: the sensitivity of sales to variations in price, referred to as the elasticity of demand, and the ease with which competitors can enter the market. In general the lower the price, the greater the demand for a product or service, but the price charged has to generate sufficient sales to recover the costs and yield a profit. If this is not possible, the cost base has to be pruned and brought under the expected revenue. Prices are determined by an assessment and reconciliation of two different approaches:

a)   Market-based pricing techniques
b)   Cost-based pricing techniques.

a)   Market-based pricing techniques

There are a number of different market-led approaches to pricing and a business has to decide which one is the most appropriate to it at a particular time, especially with regard to the life cycle of its product(s).

Market skimming

A market skimming approach is often used when pricing a new product. It aims to maximise profit in the short term by charging a premium price to consumers who are insensitive to price and really want the new product. This approach is suitable for a quality product or service or one with a high level of innovation, for which there is a good market demand and little or no competition. The price can be reduced later, if necessary, to attract a larger segment of the market. It is also easier to reduce a high price than to increase a low one. A market skimming objective is not a suitable policy if the market is large and the product has close substitutes or if entry is easy and cheap for potential competitors. A high price will attract competitors unless the product is protected by a patent or a strongly entrenched brand name.

Market penetration

Market penetration involves setting a relatively low price for a product or service to get quick acceptance and a large share of the market. This approach is adopted in a price-sensitive market where close substitutes are available, where the market is easy to enter and where the business can seek the benefits of large-scale operations. It is a dangerous policy for a new SME to follow unless its cost base is very competitive.

Target pricing

Under this procedure, price is established in relation to a satisfactory rate of return on the capital employed in the business.

Follow the leader

There is no calculation involved in this method and the business becomes a price taker.

Going rate

Some businesses adopt the going market rate for their product or service because of its nature and the present competition.

Product line promotion

Some new products extend or complement the range of products produced by a business. A new product can be priced at or near marginal cost to attract sales for other products in the range.

b)   Cost-based pricing techniques

There are three cost-orientated techniques used in pricing:

- Cost-plus pricing
- Target pricing
- Marginal pricing (Harper, 1995; Lucey, 2009).

Cost-plus pricing

The cost-plus price of a product or service is determined by adding a certain percentage to its unit cost, a widely used technique especially in job production and retailing. A profit figure expressed as a fraction or percentage of the cost price is known as the 'mark-up'; a profit figure expressed as a fraction or percentage of the selling price is called the 'margin' (or gross margin or contribution margin).

- A mark-up of 50 per cent gives a margin of $33^1/_3$ per cent
- A mark-up of $33^1/_3$ per cent gives a margin of 25 per cent
- A mark-up of 25 per cent gives a margin of 20 per cent
- A mark-up of 20 per cent gives a margin of $16^2/_3$ per cent.

If a product costs €100 and a mark-up of 25 per cent is applied, the selling price, excluding VAT, is €125. The margin is 20 per cent. The following are useful formulae applied to this example:

$$\text{Selling price} = \frac{\text{Cost}}{100 - \text{Margin on sales}} \times \frac{100}{1} = \frac{100}{80} \times \frac{100}{1} = \text{€125}$$

$$\text{Mark-up on cost} = \frac{\text{Margin on sales}}{100 - \text{Margin on sales}} \times \frac{100}{1} = \frac{20}{80} \times \frac{100}{1} = 25\%$$

$$\text{Margin on sales} = \frac{\text{Mark-up on cost}}{100 + \text{Mark-up on cost}} \times \frac{100}{1} = \frac{25}{100 + 25} \times \frac{100}{1} = 20\%$$

A mark-up is applied to the cost excluding VAT. The appropriate VAT is then applied to get the actual selling price. It is very common in retail sales to set the selling price just below the round figure planned, for example €7.99, €8.99.

Cost is the actual or expected expenditure to be incurred in producing a product or providing a service. Costing is the process of recording expenditure, classifying it and allocating it to cost centres in order to determine the cost of producing a product or service. Costs are classified as direct and indirect as well as variable and fixed. A direct cost is one which can be allocated directly to a job or cost centre; an indirect cost cannot be allocated directly, for example the cost of an overhead such as the finance office. A variable cost is one which tends to vary directly with output, while a fixed cost tends to be unaffected by changes in output up to a certain point. Increases in output and sales beyond a certain point result in extra fixed costs. A cost can also be semi-fixed, that is, one containing both fixed and variable elements, for example telephone charges. Table 5.4 is an example of cost-plus pricing (full cost pricing or absorption cost pricing).

Table 5.4: Example of cost-plus pricing

Notes			Job number 100
		€	€
i)	Direct materials		50.00
ii)	Direct labour		25.00
	Prime/variable/cost		75.00
iii)	Production overheads	15.00	
iv)	Selling and administration overheads	10.00	
			25.00
	Total cost		100.00

Table 5.4: Example of cost-plus pricing (continued

v)	Add mark-up (say, plus 25%)	25.00
		125.00
vi)	VAT (say, 21%)	26.25
	Selling price	151.25

Notes:

i)   Material used on a particular order is requisitioned from the stores department in a business and the actual cost is charged to the appropriate job number (a number used to collect the costs incurred on a particular job) using the adopted system of material pricing, for example first-in first-out price, standard price or other method deemed appropriate.

ii) Labour cost is determined by multiplying the number of productive hours spent by each operative on a specific job by the appropriate labour rate. The total annual labour cost for each operative is calculated (gross pay plus employer's PRSI) and divided by the number of hours a person is expected to spend on productive work during the year (total annual hours less annual leave, public holidays, and 'lost time' such as waiting time, starting-up time). The actual productive hours spent on each job can be controlled by job cards or other appropriate method showing the starting and finishing time on each job.

iii) Production overheads are budgeted for the year and a fair share is charged to each job undertaken during the year using whichever of the following methods is most appropriate: a rate per labour hour, a percentage of direct labour, a rate per unit of output, a rate per machine hour or a percentage of prime cost.

iv) The objective of overhead apportionment is to spread the total cost fairly over all jobs carried out during the year. Selling and administrative overheads are charged in accordance with the procedure designed to recover the total over all work carried out during the year.

v)   A mark-up is added to the total cost of each job with regard to the pricing objectives of the business, the elasticity of demand, market conditions and the terms of trade for intermediaries as appropriate.

vi) The appropriate VAT rate is added to the final cost to arrive at the selling price to be charged to customers.

vii) Calculating the cost of a product is not easy or exact; at best it is only approximate. This type of total-cost absorption is suitable only for jobs done specially to customers' requirements, but not for a process-type operation.

viii) Sometimes the appropriate wholesale and retail margins have to be included in the price. In the book business, publishers determine the final retail prices and generally allow a 50 per cent discount on cover prices to wholesalers (some require more), who in turn distribute the books to retailers and allow them a 33⅓ per cent discount. In a book costing the purchaser €36, €12 goes to the retailer, €6 to the wholesaler and the balance, €18, to the publisher. The practices and terms used in any business activity have to be considered when determining selling prices.

Limitations

The chief limitation of cost-plus pricing is that it ignores demand. The selling price of most products or services influences demand. Also, different methods are used to apportion fixed overheads, each of which gives a different figure for the same job, resulting in different total costs and selling prices. This method can also promote inefficiency. Another limitation of cost-plus pricing is that it is based on an estimated activity level. If the total sales do not reach the anticipated level, a loss can result even though each job undertaken earned a profit; the reason for this is that the activity level achieved is insufficient to recoup the total fixed overheads. Profit is not earned until all the fixed overheads are recovered in any year from sales. In recent years, activity-based costing (ABC) has become common, where overheads are charged to products in relation to their use of various activities (Clarke, 2002).

Target pricing
Under this method, price is calculated by adding a desired rate of return to total cost per unit (Table 5.5). The formula used in target pricing is as follows:

$$\text{Desired mark-up} = \frac{\text{Desired return on capital employed}}{\text{Total estimated cost of production}} \times \frac{100}{1}$$

Table 5.5: Example of target pricing

Assume Moy Co. Ltd plans to manufacture 20,000 units of product X in the following year at a budgeted total cost of €600,000, excluding VAT. You are told the following:

Capital employed:	€1 million
Expected rate of return on capital employed:	20%

The selling price can be calculated as follows:

$$\text{Mark-up} = \frac{20\% \text{ of } €1 \text{ million}}{\text{Total estimated cost of production}} = \frac{€200,000}{€600,000} \times \frac{100}{1} = 33\frac{1}{3}\%$$

		€
Cost of production per unit (€600,000 ÷ 20,000)	=	30
Add target mark-up, 33⅓%	=	10
Selling price per unit (excluding VAT)	=	40

Marginal pricing
Marginal or variable-cost, pricing is a procedure for setting prices based on a knowledge of marginal cost, the extra expenditure incurred by producing one extra unit and the sensitivity of customers to various prices. The difference between the sales price and the marginal cost is known as the 'contribution'. The contribution per unit multiplied by the sales volume in units, less fixed costs, gives the overall profit or loss. Variable and fixed costs are shown separately in a marginal cost statement because they show different

behavioural patterns in relation to changes in output. Fixed costs remain the same despite changes in output, whereas variable costs vary directly with output. The contribution goes initially to recover fixed costs and, when these are recovered, the total contribution is profit. Information about the contribution can be very useful in pricing as well as when making many management decisions such as the optimum sales mix, make or buy decisions, contribution of each product or department or contribution per limiting factor (if one is in scarce supply).

Any pricing decision has to consider the anticipated sales demand at alternative price levels, especially in a price-sensitive market. In full-cost pricing (absorption costing), one must anticipate the number of units to be sold, whereas in practice the selling price in many cases determines the demand. A marginal costing statement showing unit selling price, marginal cost, contribution per unit, expected sales volume, total contributions (contribution per unit x sales volume) less total fixed costs gives the total profit/loss, and is a very useful technique to use in pricing (see example (a) in Table 5.6). Similar statements can be used to show the profit or loss arising from expected sales at different price levels. It is very easy to determine from a comparison of such statements which selling price maximises profits.

Break-even analysis
Marginal cost statements provide useful information for break-even, profit volume, margin of safety and 'what if' analysis (Clarke, 2002). Break-even analysis is a technique for calculating the break-even point of a business (the volume or sales revenue at which neither a profit nor a loss is made) as well as providing valuable information for pricing and planning. Profit/volume (P/V) ratio is a rather confusing title for what is really the contribution-to-sales ratio. The margin of safety is the anticipated level of activity above the break-even point. In other words, it is a measure of the extent to which existing or anticipated activity can fall before a profitable operation becomes loss-making. Table 5.6 shows how useful these concepts are in decision-making.

Marginal cost statements are based on a number of assumptions:
- That the behaviour of costs and revenue is linear over the range of activity employed
- That all costs can be classified as either fixed or variable
- That the fixed costs remain the same over the volume range adopted and that the marginal cost changes in line with volume
- That the selling price and cost elements remain the same
- That there will be no change in productivity
- That the analysis deals only with one product or that any mix will remain the same
- That volume is the only factor influencing costs (Harper, 1995; Lucey, 2009).

Table 5.6: Use of marginal costing

	Per unit	Total
	€	€
Sales (10,000 units)	60	600,000
Marginal/variable cost	30	300,000
Total fixed cost		120,000

You are required to calculate the following using marginal costing:

a) Budgeted profit / loss using a marginal cost approach
b) Break-even point in units
c) Break-even position in value terms
d) Margin of safety in units
e) Margin of safety in value terms
f) Number of units to be sold in order to make a profit of €30,000
g) Sales revenue required to make a profit of €30,000

a) Profit/loss – unit data:

	€
Selling price per unit	60
Less marginal cost per unit	(30)
Contribution per unit	30
Total contributions (10,000 x €30)	300,000
Less total fixed costs	(120,000)
Total budgeted profit	180,000

Note: If sales are expected to change in response to prices, a marginal cost statement can be prepared as above for each option to determine which price is the most advantageous.

	Formula	Calculation
b) Break-even point in units	$\dfrac{\text{Total fixed costs}}{\text{Contribution per unit}}$ =	$\dfrac{€120,000}{€30}$ = 4,000 units
c) Break-even position in value terms	$\dfrac{\text{Fixed costs}}{\text{Contribution/sales ratio}}$ =	$\dfrac{€120,000}{.50}$ = €240,000
d) Margin of safety in units	$\dfrac{\text{Total profit}}{\text{Contribution per unit}}$ =	$\dfrac{€180,000}{€30}$ = 6,000 units
e) Margin of safety in value terms	$\dfrac{\text{Total profit}}{\text{Contribution/sales ratio}}$ =	$\dfrac{€180,000}{.50}$ = €360,000

Table 5.6: Use of marginal costing (continued)

f) Number of units to be sold in order to make a net profit of €30,000	$\dfrac{\text{Fixed costs + Desired net profit}}{\text{Contribution per unit}}$	=	$\dfrac{€120,00 + €30,000}{€30}$ = 5,000 units
g) Sales revenue required to make a profit of €30,000	$\dfrac{\text{Fixed costs + Desired net profit}}{\text{Contribution per unit}}$	=	$\dfrac{€120,00 + €30,000}{.50}$ = €300,000

5.5 Accounting records

The following books are usually kept by a business:

- General ledger, a book with the double-entry records of all transactions
- Receipts book, a book recording all cash, cheques and electronic receipts, with appropriate analysis columns and details of supporting records like invoices, till rolls and bank lodgements
- Payments book, a book for recording all payments made, with appropriate analysis columns for each item of expenditure and cheque number or electronic payment number
- Petty cash book, with vouchers for small payments
- Sales book, containing details of goods sold on credit
- Debtors' ledger, ongoing record of debts owed to the business
- Purchases book, containing details of goods bought on credit
- Creditors' ledger, ongoing record of amounts owed by the business
- Returns book, containing particulars of goods returned by or to the business
- VAT record, with records of relevant returns
- Payroll records, including supporting documents for gross pay, deductions, payments and relevant tax returns
- Inventories/stocks with records of receipts and transfer to work in progress or sales
- Fixed asset register, record of fixed assets with details of additions, disposals and depreciation
- Journal, containing opening and closing entries and any transactions not recorded in another book
- Capital account, the owner's account
- Bank statements, with reconciliation on a regular basis, at least every month, where the balance in the general ledger is reconciled with the bank statement as at a specific date.

Ledger accounts can be divided into two classes: personal and impersonal. A personal account is one in the name of a person or organisation, for example debtors and creditors. Impersonal accounts can be classified as real or nominal. A real account is one relating to property such as buildings, machinery and stock, while a nominal account is one relating to expenses, income and capital. There should be a supporting document for every transaction. Most payments, including salaries, are now made electronically. The payer requires bank account numbers and branch sort code numbers for all electronic payments. It is essential that a proper computerised accounting system is put in place from the start of any business (with professional help if necessary). It is also important to have a system of good internal control in operation to safeguard assets, to prevent fraud or errors and to ensure accuracy.

If the business has credit sales it is important to have a system in place to record all orders received and to track them until the goods are supplied, invoices issued and payment received. When goods are required, a purchase order has to be issued showing details of the organisation, the date, description of the goods, quantity required and the VAT number. All invoices relating to sales and purchase orders are numbered sequentially to facilitate control. Accounting records are kept on the double-entry principle of bookkeeping whereby every transaction is recorded by a debit and a credit entry in the ledger accounts (Wood and Robinson, 1999). A business has to be able to prepare financial statements from its accounting records when required. This is done at least once in every financial year, that is, the 12-month period for which the business decides to prepare final accounts.

Section 202 of the Companies Act 1990 requires every company to keep proper books of account that correctly record and explain the transactions of the company and will at any time enable the financial position of the company to be determined with reasonable accuracy and ensure that any balance sheet, profit and loss account or income and expenditure account complies with the requirements of the Companies Acts.

They must contain the following information:

- Entries relating to all money received and expended and the matters in respect of which these transactions take place
- A record of the company's assets and liabilities
- If the business involves sales of goods, a record has to be kept of all purchases and sales (except those sold for cash in a retail trade), specifying the goods, sellers and buyers and a record of all invoices relating to these transactions
- A statement of stock held at the end of each financial year, with supporting documentation
- If the business involves the provision of services, a record of the services provided and supporting invoices must be maintained (s 202.3).

Failure to keep proper records is a criminal offence and the records must be retained for six years.

5.6 Financial statements and their interpretation

The main financial statements, prepared from the books and records in a business, are the following:

a)   Trading account
b)   Profit and loss account (income statement)
c)   Balance sheet
d)   Cash flow statement.

a)   Trading account

A trading account of an organisation shows the gross profit earned during a specific period, that is, after deducting the cost of sales from the sales figure. If a business is engaged in manufacturing there is also a statement known as the manufacturing account, showing the cost of goods produced during a specific period, which is transferred to the trading account.

b)   Profit and loss account

A profit and loss account shows the net profit or loss in a business for a specific period, that is, the result after charging all expenses relating to the period against the gross profit transferred from the trading account. Accounts are prepared using what is called the 'accruals concept' of accounting. This means that revenue and costs are recognised as they are earned or incurred (not as money is received or paid), matched with one another as far as their relationship can be established and included in the accounts of the period to which they relate. Consequently it is rather different from a system of cash accounting which recognises only cash inflows and outflows. Accounts are prepared in accordance with the applicable accounting standards.

c)   Balance sheet

A balance sheet is a statement of an organisation's assets, liabilities and equity as at a certain date. It shows five key figures:

*   Fixed assets
*   Current assets
*   Current liabilities
*   Long-term liabilities
*   Net worth or owners' equity (see layout of a trading account, profit and loss account and balance sheet in Table 5.7).

d)   Cash flow statement

A cash flow statement is prepared for most businesses. It shows how cash is generated and spent during a specific period as well as reconciling the opening and closing cash balances. It is prepared in accordance with the recommendations laid down in the Financial

Reporting Standard (FRS) 1, which was introduced in 1991. Cash inflows and outflows are classified under the following standard headings:

- Operating activities
- Returns on investment and servicing of finance
- Taxation
- Capital expenditure and financial investment
- Acquisitions and disposals
- Equity dividends paid
- Management of liquid resources
- Financing.

Individual categories of inflows and outflows are to be disclosed separately, either in the statement or in notes. FRS 1 obliges all organisations required to give a true and fair view of their financial affairs to produce a cash flow statement as part of their annual accounts, with the exception of enterprises classified as 'small companies' under the Companies (Amendment) Act 1986 (see below).

Ratio analysis

Data is extracted from financial information and converted to statistics, known as ratios. Accounts are mainly interpreted by analysing various ratios under the following key performances indicators:

- Profitability
- Liquidity
- Leverage
- Activity.

Using the information given in Table 5.7, the various ratios are calculated, followed by some general comments on their meaning (Clarke, 2002; Kennedy *et al.*, 1995).

Table 5.7: ABC Co. Ltd trading/profit and loss account and balance sheet for the year ended 31 December year x

	€	€
Sales (all credit sales)	600,000	
Cost of goods sold	360,000	
Gross profit		240,000
Selling and distribution costs	160,000	
Interest paid	5,000	
Administration costs	47,000	
		(212,000)
Profit before taxation		28,000
Corporation tax		4,000
Net profit after taxation		24,000

Table 5.7 (continued)

Balance sheet as at 31 December year X

	€	€	€
Fixed assets (book value)			160,000
Current assets			
Inventory	90,000		
Debtors	120,000		
Cash	10,000	220,000	
Current liabilities			
Trade creditors	100,000		
Corporation tax	4,000		
Bank overdraft	26,000		
		(130,000)	
Net current assets			90,000
Net assets			250,000
Financed by:			
Ordinary share capital issued			120,000
Profit carried forward		66,000	
Add profit for this year		24,000	
			90,000
Bank term loan			40,000
			250,000

Note: Capital employed = net assets, or shareholders' funds plus long-term liability

Profitability ratios

Ratio	Formula		Calculation (€)		Ratio
Gross profit on sales	$\dfrac{\text{Gross profit}}{\text{Sales}}$	$\times \dfrac{100}{1}$	$\dfrac{240,000}{600,000}$	$\times \dfrac{100}{1}$	40%
Net profit on sales	$\dfrac{\text{Net profit after interest and tax}}{\text{Sales}}$	$\times \dfrac{100}{1}$	$\dfrac{24,000}{600,000}$	$\times \dfrac{100}{1}$	4%
General expenses/ sales	$\dfrac{\text{General expenses excluding interest}}{\text{Sales}}$	$\times \dfrac{100}{1}$	$\dfrac{207,000}{600,000}$	$\times \dfrac{100}{1}$	34.5%
Return on capital employed (ROCE)	$\dfrac{\text{Net profit after taxation}}{\text{Capital employed}}$	$\times \dfrac{100}{1}$	$\dfrac{24,000}{250,000}$	$\times \dfrac{100}{1}$	9.6%

OR

	$\dfrac{\text{Profit before interest and tax}}{\text{Capital employed}}$	$\times \dfrac{100}{1}$	$\dfrac{33,000}{250,000}$	$\times \dfrac{100}{1}$	**13.20%**
Return on net worth	$\dfrac{\text{Net profit after interest and tax}}{\text{Net worth (shareholders' funds)}}$	$\times \dfrac{100}{1}$	$\dfrac{24,000}{210,000}$	$\times \dfrac{100}{1}$	**11.42%**

Liquidity ratios

Current asset ratio	$\dfrac{\text{Current assets}}{\text{Current liabilities}}$		$\dfrac{220,000}{130,000}$	$\times \dfrac{100}{1}$	**1.69 : 1**
Acid test or quick ratio	$\dfrac{\text{Current assets less inventory}}{\text{Current liabilities}}$		$\dfrac{130,000}{130,000}$	$\times \dfrac{100}{1}$	**1 : 1**

Leverage ratios

Debt ratio (gearing ratio)	$\dfrac{\text{Total liabilities}}{\text{Total assets}}$	$\times \dfrac{100}{1}$	$\dfrac{170,000}{380,000}$	$\times \dfrac{100}{1}$	**44.73%**
Debt/equity ratio (gearing ratio)	$\dfrac{\text{Long-term debt}}{\text{Issued share capital and revenue (i.e. shareholders' funds)}}$	$\times \dfrac{100}{1}$	$\dfrac{40,000}{210,000}$	$\times \dfrac{100}{1}$	**19%**
Times interest covered	$\dfrac{\text{Profit before interest}}{\text{Interest charges}}$		$\dfrac{33,000}{5,000}$		**6.6%**

Activity ratios

Stock turnover	$\dfrac{\text{Stock} \times 365}{\text{Cost of goods sold}}$		$\dfrac{90,000 \times 365}{360,000}$	**91 days**
Average period of credit allowed	$\dfrac{\text{Debtors} \times 365}{\text{Credit sales}}$		$\dfrac{120,000 \times 365}{600,000}$	**73 days**
Average period of credit received	$\dfrac{\text{Trade creditors} \times 365}{\text{Cost of goods sold}}$		$\dfrac{100,000 \times 365}{360,000}$	**101 days**
Turnover on net assets	$\dfrac{\text{Sales}}{\text{Net assets}}$		$\dfrac{600,000}{250,000}$	**2.4%**

Profitability ratios

These ratios focus on profitability in relation to sales and investment. Every business-person is interested in gross profit – the higher, the better. The gross profit can be compared with the planned mark-up (profit related to cost) and any difference could indicate errors or fraud. A gross margin of 40 per cent is good, but the ratio depends on the business in question, with some in excess of that figure and many lower. The net profit-to-sales ratio tells us how much of the sales figure remains with the owners after paying all expenses. It can be calculated before interest (an allowable expense for tax purposes) and taxation or after deducting both.

The general expenses-to-sales ratio can be calculated in aggregate, as shown above and for each item. A useful technique to use in an analysis of expenses is the preparation of a '100 per cent statement', where each expense item is expressed as a percentage of the sales figure (100 per cent). Trends can then be isolated and queried.

Return on capital employed (ROCE) can be calculated in a number of different ways: net profit before interest and taxation, or after both, in relation to net assets. The return after interest and taxation can be compared with the net cost of capital. Return on net worth (shareholders' funds) is important for the owners. They expect a good return on their investment to compensate them for the risk undertaken and any inflation during the period. This return is compared with alternatives which could be received; business-people expect to earn far higher returns from their enterprises than could be earned risk-free from safe investments. Return on net worth can be increased by the use of debt finance (loans). Interest paid on a loan is an allowable expense for tax purposes; dividends, the apportionment of profits to shareholders, are not allowable. If a business earns more than the net cost of financing the debt, the surplus after taxation belongs to the owners.

Liquidity ratios

Liquidity ratios measure the ability of a business to meet its short-term financial obligations as they fall due. The current asset ratio indicates the extent to which current assets are available to meet immediate liabilities. This is a crude measure because it does not consider the quality or liquidity of the current assets. A current asset ratio of 2 : 1 is considered to be satisfactory, but the norm can vary depending on the type of business and the effectiveness of working capital management. The acid test ratio of liquidity ignores stock because it is assumed that it will take time to convert that asset into cash. A ratio of 1 : 1 is generally regarded as satisfactory, but many successful businesses operate with a lower one as a result of good working capital management.

Leverage ratios

Leverage or debt ratios measure the relationship between debt and total assets and debt and equity as well as the number of times interest charges are covered by profit before taxation. If the amount of debt exceeds the figure for equity, the business is said to be 'high geared'; if less, it is 'low geared'. Creditors like to see a low debt ratio because equity represents a cushion against possible loss. Low-geared businesses can attract more debt if required for investment. As the proportion of debt in an organisation increases, so does risk and lenders will not go beyond a certain proportion, which varies depending on the nature of the business.

Activity ratios

Activity ratios measure the efficiency of management in using the resources of a business. They include stock turnover, the average period of credit allowed on sales, the average period of credit received on purchases and the turnover on net assets. These ratios can be compared with the norm for the industry and trends over time.

Limitations of ratio analysis

Ratios give concise yardsticks to be used for comparison with planned performance (budgets), past results, similar businesses and the norms of a particular industry. Ratios are used only as guides to interpretation. They are based on historical accounts, often a few months old, and a balance sheet as at a particular date only. Fixed assets in a balance sheet may be valued at cost and not current market price, or if revalued, that figure may now be out of date. All these factors have be considered when interpreting ratios.

Value added statement

Some organisations publish a value added statement, often in the form of a pie chart. It shows in a concise manner the wealth created by an organisation (usually calculated as the difference between sales and purchased goods and services) and the way in which it is shared between employees, Government and providers of capital as well as the business itself in the form of retained profit.

5.7 Published accounts

There are special obligations on companies with regard to published accounts. The directors of a company are legally required to prepare, or have prepared, a statutory set of accounts which give a 'true and fair' view of the state of its affairs and lay those accounts before the members at an annual general meeting (s 48 CA 1963). The accounts must comply with company law and the applicable financial reporting standards. Every balance sheet and profit and loss account of a company must be signed by two directors of the company. The following obligations are considered below:

a)   Auditors' report
b)   Directors' report
c)   Annual return

d)   Published accounts
e)   Additional requirements.

a)   Auditors' report

A company is legally obliged to have its financial statements audited at least once a year unless exempted. A private company can be exempted from the requirement to have an annual audit provided it complies with certain conditions (Part III Companies (Amendment) Act, No. 2, 1999 as amended by s S53 Companies (Auditing and Accounting) Act 2003). The current conditions for audit exemption, all of which must be satisfied, are available on the Companies Registration Office website. This concession does not exempt a private company from its obligation to prepare a full set of accounts and lay them before the annual general meeting (AGM).

An audit is an independent review of the financial affairs and statements of a business carried out by a qualified auditor, usually a professional firm. The first auditors of a company are appointed by the directors at any time before the first AGM, and the person so appointed holds office until the conclusion of that meeting. Auditors are subsequently appointed at each AGM (s 60 CA 1963). Auditors have the right of access at all reasonable times to the books and records of a company and are entitled to request any information and explanations deemed necessary for the performance of their duties from the officers. If the auditors form an opinion that the company has failed to keep proper books of account, they are obliged to notify the company. If the required action is not taken within seven days, the auditors are obliged to notify the Registrar of Companies, who will inform the Director of Corporate Enforcement. The Company Law Enforcement Act 2001 established the Office of the Director of Corporate Enforcement (ODCE), which has responsibility for ensuring compliance with all company legislation. The auditors are required to provide any information or documents requested by the Director. The auditors are also obliged to notify the Director of Corporate Enforcement where they come across information which leads them to believe that any officer or agent of the company has committed an indictable offence under the Companies Acts. Auditors are required by law to report to the members of the company on the accounts and have the right to attend general meetings. The remuneration of the auditors is fixed by the company at the AGM or in the manner it may determine. The auditors' report and directors' report (see below) must be annexed to every profit and loss account and balance sheet placed before the AGM of a company.

An auditors' report is required to state the following:
•   Whether, in their opinion, proper books of accounts have been kept
•   Whether they have obtained all the information and explanations which were necessary for the purpose of the audit

- Whether the company's balance sheet and profit and loss account are in agreement with the books of account
- Whether, in their opinion, the company's balance sheet and profit and loss account have been properly prepared and give a true and fair view of the state of its affairs at the end of the financial year and for the year, respectively (Information Book, 5, Auditors, ODCE).

The auditors are also required to state whether, in their opinion, there existed at the balance sheet date a financial situation which, under s 40(1) of the Companies (Amendment) Act 1983, would require the convening of an extraordinary general meeting of the company. This arises where the net assets (total assets less total liabilities) of a company fall to 50 per cent or less of its called-up share capital.

b) Directors' report

This is a report by the directors on the company's performance and activities for the year under review. It must be signed by two directors and contain the following (s 158 CA 1963):
- The steps taken to ensure that proper books and records are kept and their location
- The recommended dividends, if any
- The amounts to be carried to reserves, if any
- Details of any change during the year in the nature of the business of the company or of its subsidiaries, or of any company in which it has an interest
- A list of subsidiary companies or companies in which it owns more than 20 per cent of the nominal value of voting shares stating where each is incorporated, and the nature of the business carried on
- A fair review of the development of the business and of its subsidiaries during the year
- Particulars of any important events affecting the company or any of its subsidiaries, if any, which have occurred since the end of the year
- An indication of likely future developments in the business of the company and of its subsidiaries, if any
- An indication of the activities, if any, in the field of research and development
- Information about the acquisition by the company of its own shares
- Particulars of all donations to an individual or to a political party exceeding €5,078.95 in value relating to the year for political purposes (s 26 Electoral Act 1997 as amended in 1998 and 2001).

Under the Safety, Health and Welfare at Work legislation, the directors' report is required to comment on the extent to which policies set out in the company's safety statement were fulfilled during the year. The auditors are required to consider the directors' report and state if it is consistent with the accounts prepared by the company for that year.

c) Annual return

Every company is required to submit an annual return to the Companies Registration Office in each calendar year (form B1), covering the period up to a date not later than the company's annual return date (ARD), a concept introduced by the Company Law Enforcement Act 2001. Every company incorporated prior to 1 March 2002 was assigned an ARD. The first annual return of a company incorporated after 17 May 2004 is required to be made up to the date that is six months after the date of incorporation and filed within 28 days of that ARD. Accounts are not required to be filed with the first annual return. Thereafter, the annual return date is the anniversary of the first return, but it may establish a new ARD by either using the extension procedures or else by making a subsequent return up to an earlier date (see the Companies Registration Office website).

The annual return, signed by the secretary and a director, is to be delivered to the Registrar of Companies within 28 days of the ARD. The accounts annexed to an annual return cannot be made up to a date more than nine months before the ARD. The penalties for failure to file an annual return, or late filing, include fines, prosecution and striking from the register.

The following information must be provided in the annual return:

- Company name
- Registered office address
- Company registered number
- Date that the return is made up to
- Financial year covered by the return
- Company secretary's name and address
- Directors' names, dates of birth, addresses and occupations
- Details of directors' other directorships
- A private company is obliged to send a certificate certifying that since the last return it has not issued any invitation to the public to subscribe for any shares or debentures and that it otherwise complies with the requirements of a private company
- Details of any political donations made by the company
- Particulars of mortgages and charges required to be registered
- Authorised share capital*
- Issued share capital
- An analysis of issued share capital between shares paid for in cash and shares paid for otherwise than in cash*
- List of members and the number of shares held by each
- List of persons who have ceased to be members since the last return*
- Details of shares transferred since the last return.*

* Note: These are required only in the case of companies with a share capital. (Information Book 1, Companies, ODCE.)

The following are required to be annexed to the annual return:
- Profit and loss account (see published accounts)
- Balance sheet (see published accounts)
- Notes to the financial statements (see published accounts)
- Directors' report (see published accounts)
- Auditors' report (except where the company avails of the audit exemption)
- Certification by the secretary and a director that the financial statements and the auditors' report submitted are a true copy of those presented to the members of the company.

d) Published accounts

A limited company is required to file an annual return together with a certified copy of the profit and loss account, balance sheet, auditors' report and directors' report as required by the Companies (Amendment) Act 1986 with the Registrar of Companies within 28 days of the annual return date. Small and medium-sized private companies may be exempt from filing some of these documents in respect of any financial year if in that year and the one immediately preceding it the company satisfies two of the three conditions shown in Table 5.8.

Table 5.8: Classification of small and medium-sized private companies for publication of accounts

Conditions	Small companies	Medium-sized companies
	€	€
Balance sheet total not exceeding	1.905 million	7.618 million
Turnover not exceeding	3.809 million	15.237 million
Number of employees not exceeding	50	250

A company qualifying as a small company is not obliged to file a profit and loss account or a directors' report with the annual returns. It is required to file a certified copy of an abridged balance sheet, with a statement signed by two directors that they have relied on the specific exemptions, a certified copy of the auditors' report together with a report by the auditors confirming that the directors are entitled to claim the small company exemption. A medium-sized private limited company is obliged to file, with its annual return, a certified copy of the profit and loss account, balance sheet and notes, all of which may be in the prescribed abridged form, directors' report, auditors' report, a statement by directors that their company is entitled to medium-sized exemptions and a special report from the auditors confirming this. All other private and public limited companies must file, with the annual return, a full profit and loss account, balance sheet and notes, together with the directors' report and auditors' report. Specified formats for the profit and loss account and balance sheet which can be used are outlined in the Companies (Amendment) Act 1986. For companies classified as small and medium-sized, two sets of accounts are prepared, one for members and the second complying with minimum publication requirements for filing with the Registrar of Companies. The annual schedule for company accounts and filing is shown in Table 5.9.

Table 5.9: Annual schedule for company accounts and filing of annual return

Item	Requirement	Timing
1.	Accounts to be prepared and audited annually up to company's year end.	As soon as possible after the company's year end.
2.	Board meeting to be convened to approve audited accounts for signature by two directors, date to be fixed and secretary to be authorised to convene the AGM.	As soon as the accounts are prepared, 2–4 months after year end.
3.	Accounts to be returned to auditor for signature.	As soon as possible after board meeting.
4.	AGM to be convened by notifying members and auditor and enclosing a copy of the accounts, auditors' report and directors' report.	Members are entitled to 21 clear days' notice of the date fixed for the AGM.
5.	Accounts to be presented to members for adoption (i.e. approval).	At AGM.
6.	Annual return to be completed.	By annual return date.
7.	Annual return, with all necessary documents including accounts in the prescribed format, and fee to be filed in the Companies Registration Office.	Within 28 days of the annual return date.

Notes:
1. The first accounts must be presented at an AGM within 18 months of incorporation.
2. Thereafter, an AGM must be held in each calendar year within nine months of the company's year end. The interval between AGMs must not exceed 15 months.

e) Additional requirements

When enacted, section 45 of the Companies (Auditing and Accounting) Act 2003 will require every public company (PLC) and every large private company to establish an audit committee, unless they have ministerial exemption or explain in the directors' report why it was not done. These companies will also be required to prepare two statements every year: a directors' compliance statement and the annual compliance statement. The former sets out the company's policies regarding compliance with all legal requirements, including tax obligations, as well as how these are implemented and reviewed. The annual compliance statement must contain an acknowledgement that the directors are responsible for ensuring compliance with all relevant obligations, specify the procedures in place to ensure compliance, and if not to give reasons. The statement has to confirm that the directors have reviewed the effectiveness of the procedures. The auditors of companies covered by this obligation must assess the fairness and reasonableness of the directors' compliance statements and give their opinion on them.

The 2003 Act also provides that the annual accounts of every company, regardless of size, must comply with the relevant financial reporting standards. Each company has to clearly state the accounting policies that it adopted in the preparation of its annual accounts. The accounts must state the total fees paid to the auditors' firm for all work, including non-audit work. If fees for non-audit work are higher than the audit figure, the directors are required to state in the annual report that the non-audit work has not interfered with the auditors' independence.

5.8 Summary

A new entrepreneur has to estimate the finance required for the purchase of fixed assets, start-up costs and working capital. Most small businesses are started with limited financial resources, provided by the entrepreneurs, borrowings and, if eligible, grants. Many other sources are available to companies. Sources of finance are classified as short term, medium term and long term.

While the financial objective of a business is to earn profits as soon as possible, it can take some time, which varies from business to business, to establish a loyal customer base and a commercially profitable business. It is important to have sufficient cash to survive the early development of a business and for cash inflow to exceed revenue expenditure thereafter. A business has to plan for its capital expenditure and the required working capital. Good cash management is essential in every business.

Pricing is one of the most important decisions to be made by the management of any business. The general objectives of any pricing policy are recovery of full costs, attainment of a satisfactory profit and value for customers. Prices are determined by an assessment and reconciliation of two different approaches: market-based and cost-based techniques.

Every person or organisation carrying on a trade, business or profession is legally obliged to keep proper books and records. These have to provide the information required to prepare the financial statements, which has to be done at least once in every financial year. The main financial statements are the trading account, profit and loss account, balance sheet and cash flow statement. These statements are interpreted mainly by analysing various ratios.

A company is obliged to prepare annual accounts and to have them audited (unless it is exempt from the audit requirement) and to lay them before members in an AGM. It is also obliged to file an annual return with the Registrar of Companies.

Questions

1. Explain the following sources of business finance.
    a) Business Expansion Scheme
    b) Seed Capital Scheme
    c) Term loan
    d) Factoring.
2. Explain the distinction between each of the following.
    a) Liquidity and solvency
    b) Capital and revenue expenditure
    c) Preference shares and ordinary shares
    d) Seed capital and venture capital
3. Discuss the procedures involved in the preparation of a cash flow budget.
4. Discuss the main factors involved in pricing a product or service.
5. Describe the obligations on a company in relation to published accounts, the AGM and an annual return.

Chapter 6

Taxation

Nothing great was ever achieved without enthusiasm.

RALPH WALDO EMERSON

Learning objectives

- To understand the chief taxation obligations for small businesses
- To comprehend PAYE and PRSI
- To explore the taxation system for self-employed people
- To understand the principles of Value Added Tax (VAT)
- To appreciate corporation tax, commercial rates, capital taxes and customs and excise
- To explore various pension options and the taxation implications.

This chapter is structured as follows:

6.1   Introduction and obligation to keep proper records
6.2   PAYE, PRSI, Universal Social Charge
6.3   Income tax for the self-employed
6.4   Value Added Tax
6.5   Corporation tax
6.6   Commercial rates
6.7   Capital taxes
6.8   Customs and excise duties
6.9   Tax clearance
6.10 Revenue audit
6.11 Patent royalties
6.12 Pensions
6.13 Summary

6.1 Introduction and obligation to keep proper records

Every person or organisation carrying on a trade, business or profession is obliged to keep proper accounting books and records, which have to be retained for a period of six years. Apart from any other requirements, every business has to comply with its taxation obligations. The records must include details of all purchases and sales of goods and services, business income and expenditure, any finance introduced to the business and/or withdrawn for private use, debtors, creditors, stocks, business assets and the matters to which they relate. All supporting documentation such as invoices issued and received, income receipts, payment records, credit or debit notes and bank statements must be kept. Failure to keep proper books and records is a Revenue offence. The following accounts have to be prepared from the accounting books and records for taxation purposes:

- A trading account showing all sales of goods or services for the period, the cost of those goods or services and the gross profit or loss
- A profit and loss account showing the gross profit, all expenses relating to the period and the net profit or loss
- A capital account for the owner(s), where relevant, showing the opening capital, net profit or loss for the period, any cash introduced, drawings, if any, and the closing balance
- A balance sheet showing the business assets and liabilities as at a certain date (the last day of the period covered by the accounts).

A person or organisation is obliged to notify the tax office when starting a business. This is done by completing registration form TR1, which covers income tax, employer's PAYE and PRSI and VAT for sole traders, partnerships, unincorporated bodies and principal contractors; form TR2 is used for companies. These forms are available on the Revenue's website. Many taxes can be paid by direct debit, with an agreed monthly figure (generally one-twelfth of estimated liability for the year) charged to the business bank account in respect of each tax, and one annual return completed for each at the end of the year. Taxes can also be paid by single direct authority for one-off payments through the Revenue Online Service (ROS), by Laser or by postal payments using the appropriate forms. The tax year is from 1 January to 31 December. The law relating to income tax, capital gains tax and corporation tax is contained in the Taxes Consolidation Act 1997 and subsequent Finance Acts. This chapter explains the various taxes applicable to businesses.

6.2 PAYE, PRSI, Universal Social Charge

a) PAYE

Pay As You Earn (PAYE) is a method of tax payment under which an employer is obliged to deduct the appropriate tax, Pay Related Social Insurance (PRSI) and the Universal Social Charge each time a payment of wages or salary is made to an employee so as to spread liability throughout the tax year. A full tax credit system was introduced from 6 April 2001, thus simplifying the procedure and giving the same credits to higher and standard rate taxpayers. Hitherto taxpayers on the higher rate gained more from any allowance.

All employers are obliged to register for PAYE and PRSI where they pay in excess of

€8 per week (€36 per month) to an employee working full time or €2 per week (€9 per month) where the person has other employment. Effectively this means that any person or organisation with an employee has to register as an employer for tax purposes. The registration system is simple: completion of form TR1 for an individual or partnership, and TR2 for a company. Failure to register will result in the employer being liable for all the tax and PRSI which should have been deducted as well as interest charges.

An employer receives a Tax Credit Certificate or a tax deduction card, or tape or disk, as appropriate, showing the total tax credits for each employee, the standard rate cut-off point (SRCOP) and the tax rates applicable. The standard rate cut-off point is 'the amount of the personal standard rate band allocated to the employee' (Revenue Commissioners, 2005). Any pay in excess of the SRCOP is taxed at the higher tax rate.

Gross pay includes the normal payment for the week or month as well as overtime, bonuses and, from January 2004, the taxable value of most benefits in kind given to employees. (For details of benefits in kind, see 'Employer's Guide to Operating PAYE and PRSI for Certain Benefits' at www.revenue.ie.) The employer taxes gross pay less superannuation deductions and it is calculated on a cumulative basis. Each week or month an employee is taxed at the standard rate up to the cut-off point shown for that date, calculated on a cumulative basis from 1 January to the date of payment, with any income in excess of that figure taxed at the higher rate. The gross tax payable in any week or month is the cumulative due from January to the payment date. This gross tax is reduced by the tax credits accumulated since 1 January to the payment date to get the net tax due. The tax deduction card has the following columns to facilitate calculations:

- Week number (from 1 to the end of the year)
- Gross pay for the week or month, cumulative gross pay to date (pay for this week or month plus total gross pay to the previous pay period)
- Cumulative standard rate cut-off point
- Cumulative tax due at the standard rate
- Cumulative tax due at the higher rate
- Cumulative gross tax
- Cumulative tax credits
- Cumulative tax
- Tax deducted this period
- Tax refunded this period.

The tax deduction card also has columns for PRSI: the employee's weekly or monthly payment, the total PRSI payable and the contribution class of the employee. The net pay of the employee is gross pay for the week or month less the tax deducted for the week or month, the employee's PRSI for the week or month and the Universal Social Charge for the week or month.

If an employee starts work for the first time in week 26 the employer operates PAYE from that week, with the cumulative standard rate cut-off point and the cumulative tax credits as at that week. If the employee leaves a previous employment, he or she is obliged to submit a P45 (parts 2 and 3) to the new employer. The new employer keeps part 2 of the P45 and completes part 3 and sends it to the local tax office. A new Tax Credit Certificate is issued for the employee and a tax deduction card or disk. Tax credits are non-refundable. Any excess of tax credits over the liability for the week or month (unused tax credits) can be carried forward to subsequent weeks or months in the tax year.

An employee receives a PAYE Notice of Determination of Tax Credits and Standard Rate Cut-off Point. This notice, generally called a Tax Credit Certificate, shows an individual's tax credits for the year based on the most up-to-date information available to the Revenue, his/her standard rate cut-off point, the appropriate figures for a month and a week and the rate(s) of tax applicable. When an employee has reliefs which qualify for relief at the higher rate of income tax, the tax credits and the standard rate tax band are adjusted accordingly.

b)   PRSI

Pay Related Social Insurance (PRSI) is a social security tax paid by employers, employees and the self-employed to partly cover the cost of providing various social welfare benefits for eligible contributors. An employer has to pay a contribution, known as the employer's PRSI, in respect of each employee (see Table 6.1). With regard to employees, there are different classes of PRSI contribution: A, B, C, D, E, H, J, K, with each divided into further subclasses. However, the most important class in the private sector is A1. PRSI class A1 covers all those aged 16 to 66 working in the private sector in industrial, commercial and service-type enterprises who are employed under a contract of service as well as civil and public servants recruited after 6 April 1995. This category qualifies contributors for a wide range of benefits, including contributory pension, widow's or widower's pension, unemployment benefit and disability benefit. The PRSI contribution is a percentage of the employee's 'reckonable earnings' (gross pay less superannuation contributions). Every person over 16 receives a Personal Public Service (PPS) number from the Department of Social and Family Affairs for the purpose of social welfare, tax, education and health services. All PRSI contributions are recorded under that number and it is required for all taxes.

Self-employed people are liable for PRSI at the class S rate. Benefits available to contributors in this class include contributory pension and widow's or widower's contributory pension, maternity benefit and bereavement grant, provided the required contributions are paid. The class S contribution is a percentage of gross income less superannuation and capital allowances (where applicable).

c)   Universal Social Charge

A Universal Social Charge was introduced from 1 January 2011 to replace the health contribution and the income levy. The income levy was introduced on 1 January 2009 and doubled on 1 May that year. The main exemptions from the income levy were medical card holders and those with total annual income under €15,028. The rates of PRSI, health contribution and income levy applicable in 2010 are shown in Table 6.1.

The Universal Social Charge is to be applied at progressive rates of 2 to 7 per cent, depending on income, as follows:

Annual income	Aged under 70	Aged 70 or over
Less than €4,004	Exempt	Exempt
First €10,036	2%	2%
Next €5,980	4%	4%
Balance	7%	4%
Balance (self-employed to €100,000)	7	4
Relevant income for self-employed over €100,000	10	7
Medical card holders	4	4

Social welfare payments are exempt from the Universal Social Charge.

With effect from 1 January 2011, the PRSI ceiling of €75,036 was abolished and the class S rate for self-employed individuals was increased to 4 per cent. From that date, public servants liable at modified rates were subject to PRSI at 4 per cent on incomes over €75,036.

Table 6.1: PRSI and levies for 2010

a) PRSI	Rate (%)	
Employer's PRSI	8.5	Where employee's gross income does not exceed €356 per week.
	10.75	Payable on all of an employee's income where it exceeds €18,512 per annum, with no ceiling.
Employee's PRSI (Class A1)	4.0	On the first €75,036 per annum (with the first €127 of weekly income disregarded). Exempt where income is €352 per week or less.
Self-employed PRSI (Class S)	3.0	On all income. Minimum PRSI contribution: €253. Exempt where income is less than €3,174 per annum.

b) Health levy payable by employees and self-employed	Rate (%)	
Health contribution	4.0	On income up to €75,036 per annum.
	5.0	On income over €75,036 per annum.

Those earning under €26,000 per annum (€500 per week) (including self-employed), medical card holders and people aged 70 or over from 1 July 2001 were exempt from the health contribution.

c) Income levy	Rate (%)	
	2.0	On income up to €75,036 per annum.
	4.0	On income between €75,037 and €174,980 per annum.
	6.0	On income over €174,980 per annum.

For the current rates of tax, tax bands, personal tax credit entitlements and information on other taxes, see the Revenue's website at www.revenue.ie. For the current PRSI rates, see SW14 at www.welfare.ie.

d) Returns

The total PAYE, PRSI and Universal Social Charge deducted from all employees during a month as well as the employer's PRSI contribution in respect of each employee for the same period is sent to the Collector-General within nine days from the end of each income tax month, that is, between the 5th and 14th day of the calendar month. The form P30 bank giro payslip is completed and returned. It is also possible to pay PAYE, PRSI and the Universal Social Charge through the direct debit scheme and make an annual return and declaration of liability using the Revenue Online Service (details on how to become a ROS user are available on the Revenue website).

The following forms have to be completed at the end of the tax year and returned to the Collector-General by 15 February:

- P35: A declaration that the particulars of tax and PRSI being returned are correct
- P35L: A list of the particulars of PAYE and PRSI for each employee in respect of that year
- P35L or T: A return of PAYE and PRSI particulars for any employee whose PPS number is not known.

In addition, form P60 must be completed and given to each employee by 15 February showing gross pay, tax deducted and the employee's PRSI contributions for the year ending 31 December. .

e) Contractors

A principal contractor in construction, forestry and meat processing operations is obliged to deduct tax (Relevant Contracts Tax) at 35 per cent from all payments made to subcontractors and remit the amount to the Collector-General unless the principal contractor holds a relevant payments card (RCT47) for that subcontractor. A subcontractor can obtain this certificate from the local Inspector of Taxes provided his or her tax affairs are in order and up to date. The withholding rate is to be reduced to 20 per cent for registered subcontractors with an established compliance record.

6.3 Income tax for the self-employed

Income tax is payable by the self-employed on the annual profits or gains from a trade, profession, vocation and any other income. The annual profits in a partnership are divided between the partners in accordance with their agreement. Each partner is treated as a self-employed person and taxed on his/her share of the profits arising in the tax year to 31 December or in his/her accounting year if different. If a person's accounting year ends on 31 October, the profits for that period are taken as the profits of the tax year. Income earned from other sources such as rental income and interest received is taxed in the current tax year, from 1 January to the following 31 December.

Special regulations apply to the commencement and termination of a business. The following apply to commencement years.

First year:
- The taxable profits are those from commencement to the following 31 December.

Second year:
- Accounts are prepared for a full 12-month period ending in the second tax year, that is, on the profits of the first full year trading.
- Where the accounts are prepared for less than a year or where more than one set of accounts are prepared to a date or dates within that tax year, the assessment is based on the full amount of the profits of one year ending on the later or latest of those dates.
- In any other case the assessment is based on the actual profits for the tax year.

Third and subsequent years:
- Profits are taxed on a current-year basis (profits of an accounting period of a year ending on any date within that tax year).

If the profits for the second year to 31 December are less than those of the first 12 months' trading, a reduction for the excess can be claimed.

With respect to the termination of a business, the following regulations apply.

Last year:
- Taxed on profits from 1 January to date of cessation.

Penultimate year:
Taxed on the higher of the following:
- Profits of the accounting year ending in the second-last year, or
- Profits of the year from 1 January to the following 31 December in the second-last tax year.

a)   Self-assessment

Self-assessment is a system of taxation administration which requires a self-employed taxpayer to complete an annual tax return, showing income from all sources, appropriate tax credits, the computation of the tax payable and payment of the appropriate tax on or before the specified date(s). The system, which was introduced in 1988, places responsibility for the payment of the correct tax firmly on the taxpayer (it also applies to other taxes like capital gains tax, capital acquisition tax and corporation tax.

The common date for the payment of tax and the filing of annual returns is 31 October following the end of the tax year. This system, known as Pay and File, allows self-employed taxpayers to file their annual returns for the previous tax year and pay their taxes at the same time. The following have to be paid by each self-employed taxpayer by 31 October:

i)   An estimate of the income tax due for the current tax year, known as preliminary tax (see below)

ii)   The balance of income tax due from the previous tax year

iii)   Any capital gains tax due on disposals from 1 January to 30 September in the current tax year.

A taxpayer can submit his/her tax return at an earlier date and the Revenue will issue a final tax assessment for the relevant year to enable the taxpayer to pay the correct liability by 31 October. Payment can be made by completing the single debit authority and personalised payslip at the back of the return form, by completing the payslip and enclosing a cheque with the form to the Collector-General or by using the Revenue Online Service (ROS).

b)   Preliminary tax

Preliminary tax is the prepayment of the current year's liability in respect of income tax, PRSI and health contribution estimated by a self-employed person to be payable in the year of assessment to avoid being charged interest. The lower of the following must be paid by 31 October to avoid an interest charge:

*   90 per cent of the final liability for the current year of assessment, or

*   100 per cent of liability for the preceding year of assessment, or

*   105 per cent of liability for the year preceding the last year, but only where tax is paid by direct debit (this does not apply if the relevant figure is nil).

Preliminary tax can be paid by instalments throughout the year so as to avoid a lump sum payment on 31 October. Most taxpayers receive a notice of preliminary tax around September each year. It is the taxpayer's responsibility to pay the correct preliminary tax regardless of the figure shown on the notice or if no such notification is received. If a taxpayer calculates that no tax is payable, the preliminary tax payslip should be returned with 'NIL' recorded. However, even where there is a nil return for income tax, liability can arise in respect of PRSI and the Universal Social Charge, which have to be included in the preliminary tax. There is no right of appeal against liability for preliminary tax.

c)   Self-employed returns

Every self-employed person is obliged to submit a completed tax return (form 11 or 11E) by 31 October following the year of assessment to which it relates. Self-employed people are required to prepare and retain the following accounts for each tax year: trading account, profit and loss account, capital account and balance sheet. These accounts are no longer required to be sent with the tax return, but extracts of the relevant information have to be recorded on the tax return. A notice of assessment based on the return is issued, showing total liability for the tax year less the amount paid in preliminary tax. Any outstanding tax has to be paid by 31 October in the year following the year of assessment. Failure to submit a tax return by 31 October will result in a surcharge being added to the tax liability. The surcharge is 5 per cent of the full tax payable for the year subject to a maximum of €12,700 where the return is less than two months late, and 10 per cent up to a maximum of €63,500 where the return is over two months late. In respect of a new business, this surcharge will not be imposed if the return for the first year is made by 31 October the following year. The payment date for capital gains tax liability is now 31 October for any gains on disposals to 30 September in that tax year and 31 January in the following year in respect of the period 1 October to 31 December in the tax year.

d) Taxable profits

Net profits are calculated by deducting the cost of sales and business expenses from the sales figure, all excluding VAT. Adjustments have to be made to the net profit figure to arrive at taxable profits. Some business expenses are allowable for tax purposes and others are not (see Table 6.2).

Table 6.2: Allowable and disallowable business expenses

Business expenses allowable for tax	Business expenses not allowable for tax
Purchase of goods for resale	Improvements to premises (see Note 1)
Wages and salaries including employer's PRSI	Depreciation (see Note 2)
Commercial rates	Any expense not wholly and exclusively incurred in running the business
Rent paid	
Lighting and heating	Some car expenses (see Note 4)
Repairs and maintenance	Entertainment expenses
Running costs of vehicles used in the business	Provisions
Professional fees	Charitable donations
Interest on borrowings for the business	Personal or domestic expenses
Lease payments on vehicles or machinery used in the business	Any salary or drawings paid to the owner and/or his/her spouse
Bad or specific doubtful debts	Interest paid on overdue taxes
All other expenses incurred in running the business unless disallowed by law	Capital grants amortised as income over a number of years
Capital allowances (see Note 3)	
Advertising and promotions	
Trade subscriptions	
Accounting or audit fees	
Certain pre-trading expenses like costs of feasibility studies, business plans, rent paid, accountancy fees	

Note 1: Only expenditure of a revenue nature is allowed for tax purposes. Any capital expenditure is not allowed. This includes the purchase or improvement of premises and assets used for several years like plant, machinery and vehicles. However, capital allowances are given in respect of certain assets (see Notes 2 and 3) to allow for wear and tear.

Note 2: Depreciation is not allowed because capital allowances are given instead.

Note 3: The following capital allowances on net cost (exclusive of any grant and VAT) apply for expenditure incurred from 4 December 2002:

a)   Straight-line calculation   %

        Plant and machinery   12.5

        Industrial buildings   4.0

        Hotels   4.0

b)   Motor vehicles: See www.revenue.ie for current regulations.

Calculating the taxable profit involves three steps:

i)   Start with the net profit shown in the profit and loss account.

ii)   Add back any expenses shown in the profit and loss account which are not allowed for tax purposes, for example depreciation (see Table 6.2).

iii)   Deduct capital allowances for the year (see Note 3 above). The Finance Act of 2009 introduced tax relief for capital expenditure incurred by companies in acquiring a range of intangible assets such as brands, trade marks, copyrights and patents.

Relief for loss is allowed as a set-off against total income of the tax year or against future profits of the same business for subsequent years. A self-employed person can claim tax relief on a contribution to an approved pension scheme subject to a maximum of 15 per cent of net relevant earnings if under 30 years; the figure increases with age (see Section 6.12 on pensions below). Tax is calculated on taxable income. This gross tax figure is reduced by the tax credits of the individual to arrive at the net tax payable. The appropriate PRSI and Universal Social Charge have to be calculated to get the total payable to the Revenue.

e)   Professional services

Tax at the standard rate is deducted at source from payments made for professional services by Government departments and State bodies.

6.4 Value Added Tax

Value Added Tax (VAT) is a consumer tax charged on value added, introduced in Ireland with effect from 1 November 1972. The relevant law is contained in the Value Added Tax Acts 1972 to 1978 as amended, various Finance Acts, regulations and orders. VAT is chargeable on the taxable supply of goods and services within the State, on goods imported into the State from outside the EU, on intra-community acquisition of goods within the State and certain services received from abroad, known as Fourth Schedule services. It is collected by registered persons on their supplies of taxable goods and services as well as by Customs and Excise officers on imports from outside the EU. Each registered person charges VAT on the supply of goods and services and is allowed credit against this liability for tax paid on business purchases. A registered person does not pay VAT except where he/she is the final consumer.

a)   Who must register for VAT?

A person is obliged to register for VAT if annual turnover (total sales less VAT) exceeds or is likely to exceed the following annual limits:

*   €75,000 in respect of the supply of taxable goods
*   €37,500 in respect of the supply of taxable services
*   €41,000 for persons making intra-community acquisitions
*   €35,000 in respect of distance sales (mail-order sales) to Ireland from another EU State.

Farmers, people engaged in sea fishing and traders whose turnover is under the above limits do not have to register, but may do so if they wish. A taxable person is a sole trader, partnership, company, co-operative or other trading entity which is required to be registered for VAT. To register, form TR1 (or TR2 if a company) is completed and returned to the Inspector of Taxes. An accountable person is a taxable person who is obliged to register for VAT. VAT is normally accounted for by the supplier of goods and services, but there are certain exceptions where the recipient is accountable. These include the intra-community acquisition of goods and services from another EU State, receipt of Fourth Schedule services from abroad (those listed in the Fourth Schedule of the VAT Act) or cultural, artistic or entertainment services, and from 1 September 2008, construction services supplied to a principal contractor by subcontractors. The various rates, with examples of some of the items covered, are shown in Table 6.3, but these are subject to change (for current information, see the Revenue's website).

b)   Zero-rated sales

Goods supplied to a registered person in another EU State can be zero-rated provided the supplier has proof of despatch and quotes his/her VAT number as well as that of the customer on a valid VAT invoice. Goods supplied outside the EU are also zero-rated. Taxable persons that derive 75 per cent or more of their sales from VAT-registered organisations in the EU or from exports outside the EU may be eligible, subject to approval, to receive most goods, services and imports at the zero rate. Application for approval is sent to the local Inspector of Taxes on form 13A. When approved, form 13B is issued. A copy of this form is then sent to all suppliers of the approved person in the State who can then zero-rate all supplies to that person and quote the authorisation number on all invoices.

Table 6.3: VAT rates from 1 January 2011

Rates	Examples of some of the items covered
Exempt category	Activities in this category are not liable for VAT on sales and do not qualify for any repayment of VAT paid on taxable purchases. These activities include medical, dental, optical, chiropody, insurance, educational services including pre-school facilities, certain banking, agency and stock exchange services, admission to sporting and circus events, transport of passengers, betting and funeral undertakings as well as certain theatrical and musical performances.
Zero rate	Goods in this category are not liable for VAT on sales, but there is an entitlement to a repayment of VAT paid on taxable business purchases. Items covered include most food and drink of a kind used for human consumption, most exports of goods and services relating to them, fertilizers, personal clothing and footwear suitable for children under 11, books, certain medical equipment and appliances.
5.2%	This is a flat rate refund designed to compensate unregistered farmers for VAT paid on purchases.
13.5%	This is the reduced rate. Items taxable at this rate include concrete blocks, most building contracts, hotel and holiday accommodation, hotel and restaurant meals, short-term hiring of cars, boats, caravans, etc., newspapers, domestic energy products including electricity, bio-fuels, agricultural and veterinary services, repair and maintenance services, admissions to cinemas, cabarets and certain live theatrical and musical performances.
21%	The standard rate is applicable to all goods and services that are not exempt or taxable at the zero or reduced rates. Examples include adult clothing and footwear, drink and certain foods, most building materials, commercial and office equipment, telecommunications, legal, accounting, advertising and some other services, stationery, furniture, jewellery, cosmetics, commercially organised sports and leisure activities.

c)   Invoices

A registered person is obliged to issue an invoice when supplying goods or services to another registered person or to a person entitled to repayment of VAT. An invoice should contain the following:

- Name, address and VAT registration number of supplier
- Name and address of customer
- Date of issue of the invoice and of the supply of goods or services
- A full description and quantity or volume of the goods or services supplied
- The amount charged excluding VAT, the tax rate and the total including VAT
- A number (based on one of a series).

An invoice has to be issued within 15 days of the end of the month in which the goods or services are supplied. It is obligatory to keep all records relating to VAT for six years.

d) Taxable period

The taxable period for VAT is every two months, beginning on 1 January. A taxable person is obliged to complete form VAT3 for every two-month period and return it with the relevant payment to the Collector-General before the 19th day of the following month (otherwise interest is payable on the overdue tax). A business with low VAT liabilities may be permitted to submit an annual VAT return and other small operators may be allowed to submit returns two or three times a year subject to certain requirements. The VAT return is completed showing:

- VAT charged for the period
- VAT paid for the period
- VAT due to the Revenue (or, if the amount paid exceeds the figure payable, the sum repayable)
- Goods supplied to or received from other States of the EU.

A taxable person can reclaim VAT charged on goods and services purchased for use in the business. However, VAT on the following are not allowed with certain trading exceptions: the provision of food, drink, accommodation (other than conference-related) or other personal services, entertainment expenses, the acquisition for hiring of any motor vehicle or the purchase of petrol otherwise than as stock in trade for resale. If a taxable person obtains goods for private use in respect of which a VAT credit was received, the amount involved, known as self-supplies, is treated as a sale (at cost price) and taxable as such. The registered person is the final consumer of such goods and accordingly liable for the VAT.

In addition to paying tax every two months, an annual return of trading details (sales and purchases) is required; this information is provided on one of the bi-monthly VAT return forms issued by the Collector-General. This form includes figures for all Irish, intra-EU and overseas trade at the various VAT rates for the year. The Revenue Commissioners have a good knowledge of a person's business from VAT returns before the annual tax return is submitted. Inspectors of Taxes expect to see a margin in line with the norm for the industry or business in question as well as sales and purchases figures in line with VAT returns submitted in respect of the year. With the approval of the Collector-General, a taxable person can pay VAT through the direct debit system (by paying one-twelfth of the previous year's liability monthly) and make an annual return and declaration of liability. There is also an option of paying flexible amounts to reflect the seasonal nature of a business.

e) Methods of calculating VAT

A taxable person can calculate VAT liability by one of two methods:

- Invoice basis
- Cash received basis.

VAT is generally calculated on the invoice or sales basis, where liability is computed by deducting the total VAT shown on all invoices received during the two-month period from the aggregate of the VAT recorded on all invoices issued during the same period. It does not matter when payment is received or made.

In respect of the second method, cash received during a two-month period is assumed to be the sales for the period. This system can be used if at least 90 per cent of a trader's turnover consists of supplies of goods and services to unregistered persons or where annual turnover is not likely to exceed €1 million. Retailers and others who do not issue invoices usually obtain permission to use this method. In respect of credit card transactions, the total amount taxable is the figure charged by the supplier (not the amount received from the credit card companies). If sales involve goods at different VAT rates and the retailer does not have facilities for segregating receipts at point of sale into different VAT rates by means of scanning bar codes or another procedure and cannot reasonably be expected to do so, there are special procedures, Retailers' Special Schemes and another one for chemists, which can be used. The receipts are apportioned on a fair basis over the different rates using one of the approved methods.

Where the cash receipts basis is used, the takings include the VAT content of each sale. These tax-inclusive figures must be converted to tax-exclusive figures for the tax return. A simple way of doing this is to apply the following formula:

$$\text{Tax-inclusive figure} \times \frac{100}{(100 + \text{VAT rate})} = \text{Tax-exclusive figure}$$

Trading accounts are prepared using VAT-exclusive figures for sales and purchases.

f) VAT reporting requirements for the EU single market

There are two VAT reporting requirements for the EU single market:

- VIES (VAT Information Exchange System)
- Intrastat VAT Return.

The VIES is a quarterly return (which can be submitted monthly) prepared by each taxable person in respect of exports to a VAT-registered trader in another member state. This return has to be submitted monthly where the value of a company's intra-community supplies exceeds €100,000 per quarter from 1 January 2010 and €50,000 from 1 January 2012. It contains the VAT number and the value of sales to each customer in a member state for the period of the return. It has to be submitted within a month of the due date.

The purpose of the Intrastat VAT Return is to provide statistical data relating to imports and exports between member states. Depending on the amount of inter-EU trade carried out by a taxable person, there are two methods of making the necessary returns. If a taxable person's exports do not exceed €635,000 annually and imports are not over €191,000 a year, the appropriate statistics can be provided on the normal VAT return form, VAT3 (boxes E1 and E2). Where either of the above export or import figures is exceeded, a special monthly return, known as the Intrastat Return, is required. This return requires information relating to the class of goods traded, country of origin, country of destination, mode of transport, nature of the transaction (sale, lease, hire, etc.), invoice value, delivery terms, ancillary costs, weight in kilograms and units in the case of certain types of goods. The Intrastat VAT Return has to be submitted to the Revenue for every calendar month between the 5th and 10th working day following the month to which it refers.

6.5 Corporation tax

The Revenue Commissioners are notified by the Companies Registration Office of all new company registrations. Every company is also obliged to notify the Revenue Commissioners within 30 days of commencing trading. Form TR2 is used to register for any or all of the following: corporation tax, employer's PAYE and PRSI and VAT.

A company is liable for corporation tax on its profits and chargeable gains. It is assessed on the profits made during its accounting period, that is, the 12-month period for which it makes up its accounts. The system used is self-assessment. The payment date for preliminary corporation tax is the 21st of the month before the end of the accounting period. A company is obliged to pay preliminary tax of not less than 90 per cent of the final liability, or in respect of a small company (where tax liability for the previous year is under the specified threshold), 100 per cent of the liability for the previous year, if this is lower, to avoid an interest charge. A company has to submit a return (CT1) no later than nine months after the end of its accounting period or by the 21st of the ninth month if earlier. The Pay and File system also applies to companies in respect of the above date. Any balance of tax due is payable on that date. If a company does not submit its tax return on time a surcharge is payable, with restrictions on certain reliefs and allowances. Where the corporation tax liability for the previous accounting period was in excess of €200,000 there are now two instalments payable. The first instalment, either 50 per cent of the liability for the previous year or 45 per cent of the final liability for the current year, is payable in the sixth month of the accounting year. The second instalment, the amount payable to bring the total preliminary tax paid to 90 per cent, is payable in the eleventh month of the accounting period.

A loss by a company cannot be set off against personal income; it can only be set off against the company's trading income for the same or the preceding accounting period, or against its non-trading income (investment and rental) on a value basis because of the different rates chargeable. Most Irish-resident companies are classified as close companies and are subject to some anti-avoidance provisions, in particular a 20 per cent surcharge on any undistributed rental and investment income 18 months after the end of an accounting period, with an additional charge in respect of a company involved in professional services. Co-operative societies are subject to corporation tax.

a) Rates of corporation tax

A reduced rate of 10 per cent corporation tax applied to profits derived from manufacturing and certain internationally traded services up to the year 2010 in respect of companies approved by July 1998. The rate applicable to the trading income of companies from 2003 is 12.5 per cent, unless it comes from certain excepted trades such as certain land-dealing activities when it is 25 per cent. The corporation tax rate applicable to non-trading company income (rental and investment income) is 25 per cent of taxable profit. The 12.5 per cent rate of corporation tax is very attractive, especially for companies engaged in traded services.

There is an exemption from corporation tax including capital gains for the first three years for certain start-up companies commencing to trade from 2009 with a corporation tax liability of less than €40,000 per annum. The relief, which is subject to European Union approval, does not apply to professional service companies and was subject to a cap from 2011 (for the current position, see www.revenue.ie).

b) Directors and tax

A company is obliged to register as an employer and operate PAYE or PRSI for certain directors and any other employees. Directors can either be employees paying PRSI at class A1 rate or self-employed under a contract for services and liable for class S. There is no employer's contribution payable in respect of an owner-director. Directors' salaries are allowable expenses against the profits of a company, just like those of any employees.

Company directors are also obliged to make income tax returns without being served with notices by 31 October of the year following the income tax year in question. Otherwise, proprietary directors are liable to a surcharge on the full tax payable for the year, including any PAYE deductions. A proprietary director is one who is the beneficial owner or in control of more than 15 per cent of the ordinary share capital of a company. In administering the relevant provision of the statute, the Revenue Commissioners have decided that until further notice, mandatory returns and surcharges will not apply to non-proprietary directors if they are not otherwise chargeable persons and all their income has been taxed directly or indirectly under PAYE. Proprietary directors do not qualify for the PAYE tax credit.

All payments to directors are examined, especially expenses, to ensure that the appropriate tax is paid. All payments to company shareholders have taxation implications (see Brennan *et al.*, 2010). A proprietary director can provide for a retirement pension from company profits. For Revenue-approved schemes, a company can make annual payments for a director into a personal pension (subject to annual and overall limits). The contribution is an allowable expense for the company against corporation tax and it is not taxable income for the director. Some insurance companies operate Self-Administered Retirement Trusts (SART) targeted at directors' pensions. There are also generous taxation concessions available on retirement (see Section 6.12 on pensions below).

c) Tax on dividends

With effect from 6 April 1999 a withholding tax at the standard rate of income tax applies to dividends paid by an Irish resident company to individuals in the State and certain non-residents. Individuals liable for tax at the higher rate are obliged to declare the gross dividends received and pay the difference between the tax liability at that rate and the amount deducted at source by the withholding tax. An individual who is not liable or fully liable for income tax is entitled to reclaim the appropriate refund.

Tax deducted by companies on dividends is payable to the Revenue within one month. The payment has to be accompanied by a return from the company giving the name, address and amount of the dividend paid to each shareholder.

d) Research and development tax credits

The 2004 Finance Act introduced a new incentive for companies to carry out research and development (R&D) in Ireland. From 1 January 2009 a tax credit of 25 per cent of allowable incremental capital and revenue expenditure on qualifying research and development activities over the base year of 2003 can be claimed. The definition of research and development includes basic research, applied research and experimental development. Research and development carried out before a company commences trading can qualify for the tax credit at a later date. This tax credit is in addition to the normal deduction of research and development expenditure in respect of corporation tax, which is an effective relief of 37.5 per cent.

6.6 Commercial rates

Businesses are liable for commercial rates payable to local authorities (domestic rates were abolished in 1978 and agricultural rates in 1984). The rate payable is determined by two factors: the rate levied by the relevant local authority and the valuation placed on the premises by the valuation office. Business premises are generally revalued following major improvements. However, a local authority has the discretion to give some remission for a period of 10 years under the Industrial Development Acts 1969 to 1986 in respect of a premises provided for an industrial undertaking.

6.7 Capital taxes

Two capital taxes are outlined here: capital gains tax and capital acquisitions tax.

a)   Capital gains tax

Capital gains tax is chargeable on capital gains arising on the disposal of chargeable assets after 5 April 1974. In calculating the gain, indexation relief for inflation was allowed up to 31 December 2002, subject to certain restrictions. Exemptions include any gain arising from the sale of a person's private residence and the first €1,270 of chargeable gains in the year of assessment for an individual. Realised taxable gains are charged at a rate of 25 per cent from 7 April 2009. Capital gains tax applies to any gain resulting from the sale of a business, regardless of whether it is sold to a third party or transferred to a family member. However, retirement relief can apply. There is no capital gains tax payable where an individual aged 55 or over transfers a business or farm to a child or to a niece or nephew who has worked full time in the business or farm for the five preceding years, provided the assets were owned for more than 10 years. If the assets are transferred through shares in a family company, the owner must have been a working director of the company for at least 10 years. The transferor must hold at least 25 per cent of the voting rights or alternatively hold 10 per cent of the shares and together with family members have at least 75 per cent of the voting rights. If the beneficiary disposes of the assets within six years, this exemption is lost. If a business or farm which is owned for at least 10 years is sold to a third party by an individual aged 55 or over, there is no capital tax payable if the proceeds do not exceed €750,000 (Martyn and Reck, 2010 (2008 figure)). Returns relating to capital gains are made with income tax or corporation tax returns as appropriate. The payment date for capital gains tax in respect of disposals between 1 January and 30 November is 15 December. The capital gains tax liability for December is payable the following January.

b)   Capital acquisitions tax

Capital acquisitions tax (CAT) was introduced in respect of taxable gifts taken on or after 28 February 1974 and on every taxable inheritance taken on or after 1 April 1975. The relationship between the disponer (donor) and the beneficiary determines the group threshold, each of which has a tax-free limit (for the current thresholds, see the Revenue website). Thresholds are indexed in line with inflation each year. The rate of tax on gifts (given during the donor's lifetime) and on inheritances (taken on death) is 25 per cent from 7 April 2009. A system of full aggregation of all benefits taken by a beneficiary from all donors applies from 2 December 1998. Gifts and inheritances taken by one spouse from the other are exempt. To improve the tax environment for transfers of businesses and farms, a reduction of 90 per cent is allowed in the value of business assets and agricultural property subject to certain restrictions (Martyn and Reck, 2010). The relevant legislation is the Capital Acquisitions Tax Act 1976 as amended.

Stamp duty is also chargeable on the disposal of a business, but a 50 per cent reduction can be claimed for a transfer to a family member, with transfers of farms to family members under 35 with agricultural qualifications exempt.

6.8 Customs and excise duties

Imported goods have to be declared to Customs. Customs duty is usually paid on the value of imports at the rate appropriate to the tariff classification of the goods involved. Each tariff classification has a 10-digit code. The EU has bilateral agreements with certain countries whereby goods satisfying specific criteria can qualify for duty-free entry, with reciprocal treatment for exports. Preferential treatment is given to goods that originate in developing countries (chiefly African and South American countries). Manufacturers who import raw material and export the finished products outside the EU can qualify for excise duty relief.

Excise duties are imposed on a range of goods, chiefly alcoholic drinks, mineral oils and tobacco products. Excise duty is also charged on certain activities which require a licence, for example betting, operating gaming and amusement machines as well as breweries and retailing spirits.

There is a Vehicle Registration Tax (VRT) on new and used vehicles registered for the first time in Ireland, which is linked from 1 July 2008 to the carbon dioxide emission level of the vehicles and not engine size.

6.9 Tax clearance

A Tax Clearance Certificate is required for Government contracts, grants and State licences to ensure that no unfair advantage is gained by a non-compliant taxpayer. The activities covered include:

a) Public service contracts valued over a specific figure in a 12-month period
b) State and public authority grants to a specific value, including industrial and farm development grants
c) FÁS employment subsidy or training schemes
d) The renewal of certain licences, for example intoxicating liquor, liquor wholesalers, road haulage and passenger transport, petroleum, gas and hydrocarbon oil, bookmakers, gaming and amusement machines as well as auctioneering.

6.10 Revenue audit

A business can be subject to a revenue audit, where all the books and records are checked with the various tax returns. Some revenue audits arise from random selection, while others emanate from target selection (for example a particular category like publicans) or tell-tale features in accounts submitted, for example margins out of line with the trade, or failure to reconcile VAT returns with accounts. In addition, the Revenue have wide powers to demand records and information, to enter premises and inspect any relevant documentation (Martyn and Reck, 2010).

6.11 Patent royalties

Exemption from income tax arising from patent royalties was introduced in 1973 to promote research and development activities in Ireland. Only certain patent royalties were exempt from tax: those received from a manufacturing activity or from non-manufacturing activities where the income came from bona fide third-party payments (where the payer and payee were not connected), subject to a number of conditions. This exemption applied to dividends paid out of royalties from manufacturing and bona fide third-party non-manufacturing activities in respect of eligible shares in a patent company (Martyn and Reck, 2010). The relief, which was subject to a ceiling of €5 million a year, was abolished from 24 November 2010.

6.12 Pensions

It is now State policy to encourage as many people as possible to make adequate provision for their retirement. Various legislative measures have been enacted to provide a new pensions framework in Ireland. The Pensions Act 1990 created a regulatory framework for occupational pension schemes and established the Pensions Board to oversee and monitor the operation of these schemes. The Act also provides for information for members of schemes, as well as the portability of accrued benefits, by permitting owners to transfer them to another approved scheme or to a buy-out bond. The Pensions (Amendment) Act 2002 updated the 1990 legislation and introduced a new type of pension scheme known as a Personal Retirement Savings Account (PRSA). It gave the Pensions Board a regulatory role in relation to all PRSA providers and established the Office of Pensions Ombudsman. An employer is obliged to produce payroll records if requested by the Pensions Ombudsman. The State also provides generous tax relief for contributions to approved pension schemes and in respect of benefits on retirement (Taxes Consolidation Act 1997, pt.30 and subsequent Finance Acts).

There are five pension options available in the private sector:
a)   State contributory pension
b)   Occupational pension scheme (also called a company scheme)
c)   Additional Voluntary Contribution (AVC)
d)   Retirement Annuity Contract (RAC)
e)   Personal Retirement Savings Account (PRSA).

a)   State contributory pension

The majority of private sector employees and those who joined the public sector after 6 April 1995 and pay the class A1 rate of PRSI are entitled to the State contributory retirement pension (where they have retired from full-time work) at 65 or the social welfare old-age contributory pension at 66 (subject in both cases to the requisite number of contributions). The self-employed pay the class S rate of PRSI at 4 per cent (plus the Universal Social Charge), which entitles them to a State contributory pension (subject to the requisite number of contributions). The only pension many self-employed people and numerous employees have is that provided through the State social insurance scheme. For those who do not qualify for this or any other pension, there is a non-contributory means-tested State pension provided at 66 or over under the social assistance scheme.

b)   Occupational pension scheme

An occupational pension scheme is one established by an employer to provide pensions for employees on retirement. There is no legal obligation on any business to establish an occupational pension scheme. Where an occupational pension scheme is established, it can be one of three types:

*   A defined benefit scheme
*   A defined contribution scheme
*   A hybrid of both.

A defined benefit scheme specifies the level of pension payable for life on retirement, based on length of service in the scheme and earnings at retirement. It is funded by the employee and employer.

A defined contribution pension scheme is where the pension payable on retirement depends on what can be purchased with the amount paid into the scheme and the returns earned. It does not promise any specific level of pension to an employee on retirement. Contributions paid to the scheme by the employee and employer are invested and the final lump sum is used to purchase an annuity (pension) from an insurance company at retirement, which is then payable for life. Under this scheme the value of a pension is determined by the amount invested, the returns earned and the cost of the pension at retirement with regard to the long-term yield on gilts and life expectancy. The annuity usually ends with the death of the contributor, but it is possible to buy one at a greater cost that continues to be paid to the surviving spouse.

A hybrid pension scheme contains a specific proportion of defined benefit and the balance a defined contribution. To qualify for income tax relief, which is available at the employee's top rate, the occupational pension scheme must be Revenue approved.

c)   Additional Voluntary Contribution (AVC)

Additional Voluntary Contributions are voluntary pension contributions made by members of a pension scheme which are additional to the amount that they are required to make with regard to the rules of the scheme. Subject to the regulations imposed by the Revenue, a employee can make AVCs and avail of any used tax relief as per the age-related scale shown in Table 6.4. They are a tax-efficient way to increase future retirement income. This can be very advantageous for employees with broken service for any reason.

d)   Retirement Annuity Contract (RAC)

A Retirement Annuity Contract is a defined contribution scheme where the pension payable depends on the contributions paid, the returns received and the cost of buying the pension. An RAC is taken out by self-employed people and those who have earnings from non-pensionable employments. The income tax relief available is shown in Table 6.4.

e)   Personal Retirement Savings Account (PRSA)

PRSAs are flexible, portable, long-term defined contribution personal pension savings schemes designed to enable people, especially those who have made no provision for their pensions, to save for retirement in a regular and flexible manner. PRSAs are available from a number of authorised providers approved by the Pensions Board and the Revenue Commissioners. Holders can change employments as often as they like with no effect on their PRSAs. A person can contribute as much as he/she wishes, but the minimum is €300 per annum and the figure can be increased or decreased as required. Financial planning for retirement involves a big commitment over many years, with the size of the retirement fund determined by the amount contributed and the returns earned.

There are two types of PRSAs available: standard and non-standard. In respect of the former, the provider cannot charge more than 5 per cent of the contribution made or more than 1 per cent per annum for the management of the fund, the contributions can only be invested in pooled funds and the member does not have to purchase any other product such as a life insurance policy. There are costs involved for the provider in respect of each contribution and in the management of the fund, which can be charged to members, but they cannot exceed these limits. In the case of a non-standard PRSA, there is no limit on charges and the contributions can be invested in a range of funds. PRSAs are open to anyone under the age of 75. A PRSA is not risk free and is not guaranteed by the Government. Its value will depend on the total contributions made, the investment returns achieved and the charges imposed.

Tax relief on pension contributions

There are generous tax reliefs at the taxpayer's top rate available to anyone contributing to an approved pension scheme, Retirement Annuity Contract, occupational pension scheme, Additional Voluntary Contribution or a PRSA. These vary with age, as shown in Table 6.4.

Table 6.4: Tax relief on pension contributions

Age	Limit of net relevant earnings or remuneration	
	a) RACs	
	b) Occupational pension scheme and PRSAs or AVCs	
	%	
Under 30	15	
30–39	20	
40–49	25	
50–54	30	
55–59	35	
60 years or over	40	

Net relevant earnings derive from trades, professions and non-pensionable employments, less certain payments and deductions (Martyn and Reck, 2010). Remuneration is gross income in respect of members of occupational pension schemes. Certain sports-people, who usually retire early, can get relief of 30 per cent regardless of age. There is a maximum amount of earnings which qualify for income tax relief in respect of pension contributions (for the current figure, see www.revenue.ie). A self-employed person may avail of the income tax relief for the preceding year by making a contribution to an approved pension scheme by 31 October following that year but subject to the limits shown in the table. From 1 January 2002 employees in an occupational pension scheme or a statutory one can make Additional Voluntary Contributions to a PRSA. It is a requirement that the PRSA is established under a rule of the main scheme or under a separate scheme approved by the Revenue. However, the maximum lump sum and pension must be within the limits set out in the approved occupational pension rules. Employees who are not in occupational pension schemes may claim tax relief on contributions up to €1,525 per year even if this exceeds the income-based limits.

Employer's obligations for PRSAs
From 15 September 2003 all employers are obliged to enter into an agreement with a PRSA provider to offer at least one standard PRSA to excluded employees. These are employees who are not offered an occupational pension scheme or are included for death-in-service benefits only, or are not eligible to join the occupational pension scheme and who will not become eligible within six months of taking up employment, or are included in a occupational pension scheme which does not allow AVCs. An employer is also obliged

to notify excluded employees of their rights and allow a PRSA provider or an intermediary reasonable access to such employees.

Under the Protection of Employees (Part-Time Work) Act 2001, part-time employees cannot be treated less favourably than comparable full-time staff. This means that if an employer provides a pension scheme for full-time staff, comparable part-time employees should also have access, unless their exclusion can be justified on objective grounds. An exception to this requirement is where the part-time employee works less than 20 per cent of the normal hours of a comparable employee. An employer is obliged to allow reasonable paid leave of absence to excluded employees, subject to the requirements of work, so that PRSAs can be arranged, to facilitate such employees in every reasonable manner to enter into a pension contract, to make pension deductions at source without charge on request and forward them to the PRSA provider within 21 days of the end of the month in which the deductions took place, and advise all such employees monthly in writing of the contributions made. Employers can contribute to employees' PRSAs, but there is no legal obligation to do so, which makes them even less popular than defined contribution occupational schemes. An employer's contribution is aggregated with the employee's to get the maximum tax-relieved figure.

PRSA benefits

A person can normally take PRSA benefits between the ages of 60 and 75. There are some circumstances where the benefits can be taken before 60, such as retirement at age 50 or over or on health grounds. Normally it is not possible to cash a PRSA before the age of 60 (or retirement). A PRSA cannot be given as a security for a loan or assigned to anyone else.

Options on retirement

An employee in an occupational pension scheme has the following options on retirement:
a)   Use all the fund to purchase an annuity (a pension for life), subject to a maximum pension of 66.67 per cent of the final year's remuneration
b)   Withdraw up to 150 per cent of the the final year's remuneration as a tax-free lump sum and purchase an annuity with the balance. A lifetime ceiling for tax-free pension lump sum payments was introduced from January 2011 (initially €200,000).

The options available at retirement to the self-employed, an employee with a PRSA who is not a member of an occupational scheme and proprietary directors are as follows:
a)   Use all the fund to purchase a retirement annuity, payable immediately
b)   Withdraw up to 25 per cent of the fund as a tax-free lump sum, subject to the ceiling, and either:
- Purchase a retirement annuity with the balance
- Draw down the balance as a lump sum, which is taxable under the PAYE system

- Invest the balance in an Approved Retirement Fund (ARF), subject to certain conditions.

When a recipient dies, the income ceases unless the pension was purchased for a guaranteed period or provision was made for a surviving widow or widower. An Approved Retirement Fund is a tax-exempt method used to hold, invest and pay out benefits in retirement. Funds invested in an ARF can be withdrawn at any time and in any amount, subject to income tax, or used to purchase a pension. Whereas an annuity is payable for life, an ARF can run out. An ARF can be transferred tax-free between spouses. Any money left in an ARF on death becomes part of the deceased person's estate. Where a retired person's regular income per annum does not exceed €12,700, he or she is required to invest €63,500, or if less, the balance in the fund after the initial withdrawal, in an Approved Minimum Retirement Fund (AMRF). Investment income from an AMRF can be taken out, subject to income tax, but the capital sum cannot be withdrawn until the holder reaches 75 years of age (again, subject to income tax). When an AMRF holder reaches 75, the fund becomes an ARF. Following the Finance Act 2006, a deemed withdrawal of 3 per cent applies to all ARFs every year from 2009 and taxed at the recipient's marginal rate of tax (and that figure was to be increased to 5 per cent in 2011). Any actual withdrawal will be deducted from the imputed figure.

From 7 December 2005 a cap was applied to all individual retirement funds and that figure was reduced from January 2011. There are major changes in relation to pensions (see www.pensionsgreenpaper.ie).

6.13 Summary

Every person or organisation carrying on a trade, business or profession is obliged to keep proper accounting books and records, which have to be retained for six years. Apart from any other requirements, every business has to comply with its taxation obligations. A person or organisation is also required to notify the tax office when starting a business and register as an employer if employing staff, for VAT if turnover is expected to exceed the specified thresholds and for income tax in the case of an individual and corporation tax in respect of a company.

Payment and return dates have to be respected, otherwise interest on outstanding tax can accrue. Income tax is payable by the self-employed on the annual profits or gains from a trade, profession, vocation and any other income. The system used is self-assessment. There are special regulations relating to starting and terminating a business as well as to allowable expenses for tax purposes. A person or organisation with a turnover in excess of the specified thresholds is obliged to register for VAT and submit the required returns. A company is liable for corporation tax. Other taxes include commercial rates, capital gains tax, customs and excise duties.

It is State policy to encourage as many people as possible to make adequate provisions for their retirement. There are generous taxation incentives for people to provide for their own pensions, with five options available to those in the private sector.

Questions

1. Using the internet, find out the current regulations in respect of the following.
    a)   Universal Social Charge
    b)   The current rates of income tax, tax bands and tax credits
    c)   Corporation tax rates
    d)   Capital allowances on energy-efficient equipment
2. Explain the following terms.
    a)   The standard rate cut-off point for personal taxation
    b)   Self-assessment
    c)   Preliminary tax
    d)   Commercial rates
3. Describe how the PAYE system operates.
4. Describe the methods used in the calculation of VAT for a registered person.
5. Discuss the pension options available to a self-employed person in Ireland.

Chapter 7

Operations management

A pessimist sees a difficulty in every opportunity; an optimist sees an opportunity in every difficulty.

Winston Churchill

Learning objectives

- To explore the main operational processes in a business
- To appreciate the importance of quality
- To consider the steps involved in new product development
- To understand what is meant by the value chain
- To comprehend some of the principles of insurance
- To appreciate some legal issues relating to the supply of goods and services as well as competition.

This chapter is structured as follows:

7.1 Introduction to operations management

Operations management refers to the range of processes required to transform various resource inputs into marketable products or services. Traditionally it was sometimes called production management because of its close association with manufacturing. It includes manufacturing, construction, extractive activities (mining, quarrying, oil, gas, peat, forestry, agriculture), an ever increasing range of services, transport and distribution in some organisations as well as maintenance and repairs to existing facilities. Operations management seeks to develop core competence in the production process, from receipt of orders to delivery to customers. The emphasis is on creating value by designing better products or services to meet the needs of customers, enhancing performance or quality and reducing costs over all the activities involved in the process.

The main activities explored are the acquisition of a premises, operations planning and control, supply chain management and quality. As research and development and new product development are generally located in the operations department of a business, they are considered here also. Some issues relating to insurance are also covered as well as an appreciation of legal issues relating to the supply of goods and services.

7.2 Premises

Many aspiring entrepreneurs lack the resources required to secure suitable premises and initially use whatever facilities they themselves or their parents possess. Some people provide various services from their own homes. Many small businesses are started by people engaging in commercial activities to supplement their income. There are stories of many successful businesses originating in their promoters' garages, including the Apple Computer Corporation. Planning permission is now required for commercial enterprises and most entrepreneurs require suitable facilities for their businesses.

There are four main considerations relating to a business premises: location, purchase or lease, facilities required and compliance with various laws and regulations. The choice of geographical area and location within it are important decisions, influenced by the requirements of a business. In the case of a retailing enterprise, the following are important considerations: convenience for a large pool of potential customers, traffic flow, shopping and spending patterns in the area, ease of access for deliveries, car parking facilities nearby, security and expected future changes. Planned developments for the district are also worth investigating (in the local planning office) and it is often helpful to identify the locations of competitors. Manufacturing organisations have specific requirements: access to raw materials, access to markets, space requirements, staff needs, general infrastructure and cost, all of which have to be carefully considered before making the location decision. Relocation can be expensive.

The purchase or lease decision is always difficult, but it depends on the nature of the business, future prospects and above all the available resources (which are usually scarce in a start-up situation). By purchasing a premises, an entrepreneur has a good security for future borrowings if required, an asset which should appreciate in value over time and one which could qualify for a grant (depending on the nature of the business). Leasing a premises enables an entrepreneur to use business facilities without any large capital outlay. The terms and conditions of any lease have to be carefully studied, especially matters relating to length (a long period may not be advisable for some new businesses), restrictions on use, floor area, storage capacity, expansion potential, maintenance and repairs, insurance, terms for renewal, rent reviews upwards, downwards or no change (depending on the circumstances), termination and, of course, the cost. A break clause can be agreed allowing for termination of the lease after a specific period. Service charges and commercial rates also have to be considered whether the premises is owned or leased. An entrepreneur can lease his/her own premises (if owned) to a company to run a business, which then becomes an operating organisation. Many entrepreneurs who own property find this to be a convenient arrangement in case of liquidation for any reason and to avoid a possible double capital gains tax liability arising. Good legal advice is important on all matters relating to leases.

Certain utilities and facilities are required for all premises: water, sewerage, electricity, heating, insulation, fire escapes, fixtures and fittings, telephone, internet, broadband and other facilities depending on the nature of the business. The capacity of a building to satisfy present needs and those of the immediate future is an important consideration also. A selected building has to have planning permission from the local authority for the proposed use and any prescribed conditions have to be acceptable. The design and construction of a building must comply with the relevant building regulations.

The building must comply with fire regulations, pollution control, health, hygiene and safety legislation as well as any special regulations, for example those relating to food production if required. In some businesses there may also be environmental regulations. Where hazardous materials are involved, Integration Pollution Prevention Control (IPPC) licences are required in an effort to prevent or reduce emissions. Waste water discharge licences, administered by local authorities, are required by a wide range of businesses. There are also regulations dealing with waste electrical and electronic equipment. Once a premises is secured, the necessary equipment has to be sourced, new or second-hand.

7.3 Operations planning and control

The production process involves two key activities: operations planning and control. It is a process of establishing production plans, scheduling the resources required and implementing and monitoring actual performance against the standards set. Its purpose is to ensure that the right products are produced in the required quantities and quality at the appropriate times as economically as possible. There are two separate elements involved in operations planning and control but they are intertwined.

Operations planning is concerned with anticipating future demand for products and organising the necessary facilities and factors of production. This consists of two related activities: strategic and tactical. The former is concerned with long-term decisions relating to what to produce as well as the facilities, technology and good design. Tactical planning is concerned with operational problems such as how to schedule production, inventory levels, staffing, subcontracting and setting output targets to ensure that incoming orders are completed promptly. Operations planning begins with predicting the short-term and long-term demand for the products of a company. Forecasts of future demand have to be prepared based on market information, feedback from staff, statistical analysis of past demand and correlation with key economic indicators. Long-term forecasts influence the provision of the required production facilities and related technology. A schedule of demand for each product for a period, for example a year, is used to plan other resources required, raw materials, inventories, labour and equipment. Annual forecasts are broken down into shorter periods, such as a week or a four-week period, to identify peaks and low points. Production requirements (outputs) are converted into corresponding inputs, with a product design specification outlining the raw material, labour and other requirements. Decisions are made with regard to optimum lot sizes, inventories, including timing of receipts, loading (filling the available capacity), scheduling, machine loadings and job assignments. This is followed by scheduling: planning the sequence of work on a timescale to ensure that it is completed by the target dates. The objective is to optimise the use of the various resources in production, which can involve altering the sales pattern where possible, arranging later delivery dates, producing for stock during slack periods or developing off-season products to use spare capacity (Wild, 2002). Outsourcing of activities that others can do cheaper and better is also a consideration. Outsourcing can involve a single task, a function or the full process. Most outsourcing takes place within the country and the ideal arrangement is better value for both parties.

While operations planning is concerned with determining the production capacity and organising the various factors at a particular time, control ensures that the available capacity is used in the optimum way to supply customers' orders. It involves monitoring the production schedules to ensure that the plans, targets and requirements of specific orders can be met on time. Scheduling of all work has to operate within the available capacity. Corrective action has to be taken if it becomes clear that schedules will not be completed on time. Actual demand for products is monitored against plans and adjustments made as required.

Traditional production can take one of four forms: job, batch, mass or continuous flow. Job production refers to products specially made to meet the specific requirements of customers. It is generally small scale, craft based and labour intensive, with little scope for standardisation. Batch production can take one of three forms: a batch produced once only for a specific order, one produced at regular or irregular intervals as required or one produced periodically at known intervals for satisfying continuous demand. This system combines standardisation with the need to satisfy the specific requirements of customers. Mass production is the automated processing of a large quantity of a standardised product, for example fast food. Continuous or flow production is the processing of products in a continuous flow. This system is widely used in the production of standardised homogenous products. A project is also a process type, a one-off high-value order, for example a construction contract.

The next issue is plant layout: the physical arrangement of all production facilities. Plant layout is influenced by the nature of the product(s), the production process, the handling methods in use, the quantity to be made and the equipment to use as well as the facilities required for receiving material, dispatching production and circulation. The main types of plant layout are fixed position (the necessary equipment remains in a fixed position during the process), process layout (used in batch production where the facilities are organised around the required process), product layout (where facilities are laid out for a particular product, for example in mass production) and group technology (where similar features can be done together to reap economies). Group technology is a technique whereby 'families' of components requiring similar operations may be processed together, thereby gaining some benefits of large-scale production (Russell and Taylor, 2005; Wild, 2002).

Productivity is the efficiency with which an organisation uses input resources to achieve its outputs. Objective indices of performance are established for individuals, units, departments and the whole organisation, against which actual results are measured so as to achieve the desired targets.

Advanced manufacturing technologies

Good design, innovation and the adoption of modern advanced manufacturing technologies can create competitive advantages for organisations. These advanced manufacturing technologies (AMTs) include computer-aided design (CAD), manufacturing, engineering, planning and control systems. CAD enables designers to experiment in a swift and cheap manner in their search for better products. Computer-aided manufacturing (CAM), consisting of robotics, computer-controlled machines and flexible production systems, is used to plan and control production processes. A flexible manufacturing system (FMS) consists of computer-controlled machines and automated material-handling equipment with the flexibility to produce a variety of products within broad parameters in a short time. Computer-integrated manufacturing (CIM) is the integration of all the elements of advanced manufacturing technologies into one system (Russell and Taylor, 2005; Slack *et al.*, 2004). Any manufacturing SME that plans to move up the value chain has to exploit the potential of new technologies.

7.4 Supply chain management

Supply chain management is the process by which the needs of customers are satisfied through the co-ordination of orders, suppliers, operations and distribution (Christopher, 2005). A business has to source the required raw materials to ensure that the necessary quantity is available when required on agreed terms. Other issues to be addressed include warehousing facilities and costs, if relevant, for raw materials and finished goods; transportation; handling; and health and safety.

The traditional system of purchasing raw materials was by continuously reviewing the stock of each item held and ordering a pre-determined quantity (called the reorder quantity) once the level fell below a specified level (known as the reorder level). This procedure led to high costs in terms of storage, insurance and deterioration as well as the cost of the big investment required in inventory.

The person responsible for the acquisition of raw materials in an organisation is called the purchasing officer. His/her role is to obtain the proper quantity of material of the proper quality at the best price for delivery at the right time. He/she has to be a person of integrity with a keen analytical mind to enable him/her to assess conditions, terms and quality. The purchasing officer is expected to seek tenders and quotations for supplies so that the best terms available can be secured. However, the lowest price is not necessarily the most economical; quality, reliability and delivery dates are other important considerations.

The routine of purchasing involves initiating a purchase requisition (usually by a storekeeper or the person who requires materials), seeking tenders or quotations if not already available, sending out a purchase order, checking incoming material against the order for quantity, quality and prices and clearing the invoice for payment. In many organisations, goods received notes are prepared in respect of receipts, against which invoices are passed for payment, after checking their terms with tenders and quotations received.

Recent developments in manufacturing have resulted in huge changes for the purchasing function. Three different operations control techniques are now used in manufacturing: materials requirements planning (MRP), just-in-time (JIT) and optimised production technology (OPT). Materials requirements planning (MRP I) is a computerised system which establishes the amount and timing of finished goods required by customers and then determines the time-phased requirements for raw materials, components and other items. It is a system used to plan and co-ordinate materials purchases with production scheduling. MRP I requires a master production schedule outlining the quantity and timing of each item to be produced; a bill of materials which specifies the raw materials, components and other items required to produce each finished product; an inventory report detailing stocks, planned receipts and items requisitioned; and a master parts file with information on lead times of all items to be purchased or made in-house. Orders for the optimum quantities to be purchased are placed at the appropriate times with regard to the lead time required in this backward scheduling of requirements. The adoption of MRP I results in low levels of inventory, a reduction in handling costs as well as better synchronisation of purchases with production and sales. MRP I has been extended to incorporate all manufacturing resources, machine capacity, labour scheduling and materials planning (Russell and Taylor, 2005; Slack *et al.*, 2004; Wild, 2002). This extended system is known as manufacturing resource planning (or MRP II).

Just-in-time (JIT) is an operations philosophy designed to have the necessary raw materials arriving just as they are needed (just in time) for use in the production process. A key feature of JIT is its objective to reduce stock levels to an absolute minimum. To achieve this objective it seeks to match demand for finished goods with production as well as securing delivery of raw materials and components from suppliers just in time for use. The organisation becomes market led. An order for goods generates activities throughout the production system back to suppliers. JIT also seeks delivery on time, zero defects, zero breakdowns, better factory layout and the elimination of waste (anything which does not add value). Organisations using JIT systems seek to develop close co-ordination and symbiotic working relationships with suppliers and customers. The emphasis is on innovation, flexibility and rapid response to customers' needs. JIT generates other economies: reduced work-in-progress, reduced space requirements, shorter throughput times and better workflows (Christopher, 2005; Slack *et al.*, 2004).

The objective of optimised production technology (OPT) is to optimise throughput as well as decrease inventory and processing costs. It identifies bottlenecks and removes them, or at least seeks as much efficiency as possible. Virtually all manufacturing is now based on the 'pull' principle, whereby customers' orders activate the production process. In its extreme form it results in the elimination of all stocks other than work-in-progress. A good example of this development is Dell Computer Corporation, where an order generates the production process and results in delivery of the finished product within a few days. The supply chain is concerned with the process from receipt of the order to materials procurement, the production process as well as distribution to the customer. The main objectives of supply chain management are innovation and creating better value for customers (Christopher, 2005).

7.5 Quality

Concern with quality is not new. Craftspeople from the earliest times set and maintained their own standards, establishing reputations for reliability on which their livelihoods depended. These craftspeople designed and produced products to meet their customers' needs and expectations, often with great ingenuity and imagination. Thinking, doing and serving the customer were an integral process performed by the same person. The Industrial Revolution, which started in England in the eighteenth century, changed the existing agrarian handicraft economy to one dominated by industry and mass production using machinery. Production was broken down into a series of narrow repetitive tasks, each the responsibility of a specialist operative. This approach was developed further and extended during the early years of the twentieth century as a result of the work of F. W.

Taylor and his principles of scientific management (Taylor, 1911). Scientific management led to specialisation, standardisation and high productivity, but quality soon became an issue. Systems of inspection, known as quality control, were introduced, with no role for operatives. Quality control was a post facto process, designed to detect defective products before they left the factory. It was an expensive and wasteful process, often involving considerable reworking and wastage.

The recent interest in quality came from the interaction of American minds and Japanese industry during the 1950s with the work of people like W. Edwards Deming (1986), Joseph Juran (1989) and many others. During the 1970s the emphasis switched to quality assurance, which was designed to build quality into the production process and return responsibility to the workforce. Quality issues became very important in Ireland from the 1980s, influenced by world developments and customers' expectations. The National Standards Authority of Ireland (NSAI) is the Irish certification body for the harmonised European and international standards of the International Standards Organisation, Geneva (ISO 9000). An applicant organisation is required to document their quality systems, procedures and work instructions. They are assessed by the NSAI and, if approved, the organisation receives certification that it has the appropriate quality standards. Excellence Ireland operates two quality mark (Q Mark) programmes: the Quality Systems Q Mark dealing with the operational standards in a business, and the Q Mark for Business Excellence, where the emphasis is on continuous improvement.

Total quality management

The quality of a product is influenced by design features, manufacture, performance, reliability, durability and value to the customer. Total quality management (TQM) is a philosophy of continuous improvement in every aspect of an organisation's activities with the objective of supplying a quality product or service. It involves everyone and every activity in the pursuit of excellence, with the objective of continually meeting and exceeding the expectations of customers. TQM stresses that every aspect of an organisation's activities and not just the product has an effect on customers' views of quality. It acknowledges the adage that 'the customer is king' (Peters, 1987; Peters and Austin, 1986; Peters and Waterman, 1982; Quinn, 2006). Acceptance of this fact requires a complete culture change in organisations and inspires an organisation to dedicate itself to continuous improvement, with the flexibility to respond quickly to customer requirements. In this context TQM can be seen as a metaphor for the management of change within an organisation, with every person endeavouring to provide an excellent service to customers.

TQM seeks a permanent shift in the focus of an organisation from short-term expediency to long-term quality improvement. It demands constant innovation, improvement and change, which are generally achieved on an incremental basis. Sallis

(1996) claims that 'the philosophy of TQM is large-scale, inspirational and all-embracing, but its practical implementation is small-scale, highly practical and incremental'. Big schemes often founder because of bad planning, poor resourcing and inert leadership, leading to cynicism and apathy. The key elements of TQM are as follows:

- Commitment and leadership from senior management
- Planning, organisation and seeking the commitment of staff
- Developing systems and procedures for continuous improvement
- Education and training
- Involvement of all employees
- Teamwork
- Measurement and feedback
- Changing organisational culture.

The implementation of TQM requires a big change in the culture of most organisations. Effective change starts with the chief executive and permeates an organisation. TQM can flourish in an organisation with a clear vision for its future, a commitment to strategic planning, a dedication to quality in all its activities and the pursuit of continuous improvement and customer service. The provision of a quality product and/or service can establish a differential advantage for an organisation (Oakland, 1993).

World-class manufacturing

World-class manufacturing (WCM), according to Schonberger (1986), is a term which describes 'the breadth and the essence of fundamental changes taking place in larger industrial enterprises'. Its primary objective is to enable an organisation to establish and maintain a competitive advantage in the marketplace by operational excellence. Features include continuous quality improvement, cellular plant/work organisation, flexible multi-skilled staff, employee empowerment, shorter delivery times, building close collaborative customer and supplier relationships, integrated information systems, automation, equipment maintenance, lean manufacturing and cost improvements, with extensive training and development. Together with improved information technology and production processes, WCM places a big emphasis on greater employee involvement, long-term symbiotic relationships with suppliers and customers, quality, value and customer satisfaction (Keegan, 1997). Some organisations require more than continuous improvement to compete effectively. They require business process re-engineering (BPR), defined by Hammer and Champy (1994) as:

> the fundamental rethinking and redesign of business processes to achieve dramatic improvements in critical, contemporary measures of performance, such as cost, quality, service, and speed.

of the process is to 're-invent the business', with a big emphasis on customer response, flexibility and empowerment.

7.6 Research and development

Many organisations have a research and development function, often based in the operations department, focused on creativity, innovation and intrapreneurship. Innovation involves the introduction of new ideas which add value for an organisation and its customers and can relate to technical, managerial, process or product developments. The two big drivers of innovation are changing market needs and new technology. Most innovations are incremental in nature; others involve radical changes and can result in doing different things or doing things in a different and more effective way. Bellon and Whittington (1996) state that innovation 'involves an attitude of mind that is always seeking to improve, that responds to customer needs, and that aims to get ahead of the competition and stay there'. Innovation incorporates new perspectives for existing products or services, leading to additional uses, better design, improved processes and the development of new products. Irish industrial policy is now focused on research and development, innovation, quality, productivity and added value as well as developing sustainable competitive advantage leading to profitable sales, exports and employment. The big emphasis is now on knowledge-based research and innovation to establish and maintain a national competitive advantage.

7.7 New product development

Product development is not the prerogative of new businesses alone, as most new products are developed by existing businesses because of the competence and resources required. Companies appreciate that their future survival and growth depend on the development of new or improved products to cater for the changing needs of customers. In the food sector, demand is changing to organic, low-fat, low-salt, low-cholesterol products. Continuous innovation is the only way to avoid obsolescence and secure the future. Many new products are technology led, but no development can ignore the marketplace. A market approach uses new technologies to meet the changing needs of customers or solve their problems better and cheaper than competing products. The emphasis is on the development of a differentiated product which can provide unique benefits to customers and better value than competitors. New product development has to have a strong customer focus, targeted at a large and growing market, preferably with export potential. It is not an easy process; the risks are high and, in many cases, the rewards modest. A large number of planned new products never reach the marketplace, and some that are launched do not survive for long. Some of this failure can be explained by inadequate research, poor screening, higher than expected costs, bad planning and, in many cases, a complete lack of commercial potential. Successful products are required to recoup the expenditure of those that do not succeed, but they can also quickly attract competitors unless protected by patents or trade marks. To reduce the risk of failure, a proposed new product is generally subjected to a seven-stage evaluation before being approved (Figure 7.1). The purpose of each successive stage is to decide whether the idea should be abandoned or developed further.

Figure 7.1: New product development process

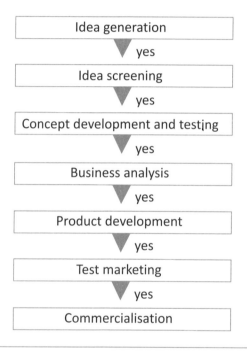

Source: Adapted from Booz-Allen and Hamilton (1982) and Kotler (2003)

a)   Idea generation

The purpose of idea generation is to suggest a number of proposals for the development of new products. The more ideas put forward, the better the chance of identifying a good one. In some cases business ideas emerge spontaneously from various people both inside and outside a business, such as staff, customers, suppliers, distributors and even competitors. They can come from anyone provided that a progressive, innovative culture is fostered. Feedback from sales and marketing personnel on customers' changing requirements is very important, as is monitoring competitors, suggestion schemes, brainstorming sessions, trade journals and exhibitions of the latest technology. Some companies adopt a more systematic approach in their search for new products with the establishment of special teams or a research and development department to consider suggestions and to take a proactive role in seeking ideas. Marketing theory tells us that customers' changing needs and wants should be the starting point in the search for ideas. A group exercise in brainstorming is often very fruitful in generating ideas. Those present are asked for suggestions, the wilder the better, and all ideas are listed and considered. No criticism or evaluation are permitted at a brainstorming session. The strategy adopted is generally an analysis of the existing industry and market, an assessment of internal resources and capabilities and the identification of potential innovation and/or new products.

b)   Idea screening

Screening involves assessing all the ideas put forward and selecting those deemed to have the most potential for more careful consideration. Each proposal is evaluated under a number of key factors on a checklist, chiefly market needs, company competence to undertake the project, supplies, production facilities and financial requirements. It is in a company's interest to abandon ideas at an early stage which do not appear to be commercially viable or compatible with its production, marketing, financial and staffing resources. Market demand, compatibility and competence to undertake the venture are the three most important criteria used in the screening of proposed new products. It is very important to know the needs of customers in the target market and how the new product can offer unique benefits when compared with competitors.

c)   Concept development and testing

An innovative idea (a proposal for a possible product) has to be developed into a product concept. A consumer does not buy a product; he/she buys an expectation of some benefits, which are known as product concepts. Most ideas can be developed into a range of product concepts by asking questions regarding potential users and benefits they expect. A business has to consider the possible concepts and select one which offers good commercial potential.

Once the product concept is chosen, the market positioning and competitive environment faced by it become obvious. The company has to consider how it could compete in that market and carve out a unique niche. Concept testing involves showing the product to groups of consumers in the target market and seeking their reactions. The business is interested in feedback on the concept itself, the benefits it offers over competing products, whether it meets consumers' specific needs, whether these consumers would purchase it and any recommendations for improvement (Kotler, 2003). In addition to researching consumers' views on the relative advantages of a new product over existing competition, further valuable information can be gathered in relation to price, promotion and distribution.

The competitive environment faced by a new product in terms of existing suppliers, prices and marketing policies has to be assessed in an effort to establish some unique differential advantage. The information enables an organisation to prepare a draft marketing strategy for the targeted market.

d) Business analysis

Under business analysis, the expected sales, costs and financial return from the proposed new product are estimated and evaluated. These key measures are also assessed throughout the remaining stages of this process as new information becomes available. Estimating sales is difficult and it is carried out by feedback from the concept testing, surveys, previous experience, general market information and the nature of the product. With regard to the market, the following are key factors: duration of consumers' needs, frequency of the needs, stage in life cycle of proposed product, market size, rate of penetration, possible market share and the demand cycle (Kotler, 2003). Products can be one-off purchases, infrequent or frequent purchases, each of which has different sales cycles. Estimates are prepared for the most optimistic, most pessimistic and likely outcomes. Once sales are estimated, costs are easier to predict as most are related to sales volume. Marketing costs can be high for a new product. After estimating fixed costs, profitability indicators are calculated and cash flow forecasts prepared, with the expected return compared with the alternatives available.

e) Product development

When a product concept is considered to be commercially viable, it is developed as a prototype, tested, branded and packaged. A prototype involves production of the product specified in the concept. This is then tested by asking some potential consumers (or panels of consumers) for their reactions, which are assessed, leading to revision and further improvement.

The brand name selected has to reinforce the product concept (its benefits to the consumer) and be distinctive, simple, easy to remember and pronounce as well as suggesting the key attributes of the product (Kotler, 2003). Packaging, an important element of new product development, has to be attractive, economical, convenient, promotional and attract the attention of consumers as well as promoting the desired image (Kotler, 2003). The packaging also has to be tested by potential intermediaries and consumers.

f) Test marketing

In test marketing the proposed new product is tried out in a number of carefully chosen sales outlets in various locations. The objectives are to acquire additional knowledge from potential customers, experiment with different promotions, identify the reactions in different locations, if any, and to get feedback from the trade. This gives some indication of the level of acceptance by customers and an indication of possible successful commercialisation.

g)   Commercialisation

If the test marketing gives positive feedback, which is no guarantee of success, the final stage is commercialisation. This involves organising the required resources for the production schedule as well as the marketing and managerial operations to launch the product in the marketplace. Some new products are not commercial successes; a well-publicised example was Guinness Light, a light stout targeted at women launched in 1978, which had to be withdrawn because of poor sales.

7.8 Value chain

Porter (1985) proposed the value chain as a means of identifying ways to increase customer value. Customers are always interested in what they perceive to be value, and organisations respond by either increasing total customer value or decreasing total cost. Value chain analysis involves identifying the activities that have to be performed in designing, producing, marketing and delivering a product or service. Porter's value chain identifies nine strategic activities that create value and cost in an organisation, consisting of five primary and four support activities. The primary activities represent the sequence of bringing materials into the business (inbound logistics), producing products (operations), supplying finished products (outbound logistics), marketing (marketing and sales) and servicing them (service). The support activities are procurement, technology development, human resource management and a firm's infrastructure (general management). An organisation has to examine the costs and performance of each activity and seek improvements. It has to consider the costs and performances of its competitors as benchmarks against which to measure its own, with the objective of achieving a competitive advantage. There is a big emphasis on the effective management of core business processes, new product development, inventory management, customer acquisition and retention, order-to-remittance activities and overall customer service.

7.9 Insurance

Insurance is a contract whereby an insurer undertakes to indemnify the insured against some loss caused by a risk covered by the agreement in return for a payment known as the premium. The details of an insurance contract are specified in a document called a policy. Insurance covers risks which may happen, whereas an assurance policy covers an event which will happen, for example death.

Insurance contracts contain a number of special provisions: insurable interest, *uberrimae fidei*, indemnity, average clause, subrogation and the principle of contribution (Doolan, 2007).

- Insurable interest means that the insured must have some legal interest in the risk insured.

- Contracts of insurance are said to be *uberrimae fidei*, 'of the utmost good faith', which means that all material facts relating to the risk must be disclosed prior to the agreement.

- A contract of insurance is one of indemnity, meaning that the insured cannot recover more than the actual loss incurred. An insured person cannot make a profit from insurance.

- Insurance contracts relating to property contain an average clause, under which the loss covered is proportional to the actual sum insured related to the total value. For example, if a person incurs a loss of €100,000 arising from damage to a premises with a market value of €400,000 but only insured for €200,000, the insurance company will reimburse only €50,000 (only half the value of the premises was insured). The purpose of the average clause is to prevent under-insurance.

- Under subrogation, the insurer can take over the legal rights of the insured against any person or organisation responsible for the loss.

- The principle of contribution means a fair apportionment of a loss between insurers where the insured has taken out more than one policy to cover the same risk.

A business has different types of insurance cover: buildings, contents, burglary/theft, motor vehicles, employer's liability, public liability, product liability if necessary, professional indemnity cover where applicable, as well as consequential loss (to make good any loss arising from interruption to the business because of a fire or other causes). Under the Road Traffic Act 1961, a person cannot drive a motor vehicle in a public place unless insured for injury caused to third parties. It is good practice to get quotations for all types of insurance. Many self-employed people also take out permanent health insurance to provide incomes for themselves if they are unable to work.

7.10 Legal issues relating to goods, services and competition

This section looks at the following:
a) Sales of goods and services
b) Competition.

a) Sales of goods and services

Contracts for the sale of goods and supply of services are modified by statute law, the Sale of Goods Act 1893 as amended by the Sale of Goods and Supply of Services Act 1980 and secondary legislation resulting from EU directives. This legislation provides for implied terms in all consumer contracts, where businesses sell goods and offer services for personal use or consumption. These implied terms include the following:

- That the seller has good title and a right to sell the goods
- That where goods are sold by description, they shall correspond with the description
- That goods sold are of 'merchantable quality' with regard to their expected use and durability
- That they are fit for their purpose
- That if goods are purchased from a sample, they should correspond with the sample.

In respect of services where the provider is acting in the course of business, the following terms are implied:

- That the supplier has the necessary skill to provide the service
- That the service will be provided with due care and diligence
- That materials used in the service are of merchantable quality
- That the service is fit for its purpose (Doolan, 2007; Keenan, 2008).

If a guarantee is given it usually provides that the manufacturer or supplier will repair or replace any defective part without charge during the specified period.

Under the Consumer Protection Act 2007 it is an offence for any retailer or professional to make false or misleading claims about goods, services or prices. This includes weight, ingredients and performance.

The National Consumer Agency (NCA) was established in 2007 to provide advice and information to consumers on their rights and to enforce the legislation. It does not become involved in individual disputes between consumers and sellers of goods or providers of services.

b) Competition

The main legislation dealing with competition in Ireland is the Competition Act 2002 as amended in 2006 and the substantive rules contained in Articles 81 and 82 of the EC Treaty, which cover anti-competitive arrangements and the abuse of dominance, respectively. The law refers to 'the relevant market', the product and geographic market in which the competitive practices take place. The market is considered from the demand side of customers and the supply side of suppliers (Collins, 2006).

Section 4(1) of the Competition Act 2002 prohibits anti-competitive arrangements and declares prohibited arrangements to be void. It states:

> Subject to the provisions of this section, all agreements between undertakings, decisions by associations of undertakings and concerted practices which have as their object or effect the prevention, restriction or distortion of competition in trade in any

goods or services in the State or in any part of the State are prohibited and void, including in particular, without prejudice to the generality of this subsection, those which –

a) directly or indirectly fix purchase or selling prices or any other trading conditions;

b) limit or control production, markets, technical developments or investment;

c) share markets or sources of supply;

d) apply dissimilar conditions to equivalent transactions with other trading parties thereby placing them on a competitive disadvantage;

e) make the conclusion of contracts subject to acceptance by the other parties of supplementary obligations, which by their nature or according to commercial usage have no connection with the subject of such contracts.

There are limited exceptions to this provision, for example where the agreement complies with the efficiency conditions of the legislation or a declaration issued by the Competition Authority. Section 5 (1) of the 2002 Act, which is based on article 82, provides as follows:

Any abuse by one or more undertakings of a dominant position in trade for any goods or services in the State or any part of the State is prohibited.

There is a responsibility on dominant businesses to ensure that they do not engage in behaviour that prevents competition. Issues to be considered in this respect are market share, any barriers to entry, barriers to expansion, customer switching costs, the ability of an allegedly dominant firm to act independently of its competitors and countervailing buyer power (Collins, 2006). Examples of the abuse of dominance include the imposition of unfair purchase or selling prices, refusal to supply or deal, applying different conditions to equivalent transactions with other trading parties, making contracts subject to acceptance of other supplementary obligations which have no connection, price fixing, exclusive arrangements and loyalty rebates.

The Competition Authority, which was established under the 2002 Act, is responsible for the enforcement of competition law, adjudicating on mergers and promoting competition.

7.11 Summary

Operations management covers the range of activities required to transform various resource inputs into marketable products or services. It incorporates securing a suitable premises and ensuring that all legal and regulatory requirements are observed.

The main function is operations planning and control: the process of establishing production plans, scheduling the resources required, implementing and monitoring actual performance against the standards set. Good design, innovation and the adoption of modern advanced manufacturing technologies can create competitive advantages for organisations. These advanced technologies include computer-aided design, manufacturing, engineering, planning and control systems.

Another function of operations management is supply chain management, the process by which the needs of customers are satisfied through the co-ordination of orders, suppliers, operations and distribution, with big developments in the application of modern technologies. The quality of a product or service is influenced by design, manufacture, performance, reliability, durability, value to the customer and continuous improvement.

Research and development has a major role in innovation and new product development, with each stage outlined from idea generation to commercialisation. Porter's value chain concept (1985) is designed to increase customer value. Insurance is an important issue. The legal aspects of the sale of goods and services have to be considered as well as the implications of the Competition Act 2002, which prohibits anti-competitive arrangements and abuse of a dominant position in the relevant market.

Questions

1.   Discuss the main issues to be considered in the selection of a premises for a business.
2.   Explain the chief elements of operations planning and control.
3.   Assess the main issues involved in supply chain management.
4.   Explain the concept of total quality management.
5.   Discuss the process of new product development.

Chapter 8

Employing staff

*A man of genius makes no mistakes. His errors are volitional and
are the portals of discovery.*

James Joyce

Learning objectives

* To provide an introduction to human resource management
* To comprehend the recruitment process
* To explore relevant employment legislation
* To appreciate the main issues in pay, conditions and staff development
* To consider the role of the various State organisations involved in employee relations.

This chapter is structured as follows:

8.1   Introduction to human resource management
8.2   Recruitment and selection (employee resourcing)
8.3   Employment law
8.4   Pay and conditions (reward management)
8.5   Staff development (employee development)
8.6   Employment relations (employee relations)
8.7   Summary

8.1 Introduction to human resource management

Human resource management (HRM) is a strategic, proactive, integrated, long-term approach to the management of staff. Whereas traditional personnel management was seen as managing an adversarial relationship in the workplace, human resource management is intended to be unitarist in nature, with a shared vision of the future. As the pace of change accelerates in a global marketplace based on high-technology communications, knowledge and learning, employers require staff with new mindsets who are focused on strategic goals, results, customer service, continuous learning, flexibility, innovation, change, enterprise, teamwork and the creation of mutually beneficial partnerships. Employers like employees who work with them rather than for them.

According to the Enterprise Strategy Group (2004):

> Employees who take responsibility for their work and its contribution to the company, who see it as their role to identify problems and solutions, who try to find ways to operate more efficiently and who work with their fellow employees and their employer to enhance the productivity of the business are particularly valuable, and especially so as the business becomes more knowledge-based.

This new approach is based on trust, empowerment, initiative and commitment to the achievement of personal and organisational goals. Effective, competent, highly motivated and customer-focused staff can give a competitive advantage to any organisation.

8.2 Recruitment and selection

The process of recruitment and selection is concerned with attracting and assessing candidates for employment. The process involves five stages:

a)   Human resource planning
b)   Job analysis
c)   Recruitment
d)   Selection
e)   Induction.

a)   Human resource planning

Competent staff with positive attitudes and good personalities who are committed to delivering a professional service are invaluable to an organisation. Consequently, the recruitment and training of such staff are a very important part of management. Human resource planning is an integral part of strategic management. It involves an accurate profile of existing staff (where applicable); a forecast of the staffing required in terms of number, qualifications, skills, experience and adaptability; and the strategic direction of the organisation. From this analysis, a human resource plan is prepared. The filling of any vacancy arising from resignation or retirement has to be considered in the context of the strategic and human resource plans. Some vacancies can be filled internally by redeployment, retraining or promotions, provided suitable staff are available. There are strong arguments in favour of this approach, as it has the capacity to motivate internal staff.

b)   Job analysis

Job analysis consists of identifying the key components of a job and the skills, competencies and attributes required for its satisfactory performance. Arising from this analysis, it is possible to prepare a job description and a person specification. A job description is a statement of the purpose, scope, duties, responsibilities and reporting relationship in a particular job. A person specification is a description of the ideal person for a specific vacancy. It includes minimum qualifications, desirable qualifications, prior experience, specific skills, competencies, aptitudes, interests and the personal attributes that are required (Gunnigle *et al.*, 2006). In practice it is common to find the person specification included in the job description.

c)   Recruitment

Recruitment is the process of inviting candidates to apply for a specific vacancy. This involves the preparation of a job advertisement which outlines the key features of a post, the application procedure and the closing date. All posts must be open to men and women, married or single. A post can be filled by internal competition amongst existing staff, by external recruitment or by advertising it internally and externally. The main methods used for external recruitment depend on whether the job is in the public or private sector as well as the nature and level of the post. All permanent jobs in the public sector are publicly advertised, a requirement which does not apply in the private sector. As a result, a large number of private sector jobs are not advertised in the public media. Sources of external supply include personal recommendations, schools, colleges, FÁS, employment agencies and public advertisements on a website, local radio, local and national newspapers, specialised journals and magazines.

An applicant is required to complete a standardised application form and/or submit a curriculum vitae (CV). The information required includes name, address, telephone number, email address, education, qualifications, membership of trade or professional bodies, employment history, achievements, interests, names of two or more referees, signature and date. The next step in the process is screening, when all applications are considered and those deemed not qualified or unsuitable are eliminated from the competition. As the selection system used by most organisations involves interviews, the number of applications is reduced to about six or eight in respect of each post. The chief criteria used for shortlisting are qualifications, experience and the competencies required. The screening and shortlisting are carried out by at least two people, with their reasons for decisions recorded and retained, together with the scoring system used. The first stage in the selection process for some organisations is psychometric testing to assess ability and personality.

d)   Selection

Selection means choosing the most suitable applicant for a post. The chief method used is to interview all candidates on the shortlist. This involves selecting an interview board, which usually consists of three (and sometimes more) people – a personnel specialist, the head of the department requiring the employee – and an expert in the activity in question, with both genders represented. All members should receive appropriate training in conducting competency-based interviews and relevant employment law. A marking scheme is prepared before the interviews with the relative weighting of the specified competence criteria. Members of the board prepare for the interview by reading the documentation submitted by the candidates on the shortlist and establish a clear understanding of the ideal type of person required from the job description.

Interviewers generally explore topics like the nature of work experience; responsibility; achievements; how well a candidate performed in previous roles; problems and how they were dealt with; mistakes made and what was learned from them; personal strengths and weaknesses; relationships with superiors, colleagues, subordinates and the general public; reasons for changing jobs; and skills, knowledge and competencies required for the post in question, all of which depend on the nature of the job. The members of the interview board are individually allocated responsibility for various aspects of the interview – one person dealing with qualifications, attainments, skills and special aptitudes, a second with prior experience and interests, the third with disposition and the specific requirements of the post. Candidates are assessed in respect of all the competence criteria specified. All members must be familiar with the equality legislation and ensure that no discriminatory questions are asked or any undesirable comments made. The task of the interview board is to identify the most suitable candidate for the job and rank others deemed suitable in order of merit, based on actual achievements and competencies. Written records of all interviews are kept, including a marking sheet for each candidate and notes taken during the interview, with evidence of achievements and competencies. In some cases, interviews are supplemented by special requirements like psychometric tests.

After the interviews a report is prepared with unanimous recommendations on a ranking of the candidates deemed suitable for approval by the human resource department or board of directors, depending on the nature of the post. The first candidate is then asked to submit evidence of qualifications if not already submitted, two character references (many employers request references prior to the interview) and for some employments, a medical examination is required. If the documentation, references and medical result are satisfactory, with regard to the provisions of the Employment Acts 1998 and 2004 regarding disability, the recommendations of the interview board are approved and the post is offered to the candidate ranked first.

Many job offers clearly specify the performance expectations for the post. A contract of employment is prepared, with all terms required by the Terms of Employment (Information) Acts 1994 and 2001, as well as clauses providing for flexibility and variation of duties from time to time, duration of probation, confidentiality (if applicable), grievance procedures, disciplinary procedures, the right to lay a person off or place him/her on short time due to temporary shortage of work (if relevant) and any other essential item. When the terms are agreed, the contract of employment is signed by both parties. The new employee is then asked to report for duty on a specified date and letters of regret are sent to the unsuccessful candidates. Instead of the traditional full-time job, several flexible work options are now in operation to facilitate better management of families and careers. These include job sharing, flexitime, term-time working, contracts for regular part-time work, career breaks, parental leave, enhanced unpaid maternity leave, paternity leave, carer's leave, emergency annual leave (for urgent domestic matters) and working from home using modern information and communications technology (teleworking), a rapidly developing trend in the EU. Family-friendly work arrangements are now one of the ways to attract and retain staff. In respect of temporary contracts, employees are informed of the purpose of the posts, their duration and the circumstances under which they will be terminated.

e)   Induction

When the successful candidate reports for duty he/she is required to undertake an induction course, which varies from business to business and with the nature of the post. It includes an introduction to the organisation, its history, mission, strategic plan, organisation, culture, health and safety obligations, regulations, pay and conditions, policies, procedures, rules, security and the necessary paperwork for tax and other matters, as well as specific training relating to the actual post and the culture, beliefs, ethos and standards of the business. Induction training is an activity which in the words of William Shakespeare is 'more honoured in the breach than the observance', but it is an essential element of good management practice. The socialisation of new employees into an organisation is important and can be facilitated by informal support networks, some of which emerge spontaneously in every organisation and others that are established for that purpose.

Most new employees are enthusiastic and it is important that good working relations are established from the start. The role of a person in a managerial capacity is crucial to this relationship. He/she has to have good interpersonal skills and develop a culture of respect, trust, fairness, ethical values and high standards. A new employee has to be integrated into an effective united team focused on achieving specified targets and objectives. The modern emphasis is on flexible teamwork with a high degree of autonomy. A good working environment is facilitated by listening, consultation, communications, influencing and empowerment. All employers want employees with a progressive 'can do' approach, focused on objectives, customer service, continuous learning, teamwork, innovation and building mutually beneficial working relationships.

8.3 Employment law

Once employment commences, the concern moves to compliance with employment law, pay and conditions (reward management), staff development (employee development) and managing the employment relationship (employee relations). (For a comprehensive treatment of the recruitment process and each of these concerns, see Gunnigle *et al.*, 2006.)

A contract of employment can be established by an express written agreement (the recommended procedure), by oral agreement or can be inferred from the conduct of the parties. It can be very difficult to prove the provisions of an oral agreement in the event of a dispute. A contract involves an offer, unconditional acceptance, consideration and the intention to create legal relations. There are two types of legal agreement for the provision of labour: a contract of service and a contract for service. The distinction is important for many reasons, chiefly because most of the protective labour legislation applies only to employees, but there are also major taxation, PRSI, insurance and other implications. In a contract of service the relationship is that of employer and employee, whereas in a contract for service the relationship is that of employer and independent contractor, where a person is self-employed and responsible for the provision of the necessary equipment, the administration of his/her own taxation, insurance and other requirements. A self-employed person usually works for a number of different employers, organising and managing his/her own activities, whereas an employee provides exclusive service to one employer in almost all cases. The terms of a contract for service are agreed by the participating parties.

It is sometimes quite difficult to establish whether a contract of employment is one of service or for service, and this has given rise to a substantial volume of litigation over the years. Each case is considered as a whole on its unique features, including working conditions, the reality of the relationship and extent to which the staff member is integrated into the business. However, a number of tests are used, including control, integration and whether the person performing the work does so as a person in business on his/her own account. The big question is who decides what, when, where and how the work will be done. Is the job integrated into the business with the employer providing all tools and equipment? In this case the relationship is likely to be that of employer and employee (a contract of service). If the person works for a number of organisations, provides his/her own tools and equipment and agrees a price or fee for each work assignment, it can generally be assumed that the relationship is with an independent contractor. It is not a matter for the parties involved to state that a contract of employment is one of service or for service. By its nature, it is either one or the other (see Table 8.1). In the event of a legal challenge to any such agreement, the courts will consider all aspects of the employment before reaching a decision.

Table 8.1: A contract of service contrasted with a contract for service

Relationship	Employer/employee	Employer/independent contractor
Work classification	Employee	Self-employed
Duration	Continuous as per the contract	Specific work assignment
Organisation and control	Employer decides what, how, when the work will be done	Independent contractor controls how and when the work will be done within the terms of the agreement
Tools and equipment	Provided by employer	Provided by independent contractor
Protective employment legislation	Applies to contracts of service	Does not apply to the independent contractor (except in respect of employees of that person)
Payment	Regular wage/salary	Contract price/fee/exposed to financial risk
Hours of work	Determined by employer	Discretion of the individual
Vicarious liability	Employer liable for vicarious acts of employees (any wrong or injury done in the course of their employment)	Employer has no liability for wrongs and injuries done by an independent contractor
Taxation	PAYE/PRSI and the Universal Social Charge deducted by employer	Self-assessment
PRSI	Employer and employee liable at the appropriate rates	Independent contractor liable for the self-employed rate
Insurance	Employer's liability	Independent contractor carries his/her own insurance
Pension arrangement	Occupational pension scheme or a nominated Personal Retirement Savings Account (PRSA) provider	Retirement annuity contract

Terms of employment

The terms of a contract of employment (of service) can originate from a number of sources, for example those agreed by both parties, terms implied by common law (general rights and duties which are now part of every such contract), terms implied by statutes (protective legislation in respect of a floor of minimum rights, equality legislation, safety law), collective agreements (national, industry or company) or terms derived from custom and practice for the industry. Once agreed the contract can be altered by agreement, acquiescence (going along with some change without challenge) or in accordance with its provisions. Before looking at pay, employment legislation, which is now very extensive, is considered. Employment legislation enacted since the 1970s has provided a floor of minimum entitlements for all employees, which are implied in all contracts of employment whether stated or not. Contracts of employment can provide for better terms, but they cannot be less than the statutory minimum specified in the relevant legislation. Some current employment rights evolved from the common law, judge-made law based on judicial precedents and previous legislation. The Department of Enterprise, Trade and Innovation has produced an excellent summary of the main employment legislation in its *Guide to Labour Law* (2007) which is an invaluable source.

The following legislation is considered below (but these details are not intended as complete):

a)   Minimum Notice and Terms of Employment Acts 1973–2001
b)   Terms of Employment (Information) Acts 1994–2001
c)   Redundancy Payment Acts 1967–2007
d)   Protection of Employment Act 1977
e)   Protection of Employees on Transfer of Undertakings Regulations 2003
f)   Payment of Wages Act 1991
g)   Unfair Dismissal Acts 1977–2001
h)   Protection of Employees (Part-Time Work) Act 2001
i)   Maternity Protection Acts 1994 and 2004
j)   Adoptive Leave Act 1995
k)   Protection of Young Persons (Employment) Act 1996
l)   Organisation of Working Time Act 1977
m)   Safety, Health and Welfare at Work Act 2005
n)   Protection of Employees (Employers' Insolvency) Acts 1984–2004
o)   National Minimum Wage Act 2000
p)   Parental Leave Acts 1998 and 2006
q)   Carer's Leave Act 2001
r)   Public Health (Tobacco) Act 2002 and 2004
s)   Protection of Employees (Fixed-Term Work) Act 2003
t)   Employment Equality Acts 1998–2007
u)   Equal Status Acts 2000 and 2004
v)   Employment Permits Acts 2003–2006
w)   Employees (Provision of Information and Consultation) Act 2006
x)   Employment Law Compliance Bill 2008.

a)   Minimum Notice and Terms of Employment Acts 1973–2001

The Minimum Notice and Terms of Employment Acts 1973–2001, as amended by the Protection of Employment (Part-Time Work) Act 2001, specify minimum periods of notice to be given by employers and employees when terminating a contract of employment. These Acts apply to employees with at least 13 weeks' continuous service with the same employer.

The minimum period of notice varies according to length of service as follows:

Length of service	Minimum notice
Thirteen weeks to two years	One week
Two to five years	Two weeks
Five to 10 years	Four weeks
Ten to 15 years	Six weeks
More than 15 years	Eight weeks

An employer is entitled to at least one week's notice from employees with more than 13 weeks' service. Any employer or employee can waive his/her right to notice and accept payment in lieu. However, the Acts do not prevent either party from terminating a contract of employment without notice due to the misconduct of the other party. Any dispute about these Acts can be referred to the Employment Appeals Tribunal (EAT).

b)   Terms of Employment (Information) Acts 1994 and 2001

These Acts require employers to provide a written statement to employees outlining certain terms of their employment within two months of the date of commencement, or after being requested to do so by those whose employment commenced before 16 May 1994. The particulars required are:

- Name of employee
- Name and address of employer
- Place of work
- Job title or nature of work
- Date employment commenced
- If a temporary contract, its expected duration
- If a fixed-term contract, date when the contract expires
- The rate of remuneration
- Whether remuneration is to be paid weekly, monthly or otherwise
- Terms and conditions relating to hours of work including overtime, rest break entitlements, paid leave, sick or injury leave, pension scheme arrangements
- Period of notice to be given before terminating employment by employer and employee
- The pay reference period in relation to the National Minimum Wage Act 2000
- Information that an employee is entitled to request a statement of his/her average hourly rate of pay for any pay reference period in the previous 12 months
- Any provision(s) in a collective agreement which affects the terms of employment. The statement must be signed by the proprietor or manager and a copy kept (Department of Enterprise, Trade and Employment, 2005).

With regard to remuneration and conditions of employment, the employer can, as an alternative to providing the information, refer the employee to any relevant employment agreement, for example an employment regulation order of the Labour Court, an employment agreement registered in the Labour Court or a collective agreement, provided the information is reasonably accessible. An employee under 18 must also be provided with a copy of the official summary of the Protection of Young Persons (Employment) Act 1996 within one month of taking up employment. There is no legal obligation on employers to pay employees who are absent from work due to sickness or injury, but it can be provided for in a contract of employment. Employers specify the procedures to be followed in relation to grievances, disciplinary issues, equality, bullying and harassment. An employer is obliged to notify an employee of any change in the written statement within one month of the change taking effect. Any complaint with regard to the Act can be referred to a Rights Commissioner, with a right of appeal by either party to the Employment Appeals Tribunal.

c)   Redundancy Payments Acts 1967–2007

These Acts oblige employers to pay compensation to certain employees who are dismissed because of redundancy (where their jobs cease to exist for any reason). To qualify for a lump sum payment, an employee must have two years' continuous service with the same employer after the age of 16 and have his/her employment terminated because of redundancy. Following the enactment of the Protection of Employment (Part-Time Work) Act 2001, part-time employees are now also eligible. The statutory redundancy lump sum is an aggregate of the following:

- Two weeks' pay for each year of service under the Acts, subject to an overall ceiling per week
- A bonus of a week's gross pay, subject to the overall statutory ceiling (for current rates, see www.entemp.ie).

The statutory lump sum must be paid by an employer, but he/she is entitled to a rebate of 60 per cent from the Social Insurance Fund, provided two weeks' notice is given to the employee on the prescribed form (RP50 part A), with a copy to the Department of Enterprise, Trade and Innovation. When the actual dismissal takes place the employee must be given a redundancy certificate (RP50 part B). To claim the rebate, an employer is obliged to submit the prescribed form (RP50) to the Department, together with a copy of the redundancy certificate. Any dispute under these Acts can be referred to the Employment Appeals Tribunal within one year. An employer and an employee can agree a payment in excess of the statutory minimum.

d) Protection of Employment Act 1977

This Act, as amended, obliges employers who are planning collective redundancies to notify the Minister for Enterprise, Trade and Innovation and employees' representatives as soon as possible but at least 30 days before the first dismissal takes place. Employers are obliged to consult with these representatives, or with the employees where there is no trade union, regarding the particular employees to be made redundant and how the proposals can be avoided or their effects mitigated. A collective redundancy means the dismissal for reasons of redundancy over any period of 30 consecutive days of at least:

- Five persons in an organisation employing more than 20 and less than 50
- 10 persons in an organisation employing between 50 to 100
- 10 per cent of employees in an organisation employing between 100 and 300
- 30 persons in an organisation employing 300 or more (*Guide to Labour Law*).

A complaint under this Act can be made to a Rights Commissioner, with a right of appeal to the Employment Appeals Tribunal. The Protection of Employment (Exceptional Collective Redundancies and Related Matters) Act 2007 was enacted to deal with collective redundancies on a compulsory basis where the employees are replaced on inferior terms.

e) Protection of Employees on Transfer of Undertakings Regulations 2003

These regulations are designed to protect the rights of employees in the event of the transfer of ownership of an undertaking or a part of it. They provide that the rights and obligations of the original owner (the transferor) under an employment contract shall be transferred to the new owner (the transferee). Following a transfer, the transferee must continue to observe these terms and conditions until they expire or a new agreement comes into effect, except for occupational pensions where special regulations apply. A transfer of an undertaking does not in itself constitute grounds for dismissal. Representatives of the employees of both organisations must be informed in good time (normally more than 30 days) before a transfer is carried out, together with the reasons and the implications. A complaint under these regulations can be referred to a Rights Commissioner within six months, with a right of appeal to the Employment Appeals Tribunal.

f) Payment of Wages Act 1991

This Act provides that every employee has a right to a readily negotiable mode of wage payment, a right to a written statement of gross pay with all deductions itemised (payslip) and protection against unlawful deductions by employers. Under the Act, wages can be paid by cheque, bank draft, postal/money order, credit transfer, cash or any other specified mode of payment. Payment by electronic Paypath, where the net amount due is paid directly into an employee's bank account, is now a common practice, but a payslip has to be given to the employee itemising all deductions. The Act applies to any person working under a contract of employment or apprenticeship or through an employment agency or subcontractor.

Deductions from gross pay can only be made where authorised by law (PAYE, PRSI), or authorised by the employee in a contract of employment (pension contribution) or made with his/her written consent (health insurance deduction, trade union subscription). Special restrictions are placed on employers in relation to any other deduction from wages which arise from a penalty or in respect of the supply of any goods or services to the employee. Complaints relating to the non-provision of payslips can be made to the Labour Inspectorate and those concerning unlawful deductions can be referred to a Rights Commissioner.

g)   Unfair Dismissals Acts 1977–2001

These Acts, which apply to most employees, provide protection against unfair dismissal and a system of redress if required. The following are the main exceptions from the protection of the legislation: those who have less than one year's continuous service (except for reasons of pregnancy, adoption, trade union membership or exercising some statutory rights), employees who have reached retirement age, those who work for a close relative in a private house or on a farm, members of the defence forces, gardaí, and some State employees, and the termination of apprenticeships or training at the completion of the specified terms. The Acts also exclude a contract of employment for a fixed term (a fixed-term contract), or for a specified purpose of limited duration (a special purpose contract), provided that it is in writing, signed by both parties and that it contains a clause that the Acts shall not apply. Such contracts are now covered by the Protection of Employees (Fixed-Term Work) Act 2003 (see below). However, since 1 October 1993 a series of two or more contracts of employment, between which there is no more than a three-month break, may be considered to have existed for the purpose of avoiding liability under the Acts, when they will be added together to calculate continuous service. The Acts do not apply to an employee who is informed in writing at the commencement of his/her employment that it will terminate when another employee who is availing of some statutory leave entitlement returns.

The Acts provide that every dismissal of an employee will be presumed to have been unfair unless the employer can show substantial grounds justifying it. This means that the onus of proof is on the employer. To justify a dismissal, an employer must show that it resulted from one or more of the following reasons:

- The capability (for example persistent absence due to ill health), competence or qualifications (for example holding a clean driving licence) of the employee for the work she/he was employed to do
- The employee's conduct
- Redundancy (provided that it is genuine redundancy and the employee was not unfairly selected ahead of others with less service)

- The fact that continuation of the employment would contravene another statutory requirement
- Other substantial grounds justifying the dismissal (s 6.4 Unfair Dismissals Act 1977).

Evidence of other substantial grounds justifying dismissal can be admitted at subsequent proceedings.

The legislation requires an employer to give an employee a written statement within 28 days of taking up employment of the procedures that will be followed if a question of dismissal arises. An employer is obliged, if required, to give an employee the reasons for his/her dismissal in writing within 14 days. An employee's conduct can be a reason for dismissal, but only the most serious cases would justify summary or instant dismissal (see below under disciplinary procedures). With respect to any lack of competence, an employee has to be informed and given a reasonable opportunity to improve. Again, an employer is expected to follow fair procedures and act in a reasonable manner.

The dismissal of an employee will be deemed unfair under the Acts if it results wholly or mainly from any of the following:

- An employee's trade union membership or activities
- Religious or political opinions
- Race, colour or sexual orientation
- The age of the employee
- An employee's membership of the travelling community
- Legal proceedings against an employer where an employee is a party or a witness
- Unfair selection for redundancy
- An employee's pregnancy or any matters connected therewith, or rights under the Maternity Protection Acts 1994/2004, the Adoptive Leave Act 1995, the Parental Leave Act 1998, the National Minimum Wage Act 2000 and the Carer's Leave Act 2001 (s 6.2 Unfair Dismissal Act 1977 as amended).

Unfair dismissal can also arise where a person's conditions of work are made intolerable, resulting in his/her resignation. This is known as constructive dismissal, but in this case the onus of proof is on the employee.

A person who considers that he/she has been unfairly dismissed can bring a claim for redress to a Rights Commissioner or the Employment Appeals Tribunal within six months of the date of dismissal or within 12 months in exceptional circumstances. The redress can result in reinstatement (former job back with no loss of entitlements), re-engagement (in the former job or in a suitable alternative post on conditions deemed reasonable), damages, where financial loss has been sustained (depending on circumstances, up to a maximum of two years' pay), or compensation of up to a maximum of four weeks' pay where no financial loss is sustained. Instead of a claim for unfair dismissal, an employee could decide to take a common law action for wrongful dismissal.

Grievance and disciplinary procedures

Even though grievance and disciplinary issues are generally considered together, they are two separate issues. A grievance is any complaint by an employee in relation to his/her work, excluding issues about pay, collective agreements and matters like bullying and harassment, which are covered under other procedures. A disciplinary issue is an allegation against an employee which could result in a sanction of some type. An employer is obliged to have grievance and disciplinary procedures in place.

Grievance procedures

The main objective of any grievance procedures is to facilitate the informal resolution of complaints in a fair and prompt manner near the point of origin. However, it may not be possible to resolve all grievances through discussion between the individuals involved and may require the intervention of a third party. Grievance procedures generally involve two options: an informal stage and/or a formal stage. In the former every effort is made to get the two people involved to meet and try to find an amicable agreement. If the informal stage is unsuccessful or inappropriate, the formal option is adopted. Most procedures specify general principles for a formal process and these generally include the following:

- The complainant is asked to put the grievance in writing and sign it.
- The person about whom a complaint is made has a right to know what the grievance is and who made it. A copy of the written complaint is given to the respondent.
- A third person is expected to meet both parties and try to get them to reach an agreement or to agree to mediation.
- If the parties fail to reach an agreement, the grievance has to be addressed through the agreed process in accordance with the principles of fairness and natural justice (see below), including a right of representation (by a colleague in most cases).
- The process generally involves progressive stages from first line superior to a senior manager trying to facilitate an agreement.
- The procedures have to include a right of appeal against any proposal made for resolution of the complaint.
- If the grievance is not resolved by then, the process often provides for an external referral to a third party like a Rights Commissioner, Labour Relations Commission or the Labour Court, as appropriate.

Disciplinary procedures

An employer is legally required to have disciplinary procedures in place and give a copy of them to new employees within 28 days of appointment. Disciplinary procedures have to respect the principles of natural justice and the due process of fair procedures. The first rule of natural justice is *nemo judex in sua causa*, no one can be a judge in their own case; in other words, the person acting as adjudicator has to be independent, with no prior involvement in the issue under dispute and must not have any close relationship with the parties involved. The second rule of natural justice is *audi alteram partem*, hear the other side; in other words, a person has to be given a reasonable opportunity to respond to any allegations made.

The disciplinary process has to follow fair procedures, which generally include the following principles:

- Informing the employee of all allegations and who made them
- A right of response and proper time to respond
- If necessary, following consideration of the response, investigating the allegations made
- A right to a fair hearing before an impartial adjudicator
- A right to be represented and to cross-examine anyone making allegations
- A right to call witnesses, if relevant
- Consideration of any special circumstances
- A decision and the reasons for it
- A right of appeal.

Disciplinary sanctions can progress in stages from counselling, to a verbal warning, to a written warning, a final warning, demotion, suspension with or without pay for a period, to dismissal. Any sanction imposed has to be proportional to the issue in question. In the case of gross misconduct, like fraud, theft or gross dereliction of duties, the question of summary dismissal can arise, but due process has to be followed. In the case of a very serious allegation, a person could be suspended on full pay pending a full investigation and due process. Any dismissal has to have regard to the unfair dismissals legislation.

h)   Protection of Employees (Part-Time Work) Act 2001

This Act provides that a part-time employee cannot be treated in a less favourable manner than a comparable full-time employee with the same or an associated employer in relation to conditions of employment. However, the legislation provides that a part-time employee may be treated in a less favourable manner than a full-time employee where this can be justified on 'objective grounds':

> A ground would be considered as an objective ground for treatment in a less favourable manner, if it is based on considerations other than status of the employee as a part-time worker and the less favourable treatment is for the purpose of achieving a legitimate objective of the employer and such treatment as necessary for that purpose.

The Act provides that a part-time employee may be treated less favourably than a comparable full-time employee in relation to any pension scheme or arrangement when his/her normal hours of work are less than 20 per cent of the normal hours of a comparable full-time employee. Any complaint under the Act can be referred to a Rights Commissioner, with a right of appeal to the Labour Court.

i) Maternity Protection Acts 1994 and 2004 (as amended)

This legislation provides for 26 weeks' maternity leave for expectant mothers and an additional 16 weeks without pay if required. The legislation also provides for time off with pay for ante-natal and post-natal medical visits and leave for fathers in the event of the death of the mother during or shortly after childbirth. A woman on maternity leave may be entitled to maternity benefit from the Department of Social and Family Affairs if she has sufficient PRSI contributions, and some contracts of employment provide for full pay less the figure payable by the Department.

When an employee takes maternity leave she must take a minimum of two weeks before the date confinement is expected and at least four weeks after. The balance can be taken at the discretion of the employee, but it must be consecutive with the core period. An employee is obliged to give at least four weeks' notice in writing to her employer stating the day maternity leave will commence. An employee who wishes to take 16 additional weeks without pay must notify her employer in writing at least four weeks in advance of the first day of the additional leave (which must directly follow the maternity leave). An employer cannot refuse this application and such leave is not considered a break in service. An employee is entitled to any public holidays that occur during maternity leave (by an extra day's leave or pay in lieu) as well as her full complement of annual leave. The employee is required to notify her employer of her intention to return to work at least four weeks in advance of the return date. An employee has to be allowed back to her usual job with the same terms and conditions of employment as she had before the leave. If a mother dies within six weeks of the birth of a living child, the father is entitled to some leave (up to 16 weeks if death took place at the birth). The father must notify his employer of his intention to take this leave (which is not paternity leave) and any further leave as well as the date he will return to work.

An employer is obliged under health and safety legislation to assess the workplace for risks to women who have recently given birth or who are breast-feeding. If a risk exists the employer is required to remove the risk, or if that is not possible, to provide suitable alternative work. If that cannot be done the employee is entitled to health and safety leave, with her usual pay, for the first 21 days. Thereafter she may be entitled to social welfare benefit subject to her PRSI contributions. Disputes under this Act may be referred to a Rights Commissioner within six months, with a right of appeal to the Employment Appeals Tribunal.

j) Adoptive Leave Act 1995

Under this Act, as amended, an adopting mother, or sole male adopter, is entitled to a minimum of 26 consecutive weeks' leave from employment following placement of the child and up to 16 weeks' unpaid additional leave. The first period may qualify for social welfare benefit. Any dispute relating to this legislation can be referred to a Rights Commissioner, with a right of appeal to the Employment Appeals Tribunal.

k) Protection of Young Persons (Employment) Act 1996

This legislation is designed to protect the health of young persons (aged between 16 and 18) and children (persons under 16). Employment of children under 16 is generally prohibited by the Act. However, a child over 14 may be allowed to do light non-industrial work during school holidays provided it is not harmful to the health or safety of the child or attendance at school, or may be employed as part of a work experience or education programme approved by the Minister of Enterprise, Trade and Innovation or FÁS. A child over 15 may do such work for up to eight hours a week during school term. A child must be allowed a 21-day break from work in the summer. Young people (16- and 17-year-olds) may not be required to work for more than eight hours a day or 40 hours in any week. There is a code of practice relating to the employment of young persons in licensed premises. The working regulations for children and young persons are summarised in Table 8.2. A licence from the Minister of Enterprise, Trade and Innovation is required before a person under 16 can be employed in film, theatre, sports or advertising activities.

Table 8.2: Maximum working hours for children and young persons

	Child aged 14	Child aged 15	16- and 17-year-olds
Maximum weekly hours during school term	None during school term	8 hours	–
Maximum weekly hours outside school term	35 hours (7 per day)	35 hours (7 per day)	40 hours (8 per day)
Maximum weekly hours on work experience programmes	40 hours (8 per day)	40 hours (8 per day)	40 hours (8 per day)
Maximum working hours per day	7–8 hours (subject to above)	7–8 hours (subject to above)	8 hours
Maximum working week	35–40 hours (subject to above)	35–40 hours (subject to above)	40 hours
Half-hour rest break after	4 hours	4 hours	4.5 hours
Weekly rest break	2 consecutive days	2 consecutive days	2 consecutive days
Starting time	Not before 8 a.m.	Not before 8 a.m.	Not before 6 a.m.
Finishing time	Not after 8 p.m.	Not after 8 p.m.	Not after 10 p.m.

Before employing a young person or child an employer must obtain a birth certificate and, in respect of a child under 16, written permission from a parent or guardian is also required. An employer is obliged to keep a record for three years of all employees under 18, showing name and date of birth as well as starting and finishing times of work, wage rate and the total wages paid to each. An employer is also obliged to give all employees under 18 copies of the official summary of this Act within one month of starting employment, together with details of their terms of employment as required under the Terms of Employment (Information) Act 1994. An employer with employees under 18 is also obliged to display a summary of the Act at a place where it can be easily read. Complaints under this Act can be referred to a Rights Commissioner, with any appeal going to the Employment Appeals Tribunal.

I)   Organisation of Working Time Act 1997

This Act establishes statutory rights for employees in respect of maximum working time, rest, holiday entitlements, public holidays and zero hours. These rights can apply either from the Act, regulations made under it or through a collective agreement, where some flexibility may be agreed subject to equivalent compensation. The maximum working time rules and the rest provisions do not apply to certain categories, including the Garda Síochána, members of the defence forces, junior hospital doctors, transport employees, workers at sea, those who control their own hours of work or family members employed on a farm or in a private house (*Guide to Labour Law*).

Maximum weekly working time

The maximum average working week is 48 hours. Averaging may be balanced out over a four-, six- or 12-month period depending on the circumstances. With effect from 1 March 1998 the maximum working time for night workers (those working between midnight and 7 a.m. who normally work at least three hours of their daily total during the night and where the hours worked at night equal or exceed 50 per cent of the annual working time) is 48 hours per week averaged over two months or a longer period specified in a collective agreement approved by the Labour Court. For those whose work involves special hazards or heavy physical or mental strain, there is an absolute limit of eight hours in a 24-hour period during which they work at night. Working time is exclusive of breaks (*Guide to Labour Law*).

Rest

With effect from 1 March 1998 every employee has a general entitlement to the following:
*   Eleven consecutive hours' rest daily in a 24-hour period
*   One period of 24 hours' rest per week following a daily rest period of 11 hours
*   A rest break of 15 minutes where more than 4.5 hours are worked and 30 minutes where more than six hours are worked, which may include the first break.

Holiday entitlements

This Act provides that most employees are entitled to four weeks' annual holidays with pay for each leave year with pay (1 April–31 March) with pro rata entitlements for periods of employment of less than a year with effect from 1 April 1999. Holiday entitlements with pay are calculated as follows:

- Four weeks in a leave year in which an employee works at least 1,365 hours for the same employer
- A third of a week per calendar month where an employee works at least 117 hours
- Eight per cent of the hours worked in a leave year (subject to a maximum of four weeks). An employer should ensure that all annual leave is taken within the year to which it relates. Under section 20 of the Organisation of Working Time Act 1997, an employer can elect, with the consent of the employee, to allow holidays to be carried over, but only for a further six months.

Public holidays

The Act also provides for nine public holidays with pay: 1 January (New Year's Day), St Patrick's Day, Easter Monday, the first Mondays in May, June and August, the last Monday in October, Christmas Day and St Stephen's Day. In respect of each, an employee is entitled to a paid day off on the holiday, another paid day off within a month, an extra day's annual leave or an extra day's pay as the employer may decide. If the public holiday falls on a Sunday the next day becomes the public holiday, and in respect of Christmas Day, the following Tuesday. Part-time employees must have worked at least 40 hours in the five weeks before the public holiday to qualify for payment.

Sunday premium

Employees are entitled to paid time off in lieu or a premium payment for work on Sunday if it is not already included in the rate of pay.

Zero hours

Where an employee suffers a loss by not working hours he/she is required to work or to be available for work (but is sent home because things are quiet), that person is now entitled to be compensated for 25 per cent of the time he/she is required to be available or 15 hours, whichever is the lesser. This provision does not apply to short-time, emergency or exceptional circumstances, employee illness or employees on call.

Records and complaints

Records to show that this Act is being complied with must be kept for a period of three years. Complaints under the Act can be referred to a Rights Commissioner, with a right of appeal to the Labour Court.

m) Safety, Health and Welfare at Work Act 2005

Many rights relating to safety, health and welfare at work came from common law and legislation, especially the Safety, Health and Welfare at Work Act 1989, which was repealed in 2005. The Safety, Health and Welfare at Work Act 2005, which applies to all employers, self-employed, directors, managers, employees and those who may be affected by risks in all places of work, establishes duties and regulations designed to improve safety, health and welfare at work. It covers public, private, commercial and voluntary organisations. The Act also imposes safety and health obligations on those designing, importing, supplying or manufacturing articles or substances for use at work. There is also a wide range of sector-specific health and safety regulations in place (for example construction regulations). Under the 2005 Act, the onus of proof is on the employer to demonstrate that the workplace was managed in a manner to prevent risk of injury or danger to the safety, health and welfare of anyone (s 81). In addition to the cost of claims and higher insurance premiums, there are heavy penalties on conviction as well as possible penalties on directors and senior managers for breaches of safety legislation, including imprisonment. A health and safety culture has to be fostered at all levels in an organisation, especially by the senior staff.

The main duties imposed on employers to ensure the safety, health and welfare of all employees include:

- Providing a safe place of work
- Providing a safe means of access to and exit from work
- Providing a safe system of work
- The provision and use of protective clothing and equipment where necessary
- The provision and maintenance of adequate welfare facilities
- The prevention of improper conduct and behaviour in the workplace
- The prevention of risks to employees from the use of any articles or substances and from noise, vibration, radiation or any other physical agent
- Proper information (including in another language if required by the ethnic origin of the workforce), instruction, training and supervision for staff, including measures to be taken in an emergency or risk of imminent danger, and ensuring that all staff are competent to carry out their duties in a safe manner (s 8).

Employers are also obliged to inform all employees and contractors' staff regarding the hazards identified in the workplace and the associated risks as well as to consult with the above groups and to take account of representations made regarding safety, health and welfare (s 12). The information to be provided includes the protective and preventative measures that must be taken to comply with safety and health legislation.

Under section 17, a person who commissions or procures construction work is obliged to appoint a competent person(s) to ensure that the project is designed and capable of being constructed in a safe manner and that it can be maintained without risk to health or safety. A person who carries out construction work is also required, as far as possible, to ensure that the structure is safe and without risk to health. The duties specified in section 17 are amplified by the Safety, Health and Welfare at Work (Regulations) made under the 2005 Act. New legislation in 2006 and 2007 made specific provisions for the following:

- Working at heights regulations
- Environmental noise regulations
- Control of vibration at work regulations
- Exposure to asbestos regulations
- Construction regulations.

The Act also requires every employer and self-employed person to prepare a safety statement covering their place or places of work (s 19). A safety statement is a policy document specifying hazards, risks and precautions to be taken to safeguard health and safety in the workplace. It must include the following:

- Identification of hazards
- Assessment of risks within the workplace
- Specification of how the safety, health and welfare of employees are to be secured at work
- Precautions to be taken
- Specification of the co-operation required from employees as regards safety, health and welfare
- The names and job titles of all persons to whom tasks are assigned in relation to health and safety
- Specification of the resources provided to secure the safety, health and welfare of all employees
- Details regarding the extent to which the safety policy is fulfilled to be included in a company's annual report
- Information to employees on the contents of the safety statement.

A safety statement consists of two parts: a statement of general policy declaring a commitment to secure a safe and healthy work environment and how that is to be achieved. The statement should be issued with the approval of the board of directors or partners and given their full support. It should be signed by the chairperson, managing director or senior partner, dated and updated regularly. The directors' report to be laid before an annual general meeting of a company must now comment on the extent to which the safety statement is put into effect.

The main duties imposed on employees (s 13) include:
- Complying with the health and safety legislation
- Taking reasonable care for their own safety and that of others

- Using all protective clothing and equipment provided for their safety
- Taking account of any instructions given with regard to safe use
- Use of protective systems established for their safety
- Not engaging in improper conduct or behaviour such as violence or bullying, which could endanger another person at work in any way
- Undertaking safety and health training provided
- Reporting any dangerous machines or practices they become aware of to their employer.

Employees must not be under the influence of any intoxicant (drugs or alcohol) in the workplace that may endanger their own or their colleagues' health, safety and welfare. Under the Act it is also necessary to appoint a safety representative and a safety committee in each workplace. The safety representative is required to investigate accidents, to communicate with safety inspectors, to carry out inspections, to investigate any potential hazards and complaints relating to health, safety and welfare at work and to make representations to management on any such matter. He/she is entitled to paid time off to discharge these functions. Employees are also entitled to appoint a safety committee to promote health, safety and welfare in the workplace.

Bullying in the workplace is a threat to the safety, health and welfare of people in the workforce. The Task Force on the Prevention of Workplace Bullying (2001) defined workplace bullying as:

> Repeated inappropriate behaviour, direct or indirect, whether verbal, physical or otherwise, conducted by one or more persons against another or others, at the place of work and/or in the course of employment, which could reasonably be regarded as undermining the individual's right to dignity at work. An isolated incident of the behaviour described in this definition may be an affront to dignity at work but as a one-off incident is not considered to be bullying.

An employer is obliged to have a policy for the prevention of workplace bullying and procedures to address complaints. This can involve two approaches: informal and formal. With an informal procedure, every effort is made to resolve the complaint as close to the source as possible in an non-confrontational, supportive manner. Where this procedure is inappropriate or is not successful, the formal procedure is adopted. The complainant makes a formal complaint in writing to his/her supervisor. The alleged perpetrator is given a copy of the complaint and a fair opportunity to respond. Here again, an effort is made to resolve the complaint amicably by mediation. If this fails, the complaint has to be investigated. The investigation is carried out by an appropriate person (or persons), with both parties given every opportunity to present their cases. Both parties should be informed in writing of the findings and given an opportunity to respond to them. It is then a matter for management to take appropriate action, which could involve counselling or invoking the organisation's disciplinary procedures (Health and Safety Authority, 2002).

The Health and Safety Authority (HSA) is a tripartite body, representative of employers, employees and the State, with responsibility for the promotion, administration and enforcement of occupational health, safety and welfare of persons at work. Employers are obliged to report any accident which causes an absence of three or more days to the HSA (form IR1). Fatal accidents must be reported immediately. The HSA also deals with workplace bullying.

n)   Protection of Employees (Employers' Insolvency) Acts 1984–2004

This legislation was enacted to protect certain outstanding entitlements relating to the pay of employees where an employer becomes insolvent in accordance with the terms of the Act. Money due to employees may be paid by the Department of Enterprise, Trade and Innovation out of the Social Insurance Fund, subject to certain limits and conditions. The scheme also protects employees' contributions to occupational pension schemes which an employer may have deducted from wages but not paid over, again subject to certain limits. The Acts apply to workers who are fully insurable for all benefits under the Social Welfare Acts and those in employment over 66 years of age. Disputes under these Acts may be referred to the Employment Appeals Tribunal.

o)   National Minimum Wage Act 2000

Pay rates and how they are to be adjusted are normally stated in the contract of employment or by reference to the terms of a collective agreement (between a trade union and the employer). Policy in relation to overtime, sick pay and sick leave, which are not covered in legislation, are generally agreed as part of the terms and conditions of employment. Any complaint in relation to an employee not being paid in accordance with the terms of his/her employment can be referred to a Rights Commissioner under the Payment of Wages Act 1991.

The National Minimum Wage Act 2000, which was enacted on 1 April 2000, provides for a minimum wage for an experienced adult employee. Legal minimum rates of pay are also laid down by Joint Labour Committees of the Labour Court and registered employment agreements. The National Minimum Wage Act 2000, and regulations made under it, apply to virtually all employees over 18 except for close relatives of the employer and recognised apprentices. Employees under 18 are entitled to 70 per cent of the national minimum wage. If they continue to work for the same employer after reaching 18 they must be paid 80 per cent of the national minimum wage for the first year and 90 per cent for the second. A similar arrangement applies to employees over 18 starting employment. Pay for the purpose of this legislation includes basic earnings, commission and bonuses, shift premia, piece and incentive rates, service charges distributed by an employer to employees as well as board and lodgings provided by an employer. It does not include tips, gratuities, overtime payments, unsociable hours premium, Sunday and public holiday premium or benefits in kind. Information regarding the current minimum rates of pay can be obtained from the website of the Department of Enterprise, Trade and Innovation.

An employee wishing to make a complaint under the Act is obliged to request a written statement from his/her employer showing the average hourly rate of pay for a pay reference period (a week, fortnight or month) and send it to a Rights Commissioner of the Labour Relations Commission or to the Labour Inspectorate. An employer is obliged to keep all relevant records for at least three years.

p)   Parental Leave Acts 1998 and 2006

This legislation provides an entitlement for mothers and fathers to avail of leave from employment to take care of their young children, but there is no legal right to payment. Such leave must be used to take care of the child concerned. Each parent is entitled to a total of 14 weeks' parental leave for each child under eight, or where a child is between three and eight years at the time of adoption, the leave has to be taken within two years of the relevant adoption order. In the case of an adopted child under three at the time of the adoption, the parental leave must be taken before the child is eight years of age. The maximum age for parental leave in respect of a child with a disability is 16 years. Parental leave may be taken as a continuous block, by agreement between the employer and employee in separate blocks or by reduced hours over an agreed period. Such leave does not affect an employee's rights to public holidays, annual leave, maternity leave or the right to return to work. The Act applies to all employees, those serving apprenticeships and people working for employment agencies. Employees must normally have worked at least one year with the same employer to qualify for parental leave, but pro rata leave can be allowed if the child is approaching eight and the parent has more than three months' service. An employee is obliged to give written notice to the employer of his or her intention to take parental leave at least six weeks before the proposed starting date, stating when and how it is proposed to take the leave. The employer is required to respond with a confirmation document no later than four weeks before the leave is due to begin, stating the following:

- The date the leave will commence
- The duration
- The manner in which the leave will be taken.

The document has to be signed by both parties. Disputes concerning parental leave can be referred to a Rights Commissioner within six months and a decision can be appealed to the Employment Appeals Tribunal within four weeks.

This Act also provides for *force majeure* leave to enable an employee to deal with an emergency arising from an injury or illness to a family member. Entitlement to *force majeure* leave is limited to emergencies where the immediate presence of the employee is indispensable. Family member includes a child, spouse, partner, brother, sister, parent, grandparent or a person to whom the employee is *in loco parentis*. An employee may not be absent on *force majeure* leave for more than three days in any 12-month period or five days in 36 consecutive months. On return to work, an employee is obliged to confirm to the employer that he/she took *force majeure* leave and the reason for doing so. An employer is obliged to keep a record of parental leave and *force majeure* leave taken by employees for eight years.

q) Carer's Leave Act 2001

The Carer's Leave Act 2001 provides an entitlement for an employee with more than 12 months' continuous service to take up to 105 weeks unpaid leave to personally provide care for a person who requires full-time care and attention, subject to the conditions specified. The minimum leave period is 13 weeks. Any complaint under this Act can be referred to a Rights Commissioner, with a right of appeal to the Employment Appeals Tribunal. (Information on the Carer's Benefit Scheme can be obtained from the Department of Social and Family Affairs.)

r) Public Health (Tobacco) Acts 2002 and 2004

This legislation requires employers to ensure that there is no smoking in places of work. Anyone contravening this legislation is liable to a criminal prosecution.

s) Protection of Employees (Fixed-Term Work) Act 2003

This Act, which came into effect on 14 July 2003, provides that a fixed-term employee (see below) cannot be treated in a less favourable manner than a comparable permanent employee with the same or an associated employer doing the same or similar work except in special circumstances. All employee protection legislation, other than unfair dismissal in certain circumstances, applies to a fixed-term employee. A fixed-term employee is a person who has a contract of employment where the duration is determined by an objective condition, such as a certain date, the completion of a specific task or the occurrence of a special event. It does not include employees in apprenticeship schemes, initial vocational training, publicly funded training or vocational retraining programmes (s 2). The employee has to be informed in writing of the objective condition at recruitment. A fixed-term employee may be treated in a less favourable manner to a comparable permanent employee where this can be justified on objective grounds.

> Under section 7(1) of the Act, a ground shall not be regarded as an objective ground for the purposes of any provision of this Act unless it is based on considerations other than the status of the employee concerned as a fixed-term employee, and the less

> favourable treatment which it involves for that employee (which treatment may include the renewal of a fixed-term employee's contract for a further fixed term) is for the purpose of achieving a legitimate objective of the employer and such treatment is appropriate and necessary for that purpose.

An example would be a person appointed to a fixed-term contract to replace a full-time person who has taken a career break. A fixed-term employee can be treated less favourably than a comparable full-time employee in relation to a pension scheme where he/she works less than 20 per cent of the normal hours of a full-time employee. Otherwise, the entitlement is to pro rata benefits related to the normal hours of work of the comparable permanent employee. The Act applies to any fixed-term employee with a contract of employment, including those holding office under or in the service of the State.

The Act provides that where an employer proposes to renew a fixed-term contract, he/she shall inform the employee in writing, not later than the renewal date, of the objective ground justifying renewal of the fixed-term contract and of the failure to offer one of indefinite duration. An employer cannot employ a series of such contracts. If a fixed-term employee completes three years of continuous service with the same or an associated employer, the employer may renew the contract for a fixed term on one further occasion only and for no longer than a year, unless there are objective grounds justifying the renewal as a fixed-term contract (*Guide to Labour Law*). Where an employee is employed on two or more fixed-term contracts, the total duration cannot exceed four years unless there are objective grounds justifying the renewal as a fixed-term contract. Any fixed-term contract in breach of this provision will be deemed to be a contract of indefinite duration. The employer is obliged to inform fixed-term employees of permanent vacancies and training opportunities. Any dispute under this Act can be referred to a Rights Commissioner within six months, with a right of appeal to the Labour Court.

t)   Employment Equality Acts 1998–2007

The Employment Equality Acts 1998 and 2004 outlaw discrimination on nine grounds: gender, marital status, family status, sexual orientation, religious belief, age, disability, race and membership of the Travelling community. Discrimination is defined in the legislation as 'the treatment of a person in a less favourable way than another person is, has been, or would be treated in a comparable situation on any of the nine grounds'.

This legislation also outlaws discrimination in access to employment, conditions of employment, training, promotion, classification of posts in collective agreements, in advertising posts, including those carried out by employment agencies, and in vocational training. It also applies to certain vocational bodies like trade unions, professional and trade associations as regards membership and other benefits. An employer is not obliged to employ someone who will not undertake the duties of the post or is not fully competent or capable of doing the job. An employer is required to take appropriate measures to enable a person with a disability to take up employment unless they would impose a disproportionate burden with regard to the scale and resources of the business.

The legislation also provides for equal pay for like work, which is defined as 'work that is the same, similar, or work of equal value'. Equal pay for work of equal value is made a term of every employment contract. Like work may be demonstrated by making a comparison between the work of one employee (who has less pay) and another employee (who has more) of the same or an associated employer. An employer may show as a defence that there are grounds, other than gender, for differences in pay. Employers can engage in positive action to promote equal opportunity for men and women by removing existing inequalities. The legislation contains a number of exclusions on gender grounds, where gender is an occupational qualification (for example an artist's model), special treatment of women connected with pregnancy and maternity or adoption, the performance of services of a personal nature and limited exclusions for the Garda Síochána in specified circumstances.

This legislation outlaws sexual harassment and harassment in the workplace, whether by the employer, an employee, a client, customer or business contact. Sexual harassment is:

> where unwanted conduct relating to the sex of a person occurs
> with the purpose or effect of violating the dignity of a person, and
> of creating an intimidating, hostile, degrading, humiliating or
> offensive environment. (Article 2, Equality Act 2004)

An employer is obliged to take all reasonable steps to ensure that there is no sexual harassment in the workplace and to prevent a person being treated differently because of rejection or acceptance of sexual harassment inside or outside the place of work. Harassment is defined in the equality legislation as:

> where unwanted conduct related to any of the discriminatory
> grounds occurs which has the purpose or effect of violating a
> person's dignity, and of creating an intimidating, hostile, degrading,
> humiliating or offensive environment.

The employer is required to take 'all reasonable steps' to ensure that there is no harassment in the workplace.

Every employer is expected to have a policy and procedures for dealing with allegations of harassment and sexual harassment. These are similar to the procedures for grievances and usually include the following steps:

- Informal procedures designed to resolve the issue as close to the source as possible, with the provision of counselling or mentoring; this approach may not be appropriate for all allegations
- Formal procedures involving an investigation by an impartial person(s)
- Decision by an independent manager or committee
- Right of appeal.

Penalties can include a verbal warning, written warning, suspension and, in serious cases, dismissal. A complainant is entitled to have the allegations investigated within a reasonable period and the defendant is entitled to due process, especially where the consequences are serious.

There are a number of general exclusions from the provisions of the Acts, some of which include requirements as to residency, citizenship and proficiency in the Irish language for public service employment; educational qualification requirements for particular jobs; where a particular characteristic related to a discriminatory ground is an occupational qualification; discrimination by religious, educational and medical institutions run by religious orders under the conditions specified; and employment for the purposes of a private household. Claims must be referred in the Equality Tribunal within six months of the last act of alleged discrimination or 12 months 'for reasonable cause'. The director of the Equality Tribunal can, with the consent of both parties, appoint an Equality Mediation Officer in an effort to resolve the dispute. If an agreement is reached, it is enforceable. If either party objects to mediation or if that process is not successful, the dispute is referred to an Equality Officer for investigation. The Equality Officer issues a determination (which can be enforced through the Circuit Court) with a right of appeal to the Labour Court within 42 days.

u)   Equal Status Acts 2000 and 2004
The Equal Status Act 2000, which came into effect on 25 October 2000, prohibits discrimination in the provision of goods, services, disposal of property and access to education on the grounds of gender, marital status, family status, sexual orientation, religious belief, age, disability, race or membership of the Travelling community. Discrimination can be direct (where a person is treated less favourably on one of the grounds), indirect (because of a practice or requirement which cannot be met) and by association (because of membership of a group). There are a number of exemptions, including compliance with any statutory provision or court order, people under 18 years, insurance, schools catering for one gender only or a specific religious ethos, mature students, certain scholarships, cosmetic services, drama and entertainment where required for authenticity, adoption and fostering (upper age limits apply), refusal of admission based on prior record, wills, gifts and some special needs. The Act as amended allows preferential treatment or the taking of positive measures which are bona fide

intended to promote equality of opportunity for disadvantaged persons. Anybody wishing to make a complaint under this legislation is obliged to notify in writing the person or organisation against whom the claim is being made within two months of the alleged incident. If there is no reply or an unsatisfactory reply, the allegation can be referred to the director of the Equality Tribunal within six months of the occurrence of the incident. The director can refer the complaint to an Equality Mediation Officer, with the consent of both parties, for mediation and settlement. If a case is not referred for mediation or that process fails, it can be sent to an Equality Officer for investigation. The Equality Officer issues a determination.

The Equality Authority
The Equality Authority was established on 18 October 1999 under the Employment Equality Act 1988 and its mandate was extended under the Equal Status Act 2000 and the Equality Act 2004. It has four main functions:

- To work towards the elimination of discrimination in employment and vocational training, in the provision of goods and services, education, property and other opportunities to which the public generally has access
- To promote equality of opportunity in employment and the provision of goods, services and facilities
- To provide information on the equality legislation to the public
- To monitor the operations of the Employment Equality Acts 1998 and 2004, the Maternity Protection Acts 1994 and 2004, the Adoptive Leave Acts 1995 and 2005, the Parental Leave Acts 1998 and 2006, the Pensions Act 1990 and the Equal Status Acts 2000 and 2004.

The Equality Authority provides a free, confidential information and advisory service in relation to the implementation of the Employment Equality Acts 1998 and 2004 as well as the Equal Status Acts 2000 and 2004.

The Equality Tribunal
The Equality Tribunal, which was initially established in 1999 under the Employment Equality Act, provides redress where unlawful discrimination is proven. The office is separate from the Equality Authority. It now deals with complaints arising under equality legislation, covering employment, occupational pensions and access to goods and services. Anyone who feels that he/she has been discriminated against under either the Employment Equality Acts or the Equal Status Acts may lodge a complaint with the director of the Equality Tribunal within six months of the alleged occurrence. If both parties agree, the director can refer the complaint to an Equality Mediation Officer, who will seek an agreement between the parties. Once signed by both parties, this agreement is legally binding and it can be enforced through the Circuit Court. If either party objects to

mediation or where the process does not result in agreement and the complaint is relodged, the director will refer the case for investigation by an Equality Officer. The Equality Officer has a right of access to all relevant records and can interview persons who may be able to help with information. When an investigation is concluded the Equality Officer will issue a legally binding decision, which is enforceable through the Circuit Court.

Any decision regarding employment may be appealed to the Labour Court within 42 days of issue. The Labour Court will issue legally binding determinations, which may be appealed to the High Court on a point of law. Where the Equality Officer finds discrimination, he/she may require that a particular course of action be undertaken and/or order equal pay and arrears of up to three years in an equal pay case; in other employment cases, equal treatment and compensation of up to a maximum of two years' pay. An appeal under the Equal Status Acts is made to the Circuit Court. Complaints regarding dismissals are dealt with by the Labour Court, which can order reinstatement or reengagement, with or without compensation.

v) Employment Permits Acts 2003–2006

The Employment Permits Acts 2003–2006 regulate the main types of employment permits available to non-nationals of the European Economic Area (EEA) (those from outside the EU, Norway, Iceland and Liechtenstein) who want to work in Ireland. Under section 2 of the Employment Permits Act 2006, a foreign national cannot obtain work in Ireland without an employment permit. An employer is expected to seek confirmation of the prospective employee's right to work in Ireland prior to recruitment. Once in employment, such employees are entitled to the normal employment rights. There are four routes by which a non-EEA national can obtain permission to work in Ireland:

- Green card
- Work permit
- Intra-company transfer permit
- Spouses and dependant permits.

The green card scheme is available for a list of occupations with specific annual salaries. With respect to work permits there is a labour market test requirement, where every effort is made to fill posts by local and national advertising. With the intra-company transfer scheme, multinational companies can transfer specific categories of employees to different countries. The spouses and dependant permits scheme allows spouses and dependants of those with valid permits to apply for permits in respect of themselves (Connolly, 2007).

w) Employees (Provision of Information and Consultation) Act 2006

This legislation provides for the establishment of a framework, with minimum requirements, to provide information and consultation for employees on matters which directly affect them in an organisation employing over 50 staff.

x)   Employment Law Compliance Bill 2008

This proposed legislation is designed to ensure compliance with employment law. The National Employment Rights Authority (NERA) is to be formally established. The Bill proposes wide powers to investigate alleged breaches and prosecute employers who do not comply with employment law. If enacted, labour inspectors can enter any workplace, demand any relevant information, ask any questions and inspect employment records, including those relating to work permits. Where evidence of non-compliance is found, inspectors could seek redress from the employers and, if deemed necessary, initiate prosecutions. Employment records have to be kept for three years and for two years after an employee leaves.

If this Bill is enacted there will be over 30 statutes, 21 EU directives and 71 statutory instruments as well as five different disputes and appeals bodies regulating employment regulations in Ireland. It is a labyrinthine maze of regulations and procedures not only for the managers of small and medium-sized enterprises but also for specialists in the field.

8.4 Pay and conditions

It is a fundamental duty of an employer to pay the wages or salaries due to employees. The rates of pay offered by an employer are important for employees in terms of retention, satisfaction and motivation. While rewards like autonomy and responsibility are important, the most attractive one is the remuneration package, covering pay, benefits and incentives. Employees are always interested in the net ('take home') pay (after tax and PRSI). Gross pay is determined by many factors: strategy of the company (low-cost producer or provider of new differentiated products), staff profile, qualifications and experience required, the ability of the organisation to pay, the going rate for the job, labour market trends, the bargaining strength of a trade union, if any, and the need to stimulate performance by incentive schemes. Establishing fair rates of pay and differentials between job categories with regard to internal and external factors are important for all organisations (Gunnigle et al., 2006).

The amount of remuneration is a matter for agreement between an employer and employee, subject to the minimum wage or any Labour Court agreement. There are three main payment systems: flat rate, piecework and performance related. A flat rate is a fixed rate per hour, week and month; it is related to time spent on the job and does not take performance into consideration. It is simple to administer and convenient for employer and employee, but provides no incentive to encourage or reward good performance. In piecework, pay is determined solely by performance. It promotes high performance, often at the expense of quality and job satisfaction. In addition, a wide range of incentive schemes may be employed where some element of pay is directly related to performance. Some employers, chiefly in the private sector, have remuneration packages linking pay more closely with performance. Other incentive schemes are based on profit sharing, employee share ownership and commission. Some employers provide a range of fringe benefits for specific employees, such as sick pay, health insurance, pensions or company cars. A series of national pay agreements from the 1970s, with the Government, employers' and trade union representatives participating in tripartite agreements, have been very beneficial for employees. (For example, under the Juries Act 1975, an employee on jury service has to be paid by the employer.)

Performance appraisal

Performance appraisal is a planned systematic procedure for evaluating each employee's actual performance in relation to expectations so as to provide feedback on a regular basis. It is used to improve performance and facilitate decisions in relation to employee development, motivation and, in some cases, actual pay. An appraisal is generally carried out once or twice a year and it can be a difficult experience for both the appraiser and the appraisee. It aims to be an assessment of performance against the objectives and goals previously agreed in an honest, fair and frank manner as well as establishing the objectives and targets for the following year and how they will be measured. An effective appraisal should be positive, optimistic, supportive and leave the appraisee feeling valued, motivated and energised as well as accepting that the objectives and goals set are realistic and attainable. Negative feedback only can be destructive and lead to defensiveness, confrontation and a 'blame culture'. If a person does not respond to a positive and supportive approach, poor performance cannot be ignored.

Coaching (a structured process of helping an employee to improve performance), mentoring (where an experienced employee provides guidance to a newcomer for a period) and employee development programmes are essential features of good performance appraisal practices.

8.5 Staff development

The purpose of staff development is to help employees become more competent at their jobs, thus increasing their job satisfaction and effectiveness. Three terms are regularly used in this context: training, development and education. Training is a job-orientated learning process designed to develop knowledge, skills and attitudes in a specific activity to enable an employee to perform his/her present job more satisfactorily. Development is a person-orientated learning process designed to enhance personal qualities for present and future requirements. Both are narrower concepts than education, the development of a person for life and work as well as cultural enrichment. Education is anchored to a wider base than the narrow requirements of a specific job. All three elements are incorporated in many programmes (Garavan *et al.*, 2003).

As organisations strive for excellence in the provision of quality products and services in an effort to gain competitive advantage, appropriate personal development is essential for all categories of staff. The increasing challenge of new technologies, greater flexibility, multi-skilling, adaptability and good customer service in a rapidly changing environment have created a greater demand for staff training and development. In addition to specific 'on-the-job' and 'off-the-job' courses, many enlightened employers facilitate staff, with time off and payment of fees, to attend various external courses leading to qualifications. Such employers have found that there is a big correlation between investment in staff development and the success of an organisation. There is now a big emphasis on upskilling and workforce development (Expert Group on Future Skill Needs, 2007).

Staff development programme

The steps involved in an effective staff development programme are enunciation of a policy, identification of training needs, development of a programme to satisfy these needs, budgeting, implementation and evaluation. A policy statement on staff development provides a framework for planned interventions and reflects the attitude and commitment of the organisation. All training interventions should have regard to established learning principles and their transfer to the work situation.

An accurate identification of training needs is essential for the planning of an effective programme. This involves an objective survey of the needs of the organisation for the implementation of its strategic plan, the future needs of each job and for all categories of staff. Each category has training requirements. A programme is then devised to cater for those needs, costed and prioritised. The organisation has to decide the most appropriate and cost-effective way in which the various elements of the approved programme can be implemented. Training and development programmes can be provided in a variety of ways: coaching, mentoring 'on the job', in-house courses, workshops, computer-aided learning, open and distance learning, external placements and studying for accredited courses. It all depends on specific requirements, the required expertise, facilities and cost. Finally, all courses have to be evaluated in relation to their specific objectives. The chief procedures used are tests, questionnaires, observation and subsequent performance. Feedback is necessary to review and revise programmes as required. Most organisations see staff development as a continuous process. There is increasing reference in the literature to the 'learning organisation', one which promotes an organisational culture committed to continuous employee development.

8.6 Employment relations

The system of industrial relations in Ireland is voluntary, which means that the terms and conditions of employment are determined by free collective bargaining between employer and employee with regard to minimum legal rights, or between an employer or employers' association and one or more trade unions, subject to incorporating or improving the minimum rights established by legislation. In recent years pay increases in general have been established by a series of national pay agreements. The role of the State has been confined to the establishment of institutions to assist the collective bargaining process and help resolve disputes. The three dispute resolution bodies are the following:

a)   Labour Relations Commission
b)   Labour Court
c)   Employment Appeals Tribunal.

a)   Labour Relations Commission (LRC)

The Labour Relations Commission (LRC) was established in 1991 under the Industrial Relations Act 1990 with general responsibility for the promotion of good industrial relations through the provision of a wide range of services designed to help prevent and resolve disputes. It is a tripartite body with employer, trade union and independent representatives, all appointed by the Minister for Enterprise, Trade and Innovation.

The Labour Relations Commission provides the following services:

*   An industrial relations conciliation service
*   An industrial relations advisory and research service
*   A Rights Commissioner service.

Industrial relations conciliation service

The main function of the LRC is to provide an industrial relations conciliation service to help resolve disputes where direct negotiations are not successful. All industrial relations disputes must be referred to the LRC, except where there is provision for referring a dispute direct to the Labour Court, or where the LRC waives its function of conciliation in a particular dispute. When a dispute is referred to the LRC it assigns an Industrial Relations Officer to help resolve the dispute at local level by mutual agreement.

Industrial relations advisory and research service

In addition to its conciliation service, the LRC's other functions include an industrial relations advisory service, drawing up codes of practice to promote good industrial relations procedures, reviewing and monitoring developments in industrial relations and commissioning relevant research.

Rights Commissioners

Rights Commissioners, who are attached to the Labour Relations Commission, are appointed by the Minister for Enterprise, Trade and Innovation. Their function is to provide a free conciliation service for personal cases in grievances referred by individuals or small groups of employees. They are prohibited from investigating disputes relating to the rates of pay, hours of work and holiday entitlements of a body of workers. As a result they deal chiefly with disputes arising from individual grievances. An investigation by a Rights Commissioner is voluntary and conducted in private. Having investigated a personal dispute, a Rights Commissioner issues a recommendation on how the dispute could be settled, but it is not binding on the parties involved. Either party to a dispute can appeal a recommendation to the Labour Court. Its decision is binding on both parties, but not legally enforceable.

In addition to their functions under the Industrial Relations Acts, Rights Commissioners can also investigate cases relating to unfair dismissals, payment of wages, terms of employment, maternity protection, adoptive leave, protection of young persons, national minimum wage, parental leave and protection of employees' rights under various Acts and the Organisation of Working Time Act 1997. They issue recommendations, or decisions under some Acts, which may be appealed to the Employment Appeals Tribunal (or the Labour Court in respect of the Organisation of Working Time Act 1997, the National Minimum Wage Act 2000, Protection of Employees (Part-Time Work) Act 2001 and the Protection of Employees (Fixed-Term Work) Act 2003). The Employment Appeals Tribunal and the Labour Court can issue binding determinations (*Guide to Labour Law*).

b) Labour Court

The Labour Court was established under the Industrial Relations Act 1946 as amended in subsequent legislation in 1969, 1976, 1990 and 2001 as well as in other employment legislation. It consists of a chairperson and deputy chairpersons as well as ordinary members nominated by the Irish Business and Employers Confederation (IBEC) and by the Irish Congress of Trade Unions (ICTU), all appointed by the Minister for Enterprise, Trade and Innovation. The Court operates in divisions, consisting of the chairperson or one of the deputy chairpersons, an employers' member and a union member, but certain issues require a sitting of the full membership. The Labour Court is not a court of law, but it acts as a body of last resort when other options to resolve industrial relations issues have been exhausted. It also acts as a court of appeal for decisions of the Rights Commissioners, Equality Officers and the Director of Equality Investigations (*Guide to Labour Law* and *Labour Court, n.d.*).

The main function of the Labour Court is the investigation of industrial disputes and the issuing of recommendations for their settlement. Normally the Court will only investigate a dispute when it either receives a report from the Labour Relations Commission that no further efforts on its part will help to resolve the dispute or the Commission waives its function of conciliation in the dispute. It may also investigate a dispute referred to it under section 20 of the Industrial Relations Act 1969. Having investigated a dispute, the Labour Court issues a recommendation setting out its opinions on the merits of the dispute and the terms on which it should be settled. Agreement is dependent on both parties accepting the Labour Court recommendation in accordance with the principle of free collective bargaining. Disputes regarding one person or small groups of employees are generally referred to the Rights Commissioners. A Rights

Commissioner makes a recommendation which can be appealed to the Labour Court, which can issue an appeal decision that is not legally enforceable.

In respect of equality cases, the Labour Court is a 'court of first instance' and also has appellate roles. An employee who considers that he/she was unfairly dismissed on grounds relating to discrimination (as defined in the equality legislation) can seek redress directly from the Labour Court. The Court's decision in this case is called a determination, which is legally enforceable. In other cases involving discrimination but not dismissal, the complaint has to be investigated by an Equality Officer or the Director of Equality Investigations and a decision made. In these cases, the Labour Court has an appellate role. Either party may appeal the decision to the Labour Court, which can issue a determination which is legally enforceable. The Labour Court also has an appellate role in relation to the Organisation of Working Time Act 1997, the National Minimum Wage Act 2000 and the Protection of Employees (Fixed-Term Work) Act 2003. Its determinations in these cases are legally enforceable (*Guide to Labour Law* and *Labour Court, n.d.*).

The other functions of the Labour Court include the establishment and servicing of Joint Labour Committees (JLCs) and making employment regulation orders arising from proposals relating to pay and conditions received from these committees. JLCs are bodies established under the Industrial Relations Act 1946 to determine minimum rates of pay and conditions of work in certain employments. When their proposals are approved by the Labour Court by making employment regulations orders, they have statutory effect for the workers and employers concerned. There is also provision for registered employment agreements with the Labour Court to be binding not only on the trade unions and employers involved, but others who are in the categories covered by the agreement. They cover the pay or conditions of employment of any class, type or group of workers which is registered with the Labour Court.

The services of the Labour Relations Commission and the Labour Court are available free to all workers covered by the Industrial Relations Act 1990, generally all employees except those in the public service included in conciliation and arbitration schemes and certain other categories.

c)   Employment Appeals Tribunal

The Employment Appeals Tribunal (EAT) was originally established as the Redundancy Appeals Tribunal and renamed under the Unfair Dismissals Act 1977. It consists of a chairperson and 31 vice-chairpersons with legal qualifications and a panel of 72 members, made up of an equal number from employer organisations and trade unions. It acts in divisions, with the chairperson or vice-chairperson and one representative from both the trade unions and employers.

The function of the Employment Appeals Tribunal is to determine matters of dispute arising in relation to redundancy payments, minimum notice, maternity protection, adoptive leave, unfair dismissals, protection of employees (employers' insolvency), worker protection (regular part-time employees), payment of wages, protection of young persons, organisation of working time, parental leave and terms of employment legislation. Disputes under the above legislation may be referred either directly or on appeal to the tribunal. A party may present his/her own case to the tribunal or be legally represented (or by a representative of a trade union or employers' body). Cases must be brought within the time limit specified in the relevant legislation. The procedure involved is like a court of law. After hearing a case, the tribunal gives a determination or decision which is legally binding on both parties. Determinations in relation to unfair dismissals and maternity protection may be appealed to the Circuit Court inside six weeks, and in relation to other legislation to the High Court on a point of law only.

Mediation

Some personal disputes between employees and employers are now settled by mediation. In this process an acceptable mediator tries to reach an agreed settlement between the parties. It is voluntary, confidential and can be very satisfactory for both parties.

Irish Congress of Trade Unions

The Irish Congress of Trade Unions (ICTU) is the central authority for the Irish trade union movement. It was established in 1959 from a merger of two bodies which operated after 1944 when the original Irish Trade Union Congress, which was inaugurated in 1894, split. There are 57 trade unions affiliated to the ICTU, which operates as an all-Ireland body. There are several organisations in the private sector with no unions, especially in multinational corporations (Gunnigle *et al.*, 2004). The main function of the ICTU is to co-ordinate the trade unions operating in Ireland, nominating members to serve on various bodies like the Labour Relations Commission and the Labour Court. It has also represented its members since 1987 as a social partner in negotiating national agreements on social and economic issues as well as pay and conditions of employment.

Irish Business and Employers Confederation (IBEC)

The Irish Business and Employers Confederation, which was established in 1993, represents employers in all matters relating to industrial relations. It also nominates to serve on various national bodies and, as a social partner, in negotiating the various national agreements. In addition, it represents business and employers on all matters relating to trade, economics, finance, taxation and social affairs. It also provides a comprehensive advisory and support service to members on all aspects of employment and employee relations.

Industrial relations disputes

The legal framework for industrial relations disputes in Ireland is contained in the Industrial Relations Act 1990, as amended. In addition to the establishment of the Labour Relations

Commission and altering the functions of the Labour Court, this Act also provides a series of immunities for acts done 'in contemplation or furtherance of a trade dispute' provided the specified procedures are followed. The immunities cover criminal and civil conspiracy, the inducement of another person to break a contract of employment, a threat to induce such a breach, a threat by a person to break his/her own contract of employment, an interference with the trade, business or employment of another person and any tortious act committed by a trade union. It also legalises picketing at the place of work of a worker's own employer under the conditions specified:

> It shall be lawful for one or more persons, acting on their own behalf or on behalf of a trade union in contemplation or furtherance of a trade dispute, to attend at, or where that is not practicable, at the approaches to, a place where their employer works or carries on business, if they so attend merely for the purpose of peacefully obtaining or communicating information or of peacefully persuading any person to work or abstain from working. (section 11)

The picketing of an employer's home is not protected, but that was a rare occurrence. The Act legalises secondary picketing, but only where a second employer acts in a way calculated to frustrate a strike or other industrial action by directly assisting the employer who is party to the dispute. All the immunities are confined to trade unions with negotiation licences and the members of such unions, but do not apply to disputes concerning one worker where agreed procedures have not been followed.

From 18 July 1992 the rules of every trade union have to contain a provision that no strike or other industrial action can take place without a secret ballot, and that the committee of management of a union has discretion in calling a strike notwithstanding a majority in favour in the ballot. The immunities already referred to will not apply to any actions contrary to the result of a secret ballot. If the ballot favours industrial action and the trade union gives at least one week's notice to the employer concerned, that employer may not seek an *ex parte* injunction to stop the action, except in the case of unlawful entry, trespass or action likely to cause death or personal injury. Every trade union is obliged to forward a copy of its rules incorporating the secret ballot provision to the Registrar of Friendly Societies. Any union failing to comply is not entitled to hold a negotiation licence.

8.7 Summary

The recruitment of competent employees with positive, creative, innovative and customer-focused minds is important in the modern business world. Such employees can give an organisation a competitive advantage. A good induction programme, incorporating specific training in relation to each post as well as the culture, beliefs, ethos and standards expected, is also important.

There is now a wide range of employment legislation, starting with the Redundancy Payments Act 1967, which has provided a statutory floor of minimum rights for all employees. Pay, conditions, performance appraisal and staff development are also essential elements of human resource management.

The system of industrial relations in Ireland is voluntary, which means that terms and conditions of employment are determined by free collective bargaining between an employer and employee, having regard to the protective legislation. In recent times, pay increases in general have been established by a series of national agreements. The State supports the process with three dispute resolution bodies: the Labour Relations Commission, the Labour Court and the Employment Appeals Tribunal. The Equality Authority and the Equality Tribunal have specific obligations in relation to equality legislation.

Questions

1. Explain the following terms in human resource management.
   a) A contract of service and a contract for service
   b) A fixed-term contract and a special purpose contract
   c) Performance appraisal
   d) Staff development
2. Discuss the main issues to be considered in interviewing a candidate for a specific post.
3. Outline the main features of the safety, health and welfare at work legislation in Ireland.
4. Discuss how you would deal with an employee who is perceived to be under-performing.
5. Discuss the role of each of the following.
   a) The Labour Relations Commission
   b) The Labour Court
   c) The Employment Appeals Tribunal
   d) The Equality Authority
   e) The Equality Tribunal.

Chapter 9

Start-up, growth and exit

Great works are performed not by strength but by perseverance.

Dr Samuel Johnson

Learning objectives

- To explore the main issues which arise for a start-up business and over various stages of business growth
- To examine the various options which arise for a business that becomes insolvent
- To consider various exit strategies for owner-managers of small businesses.

This chapter is structured as follows:

9.1 Introduction
9.2 Stages of small business growth
9.3 Insolvency
9.4 Exit strategies
9.5 Summary

9.1 Introduction

Management issues for a business depend on its stage of development. The start-up stage of any business requires considerable planning and organisation. This chapter considers the main issues which arise at the start-up stage and, if successful, at the crisis and survival stages. If successful, growth is a desirable option, but this is not within the ambition, resources and competence of all entrepreneurs. Growth, like start-up, has to be carefully planned. This requires a revised strategic plan, new organisational structure, extra finance and a management team with strengths in all the main functional activities. Growth can be organic or arise from external linkages designed to achieve various synergies and economies of scale.

Some businesses do not succeed and end up insolvent. In the case of a company, this can result in receivership. Other options that can be considered include an arrangement with creditors, examinership or, if this does not succeed, liquidation. Directors of insolvent companies can incur penalties in certain circumstances.

If a business survives and prospers, the question of an exit strategy for the owner arises at some stage. Various exit strategies are briefly outlined.

9.2 Stages of small business growth

Each small business carves out its own unique development path. A business that survives and expands could go through five stages, or variations thereof, in the process (Churchill and Lewis, 1983; Jolly, 1997):

a)   Start-up stage
b)   Crisis stage
c)   Survival stage
d)   Mature stage
e)   Growth stage
f)   Mature growth.

Each stage has its own unique features and challenges, influenced by many internal and external factors like the energy, vision and aspirations of the entrepreneur as well as economic conditions, market opportunities and technological developments. A more common development model consists of start-up, survival, growth and sale. Knowledge of possible stages enables an entrepreneur to anticipate the problems and plan accordingly with good management practices. There is considerable overlap between the stages.

a)   Start-up stage

The launch of any new business is planned for some time in advance. After an entrepreneur has perceived a business opportunity and prepared a business plan which is acceptable to himself/herself, the funding agencies and investors, he/she has to focus on the market entry strategy (where, how and when to enter the target market) and the competitive strategy to be followed to differentiate the new business from competitors. The market entry strategy can involve entering one or more market segments or the whole market. This is influenced by the resources required, possible economies of scale, patent protection, the structure of the market and competition (O'Gorman and Cunningham, 2007). Competitive strategy is how a business plans to compete with existing suppliers in a chosen market. It involves a choice between providing a better product or service than existing suppliers in the market, or at a lower cost, or both.

The promoter then has to acquire and organise all the resources required to launch the enterprise (premises, equipment, supplies, finance and staff) as well as complying with all regulatory requirements like health, safety, fire and planning permission. Premises may have to be acquired, planning permission obtained, equipment provided, supplies ordered, staff recruited and trained and the production process, if applicable, organised. Insurance cover has to be arranged and various services like electricity, water, telephone and other requirements connected. A good lead time is required. With good planning and organisation, most work relating to the provision of essential facilities can be done concurrently rather than sequentially. A bank account has to be opened for the business (by completing the necessary form and providing any documentation required). It is important that all aspects of the business are in place for the launch date. The launch is preceded by a good promotional campaign, the exact nature of which will vary from one business to another, designed to persuade potential customers to try the new product or service and to come back with repeat business as well as communicating a positive reaction to their friends. The launch is an opportunity for a new business to get good publicity, but it has to be planned carefully. Some businesses start trading in advance of the launch date. Many small production businesses have no official launch.

After the launch or start, a business enters a period of great anxiety and expectations. The big question is, how are customers going to react to the product or service? Customers are generally very slow to change from an existing product or service provider for a variety of reasons: loyalty, habit or convenience. This has to be considered before a business is started to establish a unique selling proposition and competitive advantage. The main objectives at this stage are to promote the unique selling proposition of the product or service to attract customers, to get them to convey positive responses to others and to deliver the promised benefits. New benefits and value for customers are very important in early promotions so as to build a base of loyal supporters. In all the euphoria concerning the launch or commencement it is important to adhere to the business plan in relation to promotional activity, facilities, margins, prompt payment and all other matters. Good cash management is essential from the start. It is very easy to concentrate on the product or service and forget other important matters at this hectic time. The reaction of competitors has to be monitored. Some try to react in various ways: reduced prices, special offers, special promotions or endeavouring to restrict access to suppliers or distributors. The two big challenges for a new business are attracting customers and overcoming the market reactions of competitors.

Often a new business can attract early support from customers for a variety of reasons, but keeping them and increasing the number require considerable effort. This phase requires an inordinate time commitment from the entrepreneur and dedicated service by staff to make the enterprise a success. The organisation is simple, with the entrepreneur doing everything and directing all the staff. Systems and procedures are simple, often invented as the need arises. Regardless of the pressures it is essential for the entrepreneur to ensure that proper records, accounts and controls are operated from the commencement of an enterprise. Neglect of such important obligations can be costly. Regardless of how well the planning is done, every entrepreneur gets some surprises at this stage and some shocks, but hopefully ones which can be overcome. Early goodwill from friends and potential customers, effective marketing and promotion, adequate resources, huge personal commitment and good cash management can bring most businesses through this start-up stage.

b)   Crisis stage

The next stage can be chaotic as the business strives to win a market share or obtain a niche position. The business has to attract enough customers to generate sufficient turnover and profit to create a viable enterprise. Customers purchase goods and services for their perceived benefits; consequently there must be value for customers which will attract and retain them. After the honeymoon period which some businesses experience, an enterprise has to carve out its own destiny based on value to customers and its reputation for quality, service and reliability. Its objective is to build up a solid customer base. The key marketing issues at this stage are the reaction of customers to the product or service (quality, price and suitability), the feedback from distribution channels and the reaction of competitors. With regard to production, the key issues are that the facilities can produce the quantity and quality required by customers on schedule and within the established cost parameters. On the financial side, the key measures are liquidity and profitability.

Anecdotal evidence from entrepreneurs about the early development of their businesses is very enlightening; there are stories of marketing difficulties relating to distribution channels, packaging and promotional material, problems with supplies, production delays and cash flow shortages arising from overspending and slow payments. The list is endless. Comparing actual performance at this stage against the business plan can be enlightening. The most common problems arise from overestimating sales, underestimating costs, overspending on capital investments, facilities not completed on schedule, naïve assumptions about cash flow projections, poor research and inadequate contingency planning. However, most entrepreneurs discover that the business plan is an invaluable exercise in ensuring that fewer and less costly problems arise than might otherwise be the case. Every entrepreneur makes mistakes at this stage, some of which are costly, and there is considerable learning involved. An entrepreneur with experience in the business has a big advantage over a neophyte at this important phase of development. The business strategy is survival; however, up to 30 per cent of businesses fail at this stage. Their demise can result from market failure (not attracting sufficient customers), product failure (wrong product for the market), financial failure (cash flow) or owner-manager failure (lack of competence).

c)   Survival stage

If a business overcomes the crisis stage, it has demonstrated that it has the capacity to attract a loyal customer base and survive in the chosen marketplace. The objective now is to consolidate its survival.

Market opportunities and the aspiration of the entrepreneur are the main determinants of growth. The majority of new businesses remain small, often simply providing self-employment. Growth depends very much on the nature of each business, its location and resources as well as the ambition and skills of the promoter concerned. Most solo entrepreneurs survive because they provide a unique local service, a phenomenon likely to increase in the future as the number of new, permanent, pensionable jobs declines. Recent trends such as short-term contracting and outsourcing are creating more opportunities for self-employment; more people will become self-employed and market their portfolio careers to a number of employers rather than enter the traditional employer–employee relationship. In this context the ability of people to earn their livelihoods will depend on their own self-reliance, personal development, imagination, creativity, flexibility and enterprise. The objective of a solo entrepreneur is to make a good living, which the vast majority are well able to achieve.

To survive, small enterprises have to be responsive to market needs, agile and innovative, constantly seeking smarter, faster, better, cheaper and more efficient ways to offer competitive products and services. The majority of small businesses are family owned, managed and controlled (Fullard, 1999). The objectives of many family businesses are to attain and sustain a certain lifestyle rather than seek to maximise financial returns. Entrepreneurs recruit extra staff as their businesses grow. Most high-technology firms recruit a strong management team from the start. Once started, a business tries to establish a solid niche for itself by developing good relationships with customers, staff, suppliers and the general public. The most dangerous period is the first three years, when many new businesses, outside self-employment, fail to attract sufficient customers and do not survive. In Ireland there is pressure on small businesses to grow and increase employment, which is of course desirable, but it is not within the aspirations, competence or resources of all entrepreneurs. Providing additional employment, however altruistic the motive, is not a major objective of many entrepreneurs, but it may be the consequence of extra business arising from an increased base of satisfied customers. This involves keeping the maximum possible number of existing customers as well as attracting new ones, with satisfied customers referring new business opportunities to a deserving enterprise.

The emphasis at the survival stage for many small enterprises turns to ensuring that profitability reaches its target by focusing attention on costs, revenues, operating efficiency and productivity. Professional staff are often recruited to head up key functional activities and the entrepreneur has to adjust his/her mindset and role to that of a managing director, with proper delegation. Many entrepreneurs find it difficult to make this adjustment. Improved procedures, systems and controls are generally introduced and the organisation becomes more professional in all its activities. Some businesses do not progress further and consolidate, happy with their existing markets and financial returns, where the owner-managers can retain control and enjoy comfortable earnings. Some businesses also fail at this stage or are sold as going concerns.

d) Mature stage

The next phase is the mature stage, where a business can decide to exploit its existing market opportunities to their potential, disengage or expand further. A business can decide to enjoy its consolidated place in a market niche and earn average or acceptable profits indefinitely. Some markets have no growth potential and seeking opportunities elsewhere brings risks which some mature businesses are unwilling to take. A business can remain at this stage, provided it has the capacity to respond to changes in its marketplace over time. The organisational structure has professional managers in all key functional activities. Procedures, management information systems and controls are all developed in line with good business practices. Many entrepreneurs are happy to enjoy the fruits of their creations, but the big threats are complacency and slow response to market changes.

At maturity, some entrepreneurs decide to harvest their enterprises by selling them as going concerns and disengaging. Some of these entrepreneurs stay on as employees of the new owners or start up new enterprises. Another option is growth.

e) Growth stage

Many entrepreneurs decide to start as small businesses and, if successful, to grow. There are barriers which can inhibit growth, such as market size, competition, operating costs, resources, profitability and competence as well as the need for innovation and new product development. For many businesses there is a critical size of operation which enables them to reap the necessary economies of scale to compete successfully in the marketplace. Establishing value-added relationships, to the mutual benefit of each party, is an effective way of developing a business. More and more businesses are endeavouring to establish symbiotic long-term relationships with their customers, suppliers and distributors to achieve growth. Most small businesses grow organically within their existing market sectors by attracting more customers and/or by developing exports. As the Irish market is small, most growth-orientated businesses must develop export markets.

Various reports, especially the Enterprise Strategy Group report, *Ahead of the Curve: Ireland's Place in the Global Economy* (2004) and *Building Ireland's Smart Economy: A Framework for Sustainable Economic Renewal* (Department of the Taoiseach, 2008), recommend that far more Irish small and medium-sized enterprises should explore international markets. They recommend building technological and applied research and innovation capability to support the development of high-value products and services for which there is international demand. It is also planned that the big Irish investment in research and development will lead to the commercialisation of new knowledge in products and services on a global scale. The development of growth and export markets requires ambition, enthusiasm, competence and resources. More Irish businesses have to think and plan globally, identifying barriers and overcoming them. In many cases there is a poverty of ambition. More Irish enterprises have to adopt the philosophy of President Barack Obama: 'Yes, we can.' Growth, like start-up, has to be planned carefully. Many entrepreneurs find it difficult to make the transition from owner-manager to manager to a growing enterprise. Accordingly to Storey (1994), only about 4 per cent of all start-ups achieve high growth levels, measured by numbers employed.

According to O'Gorman (2001), successful small and medium-sized companies pay particular attention to market choice (industry, sector and segment) and their competitive strategies. Successful SMEs pursue strategies of differentiation, innovation, customer service and quality and grow organically. A key factor is the positioning of the business in a growth market. A business will generally have established a distinctive competence and customer success before going for growth in new markets. There are many reasons for pursuing growth: economies of scale, consolidation of the business in the long term, stability in dealing with changes in demand over time, reducing competition and especially increased profits. A growth policy brings extra risks, but the possible returns are also greater. The organisational structure becomes more formal and complex, with some slack to enable a business to engage in strategic planning. Often the owner-manager appoints a new chief executive and becomes chairperson of the board of directors with time to explore and develop strategic agreements. Increased profits are essential for growth, as it is dangerous to be over-dependent on borrowings, and raising finance for growth generally means selling more shares in a company. The main sources of finance for business growth are share capital, preference shares, loans and retained profits. A business has to grow within the limits of its financial resources, otherwise it could run out of cash and result in receivership, a common occurrence with overtrading and rapid growth. Factors to be considered for planned growth include market opportunities, a distinctive competitive strategy, building a competent management team with strengths in the key functional areas, ensuring that operations can deliver on the scale and quality required, and good management information and control systems together with adequate finance, satisfactory additional profits and positive cash flow.

Growth can be organic or involve external linkages such as a joint venture (a separate entity formed by two or more organisations), a merger (two or more firms becoming one organisation) or an acquisition (one organisation taking over another) where various synergies and possible economies of scale are identified. Irish SMEs can exploit some new international opportunities by forming joint ventures with multinational corporations. Growth can be achieved by intensive, integrative or diversification strategies (Ansoff, 1957; Kotler, 2003). Intensive growth incorporates the following:

- Market penetration (increased sales of existing product(s) in the present markets)
- Market development (increased sales for existing product(s) in new markets)

- Product development (increased sales by developing new product(s) for the existing markets).

Integrative growth involves:
- Backward integration (acquiring suppliers)
- Forward integration (acquiring control of distribution outlets)
- Horizontal integration (acquiring ownership or control of competitors).

Diversification incorporates three options:
- Concentric (new products with synergies to existing operation)
- Horizontal (new products for existing customers)
- Conglomerate (new products for new customers).

In considering diversification strategies where an organisation has a number of businesses or products, a portfolio management technique is followed, the best known of which is the Boston Consulting Group (BCG) matrix (1970). The matrix is a framework to review the performance of each business or product with regard to growth and market share. This matrix classifies products into four categories: stars, question marks, cash cows and dogs. Stars are market leaders in growing markets, but considerable funds are required to satisfy the market growth and to fight off attacks from competitors. Question marks are products with low market shares in high-growth markets. They usually require big investment to satisfy the growing market. Cash cows are products at the mature stage of their life cycles, enjoying economies of scale and good returns but with slow or declining growth rates. Dogs have low market shares and low growth rates. The options facing a business are to phase out such products, reinvent or reposition the products so as to prolong their life cycles. After considering the various products in the growth-share matrix, a business has to decide on its strategic portfolio, with a preference for more cash cows and stars and fewer dogs and question marks (Kotler, 2003). Johnson *et al.* (2005) identify three criteria by which the various growth options can be evaluated: suitability (with regard to the opportunities and threats in the environment and the strengths of the company), feasibility (in relation to resources, the market and competition) and acceptability (in relation to risk and potential profitability).

f) Mature growth

The objective of an organisation at this stage is to consolidate its growth position and reap appropriate returns. It has the professional staff and resources to engage in good management practices at all levels as well as strategic and operational planning, effective organisation, good leadership, motivation, communications and sophisticated control procedures, with the emphasis on achieving specific objectives and goals. It endeavours to keep close to customers, with the flexibility to respond quickly to changing needs and to remain entrepreneurial.

9.3 Insolvency

Some businesses do not succeed and end up in 'financial trouble', a euphemism for insolvency, or a shortage of cash to meet obligations. This may arise for many reasons, such as declining demand, uncompetitive prices, high cost base, managerial inexperience, poor control systems, under-capitalisation, overtrading, recruiting staff on the basis of nepotism and not ability, failure to change management practices as the business grows, product obsolescence and failure to respond promptly to changes in the market. In most businesses there are early warning signs, such as complaints from customers regarding price, quality, or service; credit curtailed; delay in paying creditors; suppliers demanding payment in advance; and staff turnover. Some businesses survive this traumatic experience with difficulty, but many perish. Every effort has to be made to address the crisis by first identifying the sources of the problems and possible remedial actions. Options to be considered include reducing prices and expanding sales at planned margins, improving quality, reducing costs, increasing productivity, eliminating waste, dropping loss-making products, downsizing and, if overtrading, to scale back operations within existing resources. To survive, a business has to be competitive in the marketplace, offer value to its customers and generate profits together with a positive cash flow. If these actions do not succeed, insolvency can lead, in the case of a company, to the appointment of a receiver, an examiner or a liquidator, with possible penalties on directors (see below). A company has no say in the appointment of a receiver; that is a matter for a secured creditor if a borrower defaults on repayments.

The issues that arise in an insolvency situation are as follows:

a) Receivership
b) Arrangements with creditors
c) Examinership
d) Liquidation
e) Penalties on directors
f) Strike-off
g) Bankruptcy.

a) Receivership

A receiver is a person appointed under a debenture (loan agreement) or a Court order to take control of the assets of a company which have been mortgaged or charged in favour of a lender and to sell them to discharge the debt due to the creditor. A receiver is normally appointed, following due notice, by a secured creditor, usually a financial institution, under powers contained in a valid deed of debenture, executed by the company in favour of the lender, creating at least a floating charge over all the assets of the company and often a specific charge over fixed assets. This procedure can be brought into operation in the event of the borrowing company continuing to default in the repayment of a loan secured in this manner. A receiver can also be appointed by the High Court, in which case instructions are taken from the Court. Where a specific asset is mortgaged and charged, a receiver is appointed in respect of that asset. Where the charge covers all the assets, a receiver-manager is appointed, who acts as receiver and manager of the business during the receivership. The receiver's primary duty is to the debenture-holder who appointed him or her. Where there appears to be a good reason, a receiver can apply to the High Court for an order to prevent a director or other officer of the company from removing his/her assets from the State or reducing them below a figure specified by the Court (see Note 1 on page 264).

The powers of the company and the directors' authority are suspended in respect of the assets covered by the debenture, but they do not cease to be directors. Upon the appointment of a receiver any floating charge crystallises (that is, it becomes in effect a fixed charge in respect of the assets secured). The company is obliged to provide the receiver with a statement of affairs in the prescribed form within 14 days. After the appointment of a receiver every invoice, order or business letter issued by or on behalf of the company must contain a statement that it is in receivership.

The objective of a receiver-manager is to run the company while trying to find the easiest way to repay the debenture holder who appointed him/her. If the receiver is appointed under a fixed charge, the debenture holder is paid first, with any surplus going back to the company. If the appointment arose from a floating charge, preferential creditors (for example, the Revenue Commissioners and employees) are paid first and then the debenture holder. If, after redeeming the secured loan, the company cannot be continued or sold as a going concern, the remaining assets are given to a liquidator who proceeds from there, pays the other creditors in so far as the assets permit and winds up the company. Where it appears that any director or officer may have committed a criminal offence in relation to the company, a receiver is obliged to report the matter to the Director of Public Prosecutions (DPP). A receiver is obliged to act in good faith to the debenture holder and to the company. There are several companies operating in Ireland that have survived receivership.

b)   Arrangement with creditors

Where receivership does not arise, companies consider all possible rescue options first, with liquidation a last resort. This is advantageous for creditors, who generally receive more in a rescue operation than when liquidation occurs, and for directors because it minimises their exposure to possible penalties. It may be possible for a company to negotiate an arrangement with creditors. This option depends on many factors: the integrity of the directors, acceptance of insolvency, a new viable business plan and agreement with the various types of creditors – preferential (for example, the Revenue

Commissioners, who are generally paid in full), secured and unsecured. A company undertaking this route has to receive good professional advice. First, an evaluation is carried out to find the causes of the current difficulties, to establish if the company is viable provided specific actions are taken and that it has good relationships with its key stakeholders, such as suppliers, customers, shareholders, staff and banks. Secondly, decisions are taken to stop the situation getting worse and every effort is made to prune costs and generate additional cash. The third step is to devise a rescue and restructuring scheme. This can involve some of the following: introduction of new investment with specific conditions, such as the appointment of non-executive directors and new management; creditors writing down their debts; outsourcing certain activities; disposal of some assets or underperforming units; and the introduction of good management practices. If the majority of the creditors agree to the scheme and others do not, it may be possible to use the procedure outlined in section 201 of the Companies Act 1963, which states:

> If a majority in number representing three-fourths in value of the creditors, or class of creditors . . . vote in favour of a resolution agreeing to any compromise, or arrangement, the compromise or arrangement shall, if sanctioned by the Court, be binding on all the creditors or the class of creditors, or on the members or class of members, as the case may be, and also on the company.

A scheme of arrangement under section 201 requires the approval of the Court. If these options are not feasible there are only two possible considerations:
- Examinership
- Liquidation.

c)   Examinership

The Companies Act of 1990 and the Companies (Amendment) Acts of 1990 and 1999 provide a legal mechanism whereby a company in financial difficulty can obtain short-term protection from its creditors to enable a person, known as an examiner, to assess if a possible rescue arrangement could be put in place to save it from liquidation (see Note 2 on page 264). The Court may appoint an examiner if it considers that such an order would facilitate the survival of a company, or any part of its undertaking, as a going concern. If a receiver has been appointed to the company for three days, it is not possible to make an application for the appointment of an examiner. A petition to the Court for such an appointment can be presented by the company or its directors, a creditor or members holding not less than one-tenth of the paid-up capital with voting rights. The petition must nominate a person who is willing to be appointed as examiner and satisfy the Court that the company is unable to pay its debts. It must be accompanied by an independent accountant's report containing the information specified in the Companies (Amendment) (No. 2) Act 1999. This has to show that the company has a 'reasonable prospect of survival' and that it can be funded during the examinership. On hearing such a petition the High Court has the discretion to appoint an examiner, dismiss the application, adjourn the hearing, make an interim order or any order it thinks fit. If an examiner is appointed, the petitioner is obliged to notify the Registrar of Companies within three days and publish a notice to that effect in *Iris Oifigiúil* as well as in at least two daily newspapers circulating in a district where the registered office of the company is situated.

An examiner is appointed for 70 days and an extension of 30 days can be granted by the High Court, during which time the company is under the protection of the Court. In that period no liquidator or receiver can be appointed and the company's assets cannot be attached or sequestrated, nor can a secured creditor realise a security without the consent of the examiner. No steps can be taken to repossess goods under a hire purchase agreement or a reservation of title clause or to initiate legal action to recover debts. During the period of an examiner's appointment the directors continue to act and manage the company, but the Court has the authority to vest such powers in the examiner if considered appropriate. An examiner may or, if so directed by the Court, must appoint a committee of creditors to assist. Once appointed, the examiner is obliged to conduct an examination of the affairs of the company and report to the Court within 35 days of the appointment. Officers and agents of the company or related organisation are required to produce to the examiner all books and documents in their custody or power, including details of personal bank accounts if required, and to co-operate in every respect. They can be examined on oath if necessary. The examiner can convene, attend or preside at meetings of directors and shareholders and is entitled to all the information and co-operation which an auditor would expect. The examiner's report must include the names and addresses of all officers of the company, a statement of affairs, comments on any deficiency or disappearance of property and a statement of opinion as to whether the company, or part of it, is capable of survival as a going concern. He/she is obliged to state whether such a course would be more advantageous for members and creditors than winding up.

If the examiner recommends continuation of the business, he/she is obliged to draft proposals for a compromise, or scheme of arrangement, which generally consists of a new investor with diminution of control for the existing owners and creditors writing down debts. However unpalatable the proposals, they are generally more acceptable than liquidation. Where the High Court accepts proposals for a scheme of arrangement, the examiner convenes meetings of each class of members and creditors. The notice of such meetings must contain a statement fully explaining the effects of the proposals. Creditors and members are free to accept or reject the proposals. The proposals are deemed to be accepted when a majority in number representing a majority in value of the claims adopts them. A comprehensive report on these meetings is made to the Court and any interested party has a right to object. If the Court rejects the proposals it can order the winding up of the company; if it approves, the proposals become binding on all members and creditors of the company with effect from a date fixed by the Court. When the proposals are implemented the examiner's appointment is terminated and the company loses the protection of the Court. The Court determines the fees, costs and expenses of the examiner, which are paid in full in priority to any other claim. While examinership has proved to be effective for some big corporations, such as the Goodman International Group in 1990, it can be an expensive process for small companies. By the end of the first decade of the twenty-first century, the failure rate of examinerships was high because it became difficult to attract new investors.

d) Liquidation

Liquidation, or winding up, is the process whereby the life of a company is terminated. The work is performed by a person called a liquidator, who takes over the function of the directors, ceases trading, conducts an investigation into the company's affairs, sells off all the assets, pays the creditors as far as possible in accordance with the relevant law and distributes any surplus to members. When the process is complete, the company is legally dissolved. Where a company cannot be saved it should be wound up in a responsible manner. Companies can be wound up in two ways:

- A compulsory liquidation by the Court
- A voluntary liquidation (see Note 3 on page 264).

The Registrar of Companies can strike defunct companies from the register and also those that do not file annual returns for two successive years or do not register with the Revenue Commissioners for tax purposes.

Compulsory liquidation by the Court

A company may be wound up by the High Court on the petition of a creditor, the company, a contributory (any person liable to contribute to the assets of the company in the event of its being wound up) or the Minister for Enterprise, Trade and Innovation. There are a number of grounds for such a petition, including the following: where the company passes a special resolution that it should be wound up by the Court, the company is unable to pay its debts (the chief reason and sometimes initiated by the Revenue Commissioners), the Court is of the opinion that it is just and equitable that the company should be wound up and where the company's affairs are being conducted in an oppressive manner. Notice of any such petition must be publicised in *Iris Oifigiúil* and in at least two daily newspapers seven clear days before the hearing. The Court has the discretion to refuse a petition for winding up a company and will not entertain frivolous requests. High Court liquidations are not common. If the Court grants an application it appoints a liquidator, who becomes an officer of the Court. The company is obliged to file a statement of its affairs in Court within 21 days from the date of winding up. A committee of inspection (representatives of contributors and creditors) may be appointed to supervise and assist in the conduct of the winding-up. The liquidator takes over the functions of the board of directors and is in a fiduciary relationship with the creditors and the company. He or she takes possession of all company assets, makes out lists of creditors and contributories, realises the assets and distributes the proceeds in so far as funds are available in accordance with the priority determined by law. The priorities between creditors in a winding-up is a complex topic and the following is only a general outline. Debenture holders with fixed charges are paid out of the proceeds of the sale of their secured assets. The remaining assets, when realised, are distributed with the following order of priority: the costs and expenses of winding up, preferential debts, floating charge-holders, unsecured creditors and, last, shareholders. Any conveyance, mortgage, delivery of goods or payment of execution by a company within six months of winding up made with the dominant intention of preferring one creditor over others could be held to be fraudulent preference and deemed invalid. The Court makes an order that a company is dissolved on an application from the liquidator.

Voluntary liquidation
A company can be wound up voluntarily for a wide variety of reasons. There are two types of voluntary winding-up: one initiated by members and the other by creditors. A members' voluntary winding-up can only be carried out if the company is solvent. It may be carried out if the directors (or the majority of them) make a statutory declaration of solvency to the effect that they have made a full inquiry into the affairs of the company and, having done so, have formed the opinion that the company will be able to pay its debts in full within a specified period not exceeding 12 months from the commencement of the liquidation. This declaration must be accompanied by a report from an independent person who is qualified to act as the company's auditor stating that the directors' opinion regarding solvency is reasonable. Where such a declaration is made, the company is required to pass a special resolution in a general meeting within 28 days to wind itself up, to publish a notice to that effect in *Iris Oifigiúil* and notify the Registrar of Companies. If the declaration of solvency is not challenged in an application to the Court within 28 days or survives the challenge, the members in a general meeting can appoint a liquidator (who is not subject to the supervision of creditors) and determine his or her remuneration. The liquidator then proceeds to liquidate the company. If the company is unable to pay its debts within 12 months, the members' voluntary liquidation is turned into a creditors' voluntary liquidation.

If the directors are unable to make a declaration of solvency, the liquidation must be a creditors' voluntary winding-up. A meeting of creditors must be convened for the same day or the day after the company meeting at which a resolution for voluntary liquidation is passed and a liquidator nominated. Notices are sent to creditors by post at least 10 days before the meeting and advertised in two daily newspapers. If a creditor cannot attend a creditors' meeting, he/she can nominate a proxy. The directors of the company are obliged to submit a statement of affairs to the meeting, together with a list of the creditors and the estimated amount of their claims, and appoint one of them to preside at the meeting. The statement of affairs will also show the book values of all assets with the estimated realisable value of each in a liquidation.

The usual agenda for a meeting of creditors is as follows:

- To consider the statement of affairs
- To appoint a liquidator
- To nominate creditors to a committee of inspection.

Creditors generally question the directors on all aspects of the company's affairs, and there is often considerable acrimony at such a meeting. The creditors can accept the shareholders' nominee for liquidator or replace the nominee with their own liquidator where a majority of creditors in value desire to do so, but the Court, on application, may appoint somebody else. The creditors may appoint a committee of inspection to supervise the liquidation (with creditors nominating up to five members and three shareholders). The committee of inspection, or if there is no such committee, the creditors, may fix the remuneration of the liquidator. The liquidator's duties in a voluntary winding-up are similar to the position in a compulsory winding-up. He/she must take possession of all the assets and records of the company, realise the assets, pay the costs of the liquidation and the creditors in accordance with the order of priority determined by law and distribute the remainder, if any, amongst the company members. The order of priority is as follows: secured creditors, liquidator's remuneration and expenses, preferred creditors including the Revenue Commissioners and employees, holders of floating charges, unsecured creditors and the shareholders. If no application is made to the Court for an order deferring the date, the company is dissolved on the expiration of three months from the registration of a return relating to the liquidation.

A liquidator is obliged by the Company Law Enforcement Act 2001 to provide a report to the Director of Corporate Enforcement on the conduct of the directors of an insolvent company. The Office of the Director of Corporate Enforcement (ODCE) is responsible for ensuring compliance with the Companies Acts and the prosecution of persons for suspected breaches. If it appears to a liquidator that any director or other officer of the company may have committed a criminal offence, a report has to be sent to the Director of Public Prosecutions. A liquidator can apply to the Court for an order to freeze company assets if deemed necessary and, in exceptional situations, to ask the Court to carry out an examination of any person whom it considers can provide information about the affairs of the company.

e)   Penalties on directors

The Companies Act 1990 introduced significant provisions relating to the directors of insolvent companies to deal with the 'phoenix syndrome', as it was called: a practice whereby the directors of some companies that went into liquidation leaving large debts started new companies with similar businesses soon afterwards, much to the chagrin of creditors. In addition to the financial penalties for breaches of the Companies Acts, directors and shadow directors (persons on whose directions the directors are accustomed to act) of insolvent companies may be subjected to three other penalties:

i)   Personal liability

ii)   Restriction

iii) Disqualification (see Note 4 on p. 264).

i)   Personal liability of directors

Under previous legislation it was generally necessary to prove conscious fraud before a director could be held personally liable for the debts of a company. Now such a person is potentially liable in the following circumstances:

*   The director is knowingly a party to the carrying on of the business of the company in a reckless manner
*   The director is knowingly a party to the carrying on of the business of the company with intent to defraud the creditors or for other fraudulent purposes
*   The company has failed to keep proper books of account and this has contributed to uncertainty about assets or its inability to pay its debts
*   The director is the beneficiary of a loan from the company which is prohibited under the Companies Acts
*   In a members' voluntary winding-up he/she makes a statutory declaration of solvency without having reasonable grounds for his/her opinion that the company is solvent
*   If a person acts as a director while restricted (except as permitted by legislation) or disqualified, he/she can be made personally liable if the company becomes insolvent during or within 12 months from the date he/she acted as a director while under restriction or disqualification (CA 1990).

Under the Companies Act 1990 a director will be regarded as knowingly a party to the carrying on of business in a reckless manner if:

> having regard to the general knowledge, skill and experience that
> may reasonably be expected of a person in his position, he ought
> to have known that his actions or those of the company would
> cause loss to the creditors of the company, or any of them, or he

> was a party to the contracting of a debt by the company and did
> not honestly believe on reasonable grounds that the company
> would be able to pay the debt when it fell due for payment as well
> as all its other debts. (s 138)

In addition to personal liability, fraudulent trading is also a criminal offence. A person could be deemed by a court to be guilty of fraudulent trading if he/she is knowingly a party to the carrying on of the business of a company with the intention of defrauding creditors.

ii) Restriction of directors

If a company goes into liquidation or receivership and is insolvent, a restriction order could be obtained for any person who is a director of the company when the winding-up commenced, or who was a director or shadow director at any time within the preceding 12 months. The Court will make such an order unless the person can show that he/she acted honestly and responsibly in relation to the conduct of the company's affairs and that there is no other just or reasonable reason for imposing a restriction order. If a director is subject to a restriction order, he/she cannot, for a period of five years, be appointed or act in any way as a director or secretary of any company, or be concerned or take part in the promotion or formation of a company unless it is adequately capitalised. This requires that the allotted share capital of a private company is not less than €63,487 and €317,435 in the case of a public company. Each allocated share must be fully paid. Such companies are subject to strict rules regarding capital maintenance (s 50 CA 1990).

iii) Disqualification of directors

Disqualification is an order imposed on a person preventing him or her from acting as a director, auditor, officer, receiver, liquidator, examiner or being involved in the promotion, formation or management of a company for a period of five years, or such other period as determined by the Court. Disqualification is automatic in certain circumstances and discretionary in others. Automatic disqualification applies in the following circumstances:

- Where a person is convicted of an indictable offence in relation to the company or one involving elements of fraud or dishonesty
- Where a person fails to notify the Registrar of Companies that he/she was disqualified in another state
- Where a person was convicted of acting while the subject of a restriction order except as allowed by the legislation
- Where a person is convicted of acting as a director, auditor, liquidator or examiner while an undischarged bankrupt.

The Court has the discretion to disqualify a person for such a period as it deems appropriate in the following circumstances:

- A conviction for fraud in relation to the company, its members or creditors
- A breach of duty in relation to the company
- Conduct which makes a person unfit to be concerned with the management of a company, or fraudulent or reckless trading which resulted in a declaration of personal liability for some or all of the company's debts
- Persistent default in relation to obligations under the Companies Acts
- Two or more offences of failing to keep proper books and records
- In the case of an insolvent company, failure to file all outstanding annual returns on request (s 160 CA 1990).

The Registrar of Companies maintains a register of restricted persons and a register of disqualified persons.

f)   Strike-off

The Registrar of Companies can strike a company off the Register of Companies for default in carrying out certain legal obligations such as failing to file an annual return. The directors of such companies could be disqualified by the High Court on application by the Director of Corporate Enforcement, unless they can prove that the companies had no outstanding liabilities when they were struck off. Directors can avoid strike-off and any sanctions by acting in a responsible manner. There are procedures whereby such a company can be reinstated on to the register (see the Companies Registration Office website at www.cro.ie).

g)   Bankruptcy

An individual who is insolvent could be declared a bankrupt by the High Court. A debtor or a creditor may petition the High Court to have a debtor declared a bankrupt. Bankruptcy is a legal process whereby all the assets of an insolvent individual (with minor exceptions) are transferred to a trustee, known as an official assignee, for distribution to creditors in accordance with a hierarchy of preference specified in the Bankruptcy Act 1988. Normally the process is initiated by a creditor, but it is also possible for an insolvent individual to file for bankruptcy seeking protection from creditors. If granted it allows a debtor time to prepare a scheme of arrangements whereby creditors could be paid some or all of the outstanding debts over a period. The scheme of arrangement has to be approved by three-fifths of creditors, both in value and number. It would then avoid outright bankruptcy. Bankruptcy is a long and expensive process. A person declared a bankrupt remains a bankrupt unless discharged by the High Court, and this can also happen after a period of 12 years provided certain conditions are satisfied. A bankrupt cannot stand for election to a public office or become a director of a company. Bankruptcy does not prevent a person from earning a living, as it is designed to allow for a fresh start. If the bankrupt becomes financially successful, outstanding debts have to be paid.

9.4 Exit strategies

An entrepreneur is interested in the rate of return earned on his/her investment and in the free cash flow, that is, the cash generated by operations which is available to the owner and any external investors. Surplus cash flow can be taken out as dividends, reinvested in the business or used to reduce debt, develop new products or services, make acquisitions or a combination thereof. The purpose of reinvestment is to finance growth and build a business of value. It can take several years to establish a sustainable business, when it may be considered for harvesting, that is, realising its value. This usually happens when the owner-manager is made an attractive offer for purchase or when he/she wishes to retire. An owner-manager has a number of exit options:

a)   Succession by a family member

b)   Appointment of a professional chief executive

c)   Sale

d)   Management buy-out

e)   Merger or acquisition

f)   Initial public offering (IPO).

In each case, good professional advice is required.

a)   Succession by a family member

Succession planning for a small business involves preparation for transferring the ownership to family members and the management to a chosen person to ensure that it survives when the owner-manager retires or dies. It also involves action to ensure that the owner-manager and his/her spouse have pensions or income in retirement. If it is decided to keep ownership of a company within the family, this can be achieved by transferring shares in an equitable manner where there are a number of siblings. Most owner-managers favour transfer of the management to a family member, preferably one that was involved in the business for as long as possible prior to the change. However, this option is not available where no family members are willing to undertake the responsibility or do not possess the commitment and competence required.

Directors of private companies often have a shareholders' agreement specifying who can purchase each member's share of the business as well as when it can happen and how the price will be calculated. Such agreements can prevent future disputes. Advance planning, with good legal and taxation advice, is important in the process. There are generous thresholds for the transfer of family businesses in respect of capital gains tax and capital acquisitions tax provided certain conditions are satisfied (see www.revenue.ie).

b)   Appointment of a professional chief executive

If there is no family member willing to succeed and the owner wants to retain control, the appointment of a professional chief executive is required, often with the founder becoming chairperson of the board of directors. This can be a very successful option if the right person is recruited as chief executive. It can also provide regular income for the founder.

c) Sale

In this case the business is sold as a going concern. This can be a straight sale, a controlling interest or one where the owner stays on either as manager or as a consultant for a fixed period. The chief valuation methods used in a sale are a multiple of maintainable earnings (price/earnings ratio), the market value of net assets and discounted cash flows. (The price/earnings (P/E) ratio represents the length of time required to recover the purchase price provided the earnings remain the same. In discounted cash flow, future cash flows are discounted to their present value using the required rate of return.)

d) Management buy-out

The business can be purchased by one or more managers, usually with debt finance. A management buy-out is a popular means of unlocking the value of a business and providing opportunities for the key members of staff who developed it.

e) Merger or acquisition

The company could merge with another or be acquired by another business.

f) Initial public offering (IPO)

This is where a private company goes public to raise equity finance by selling shares to the public. It can increase access to further finance and enhance the credit rating of the company. It also provides a market for any existing shareholders who wish to sell their shares and realise their value. Many SMEs will never be able to go public because of size, cost and not being able to meet the requirements, but it is an option for some and may require significant additions to the management team.

9.5 Summary

The start-up stage of any business is difficult and requires good planning. If a business survives during its early stage it can evolve over a number of other stages, each of which has its own challenges. Many entrepreneurs are satisfied to operate on a small scale, while others opt for growth. Factors to be considered for planned growth include market opportunities, a distinctive competitive strategy, a competent management team, operations which can deliver on the scale and quality required, good management information and control systems together with adequate finance as well as satisfactory additional profits and positive cash flow.

Some businesses do not succeed and become insolvent. A company has no say over the appointment of a receiver if it is unable to meet its obligations to a secured creditor.

An insolvent company may be able to organise a special rescue operation or appoint an examiner (depending on size). However, if these options fail the final step is liquidation, a development which has to be undertaken in a responsible manner. In addition to financial penalties for breaches of the Companies Acts, directors of insolvent companies may be subjected to other penalties like personal liability, restriction or disqualification.

An entrepreneur is interested in the rate of return earned on his/her investment and in the free cash flow. Surplus cash can be taken out as dividends, reinvested or used to reduce debt, develop new products or services, make acquisitions or a combination thereof. Every entrepreneur plans to be able to harvest the value of their investment at a future date. An owner-manager has a number of exit strategies available: succession by a family member, the appointment of a professional chief executive, sale, management buy-out, merger, acquisition or an initial public offering.

Questions

1. Critically assess why some businesses succeed and others fail.
2. Discuss the main issues which arise at various stages in the growth of a business.
3. Explain the difference between each of the following.
    a) A bankrupt and an insolvent person
    b) A receiver and an examiner
    c) A members' liquidation and a creditors' liquidation
    d) Restriction and disqualification of a director
4. Consider the options that arise when an owner-manager wishes to retire from a business.
5. Write a case study of a business which developed export markets.

Notes

1. The main legislation dealing with receivers is contained in Part VII of the Companies Act 1963 and Part VIII of the Companies Act 1990.
2. The law relating to examiners is contained in the Companies (Amendment) Act 1990, Part IX of the Companies Act 1990 and Part II of the Companies (Amendment) (No. 2) Act 1999.
3. The law dealing with liquidations is contained in Part VI of the Companies Act 1963, Part VI of the Companies Act 1990 and Part V of the Company Law Enforcement Act 2001.
4. Part VII of the Companies Act 1990.

Chapter 10

Management

It is not the strongest of the species that survives, nor the most intelligent; it is the one that is most adaptable to change.

CHARLES DARWIN

Learning objectives

- To assess what is meant by management
- To explore the main elements of management practice, planning, organising, motivation, leadership and control
- To comprehend issues involved in time management
- To examine the need for and the process of change management.

This chapter is organised as follows:

10.1 Introduction to management

Aspiring entrepreneurs have business ideas or visions of what will sell and then decide what market sectors to enter, when, where and how. They must also decide what they want from their businesses (goals), how they are going to compete in the target markets (strategy) and the resources (human, physical and financial) required. The key factors in the management of any business are customers, staff, a quality product or service, operations including customer service, innovation, competitiveness, provision of value, turnover, prices, costs, net profit and positive cash flow. All new entrepreneurs have to get these right to survive and prosper. Owner-managers are soon faced with a changing macroeconomic environment, uncertainty and possible new opportunities. They have to be able to consider these issues and make the most appropriate decisions for their businesses. If business expands, the issues become more complex, with several production, marketing, financial and human resource considerations, but the main focus at all times has to be on existing and potential customers.

People have managed businesses and projects from ancient times, but the impetus for the establishment of principles of management emerged during the Industrial Revolution from the last quarter of the eighteenth century. Later, four main theories of management emerged: classical, behavioural, quantitative and contemporary (Griffin, 2008). The classical approach sought to find the best ways to manage manual work and organisations in an efficient manner. Its chief pioneer was an American engineer, Frederick Taylor (1856–1915). Max Weber (1864–1920) developed what became known as the bureaucratic approach to management, with a hierarchical structure and clear rules and procedures. A French engineer, Henri Fayol (1841–1925), suggested that five functions and 14 principles of management were applicable in every big organisation. His functions were forecasting and planning, organising, commanding, co-ordinating and controlling (functions which dominate the literature on management to this day). His 14 principles are shown in Table 10.1.

Table 10.1: Fayol's principles of management

1.	Division of work – specialisation and allocation of responsibility to individuals.
2.	Authority and responsibility – authority to give instructions, responsibility and accountability.
3.	Discipline – clear and fair agreements and appropriate penalties.
4.	Unity of command – each employee with one superior.
5.	Unity of direction – one plan for a group of activities with the same objective.
6.	Subordination of individual interests to the general interest – employees to follow organisational goals rather than their own.
7.	Remuneration – fair reward for work done.
8.	Centralisation – decide what to centralise so as to obtain the optimum return from an organisation.
9.	Scalar principle – clear lines of authority throughout an organisation.
10.	Order – a sense of order throughout an organisation.
11.	Equity – all employees treated fairly.
12.	Stability of tenure for employees – to facilitate employees to give their best.
13.	Initiative – freedom and support for initiative.
14.	*Esprit de corps* – team spirit and unity of purpose.

Source: Adapted from Fayol (1949)

The behavioural approach concentrated on human relations in management and the factors which influence performance, with researchers and writers like Elton Mayo (1949), Abraham Maslow (1954), Douglas McGregor (1960), Frederick Hertzberg (1959) and Rensis Likert (1961, 1967).

The quantitative viewpoint was based on mathematics, statistics and the use of management information. Contemporary perspectives of management include systems theory, where organisations are viewed in terms of inputs, processes, outputs and feedback, and contingency theory, which suggests that there is no one best way of managing as actions depend on the special circumstances of a specific situation, put forward by writers such as Burns and Stalker (1961) and Laurence and Lorsch (1969). Other developments were total quality management (Deming, 1982) and the importance of organisational culture in influencing behaviour. William Ouchi (1981) developed what he called Theory Z, combining the positive aspects of American and Japanese management practices into a modified form compatible with the norms, culture and values of American society. All managers can find useful theories and insights in the literature, but they have to be able to adapt them to their own specific requirements.

Management is not a science; it provides no magic formula as to what decision should be made in a given situation. This requires appropriate knowledge, skills, experience and a considerable amount of intuition. There is no generally accepted definition of management. The most widely quoted is that of Henri Fayol (1949): 'To manage is to forecast and plan, to organise, to command, to co-ordinate and to control.' Brech (1953) is also widely quoted: 'Management is a social process entailing responsibility for the effective and economical planning and regulation of the operations of an enterprise.' Most definitions are developments of those of Fayol and Brech. Management can be defined as a process of planning, organising, leading and controlling an organisation so as to achieve its goals in an effective and efficient manner having regard to the perceived opportunities in a changing external environment. Effectiveness is the ability to choose appropriate goals having regard to the rapidly changing market environment. Efficiency is concerned with making the best use of all available resources. According to Drucker (1995), effective management is concerned with doing the right things rather than doing things right (efficiency). It is concerned with strategic intuition, that is, positioning an organisation to be in the right product or service, in the right place, at the right time, with competitive advantage. Management is a proactive process required at all levels of an organisation.

Managerial work does not follow an orderly, systematic model; it is fraught with the unexpected, constant interruptions, fragmented activities and demands to deal urgently with a number of issues (Mintzberg, 1973). In this complex environment it is important to be able to focus on the key goals while dealing with the multiplicity of other issues which arise. Mintzberg (1973) classifies the roles of senior managers into three groups: interpersonal, informational and decisional. He lists three roles under the interpersonal category:

- *Figurehead* (representing the organisation to the external community)
- *Leader* (motivating staff)
- *Liaison* (a link between the organisation and external groups).

The informational roles identified are:

- *Monitor* (for information relevant to the company)
- *Disseminator* (of information relevant to employees)
- *Spokesperson* (for the organisation with the external community).

Four decisional roles are listed:

- *Entrepreneur* (innovative and proactive)
- *Disturbance handler* (dealing with problems and conflicts)
- *Resource allocator* (allocator of resources)
- *Negotiator* (entering agreements with suppliers, distributors, unions and staff).

Mintzberg's research highlights the constant interruptions which are a feature of all managerial work. A manager has to undertake a variety of roles almost daily.

Most managers have qualifications and/or relevant experience. In addition to good business management skills, managers need a number of other skills to enable them to carry out their work effectively:

- Technical – relevant to the activity of the organisation
- Interpersonal – the ability to interact in a pleasant manner with people at all levels inside and outside the organisation
- Conceptual – the ability to think in the abstract
- Analytical – the ability to analyse issues
- Decision-making – the ability to make decisions based on an analysis and assessment of various options.

Managers have to be able to make rational decisions in the best interest of their organisations, regardless of other pressures. While procrastination is not an ideal quality in a manager, neither is instant decision-making without full information and consideration of the likely consequences. Decisions made are not always the correct ones, but good managers have to be able to recognise that fact and act accordingly. A senior manager has to allocate sufficient time to think strategically and focus on the big long-term goals as well as dealing with ongoing operational activities. In addition, a manager has to be a good communicator, a keen listener, a good networker, a problem-solver, able to work under pressure and constantly focused on the achievement of key goals. She/he has to have a high degree of professionalism and ethical standards as well as a keen sense of responsibility to all the main stakeholders, such as consumers, shareholders, staff and the public good.

An effective chief executive has to be a strategic thinker, a leader and a person who is able to synthesise various theories and techniques as well as a variety of economic and other forecasts to position his/her own organisation for an uncertain future. This is a big challenge. Most senior managers try to foster a strong entrepreneurial culture and responsible risk-taking. Rapid change is bringing new challenges to the global village with market liberalisation, an enlarged European Union, mobile international investment, increasing competition and the emergence of the new vibrant BRIC economies (Brazil, Russia, India and China). Modern communications, especially the internet and other new technologies, have altered the way business is done. Social networking is now widely used in business. Customers are becoming less loyal and are constantly seeking better value. It is becoming more difficult to predict and exceed the new expectations of customers – the big challenge for effective managers. Management thinking and practices have to evolve with the new reality.

The main elements of management are:

- Planning
- Organising
- Motivation and leadership
- Control.

10.2 Planning

Planning is a management process that involves thinking before doing, establishing goals and how they should be achieved. The purpose of business planning is to identify opportunities in the marketplace as well as developing a strategy and organisational structure to exploit them. Without planning, activities lack direction, problems are not anticipated, the demands of the present are given precedence over future considerations and an organisation drifts along like a rudderless ship. A plan is a predetermined course of action, the methodology devised to achieve specific goals. There are three main types of planning:

a) Strategic
b) Tactical/business
c) Operational.

a) Strategic planning

Strategic planning is the process of developing the future long-term direction of an organisation with regard to perceived business opportunities in a changing external environment and creating a sustainable competitive advantage that is not easy to replicate. The key factors for a business are the chosen industry, the targeted market sector and segments as well as the generic strategy to be adopted (O'Gorman and Cunningham, 2007). Strategic planning has to embrace a high degree of uncertainty about the future, complex options and in many cases significant change in an organisation (Johnson et al., 2005). It provides a framework to bring an organisation from where it is to where it desires to be within a specific timeframe. The process is focused on identifying future business opportunities, developing core competence for the new environment and establishing the generic strategy to be followed with competitive advantage. It has to introduce competitiveness, flexibility, agility, creativity, innovation and responsiveness in an organisation to enable it to adapt quickly to change and new opportunities. A strategy is then a map charting how a business will develop over a number of years. It has to be based on reality and commitment rather than mere aspirations. Strategic planning incorporates a number of related activities, as shown in Figure 10.1.

Figure 10.1: Strategic planning process

| Vision, mission, values |
| SWOT analysis |
| Identify target market segment and establish core competence |
| Goals and objectives |
| Formulate strategic options |
| Strategic plan |
| Implementation |
| Feedback, control, continuous reappraisal |

Vision, mission, values

A vision is a mental picture of a possible and desirable future state for an organisation which is realistic, challenging and attainable. It should be inspirational so that all members of an organisation are influenced to work towards it with unity of purpose, total commitment, pride and confidence.

A mission statement defines the purpose of an organisation's existence. It answers the following questions: What business are we in? Where are we going? What should our business be? Where should we be going? (Drucker, 1973) Once an organisation has clearly established its mission, it finds it easier to scan the relevant external environment for business opportunities. Levitt (1975), in an influential article, 'Marketing Myopia', cautioned against defining a mission too narrowly. He argued that a market-based definition, viewed as satisfying the changing needs of customers, is superior to one focused on products or services, which are transient. However, a mission statement should not be too broad. Most banks see themselves in the financial services business rather than just banking. A good mission statement should provide a vision for future direction, a sense of purpose, opportunities, challenges, meaning and motivation as well as being congruent with the distinctive competence and values of the organisation. It should focus on a business's competitive advantage in providing value for customers in its targeted market sector (Campbell and Tawadey, 1992).

Values are the beliefs and ethics which underpin an organisation's behaviour and express its relationship with various stakeholders. A code of business ethics is important for every organisation.

SWOT analysis

The external environment for any organisation is in a state of change, with predictions for the economy in respect of expected growth or recession, trends in the global economy, uncertainty in various markets, new consumer tastes and needs, use of modern information technology and other technological developments, taxation and other matters specific to each business. Timely and accurate market information is important for planning in every business. The internal organisation also has to be reviewed to assess its agility to respond to change in a competitive manner. The purpose of SWOT analysis – strengths, weaknesses, opportunities and threats – is to assess the external and internal environments for the purpose of identifying new business opportunities. This involves a review of the external macroeconomic environment in a PEST analysis. PEST stands for political-legal, economic, socio-cultural and technological analysis of the external environment, especially with regard to the targeted business sector. (It is sometimes referred to as a PESTLE analysis, with legal and environmental factors also included.) The motive is to identify opportunities and threats as well as assessing the competitive positions of market participants. This external review is followed by an analysis of the internal organisation, financial resources (long term and working capital), human resources, current products (competitiveness, life cycles, profitability, suppliers, distributors), operating systems and internal organisational structure as well as marketing (customers and their profiles), production, location, technology and management competence so as to identify competitive strengths and weaknesses.

Identify target market segment and establish core competence

From the SWOT analysis, the main factors for success in the business are identified. An effective business strategy begins with selecting which customers to serve (Abell, 1980). In many businesses it may not be possible to serve all potential customers and a decision has to be made to focus on a specific range. Careful selection of a market segment, targeting and positioning are essential elements of effective business planning so as to minimise competition. Many service organisations try to serve too many different groups, often with conflicting needs, and end up satisfying none. The core competences of the business are established, for example innovation, flexibility and customer service, which are intended to deliver better value for customers. Every effort is made to align business competence with market opportunities while endeavouring to overcome weaknesses and mitigate threats. This exercise is an essential prerequisite for deciding on market choice (industry, sector and segment), for building long-term business relationships with suppliers, distributors and customers and for developing sustainable competitive advantage in the marketplace. The capability of the organisation has to be matched with the needs and opportunities of the target market in a coherent and profitable manner.

Goals and objectives

Strategic goals and objectives have to be established. Goals are general statements of what an organisation wants to achieve over a specific period having regard to its distinctive competence and competitive advantage. Drucker (2001) lists a number of activities where goals and performance targets need to be established, such as marketing, physical resources, financial resources, innovation, productivity, profitability, manager performance and development, worker performance and attitude as well as social responsibility. Each organisation has to establish its own goals under appropriate activities for up to three, four or five years, as appropriate.

Strategic goals are translated into measurable objectives and action plans. Objectives are specific targets of performance in relation to a timeframe. A number of specific objectives, with timeframes and performance measures, are devised for each goal. It is advisable to involve staff in the process of setting objectives, which should be measurable and challenging, with a mechanism for regular feedback on performance. Objectives clarify goals, promote unity of purpose, establish targets, provide benchmarks for assessment of progress, motivate staff and increase productivity. Ideally objectives should be SMART: specific, measurable, attainable/achievable, realistic and time-bound.

Formulate strategic options

In formulating strategy an organisation has to decide where it wants to be in three to five years' time. It has to decide how it can best achieve its goals and objectives, matching its strengths with opportunities in the marketplace, overcoming its weaknesses and building competitive advantage. A product usually goes through four stages in its life cycle – introduction, growth, maturity and decline – and the stage of each has to be considered in the strategy to be adopted. Alternative strategies by which an organisation can achieve its goals are formulated and evaluated.

Miles and Snow (1978) identified four different strategies for a single business: prospector, defender, analyser and reactor. A prospector strategy is focused on new opportunities, innovation and growth. Where a business concentrates on its existing market, it follows a defender strategy. In respect of an analyser strategy, a business tries to serve its existing market well while engaging in some innovation and development. In a reactor strategy, a business has no clear focus and just reacts to changes in the market-place, which is a very dangerous option.

Porter (1980, 1985) made a big contribution to strategic management. He proposed the Five Forces Model for the analysis of an industry (discussed in Chapter 4):

- The degree of rivalry among existing competitors
- The threat of new entrants
- The bargaining power of customers/buyers
- The bargaining power of suppliers
- The threat of substitute products or services.

The objective of this analysis is to establish a strong position in an attractive market, which is difficult to replicate, hard to enter and where there is no threat of substitutes. The next challenge is to develop a strong competitive position in the chosen market. Porter identified three generic strategies for creating and sustaining competitive advantage in a market:

- Cost leadership, where an organisation aims to achieve the lowest production and distribution costs within the industry, with low overheads and economies of scale.
- Differentiation, whereby an organisation seeks to develop customer loyalty by value enhancement with some unique benefit which can attract a premium price.
- Focus strategy, where an organisation concentrates on one or more narrow market niches and becomes the best in the business. A business can pursue either cost leadership or differentiation within that market.

A business can opt for one of these strategies and establish its supporting business model. The generic strategy chosen is influenced by marketing considerations, the core competence of the business and its resources as well as the expected returns and risks involved.

Competitive advantage can emanate from all the various activities undertaken by a business: designing, acquiring all the required resources, producing, marketing and delivering a product or service. Porter (1985) proposed the value chain as a means to understand costs and possible sources of differentiation (see Chapter 7). Later, Porter (1996, 2001) suggested six principles of strategic positioning:

i)   The right goals (focused on long-term profitability)
ii)   A clear value proposition (providing unique value to specific customers)
iii) A distinctive value chain (different activities from competitors)
iv)   Accepting the necessity of trade-offs (selecting which customers to serve)
v)   Activity fit/alignment (goals and strategy consistent, aligned and mutually supportive)
vi)   Continuity of direction (keeping to the strategy).

Ryanair is an excellent example of the application of these principles of competitive positioning.

Instead of focusing on an existing market, Kim and Mauborgne (2005) argue that the strategic objective should be on creating 'blue oceans' of 'uncontested market space' with growth and profit potential. They recommend value innovation, creating exceptional value both for the organisation and its customers, thus making existing competitors irrelevant and attracting many new buyers. Value innovation applies to the entire range of an organisation's activities: product, service, delivery and the business model. According to Kim and Mauborgne, strategy should focus on attracting non-customers by redefining the target market and reconstructing the boundaries, with innovative new product and service offerings. They suggest that an organisation should be aligned to pursue both differentiation and low cost as well as establishing barriers to imitation. This can involve co-creating value with customers. Their research found that there were no excellent companies on a permanent basis. According to Leavy and McKiernan (2009), 'The average life expectancy of Fortune 500 companies from birth to death is between forty and fifty years'. They suggest the following reasons:

> corporate arrogance and hubris, lack of vision and risk taking, insufficient attention to weak signals, constraints arising from the business models of yesterday, biases inherent in internal decision-making processes and a failure to see and grasp opportunities emerging in other sectors.

Similar reasons can apply to SMEs. Consequently, strategy has to be creative and innovative as well as attracting the trust, commitment and enthusiastic co-operation of the organisation.

Strategic plan

After a careful evaluation of the possible options, management has to select its generic strategy, the one with the greatest potential to achieve the specified goals and objectives. It is the one that provides the best fit between the emerging market needs and the core competence of the business. The future is very uncertain and all planning involves assumptions, forecasting and considering various scenarios, that is, looking at different possibilities. Once the generic strategy is agreed, all other elements of the business have to be planned accordingly. A strategic plan specifies how a business will move from its current position to its desired future state under each key activity. It is a broadly defined programme of actions to achieve specified goals with regard to matching organisational strengths with opportunities in the marketplace and building competitive advantage. Every business has to promote its competitive advantage and establish that unique image in the minds of its potential customers. Any strategy involves many decisions, all of which have to be integrated, aligned and, in a rapidly changing environment, dynamic and innovative.

A good strategic plan must have vision and direction, challenging goals, co-ordination, integration and alignment between all key elements as well as distinctiveness, competitive advantage and sustainability. Vision, mission, values, goals and strategy have to be consistent, aligned and mutually supportive.

Implementation

Once approved, the strategic plan is implemented, the necessary resources provided and the appropriate organisational structure developed. This is usually achieved by means of tactical plans and an annual operating plan within the overall framework of the strategic plan. The plan has to be communicated to all stakeholders and their enthusiastic support obtained for its implementation.

Feedback, control, continuous reappraisal

Performance is monitored on a regular basis against the objectives and goals, with various controls devised to review performance in relation to targets, usually key performance indicators (KPIs). Appropriate performance measures are established for each objective and goal, short term, medium term and long term. These are established for all activities within an organisation in accordance with its strategic plan. Effective KPIs are linked to individuals and a performance culture with good communications is developed. Performance is monitored on a regular basis and early corrective action taken if required. The strategic plan is subject to continuous reappraisal. Goals and objectives can be changed if the need arises from unforeseen developments, especially in the macroeconomic environment, which is normal occurrence. An effective strategic plan has to provide an organisation with the flexibility and agility to be able to respond quickly to new market opportunities as they arise.

An organisation's culture is the pattern of beliefs and expectations that shape the behaviour of its members. These beliefs and expectations establish norms that shape the behaviour of individuals and groups. It is important that this culture is committed to the objectives and goals of the organisation as well as fostering innovation, risk-taking and openness to new ways of doing things. Most organisations have written policies, procedures and rules to facilitate decision-making and promote consistency. Administration is the interpretation and implementation of policies and procedures.

b)   Tactical/business planning

An organisation usually prepares a tactical plan or business plan specifying how it will compete in its target market. This contains tactical goals and objectives for a shorter period of one to three years, with specific targets, measures, timeframes and the names of the people responsible for each. It is prepared as an integrated business plan, generally a 'rolling plan', with projected financial accounts, balance sheets and cash flow statements.

c)   Operational planning

An operational plan encapsulates the specific strategic priorities and associated action plans which have to be undertaken to implement a segment of the business plan and to co-ordinate all the activities involved. It is an integrated short-range plan for a specific timeframe, generally one year. An operational plan specifies the goals and objectives to be achieved in a specified short timeframe, how they are to be accomplished, who is responsible for the various elements, the resources required, together with deadlines and measures of performance. Some elements of an operational plan can be a series of discrete tasks. Performance is considered on a regular basis against the targets set and corrective action is taken if required. The focus is on results and accountability in a high-performance, customer-driven culture. There can also be operational plans for days or weeks.

Many organisations implement their operational plans within the framework of an annual budget. A budget is an integrated plan covering all functional areas of a business quantified in monetary terms, prepared and approved prior to a defined period of time, usually one year. It is prepared within the framework of the strategic and tactical plans. In effect it is a detailed operational programme for the implementation of a segment of the tactical plan, with specified targets, especially for net profit. A draft budget is often revised on a number of occasions to ensure that the desired net profit can be attained. When a budget is approved, all activities have to be organised and implemented from the start of the appropriate period. It is important to remember that the targets specified in a budget, especially the projected net profit, are objectives which the management team are enthusiastically committed to achieve, rather than mere aspirations.

The actual performance achieved is ascertained and compared with the budget on a regular basis, usually monthly. An appropriate budget for each month is first determined in a sensible and pragmatic manner. After making allowance for any seasonal factors, sales, production and other budgets for each month are determined by the number of working days in each month, the labour budget by the number of paydays in each period and the monthly overhead budget by the timing of payments for each cost element. Past experience can be very helpful in establishing realistic monthly budgets. Actual performance for each month can be determined quite easily from the appropriate accounting records. Each month, the accounting department prepares management accounts which are used to monitor financial performance on a regular basis, especially sales, costs, gross margin, net profit and cash flow. Differences, or to use the accountancy term, variances, are identified, and the reasons investigated, with corrective action taken as required. Contingency plans – different courses of action to take if specific targets are not reached – are also prepared. All other objectives specified in the operational plan are also monitored on a monthly basis and action is taken if necessary.

A budget is a navigational aid for management, but its use does not have to be completely rigid. Any strategic or operational plan can be altered if circumstances change.

A budget must be respected, but it does not have to be so revered that it stops management from taking prudent decisions as the need arises. Properly used, a budget is a management technique for operational planning, for setting targets and standards, for co-ordinating all the activities in an organisation, for motivating staff, measuring performance and taking corrective action when required. Budgets are now regularly complemented by the use of non-financial measures of performance (see below).

10.3 Organising

All aspects of the strategic plan have to be organised and implemented. Organising is the process of defining various tasks and duties, arranging them in groups, assigning responsibility to individuals, establishing their formal inter-relationships and co-ordinating all the activities to achieve the specified goals. The appropriate staffing and organisational structures have to be considered in the preparation of the strategic plan. The organisation can range from a simple structure to a complex one, depending on the size and nature of the business as well as its environment. A business always has to focus on its competitiveness and how it is going to provide value for customers. A major consideration in this respect is the recruitment of competent staff with good personalities, the right attitudes, common sense and the ability to relate well with everyone. They are expected to have pride in their work, be flexible, highly productive and professional and committed to excellent customer service. A good induction programme is important to ensure that the desired values, beliefs and ethos are transmitted to all staff and that they know the standards expected. A highly productive, dedicated, motivated, innovative, responsive and customer-focused staff gives an organisation a significant competitive advantage.

As the number of staff employed in an organisation increases, the reporting relationships between employees have to be established. Fayol (1949) recommends that an organisation should have unity of direction (all staff in the organisation working towards the same goals), unity of command (one person, one boss) and a clear line of authority in all parts of the organisation (the scalar principle). The span of control (the number of staff reporting directly to any individual) has to be reasonable in relation to the nature of the work involved, the degree of specialisation, the need for interaction, the need for personal autonomy and the competence of staff. An organisation chart is a graphical representation showing the relationship between people in a big organisation. Organisational charts are now despised by many chief executives, especially since the publication of *In Search of Excellence* by Thomas Peters and Robert Waterman (1982), who found that the best companies do not have them. Feargal Quinn (2006) told us in his book *Growing the Customer* that he did not believe in organisation charts.

Organisations with many levels of reporting relationships are known as 'tall structures' while those with few are called 'flat structures'. In recent years there has been considerable delegating, with a big emphasis on flat, flexible, responsive structures and wide spans of control. More work is now done by flexible, multi-skilled employees operating in teams with a high degree of group autonomy rather than the old command and control system. The job of management is moving away from commanding and close supervision to empowering employees to use their own initiative and intelligence to achieve specified targets. Such developments increase job satisfaction and productivity. All managers delegate some work to others. Delegation involves transferring work and the authority to do that work to others, but it is the delegator's duty to ensure the employees are properly trained to undertake such work and that it is performed on schedule. All the activities, sections and departments in an organisation have to be co-ordinated and linked together with one unified aim: to achieve the objectives and goals specified in the strategic plan. There are more complex organisational structures in large organisations.

10.4 Motivation and leadership

Motivation and leadership are two interdependent aspects of management. A person's work performance is influenced by a number of factors: motivation (the desire to do a good job), leadership (nature of the employment culture), ability (capacity to do the job) and the general work environment (premises, equipment and working conditions).

a) Motivation

Motivation is the process of stimulating employees to give their best. Significant theories of motivation include Maslow (1943), McClelland (1961), McGregor (1960), Herzberg (1962) and Alderfer (1972). The most widely quoted theory is Abraham Maslow's hierarchy of needs (Figure 10.2). Maslow's work suggests that human needs can be grouped into five categories which can be arranged in a hierarchy of importance, starting with basic needs for food, shelter and clothes, and culminating in self-actualisation, when people realise their potential with fulfilling work. An unsatisfied need generates certain wants until it is satisfied. Once an unsatisfied need is met, it is no longer a motivator. In addition to satisfactory income, a person may also need a challenging job to satisfy his/her self-actualisation needs. While Maslow's theory has some merit, all human beings do not behave in the same rational, predictable manner.

David McClelland (1961) suggests that an organisation should offer a person the opportunity to satisfy three sets of needs: *achievement* (a desire for challenging tasks and high performance), *affiliation* (a desire for friendship, acceptance and social interaction) and *power* (a desire to be influential and control one's environment).

Douglas McGregor (1960) discussed managerial assumptions about employees and the implications of such beliefs in the process of motivation. He outlined two alternative sets of assumptions about human beings: Theory X and Theory Y. McGregor suggests that autocratic managers are likely to have the assumptions contained in Theory X: that employees are inherently lazy, dislike work and will do as little as possible. Consequently, they have to be managed and controlled to secure an acceptable level of performance. Theory Y has positive assumptions about employees: that they like work and are capable, energetic, creative and fully committed to achieving the objectives of the organisation if given the opportunity.

Figure 10.2: Maslow's hierarchy of needs

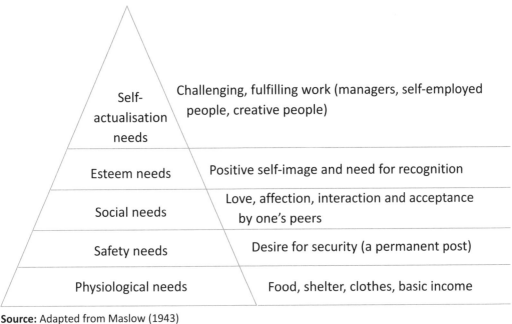

Source: Adapted from Maslow (1943)

Frederick Herzberg (1959, 1966) suggests that there are two dimensions to motivation: hygiene factors such as pay and working conditions and satisfying factors: opportunities for achievement and recognition. Getting what he called the 'hygiene factors' correct will not motivate staff; it just removes the causes of dissatisfaction. This perspective is called the 'two-factor theory'. From his research, Herzberg concluded that the motivation process involves two stages: firstly ensuring that the hygiene factors are appropriate and then providing opportunities for achievement, recognition, responsibility and advancement.

Existence-related growth (ERG) theory, developed by Clayton Alderfer (1972), reduces Maslow's five levels to three and arranges them along a continuum rather than in a hierarchy. Alderfer identified three groups of core needs: existence (physiological well-being), relatedness (good social relationships) and growth (desire for personal development). This theory suggests that more than one need can motivate a person at the same time and that a need already satisfied could become a motivator when another desired need cannot be attained.

Process theories focus on how motivation occurs. The two popular process theories of motivation are expectancy theory and equity theory. Expectancy theory suggests that motivation depends on two factors: how much a person wants something and how likely he/she is to get it. According to Vroom (1964), people are motivated to perform if they believe that their work will lead to desirable outcomes and rewards. A manager has to understand the desires of employees before trying to motivate them. Equity theory suggests that people are motivated to seek fair treatment relative to others for the rewards they receive for their work (Adams, 1963). The implication of equity theory for managers is that if rewards are to motivate staff, they must be perceived as being fair and equitable.

Schein (1965) suggests that a 'psychological contract' between an employee and an organisation, whereby both can realise their expectations, is a big motivator. Motivating staff is a complex subject with something to be learned from each theory, but there is no magic formula. In addition to basic pay, various systems of reward based on performance are being operated in many organisations. Good open two-way communications are also essential, with feedback always welcome, regardless of its source or content.

b)   Leadership

Leadership is a dynamic process of charting the future direction of an organisation to exploit new opportunities with regard to a rapidly changing external environment by focusing on 'the right things'. The traditional view of leadership was the omniscient, omnipotent chief executive, but in recent times the role is seen very much as that of a catalyst, a person who is able to think strategically as well as to empower and inspire staff in all categories to give their best to achieve the new goals specified. An effective leader has to develop a high-performance culture and ensure as far as possible that the goals and objectives are achieved. An excellent example of this new style from the world of sport was the leadership of Declan Kidney in managing the Irish rugby team to win the Grand Slam on 21 March 2009, and immediately after the victory he had the grace and humility to praise everyone except himself! The former President of South Africa, Nelson Mandela, said that the task of a good leader is to inspire people 'to perform better than they think they can'. Despite future uncertainty, a leader has to be proactive in anticipating change and adapting their organisation to be able to compete effectively in the new environment. A leader has to be able to chart a shared sense of purpose and inspire an organisation to be innovative, responsive, flexible and adaptable to new opportunities. A good leader instils hope, pride, confidence and commitment and develops a culture where staff can achieve the goals set as well as realising their own potential by using their imagination and creativity. There has to be good leadership in all sections of an organisation to achieve planned goals.

In addition to technical, managerial and leadership skills, effective leaders have a high degree of emotional intelligence (Goleman, 1996, 1998). Goleman identified five components of emotional intelligence: self-awareness, self-regulation, motivation, empathy and social skill. Self-awareness is the ability to understand one's own moods, emotions and drivers; self-regulation is the ability to control disruptive and impulsive moods as well as thinking before reaching conclusions; motivation is the drive to achieve and succeed; empathy is the ability to listen, understand and relate to the emotional responses of others; while social skill is the ability to manage relationships and establish rapport.

There are five main types of leadership behaviour:

- Authoritarian
- Democratic
- Paternalistic
- Transformational
- Situational.

The authoritarian leader is autocratic in behaviour, making unilateral decisions, dictating work practices, maintaining control and engaging in little or no communications. Generally, performance is fairly high under such a leader, but job satisfaction and morale are low. A democratic leader believes in good communications, consultation and tries to get a consensus for important decisions, but if that is not possible, they still have to be made. Performance with such a leader is generally not as high as under an authoritarian one, but job satisfaction and morale are high. A paternalistic type of leader adopts a fatherly approach to all staff, a type often found in family-run businesses. Research by Likert (1961) suggests that employee-centred leadership behaviour (developing good job satisfaction) is more effective than a job-centred approach, where the emphasis is placed on work and the procedures involved. A transformational leader is one who makes radical changes in an organisation to adapt it for a changed external environment. Such a leader has a certain charisma, a vision with a keen sense of mission and the competence to inspire staff to change rapidly and achieve new goals. It involves creatively adapting, shaping and aligning an organisation to meet new challenges and opportunities (Griffin, 2008; Naylor, 2002). The most appropriate leadership style is the one which gets the best results having regard to current conditions as well as the objectives and goals to be achieved. With this style, known as situational leadership, the person has to adapt his/her behaviour to the current and future needs of an organisation at a specific time with regard to the external environment. The focus here is on leadership with mutual and collective responsibility, rather than on leaders. The style and competence have to fit the purpose with regard to the environment, stage of development and the changes expected. Leadership and management are not synonymous. The former is concerned with influencing future direction and change, while the latter is focused on organising and controlling the operations of a business. According to Kotter (1990), management is about coping with complexity; leadership, by contrast, is about coping with change.

10.5 Control

Control is the continuous management process of measuring the performance of an organisation in relation to the objectives and goals set for it as a whole and for its constituent parts as well as taking whatever consequent action is most advantageous. Good management information systems are essential in all organisations to facilitate planning and control, with regular reports showing actual performance with planned targets. Causes of deviation have to be identified and corrective action taken if required. The main purpose of control is to improve performance and it involves five essential elements, as shown in Figure 10.3.

Figure 10.3: The control process

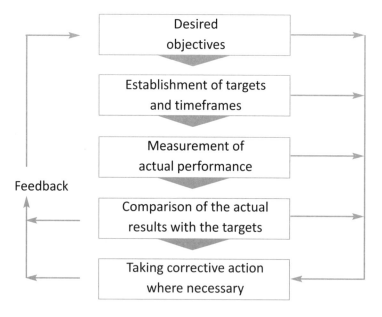

The first step in the control process is to state the desired objectives with regard to the various plans. The second step is to establish standards of performance with targets for individuals, sections, departments and the overall organisation, together with a timeframe. Once agreed, the targets have to be properly communicated to all concerned. It is important that each person clearly understands what is required. The next stage involves measurement of actual performance and this feedback system has to be accurate, simple and timely. Actual performance is then compared with the standards and targets set. Deviations are identified, with causes and consequences investigated. The last element is taking corrective action if necessary.

Control systems are devised for all operations, especially the strategic, tactical and operational objectives, as well as numerous other operations like inputs, outputs, processes and the performance of staff on a weekly or monthly basis, as appropriate. The behavioural implications of control systems have to be considered and every effort made to secure the support of all staff by good communications, consultation and involvement in the process. Controls which overemphasise blame are likely to create resistance. A system of management by objectives (MBO), whereby personal targets are established and agreed with each employee within the desired overall framework, can be very effective. Effective control systems are economical, easily understood, flexible and designed to suit each specific activity.

The main methods of control are classified as financial and non-financial, with examples of each shown in Table 10.2.

Table 10.2: Methods of control

Financial		Non-financial	
a)	Budgetary control	a)	Balanced scorecard
b)	Cash flow forecasts	b)	Benchmarking
c)	Gearing	c)	Management audit
d)	Cost/price changes	d)	Marketing audit
e)	Financial analysis	e)	Production control
f)	Break-even analysis	f)	Inventory control
g)	Internal audit	g)	Debtor control
h)	External audit	h)	Quality control

a)   Financial controls

Budgetary control

Effective financial control is essential in every organisation. In many organisations the only financial statements prepared are the annual accounts, which are usually available several months after the end of the accounting year, but as a control device, such statements have limited value. Regular (usually monthly) management accounts with associated balance sheets are required, which show the following:

- The budget for the month (where activity varies, a flexible budget is prepared with regard to variable costs and actual outputs)
- The actual performance for the month
- The variances (differences) under each heading for the month
- The budget for the year to date
- The actual performance for the year to date
- The variances under each heading for the year to date
- Balance sheet data.

Management accounts, produced in a timely manner, provide essential up-to-date financial information to facilitate good decision-making. If budgeted targets are not being attained it is up to the management team to take action. This process enables managers to adopt 'management by exception', whereby they concentrate their attention on the main deviations rather than considering every aspect of the report. A business has to be managed to yield a satisfactory profit and a positive cash flow, which enables it to survive and grow.

In reviewing management accounts, the key measures are the following:

- Turnover
- Gross margin
- Costs
- Net profit.

Under-performance in any of these is carefully considered and prompt action taken if required. In many cases, cost increases cannot be recovered by increasing prices because of the competitive position. If profitability is declining, remedial action is necessary. Actions to be considered include increasing sales if possible, increasing productivity, reducing costs, eliminating waste and adopting flexible work practices. To increase sales a business may be required to reduce prices, margins and costs so as to provide value to attract and keep customers. Other considerations for some organisations include eliminating loss-making products or services, selling under-performing units, outsourcing, downsizing the organisation and re-engineering activities. If management does not respond quickly and effectively to a changing situation, the 'bottom line' target will not be achieved and, if allowed to deteriorate, it could result in insolvency. Regular management accounts and early corrective action can prevent business failure. If a small business lacks the resources to provide management accounts, the service can be outsourced.

Cash flow forecasts

Cash flow statements are also monitored on a monthly basis. The big danger for an expanding business is overtrading: increasing turnover with insufficient resources, which can result in disaster. As a business expands extra working capital is required to finance additional stocks, debtors and other activities. Capital investment may also be required. Overtrading results in excessive demands on banks and creditors. Cash flow forecasts have to be carefully monitored on a regular basis to ensure that there is sufficient cash available to meet commitments.

Gearing

Organisations regularly review their gearing position, debt/equity ratio and its implications with regard to a changing macroeconomic environment. It can be dangerous to rely excessively on borrowed finance, as many construction companies discovered when the 2008 recession started.

Cost/price changes

Most business organisations require good costing systems, especially those engaged in competitive quotations, tenders and price-sensitive markets. Costs in every organisation always have to be closely monitored and controlled. In general, demand for products and services is price sensitive and lower costs enable a business to charge lower prices.

Financial analysis

Financial statements are analysed using ratio analysis, with appropriate action taken based on the findings.

Break-even analysis

Break-even analysis is also an important technique used in financial control.

Internal audit

Internal audit is concerned with establishing proper systems of internal controls to ensure that there is no fraud and that all operations are carried out correctly.

External audit

Almost all companies, co-operative societies and many other trading organisations have their accounts audited each year.

b)   Non-financial controls

Balanced scorecard

To counteract the big emphasis on financial measures of performance, increasing attention is being given to various non-financial indicators. Kaplan and Norton (1992), in an effort to integrate financial and non-financial measures of performance, devised the balanced scorecard, a procedure for measuring results against the strategic plan and goals in relation to a number of balanced performance indicators. They suggest performance measures from different perspectives: customers, employees, internal business process and finance, as outlined in Figure 10.4.

Figure 10.4: Balanced scorecard

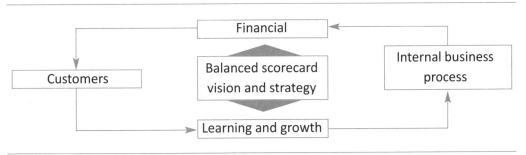

The balanced scorecard takes a strategic multi-perspective view of an organisation. Four or more major goals linked to the strategic plan are identified under the different perspectives, with targets and specific performance measures. Marketing measures could include sales, market share, customer acquisition, customer profitability, customer retention, customer complaints and how they are addressed as well as the effectiveness of the strategies adopted. Marketing and sales are so important that many organisations review performance on a weekly basis, which is essential in a very competitive environment. Accurate and reliable market information is essential in any organisation. Examples of possible financial measures include return on capital employed, return on net worth, cash flow, margins and profit growth. The internal business process perspective includes innovation, operations, quality and after-sale services. The learning and growth enablers are employee competence, information capabilities, motivation, empowerment and organisational alignment with strategy. It is up to each organisation to define its own scorecard. The same procedure can be extended to departments and sections within an organisation. The aim of a balanced scorecard is to provide a range of coherent performance indicators against which an organisation's results can be measured in relation to its strategic and tactical plans. It reflects the old adage: what gets measured gets done. Kaplan and Norton (1996) recommend that organisations move to a balanced scorecard approach in measuring performance, where the drivers of financial performance, and not just the results, are measured, evaluated and managed, as well as developing a longer-term control perspective.

Benchmarking

Benchmarking is a process of identifying and adopting, where possible, the recognised best practice in the internal and/or external environment in specific activities with the objective of continuous improvement. Sources of benchmark information include annual reports, industry/trade publications, professional associations, library databases, consultancy firms and research. Adopting new, improved practices requires change, flexibility, motivation and positive attitudes by all staff.

Management audit

Management can undertake regular reviews of its strategic, tactical and operational planning as well as its organisation, leadership, motivation, communications (internal and external), co-ordination and general control procedures.

Marketing audit

A marketing audit is defined by Kotler (2003) as:

> a comprehensive, systematic, independent and periodic examination
> of a company's or business unit's marketing environment, objectives,

strategies, and activities, with a view to determining problem areas and opportunities and recommending a plan of action to improve the company's marketing performance.

Production control, inventory control, debtor control and quality control are dealt with in Chapters 5 and 7.

10.6 Time management

Time management is concerned with the effective and productive use of a person's working time. It focuses attention on objectives and results rather than on work. The main objective is to work smarter rather than harder or longer.

Table 10.3: Steps in effective time management

a)	A commitment to manage one's time
b)	A review of existing activities
c)	Identification of the main 'time wasters'
d)	Elimination or reduction of 'time wasters'
e)	Focus on effectiveness
f)	Prioritised planning
g)	Regular evaluation of the time management plan

The first step in the process of good time management, as shown in Table 10.3, is a commitment to a plan and good organisation. This is followed by a review of all existing activities over a two- to four-week period, when 'time wasters' are identified. These usually include telephone calls, visitors, meetings, emails, diary commitments and travel. A manager has to review each 'time waster' and decide the best approach to adopt in stopping or reducing the activity. Every manager wants time each day to focus on key objectives and goals. Meetings, if not organised and conducted properly, are notorious time wasters. A business meeting should be held only if it is necessary, and it should have a definite starting and finishing time so that those attending can plan their day. Each item on the agenda has to be planned carefully, with the necessary background information provided in advance to facilitate decision-making.

A manager has to be careful in not allowing his/her life and work to be controlled by diary engagements. It is up to each person to decide his/her own programme of work for a day, week or month; other engagements fall into his/her schedule and not the other way around. Travel, especially in cities with modern traffic congestion, is another great time waster which has to be carefully controlled, and alternatives such as conference calls, Skype and other uses of modern communications technology considered. Some existing work may be unnecessary or could be planned better in advance or delegated. All work has to be examined on a regular basis to see if it can be undertaken more efficiently or simplified and standardised, especially with regard to changes in information communications technology. Procrastination is a problem for many, especially in relation to difficult assignments. Delaying a difficult job does not make it any easier to undertake.

The fifth step focuses attention on effectiveness, results and achievements. A manager has to have regard for the 'big picture', planning, organisation, goal-setting and ensuring that all the key objectives are achieved on schedule. It is very easy to get carried away by trivial issues which are insignificant in relation to the big picture. The next step is prioritised planning, identifying the main activities to be performed each day, week, month and their priority. Many managers find it useful to prepare a 'to do' list for each day, week and month to keep their attention on the key objectives and goals. The final step is a regular review of the time management plan in an effort to improve it. A person has to strike a balance between work, leisure and family obligations. Effective time management can result in the attainment of specific objectives and goals, adherence to deadlines, improved productivity, increased job satisfaction and better interpersonal relations, with less tension and stress.

10.7 Managing change

Organisations are not stationary entities. They now face a complex, uncertain and dynamic environment which demands innovation and continuous change. They all have a life cycle with four stages – formation, growth, maturity and decline – although with good leadership the latter stage may be one of renewal and revitalisation. The mature stage is potentially a very dangerous one, where organisations can rest on their laurels and stifle initiative, resulting in complacency, inertia and reaction to events with little or no innovation. Change can come through external or internal forces and can be incremental or transformational. The former involves gradual movement in the existing practices, while the latter requires a radical change to survive in the changing environment.

Even with good planning, organisations usually resist change because of uncertainty about the future. Managers experience this resistance to change, which can come from the organisation and individuals. Organisational resistance can originate from its own hierarchical structure, group inertia, threatened expertise or threatened influence (Katz and Kahn, 1978). Individual resistance to change can be caused by uncertainty, threatened self-interests, different perceptions, a lack of understanding and little or no confidence in management to create a better future. In general people resist change when they are comfortable with the status quo, when they do not understand why it is necessary and when they are doubtful about an organisation's ability to achieve the desired results. It is essential to understand and plan for the alleviation of resistance before the change process begins. Resistance can be overcome, or at least alleviated, by good communications, consultation, participation and the establishment of trust.

Figure 10.5: Steps in managing change

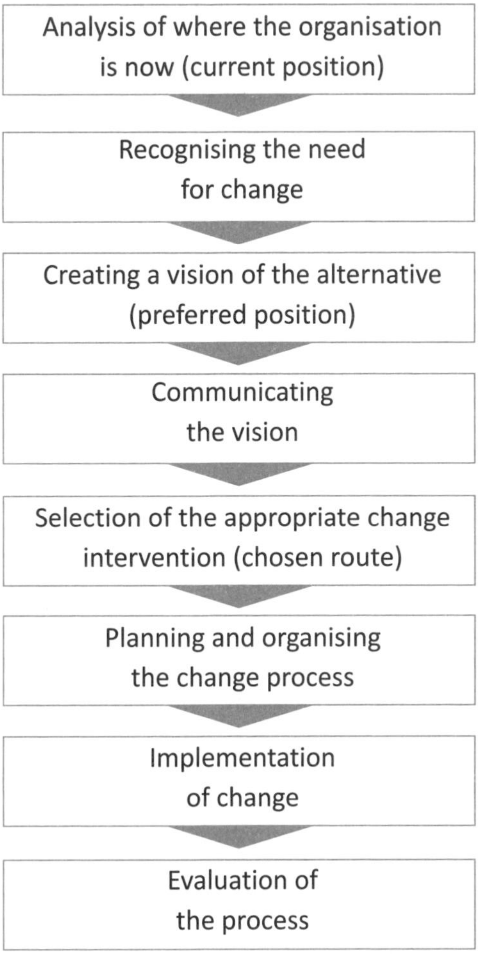

```
┌─────────────────────────────────────┐
│   Analysis of where the organisation  │
│      is now (current position)        │
└─────────────────────────────────────┘
              ▼
┌─────────────────────────────────────┐
│       Recognising the need            │
│           for change                  │
└─────────────────────────────────────┘
              ▼
┌─────────────────────────────────────┐
│  Creating a vision of the alternative │
│       (preferred position)            │
└─────────────────────────────────────┘
              ▼
┌─────────────────────────────────────┐
│         Communicating                 │
│           the vision                  │
└─────────────────────────────────────┘
              ▼
┌─────────────────────────────────────┐
│  Selection of the appropriate change  │
│     intervention (chosen route)       │
└─────────────────────────────────────┘
              ▼
┌─────────────────────────────────────┐
│      Planning and organising          │
│        the change process             │
└─────────────────────────────────────┘
              ▼
┌─────────────────────────────────────┐
│         Implementation                │
│           of change                   │
└─────────────────────────────────────┘
              ▼
┌─────────────────────────────────────┐
│          Evaluation of                │
│           the process                 │
└─────────────────────────────────────┘
```

A change process model is shown in Figure 10.5, with the first step being an analysis of where the organisation is now, as well as its own strengths and weaknesses. This is followed by recognising the need for change arising from an analysis of the external competitive environment. Management then have to create a vision of the alternative assuming a successful change, which can involve all or part of any organisation. This vision has to be communicated to staff and their support elicited. The reasons for the change, the process involved and the expected benefits have to be fully explained to staff. They must be convinced that the alternative is far superior to the present position. The next step is to select the most appropriate intervention to achieve the desired change; common methods include business planning, organisational design, new technology, operations, staff or a combination thereof. The change process then has to be planned, organised and implemented. Finally, the process is evaluated in relation to the original plan. Any change intervention has to have a champion, a person with a vision of what is required, the reasons for it and a good understanding of the context for the change as well as appropriate managerial and interpersonal skills to achieve the transformation.

Pettigrew and Whipp (1991) state that successful strategic change depends on five interrelated elements: proper environmental assessment, appropriate leadership in the cultural context of the organisation, strategic human resource management, a link between strategic and operational change and, above all, coherence between all the elements. Similar approaches are suggested by Kanter *et al.* (1992) and Kotter (1996). As the pace of change accelerates, major paradigm shifts are required in the way things are done, evolving into a continuous innovative process. With radical developments in the macroeconomic environment and the current emphasis on innovation in a 'smart economy', the only certainty in business management is continuous change.

10.8 Summary

An entrepreneur has to decide what business sector to enter, when, where and how. He/she has to establish goals and strategies to achieve them. The key factors in the management of a business are customers, staff, a quality product or service and operations including customer service, innovation, competitiveness, provision of value, turnover, prices, costs, net profit and a positive cash flow.

Managers will find useful theories and insights in the literature, but they have to be able to make sound decisions in the best interests of their organisations with regard to the present and expected macroeconomic environment. The main elements of management are planning, organising, motivation and leadership as well as control. Planning is the process of developing the long-term direction of a organisation to exploit perceived opportunities in a rapidly changing external environment. It incorporates strategic, tactical and operational plans. All aspects of a strategic plan have to be organised and implemented, including recruiting and training the required staff. Motivation and leadership are important in all organisations. Various control procedures have be used to ensure that agreed objectives and goals are accomplished.

Good time management is essential for everyone in an organisation. It can result in the attainment of objectives and goals, adherence to deadlines, improved productivity, increased job satisfaction and better interpersonal relations with less tension and stress.

All organisations now face a complex, uncertain and changing environment. Managers have to prepare their organisations for this changing environment. According to Drucker (1995), effective strategic management focuses on doing the right things rather than 'doing things right' (efficiency). It is concerned with positioning an organisation to be in the right business, with the right product or service, in the right place at the right time, with competitive advantage. It is the process of preparing an organisation to foresee change, to be innovative and adapt quickly to exploit new opportunities in a complex new environment. An effective manager has to be able to synthesise various theories, techniques and a variety of economic and other forecasts to position his/her organisation for an uncertain future. Rapid change is bringing new challenges to the global village: market liberalisation, an enlarged European Union, mobile international investment, the emergence of the new vibrant economies, new technological developments and an increasingly competitive marketplace. Customers are getting more demanding, becoming less loyal, have more choices – especially in the modern electronic world – and are seeking better value. It is becoming more difficult to predict and exceed the new expectations of customers at a profit – the big challenge for effective managers.

Questions

1. Explain what you understand by management.
2. 'To manage is to forecast and plan, to organise, to command, to co-ordinate and to control.' Discuss.
3. Consider the main issues involved in strategic planning.
4. Assess the advantages and disadvantages of budgetary control in the management of a business.
5. Consider the main issues which arise in managing change.

Layout of a feasibility study

1. Name(s), address(es), qualifications, experience of promoter(s)

2. Business proposal

3. Market
   a) Analysis of the industry, target market segment, trends and barriers to entry, if any
   b) Competitive analysis
   c) Market research using primary and secondary information
   d) Customer profiles and requirements in relation to possible product/service offerings
   e) Possible selling price for product/service
   f) Measurement of market size and possible share
   g) Market opportunity
   h) Nature of distribution system, including:
      • General requirements
      • Packaging
      • Technical support
      • Delivery
      • Terms/costs
      • Procedures
      • Promotion methods and costs
   i) Seasonality (if applicable)
   j) Sources of competitive advantage/unique selling proposition

4. Product
   a) Description
   b) Prototype to meet the product concept requirements of potential customers

5. Production
   a) Location: Options

b)   Premises: Available options
                  Purchase vs. lease, cost, title, suitability
                  Potential for expansion
                  Planning permission
                  Special requirements and costs
c)   Plant and equipment: descriptions, sources, costs
d)   Raw materials: description, sources, supply arrangements, costs, terms
e)   Production scheduling/layout
f)   Warehousing
g)   Transportation, options, suitability, costs
h)   Health, safety and welfare obligations as well as any special legal or regulatory
      requirements relating to the business
i)   Technological changes

6. Staffing
    a)   Number of staff required
    b)   Desired qualifications/skills/experience in respect of each
    c)   Contract work options

7. Finance   €
    a)   Requirements: i)   Fixed assets
                          ii)   Start-up costs
                          iii)   Working capital

    b)   Possible sources of finance:
                          i)   Promoter(s)
                          ii)   Grants (sources and conditions)
                          iii)   Borrowing (source, terms, security required)
                          iv)   Other
    c)   Costings of the product/service/margins/profitability/cash flow analysis
    d)   Break-even analysis

8. Project plan and timetable for the proposed business

9. Recommendations

Appendix 2

Business plan layout

Cover page

Table of contents

1. Promoter(s)
    a) Name(s), address(es), telephone number(s), email address, webpage of the promoter(s)
    b) Type of business organisation
    c) Brief introduction to the business, its product/service/rationale of proposal

2. Executive summary
    a) Proposed business
    b) Description of product/service
    c) Target market
    d) Description of the market opportunity
    e) How it is proposed to exploit the opportunity
    f) Capabilities to exploit the opportunity
    g) Unique features of the project which makes it attractive to customers and differentiates it from competitors
    h) Proposed investment   €
        i) Fixed assets   _____
        ii) Start-up costs   _____
        iii) Working capital requirements   _____
    (i) Finance required
        Sources (capital structure)
        i) Own funds   _____
        ii) Grants   _____
        iii) Borrowings   _____
        iv) Other: State source   _____
        Total   _____
    j) Finance projections   _____

	Year 1	Year 2	Year 3
Projected sales			
Gross profit			
Net profit			
Capital employed			
Return on capital employed (ROCE)			
Return on net worth			
Break-even projection			

Detailed plan

3. Product/service description
    a) Industry/sector/segment(s) targeted
    b) Unique features of product/service
    c) Advantages of product/service over existing competitors
    d) Unique selling proposition
    e) How your business creates value for customers

4. Industry and competitor analysis
    a) Environmental analysis: Political, economic, social, regulatory and technogical trends relevant to the targeted industry and sector
    b) Industry analysis
        i)   Type, features, market segments, current marketing practices, product offerings and their life cycles, profitability, main trends, possible market opportunity
        ii) Factors which determine the level of profitability in the industry at present
        iii) Opportunities and threats in target market(s)
    c) Competitor analysis
        i)   Market positioning of competitors
        ii) Strengths and weaknesses
        iii) Marketing practices in relation to product, distribution, price, promotion
        iv) Possible barriers to market entry
        v)   Possible reaction of competitors
        vi) Possible market opportunity

5. Strategic analysis
    a) Core competence of business
    b) SWOT analysis
        - Strengths
        - Weaknesses
        - Opportunities
        - Threats
    c) Business strategy adopted
        - Cost leadership
        - Differentiation
        - Focus strategy

6. Marketing plan
    a) Market segment(s) targeted
    b) Market size/growth potential/structure/trends/nature of the purchasing cycle
    c) Targeted customer profiles, specific preferences and behaviour
    d) Market research findings
    e) Possible market share and basis on which it is calculated
    f) How is it proposed to capture the planned market share?
    g) Competitive advantage of new product/service
    h) How is it proposed to enter the target market and compete profitably?
    i) Sales forecasts
    j) Commitments received from potential customers
    k) Marketing strategy
        i)   Market positioning
        ii)   Product: unique features; benefits new product/service has for customers
        iii) Price: proposed price and how it compares with competitors
        iv)   Place: how is it intended to sell and distribute the product/service? Agreements made, terms and conditions, export plans, if any
        v)   Promotion: how is it proposed to inform people about the product/service? Costs

7. Operations plan
    a) Location, where, why
    b) Premises, where, why, purchase or lease, title, size, cost
    c) Production/operations, process/capacity/subcontracts, if any
    d) Physical plant, machinery, equipment, requirements and costs
    e) Raw materials, sources of supply and costs

f)   Production schedules, warehousing, transport/distribution

g)   Quality strategy

h)   Legal requirements

8.   Human resources

a)   Promoter(s) and management team

The following information is required in respect of each person:

i)   Name

ii)   Qualifications

iii)   Work experience to date

iv)   Experience of managing a business

v)   Experience in this type of business

vi)   Other commitments (if any)

b)   Other staffing and skills required: Full time

Part time

c)   Roles and responsibilities of members

d)   Contract work (if any)

e)   Names of advisors

i)   Solicitor

ii)   Accountant

iii)   State agency

iv)   Non-executive directors (if applicable)

9.   Financial plan

a)   Investment required for start-up

i)   Fixed assets

ii)   Start-up costs

iii)   Working capital required   _____

Total investment   _____

b)   How it is proposed to raise the required finance

Amount subscribed by promoter(s)   _____

Amount sought by way of grant (if any)   _____

Amount to be raised by borrowings   _____

Other: State sources   _____

Total finance required for project   _____

c) Profitability

	Year 1	Year 2	Year 3
Projected sales			
Projected gross profit			
Projected net profit/sales			
Projected capital employed			
Projected return on capital employed (ROCE)			
Return on net worth			
Break-even projection			

10. Critical risks
    a) State key assumptions made in the plan
    b) State key risks involved in the plan
    c) Sensitivity analysis of some key assumptions
    d) Contingency plans

11. Start-up schedule
    Critical path of the start-up schedule

12. Appendices
    a) Market research data
    b) i) Projected trading, profit and loss accounts and balance sheets for the first three to five years
       ii) Cash flow forecasts for three to five years
       iii) Costing/pricing policy/margins
       iv) Break-even analysis data
       v) Audited accounts for the past three years, if applicable

Projected trading, profit and loss accounts for years 1, 2 and 3

		Year 1	Year 2	Year 3
a)	Sales	X	X	X
	Opening stock	X	X	X
	Add purchases	X	X	X
		X	X	X
	Less closing stock	(X)	(X)	(X)
b)	Cost of goods sold	X	X	X
	Gross profit (a – b)	X	X	X
	Gross profit % (gross profit/sales)	–	–	–
c)	Gross profit carried down	X	X	X
	Less overheads			
	Production	X	X	X
	Buildings	X	X	X
	Depreciation	X	X	X
	Selling and promotion	X	X	X
	Transport	X	X	X
	Wages and salaries including employer's PRSI	X	X	X
	General administration	X	X	X
	Interest paid	X	X	X
	Other expenses	X	X	X
d)	Total overheads	(X)	(X)	(X)
e)	Net profit before taxation (c – d)	X	X	X
	Taxation	(X)	(X)	(X)
	Net profit after taxation	X	X	X
	Net profit/sales %	-	-	-

Projected balance sheets as at the [date] of years 1, 2 and 3

	Year 1		Year 2		Year 3	
	€	€	€	€	€	€
Fixed assets (book value)		X		X		X
Current assets						
Inventory	X		X		X	
Debtors	X		X		X	
Cash	X		X		X	
a) Total current assets	**X**		**X**		**X**	
Current liabilities						
Trade creditors	X		X		X	
Current tax	X		X		X	
Liabilities	X		X		X	
b) Total current liabilities	**X**		**X**		**X**	
Net current assets (a − b)		**X**		**X**		**X**
Net assets		**X**		**X**		**X**
Financed by:						
Ordinary share capital		**X**		**X**		**X**
Reserves		**X**		**X**		**X**
Retained profit c/f	X		X		X	
Add retained profit for year	X		X		X	
Profit brought forward		**X**		**X**		**X**
Long-term liabilities (term loans)		**X**		**X**		**X**
		X		**X**		**X**

Note 1: The details can be provided in supplementary notes.

Note 2: State all assumptions made.

Note 3: A business plan for services is prepared in a similar manner, excluding those items which are not relevant.

Public procurement

Public procurement is the acquisition of works (civil engineering contracts), supplies (goods) and services by public bodies. In order for the State to obtain the best value for public funds in a competitive manner, there are guidelines relating to public procurement which have to be observed. It is important that businesspeople are familiar with the guidelines if they want to trade with the public sector. The general principles involved in public procurement are transparency, equal treatment, proportionality (any special requirements have to be necessary and appropriate) and best value. There are two thresholds involved:

a) Purchases below the European Union (EU) threshold value to which specific EU directives, now adopted in Irish Law, apply

b) Purchases above the EU threshold, which must comply with specific regulations.

a)   Purchases below the EU threshold value

There are two guidelines in operation (see *Public Procurement Guidelines* at www.etenders.gov.ie).

- Supplies or services under €5,000 are to be purchased on the basis of a written quotation from one or more competitive suppliers. For contracts up to €50,000, at least three written quotations are required from competent suppliers or from those on a panel established in an open and transparent manner.

- Purchases above €50,000 and under the EU threshold are to be obtained by a tendering process. All such purchases are first advertised on the National Public Procurement website (www.etenders.gov.ie), which satisfies the national publicity requirements, and other media can be used if desired. The procedure used can be open, restricted or panel based. Under the open procedure, tender documents are sent to any supplier who requests them. Selection, specification and award criteria are provided on the website. Under the restricted procedure, potential suppliers are required to submit qualitative selection information or complete a questionnaire, after which tender documentation and award criteria are issued. All tenders returned are evaluated against the selection, specification and award criteria. With the panel-based procedure, invitations are sent to organisations on a panel established in a open and objective manner. At least five organisations are invited to tender in a competitive process. Some contracts are awarded on the basis of the most economically advantageous tender (MEAT) in accordance with stated award criteria.

b)   Purchases above the EU threshold

Purchases above the EU threshold are required to comply with revised EU public sector procurement directives (for the current threshold and procedures, see www.etenders.gov.ie and the EU public procurement website, http://simap.en.int). Contracting authorities are required to advertise their requirements in the *Official Journal of the European Union* (*OJEU*) and use the procedures in an open and transparent manner to ensure fair competition. All advertisements in the *OJEU* are also to be published on the etenders website. These obligations also apply to private organisations which are subsidised 50 per cent or more by a public body. A contracting authority (Government department, public body or a body financed largely by public funds) with a purchase requirement in excess of a specified figure for any product or category of services is required to publish an annual notice called a Prior Information Notice (PIN) in the *OJEU* at the start of a year.

The EU Directives on Public Procurement contain four tendering procedures: open, restricted, competitive dialogue and negotiated. Under open procedures, any supplier who requests to be considered before the specified date is entitled to receive tender documents and submit a tender. In restricted procedures, any supplier can express interest and seek information, but only those suppliers that meet specific minimum requirements (like technical competence, experience and financial capacity) are invited to tender. Competitive dialogue is a procedure which can be used in complex contracts to provide some flexibility, for example public–private partnerships (PPPs). Requirements are advertised and dialogue can take place with interested parties prior to the submission of tenders. In the negotiated procedure, which is rarely used and only after the tender process fails, the contracting authority advertises for tenders with the right to negotiate the terms with at least three to ensure a competitive process. There are minimum time limits for the various stages of the EU procurement process. Contracting authorities can award contracts on the basis of the lowest tender or the most economically advantageous. Tax clearance is required from all successful organisations and they must comply with statutory obligations in respect of minimum pay, industrial agreements and health and safety issues.

The Government Procurement Agreement (GPA) of the World Trade Organization (WTO) gives equal rights of access to GPA countries, EU and European Economic Area (EEA) tenders and vice versa.

European Union Countries (27)

Austria, Belgium, Bulgaria, Cyprus, Czech Republic, Denmark, Estonia, Finland, France,

Germany, Greece, Hungary, Ireland, Italy, Latvia, Lithuania, Luxembourg, Malta, Netherlands, Poland, Portugal, Romania, Slovakia, Slovenia, Spain, Sweden and the UK.

European Economic Area (EEA)

European Union countries as well as Norway, Liechtenstein and Iceland.

Government Procurement Agreement with the WTO

The World Trade Organization (formerly General Agreement on Tariffs and Trade) was established in 1995. With a membership of 147 countries, it is the international body responsible for the rules of trade between nations. The Government Procurement Agreement with the WTO includes the following non-EU and non-EEA countries: Canada, China, Hong Kong, Israel, Japan, Netherlands for Aruba, Singapore, South Korea, Switzerland and the United States.

References/Bibliography

Abel, D.F., *Defining the Business: The Starting Point of Strategic Planning*, Englewood Cliffs, NJ: Prentice Hall 1980

Adams, G.S., 'Towards an Understanding of Inequity', *Journal of Abnormal and Social Psychology*, November 1963

ACSTI, *National Code of Practice for Managing and Commercialising Intellectual Property from Public–Private Collaboration Research*, Dublin: Advisory Council for Science, Technology and Innovation 2005

Alderfer, C.P., *Existence, Relatedness and Growth*, New York: Free Press 1963

Ansoff , I., 'Strategies for Diversification', *Harvard Business Review*, Sept–Oct 1957

Ansoff, I., *Implementing Strategic Management*, Englewood Cliffs, NJ: Prentice Hall 1990

Appleby, T. and O'Hanlon, F., *The Taxation of Capital Gains*, Dublin: Irish Taxation Institute 2010

Armstrong, M., *A Handbook of Personnel Management Practice*, London: Kogan Page 2003

Baker, M.J., *Marketing: An Introductory Text*, Basingstoke: Macmillan 1991

Bellon, B. and Whittington, G., *Competing through Innovation,* Dublin: Oak Tree Press 1996

Bennis, W.G., *On Becoming a Leader,* Cambridge: Perseus Publishing 1994

Berry, L.L. and Parasuraman, A., *Marketing Services Competing through Quality,* New York: The Free Press 1991

Bessant, J. and Tidd, J., *Innovation and Entrepreneurship,* Chichester: John Wiley & Sons Ltd 2007

Bohan, P., *Notes on Enterprise Development*, Dublin: The Marketing Institute 1996

Bolton, B. and Thompson, J., *Entrepreneurs, Talent, Temperament, Technique*, Oxford: Butterworth-Heinemann 2005

Bolton, J.E., *Report of the Committee of Enquiry on Small Firms*, CM 4811, London: HMSO 1971

Booms, B.H. and Bitner, M.J., 'Marketing Strategies and Organizational Structures for Service Firms' in Donnelly, J. and George, W.R. (eds), *Marketing of Services*, Chicago: American Marketing Association 1981

Booz-Allen and Hamilton, *New Product Management for the 1980s*, New York: Booz-Allen and Hamilton 1982

Boston Consulting Group, *The Product Portfolio Matrix*, Boston: Boston Consulting Group 1970

Bowman, C. and Asch, D., *Managing Strategy*, Basingstoke: Macmillan 1996

Bradley, F., *International Marketing Strategy*, Hemel Hempstead: Prentice Hall 1991

Bradley, F. and Kennelly, J.J., *Capitalising on Culture, Competing on Difference – Innovation, Learning and Sense of Place in a Globalising Ireland*, Dublin: Blackhall Publishing 2008

Bradley, J.A., *PRSI and Levy Contributions*, Dublin: Irish Taxation Institute 2010

Brannick, T. and Roche, W.K., *Business Research Methods*, Dublin: Oak Tree Press 1997

Brech, E.F.L., *The Principles and Practice of Management*, London: Longman 1953

Brennan, F., Moore, P. and O'Sullivan, H., *Corporation Tax*, Dublin: Irish Taxation Institute 2010

Bridge, S., O'Neill, K. and Cromie, S., *Understanding Enterprise, Entrepreneurship and Small Business*, Basingstoke and London: Macmillan Press 1998

Brodie, S. and Dillon, G., *Value Added Tax*, Dublin: Irish Taxation Institute 2010

Buchanan, C. and Partners, *Regional Studies in Ireland*, Dublin: An Foras Forbartha 1968

Burke, A.E., *Enterprise and the Irish Economy*, Dublin: Oak Tree Press 1995

Burns, P. and Dewhurst, J. (eds), *Small Business and Entrepreneurship*, Basingstoke and London: Macmillan Press 1996

Burns, T. and Stalker, G., *The Management of Innovation*, London: Tavistock 1961

Bygrave, W.D., *The Portable MBA in Entrepreneurship*, New York: John Wiley & Sons Inc. 1994

Callanan, G., *Irish Company Law,* Dublin: Gill & Macmillan 2007

Campbell, A. and Tawadey, K., *Mission and Business Philosophy*, Oxford: Butterworth-Heinemann 1992

Cannon, T., *Enterprise: Creation, Development and Growth*, Oxford: Butterworth-Heinemann 1991

Cantillon, R., *Essai sur la Nature de Commerce en General*, 1755, translated by Higgs, H., London: Macmillan 1931

Carnall, C., *Managing Change in Organizations*, New York: Prentice Hall 1990

Carter, S. and Jones-Evans, D. (eds), *Enterprise and Small Business Principles, Practice and Policy*, Harlow: Pearson Education Ltd 2000

Central Statistics Office, *Quarterly National Household Survey*, Dublin: 2006, 2007, 2008

Central Statistics Office, *Small Business in Ireland*, Dublin: Stationery Office 2007

Chesbrough, H.W., *Open Innovation: The New Imperative for Creating and Profiting from Technology*, Boston: Harvard Business School 2006

Chisnall, P.M., *Market Research*, Maidenhead: McGraw Hill 1992

Christopher, M., *Logistics and Supply Chain Management,* London: *Financial Times*/Pitman 2005

Churchill, N.C. and Lewis, V.C., 'The Five Stages of Small Business Growth', *Harvard Business Review*, May–June 1983

Clarke, P. and McDermott, E., *Financial Accounting: An Introduction*, Dublin: Gill & Macmillan 2000

Clarke, P.J., *Accounting Information for Managers*, Dublin: Oak Tree Press 2002

Coleman, M., *The Best Is Yet to Come,* Dublin: Blackhall Publishing 2007

Collins, D., 'Irish Competition Law', in Collins, D. (ed.), *Business Law*, Oxford: OUP 2006

Companies Registration Office, *Information Leaflets*, Dublin: CRO 2006

Condon, J.F. and Muddiman, J., *Capital Acquisitions Tax*, Dublin: Irish Taxation Institute 2007

Connolly, G., 'Foreign Workers – How to Get It Right', *People Focus*, CIPD in Ireland, Vol. 5, No. 3, 2007

Connolly, P. and McGing, G., 'The Special Olympics 2003', in Cooney, T.M., *Irish Cases in Entrepreneurship*, Dublin: Blackhall Publishing 2005

Cooney, T.M., 'Eamonn and Brian Fallon-Daftie', in Henry, C. (ed.), *Ernst & Young Entrepreneur of the Year Case Series*, Dublin: Blackhall Press 2007

Cooney, T.M. (ed.), *Irish Cases in Entrepreneurship*, Dublin: Blackhall Publishing 2005

Cooney, T.M. and Hill, S. (eds), *New Venture Creation in Ireland,* Cork: Oak Tree Press 2002

Cooper, M., *Who Really Runs Ireland?,* Dublin: Penguin Ireland 2010

Courtney, T., *The Law of Private Companies*, London: Butterworths 1994

Creaton, S., *Ryanair: How a Small Irish Airline Conquered Europe*, London: Aurum Press 2005

Creaton, S., *A Mobile Fortune: The Life and Times of Denis O'Brien*, London: Aurum Press 2010

Cunningham, J. and Harvey, B., *Strategic Management of Technology Transfer*, Cork: Oak Tree Press 2006

Cunningham, J.B. and Lischeron, J., 'Defining Entrepreneurship', *Journal of Small Business Management*, Vol. 29, No. 1, 1991

de Bono, E., *Lateral Thinking: Creativity Step by Step*, New York: Harper and Row 1973

de Bono, E., *Opportunities: A Handbook of Business Opportunity Search,* London: Associated Business Programmes 1978

De Búrca, S., Fletcher, R. and Brown, L., *International Marketing: An SME Perspective,* Essex: Pearson Education 2004

De George, R., *Business Ethics,* Englewood Cliffs: Prentice Hall 1999

Deming, W.E., *Out of the Crisis*, Cambridge: CUP 1986

Deming, W.E., *Quality Productivity and Competitive Position*, Cambridge: MIT 1982

Department of Enterprise, Trade and Innovation, *Guide to Labour Law*, Dubin: DETI 2007

Department of the Taoiseach, *Building Ireland's Smart Economy: A Framework for Sustainable Economic Renewal,* Dublin: Stationery Office 2008

Dibb, S., Simkin, L., Pride, W.M. and Ferrell, O.C., *Marketing: Concepts and Strategies*, Boston: Houghton Mifflin 2006

Dolan, D., *Payroll – Manual and Computerised,* Dublin: Gill & Macmillan 2004

Domegan, C. and Fleming, D., *Marketing Research in Ireland: Theory and Practice*, Dublin: Gill & Macmillan 2007

Doolan, B., *Principles of Irish Law*, Dublin: Gill & Macmillan 2007

Drucker, P.F., *The Practice of Management*, New York: Harper Row 1972

Drucker, P.F., *Management: Tasks, Responsibilities and Practices*, New York: Harper Row 1973

Drucker, P.F., *Managing for Results,* London: Heinemann 1983

Drucker, P.F., *Innovation and Entrepreneurship*, Oxford: Butterworth-Heinemann 1985

Drucker, P.F., *The Effective Executive*, Oxford: Butterworth-Heinemann 1995

Drucker, P.F., *The Essential Drucker,* Oxford: Butterworth-Heinemann 2001

Drury, C., *Management and Cost Accounting*, London: Chapman & Hall 2006

Duffy, P., 'Business Expansion Scheme Revisited', Part 2, *Irish Tax Review*, Vol. 21, No. 3, May 2008

Ellis, H., *Irish Company Law for Business*, Bristol: Jordans 1998 and 2003

Enterprise Strategy Group, *Ahead of the Curve: Ireland's Place in the Global Economy*, Dublin: Forfás 2004

Equality Authority, *The Employment Equality Acts,* 1998 and 2004, Clonmel: Equality Authority 2007

Equality Authority, *The Equal Status Acts 2000 to 2004*, Clonmel: Equality Authority 2007

Equality Authority, *About the Parental Leave Acts*, Clonmel: Equality Authority 2009a

Equality Authority, *Code of Practice on Sexual Harassment and Harassment at Work*, Clonmel: Equality Authority 2009b

ESRI, *Macroeconomic Context for a Sustainable Recovery*, Dublin: ESRI 2009

European Commission, *More Research for Europe*, Brussels: European Commission 2003

European Commission, *Europe 2020: A Strategy for Smart, Sustainable and Inclusive Growth*, Brussels: European Commission 2010

European Council, *Report of the European Council*, Lisbon: European Commission 2000

Expert Group on Future Skills Needs, *Tomorrow's Skills: Towards a National Skills Strategy*, Dublin: Forfás 2007

Fayol, H., *General and Industrial Management* (translated from the French edition, 1916), London: Pitman 1949

Fennell, C. and Lynch, I., *Labour Law in Ireland*, Dublin: Gill & Macmillan 1993

Forde, M., *The Law of Corporate Insolvency*, Dublin: Round Tree Press 1993

Forde, M. and Kennedy, H., *Company Law in Ireland*, Dublin: Round Hall 2007

Forfás, *Shaping our Future: A Strategy for Enterprise in Ireland in the 21st Century*, Dublin: Forfás 1996

Forfás, *Broadband Investment in Ireland*, Dublin: Forfás 1998a

Forfás, *Telecommunications: A Key Factor in Electronic Commerce and Competitiveness*, Dublin: Forfás 1998b

Forfás, *E-Commerce: The Policy Requirements*, Dublin: Forfás 1999a

Forfás, *Entrepreneurship in Ireland*, Dublin: Forfás 2002

Forfás, *Building Ireland's Knowledge Economy – Irish Action Plan for Promoting Investment in R&D to 2010,* Dublin: Forfás 2004a

Forfás, *From Research to the Marketplace – Patent Registration and Technology Transfer in Ireland*, Dublin: Forfás 2004b

Forfás, *Outward Direct Investment*, Dublin: Forfás 2007a

Forfás, *Tomorrow's Skills: Towards a National Skills Strategy*, Dublin: Forfás 2007b

Forfás, *Towards Developing an Entrepreneurship Policy for Ireland,* Dublin: Forfás 2007c

Forfás, *Regional Competitiveness Agendas – Overview, Findings and Actions,* Dublin: Forfás 2010

Fullard, F., 'The Importance of Family Business', *Accounting and Business*, 1999

Garavan, T., Costine, P. and Heraty, N., *Training and Development in Ireland: Context, Policy and Practice*, Dublin: Oak Tree Press 2003

Garavan, T.N. *et al.*, *Entrepreneurship and Business Start-ups in Ireland*, Vol. 1 and 2, Dublin: Oak Tree Press 1997

Ghauri, P. and Cateora, P., *International Marketing*, Berkshire: McGraw-Hill 2006

Gibson, A. and Nielson, M., *Tourism and Hospitality Marketing in Ireland*, Dublin: Gill & Macmillan 2000

Global Entrepreneurship Monitor (GEM), *Irish Annual Report*, available online at www.gemconsortium.org (2006, 2010)

Glynn, W.J. and Barnes, J.G. (eds), *Understanding Services Management*, Dublin: Oak Tree Press 1995

Goleman, D., *Emotional Intelligence: Why It Can Matter More than IQ*, London: Bloomsbury 1996

Goleman, D., 'What Makes a Leader?', *Harvard Business Review,* November–December 1998

Government Publications, *Programme for Economic Expansion*, Dublin: Stationery Office 1958

Government Publications, *Task Force on Small Business*, Dublin: Stationery Office 1994

Government Publications, *Delivery of Better Government: Strategic Management Initiative* Dublin: Stationery Office 1996

Government Publications, *National Development Plan 2000–2006,* Dublin: Stationery Office 2000

Government Publications, *National Development Plan 2007–2013*, Dublin: Stationery Office 2007a

Government Publications, *Strategy for Science, Technology and Innovation 2006–2013,* Dublin: Stationery Office 2007b

Government Publications, *Public Procurement Guidelines*, available online at www.etenders.gov.ie

Griffin, R.W., *Management*, Boston: Houghton Mifflin 2008

Gunnigle, P. (ed.), *The Irish Employee Recruitment Handbook*, Dublin: Oak Tree Press 1999

Gunnigle, P. and Roche, W.K., *New Challenges to Irish Industrial Relations*, Dublin: Oak Tree Press 1995

Gunnigle, P. *et al.*, *Continuity and Change in Irish Employee Relations*, Dublin: Oak Tree Press 1994

Gunnigle, P., Heraty, N. and Morley, M., *Human Resource Management in Ireland*, Dublin: Gill & Macmillan 2006

Gunnigle, P., McMahon, G. and Fitzgerald, G., *Industrial Relations in Ireland: Theory and Practice*, Dublin: Gill & Macmillan 2004

Haccius, C. and O'Brien, P., *Double Taxation Agreements*, Dublin: Irish Taxation Institute 2010

Hammer, M. and Champy, J., *Re-engineering the Corporation*, New York: Free Press 1994

Handy, C., *The Empty Raincoat: Making Sense of the Future*, London: Hutchinson 1994

Handy, C., *The Future of Work: A Guide to a Changing Society*, Oxford: Blackwell 1994

Harper, W.M., *Cost and Management Accounting*, Essex: Pearson Education Ltd 1995

Harvey, N., *The Challenge of Supervisory Management*, Dublin: Oak Tree Press 1997

Haughton, J., 'Growth in Output and Living Standards', in O'Hagan, J. and Newman, C. (eds), *The Economy of Ireland: National and Sectoral Policy Issues*, Dublin: Gill & Macmillan 2008

Health and Safety Authority, *Code of Practice on the Prevention of Workplace Bullying*, Dublin: HSA 2002

Health and Safety Authority, *Guidance for Directors and Senior Managers on their Responsibilities for Workplace Safety and Health*, Dublin: HSA 2007

Health and Safety Authority, *Guidance on Safety Representatives and Safety Consultation*, Dublin: HSA 2006

Health and Safety Authority, *Guidance on Safety Statements and Risk Assessments*, Dublin: HSA 2006

Health and Safety Authority, *Guidance on Workplace Safety and Health Management*, Dublin: HSA 2006

Health and Safety Authority, *Guide to the Safety, Health and Welfare at Work Act,* Dublin: HSA 2005

Hennessey, P. *et al.*, *How to Finance Your Business*, Dublin: Department of Enterprise, Trade and Employment 1999

Hennessy, L. and Moore, P., *Taxes Consolidation Act 1997: The Busy Practitioner's Guide*, Dublin: Irish Taxation Institute 1998

Henry, C. and McGowan, P. (eds), *Irish Cases in Entrepreneurship*, Dublin: Blackhall
     Publishing 2007

Herzberg, F. *et al.*, *The Motivation to Work*, New York: Wiley 1959

Herzberg, F., *Work and the Nature of Man*, New York: Staples 1966

Higgins, E. and Keher, N., *Your Rights at Work*, Dublin: Institute of Public Administration
     1999

Higgins, J., *The Kiltimagh Renewal: Best Practice in Community Enterprise*, Dublin: Oak
     Tree Press 1996

Higher Education Authority, *The Programme for Research in Third Level Institutions (PRTLI):
     Transforming the Irish Research Landscape*, Dublin: Higher Education Authority 2003

Hisrich, R.D. and Peters, M.P., *Entrepreneurship: Starting, Developing and Managing a
     New Enterprise*, Boston: Irwin 1995

ICSTI, *Technology Foresight Ireland*, Dublin: Forfás 1999

Industrial Development Authority, *Regional Industrial Plans 1973–77*, Dublin: IDA 1973

Industrial Policy Review Group, *A Time for Change: Industrial Policy in the 1990s*, Dublin:
     Government Publications 1992

Innovation Taskforce, *Innovation Ireland*, Dublin: Stationery Office 2010

Investment in Education, Vol. 1 and 2, Dublin: Stationery Office 1965 and 1966

'Iona Technologies sold to US Software Group', *Irish Times*, 26 June 2008

Irish Council for Science, Technology and Innovation, *Technology Foresight*, Dublin: ICSTI
     1999

Johnson, G., Scholes, K. and Willington, R., *Exploring Corporate Strategy*, Hemel
     Hempstead: Prentice Hall 2005

Jolly, N.K., *Commercialising New Technologies*, Boston, MA: Harvard Business School Press
     1997

Juran, J.M., *Introduction to Quality Control*, London: Chapman Hall 1989

Kanter, R., Stein, B. and Jick, T., *The Challenge of Organizational Change,* New York: Free
     Press 1992

Kaplan, R.S. and Norton, D.P., 'The Balanced Scorecard – Measures That Drive
     Performance', *Harvard Business Review*, January–February 1992

Kaplan, R.S. and Norton, D.P., *The Balanced Scorecard: Translating Strategy into Action*,
     Cambridge: Harvard Business Press 1996

Katz, D. and Kahn, R., *The Social Psychology of Organizations*, New York: Wiley 1978

Keane, R., *Company Law in the Republic of Ireland*, London: Butterworths 2000

Keegan, R., *An Introduction to World Class Manufacturing*, Dublin: Oak Tree Press 1997

Keegan, R. and Lynch, J., *World Class Manufacturing in an Irish Context*, Dublin: Oak Tree
     Press 1995

Keenan, Á., *Essentials of Irish Business Law,* Dublin: Gill & Macmillan 2008

Kennedy, T.M., Mac Cormac, M.J. and Teeling, J.J., *Financial Management*, Dublin: Gill & Macmillan 1995

Kenny, I., *Out on their Own: Conversations with Irish Entrepreneurs,* Dublin: Gill & Macmillan 1991

Kenny, I., *Freedom and Order: Studies in Strategic Leadership*, Dublin: Oak Tree Press 1999

Kerin, R.A., Mahajan, V. and Varadarajan, P.R., *Contemporary Perspectives on Strategic Planning*, Boston: Allyn & Bacon 1990

Kerr, A. (ed.), *Irish Employment Legislation*, Dublin: Round Hall 2000

Kim, W.C. and Mauborgne, R., *Blue Ocean Strategy,* Boston: Harvard Business School Publishing Corporation 2005

Kinsella, R., *Fast-Growth Small Firms: An Irish Perspective*, Dubin: IMI 1994

Kotler, P., *Marketing Management*: New Jersey: Prentice-Hall 2003

Kotler, P. and Armstrong, G., *Principles of Marketing*, New Jersey, Pearson Prentice Hall 2008

Kotler, P. and Keller, K.L., *Marketing Management,* New Jersey: Pearson Prentice Hall 2009

Kotter, J.P., *Leading Change*, Boston: Harvard Business School 1996

Kotter, J.P., 'What Leaders Really Do', *Harvard Business Review*, May–June 1990

Labour Court, *Guide to the Labour Court*, available online at www.labourcourt.ie

Labour Relations Commission, *Grievance and Disciplinary Procedures*, Dublin: LRC 2008

Lambing, P.A. and Kuehl, C.R., *Entrepreneurship*, New Jersey: Pearson Prentice Hall 2007

Lambkin, M. and Meenaghan, T. (eds), *Perspectives on Marketing in Ireland*, Dublin: Oak Tree Press 1994

Laurence, P. and Lorsch, J., *Organizations and Environment: Managing Differentiation and Integration,* Illinois: Irwin 1969

Leavy, B. and McKiernan, P., *Strategic Leadership, Governance and Renewal,* Basingstroke: Palgrave Macmillan 2009

Leavy, B. and Walsh, J.S. (eds), *Strategy and General Management: An Irish Reader*, Dublin: Oak Tree Press 1995

Levitt, T., 'Marketing Myopia', *Harvard Business Review*, September 1975

Likert, R., *New Patterns in Management*, New York: McGraw Hill 1961

Likert, R., *The Human Organization: Its Management and Values*, New York: McGraw Hill 1967

Lordan, M. and Cooney, T.M., 'Finding the Business Idea', in Cooney, T.M. and Hill, S., *New Venture Creation in Ireland*, Cork: Oak Tree Press 2002

Lovelock, C.H., *Services Marketing*, Englewood Cliffs, NJ: Prentice Hall 1999

Lucey, B., *Financial Management: An Introduction in the Irish Context*, Dublin: Folens 1996

Lucey, T., *Costing*, London: Cengage 2009

Lynch, J.J. and Roche, F.W., *Business Management in Ireland: Competitive Strategy for the 21st Century*, Dublin: Oak Tree Press 1995

Lynch, J.J. and Roche, F.W., *Understanding Business in Ireland,* Dublin: Purple Foot Publishing 1999

MacCormac, M., 'The Role of Boards of Directors and Board Practice', *Journal of Irish Business and Administrative Research*, Vol. 4, No. 1, 1982

MacDonnell, C. and McEvoy, B., *International Trade: Policy and Practice*, Dublin: Institute of International Trade of Ireland 2003

MacSharry, R., White, P.A. with O'Malley, J., *The Making of the Celtic Tiger*, Cork: Mercier Press 2000

Martyn, J. and Reck, P., *Taxation Summary*, Dublin: Irish Taxation Institute 2010

Maslow, A.H., *Motivation and Personality*, New York: Harper & Row 1954

Mayo, G.E., *The Social Problems of an Industrial Civilisation*, Boston: Harvard University Press 1945

McAteer, W., Reddin, G.and Deegan, G., *Income Tax*, Dublin: Irish Taxation Institute 2010

McCarthy, E.J., *Basic Marketing: A Managerial Approach*, Homewood, IL: Irwin 1978

McClelland, D.C., *The Achieving Society*, Princeton, NJ: Van Nostrand 1961

McClelland, D.C., 'Characteristics of Successful Entrepreneurs', *Journal of Creative Behavior,* Vol. 21, No. 3, 1987

McGarry, S. and Prendergast, G., *Franchising in Ireland*, Dublin: McGarry Consulting 1997

McGoey, I., *Marketing on the Internet: Winning Global Competitive Advantage*, Dublin: Oak Tree Press 1998

McGregor, D.V., *The Human Side of Enterprise*, New York: McGraw Hill 1960

FitzGerald, J. *et al.*, *Medium-Term Review 2008–2015,* Dublin: Economic and Social Research Institute 2008

Meenan, F., *Working within the Law: A Practical Guide for Employers and Employees*, Dublin: Oak Tree Press1999

Miles, R. and Snow, C., *Organizational Strategy, Structure and Process*, New York: McGraw-Hill 1978

Mintzberg, H., *The Nature of Managerial Work*, New York: Harper & Row 1973

Mitton, D.G., 'The Complete Entrepreneur', *Entrepreneurship Theory and Practices*, Vol. 9, No. 3, 1989

Morley, M.J. and Heraty, N. (eds), *Strategic Management in Ireland*, Dublin: Gill & Macmillan 2000

Morrison, A. (ed.), *Entrepreneurship: An International Perspective*, Oxford: Butterworth-Heinemann 1998

Murphy, E., *Business and Company Law for Irish Students,* Dublin: Gill & Macmillan 2004

Murphy, T.V. and Roche, W.K., *Irish Industrial Relations in Practice*, Dublin: Oak Tree Press 1994

Murray, J.A. and O'Driscoll, A., *Managing Marketing: Concepts and Irish Cases*, Dublin: Gill & Macmillan 1999

Murray, J.A. and O'Gorman, C., 'Growth Strategies for the Smaller Business', in Leavy, B. and Walsh, J.S., *Strategy and General Management: An Irish Reader,* Dublin: Oak Tree Press 1995

Naylor, J., *Management*, London: Financial Times Professional Ltd 2003

Nevin, D. (ed.), *Trade Union Century*, Cork: Mercier Press 1994

Nickerson, R.S., 'Enhancing Creativity', in Sternberg, R.J., *Handbook of Creativity*, Cambridge: CUP 1998

O'Connor, J. and Lyons, M., *Enterprise: The Irish Approach*, Dublin: IDA 1983

O'Farrell, P., *Entrepreneurship and Industrial Change*, Dublin: Irish Management Institute 1986

O'Gorman, C., 'The Sustainability of Growth in Small and Medium-Sized Enterprises', *International Journal of Entrepreneurial Behavior & Research,* Vol. 7, No. 2, 2001

O'Gorman, C. and Cunningham, J., *Enterprise in Action: An Introduction to Entrepreneurship in the Irish Context*, Cork: Oak Tree Press 2007

O'Hagan, J. and Newman, C. (eds), *The Economy of Ireland: National and Sectoral Policy Issues*, Dublin: Gill & Macmillan 2008

O'Halloran, M., *Irish Taxation Law and Practice*, Dublin: Irish Taxation Institute 2010

O'Kane, B., *Starting a Business in Ireland: A Comprehensive Guide and Directory*, Cork: Oak Tree Press 2004

O'Malley, E. and Van Egeraat, C., 'Post-Porter: Exploring Policy for the Irish Context', in *Sustaining Competitive Advantage*, Dublin: NESC 2000

Oakland, J.S., *Total Quality Management: The Route to Improving Performance*, London: Butterworth-Heinemann 1993

Office of the Director of Corporate Enforcement, *Information Books* 1–7, Dublin: ODCE n.d.

Ouchi, W., *Theory Z: How American Business Can Meet the Japanese Challenge,* Addison-Wesley 1981

Patents Office, *General Information Concerning Patents for Inventions*, Dublin: Patents Office 1998a

Patents Office, *General Information Concerning the Registration of Trade Marks*, Dublin: Patents Office 1998b

Patents Office, *The Patents Office Journal*, Dublin: Patents Office 2010

Peters, T., *Thriving on Chaos*, London: Pan Books 1987

Peters, T.J. and Austin, N., *A Passion for Excellence*, Glasgow: Fontana/Collins 1986

Peters, T.J. and Waterman, R., *In Search of Excellence*, New York: Harper & Row 1982

Pettigrew, A. and Whipp, R., *Managing Change for Competitive Success*, London: Blackwell 1991

Porter, M.E., *Competitive Strategy: Techniques for Analyzing Industries and Competitors*, New York: Free Press 1980

Porter, M.E., *Competitive Advantage: Creating and Sustaining Superior Performance*, New York: Free Press 1985

Porter, M.E., 'What Is Strategy?', *Harvard Business Review*, November–December 1996

Porter, M.E., 'Strategy and the Internet', *Harvard Business Review*, March 2001

Power, T. and Scully, E., *The Law and Practice of Irish Stamp Duties*, Dublin: Irish Taxation Institute 2010

Power, T., Walsh, S. and O'Meara, P., *Financial Management: An Irish Text,* Dublin: Gill & Macmillan 2005

Quinn, F., *Growing the Customer: How to Become Customer-Driven,* Dublin: O'Brien Press 2006

Revenue Commissioners, *A Guide to Personal Retirement Savings Accounts,* Dublin: Revenue Commissioners 2003

Revenue Commissioners, *PAYE/PRSI for Small Employers*, Dublin: Revenue Commissioners 2005

Revenue Commissioners, *Employers' Guide to PAYE*, Dublin: Revenue Commissioners 2010a

Revenue Commissioners, *Guide to Completing Pay and File Returns*, Dublin: Revenue Commissioners 2010b

Revenue Commissioners, *Starting in Business: A Revenue Guide*, Dublin: Revenue Commissioners 2010c

Revenue Commissioners, *VAT for Small Business: A Revenue Guide*, Dublin: Revenue Commissioners 2010d

Revenue Commissioners, *VAT Guide*, Dublin: Revenue Commissioners 2010e

Roberts, J., *The Modern Firm: Organisational Design for Performance and Growth*, Oxford: University Press 2004

Roche, W.K., Monks, K. and Walsh, J. *Human Resource Strategies*, Dublin: Oak Tree Press 1998

Rogan, D., *Marketing: An Introduction for Irish Students,* Dublin: Gill & Macmillan 2007

Rogers, E.M., *Diffusion of Innovations*, New York: Free Press 2003

Roper, S. and Hewitt-Dundas, N., *Business Innovation in Ireland: Lessons for Managers*, Cork: Oak Tree Press 1998

Ross, S., *The Bankers*, Dublin: Penguin Ireland 2010

Rotter, J.B., 'Generalized Expectations for Internal versus External Control of Reinforcement', *Psychological Monographs*, Vol. 80, No. 609, 1966

Ruddock, A., *Michael O'Leary: A Life in Full Flight*, Dublin: Penguin Ireland 2007

Russell, R. and Taylor, B., *Operations Management,* New Jersey: Wiley 2005

Sallis, E., *Total Quality Management in Education*, London: Kogan Page 1996

Sathe, V., *Corporate Entrepreneurship: Top Managers and New Business Creation*, Cambridge: CUP 2003

Schein, E.H., *Organizational Psychology*, Englewood Cliffs, NJ: Prentice Hall 1965

Schonberger, R.J., *World Class Manufacturing: The Lessons of Simplicity Applied*, New York: Free Press 1986

Schumpeter, J., *Capitalism, Socialism and Democracy,* New York: Harper & Row 1950

Slack, N., Chambers, S. and Johnson, R., *Operations Management,* Essex: Pearson Education Ltd 2004

Small Business Forum, *Small Business Is Big Business,* Dublin: Forfás 2006

Stevenson, W.J., *Operations Managements*, New York: McGraw Hill 2002

Storey, D.J., *Understanding the Small Business Sector*, London: Routledge 1994

Task Force on the Prevention of Workplace Bullying, *Dignity at Work – The Challenge of Workplace Bullying*, Dublin: Stationery Office 2001

Taylor, F.W., *The Principles of Scientific Management*, New York: Harper & Row 1911 and 1985

Telesis Consultancy Group, *A Review of Industrial Policy*, Report No. 64, Dublin: NESC 1982

Tiernan, S., Morley, M. and Foley, E., *Modern Management: Theory and Practice for Irish Students*, Dublin: Gill & Macmillan 2007

Timmons, J., *New Business Creation: Entrepreneurship for the 21st Century,* Boston: Irwin 1999

Turner, T. and Morley, M., *Industrial Relations and the New Order*, Dublin: Oak Tree Press 1995

Vesper, K., *New Venture Strategies*, Englewood Cliffs, NJ: Prentice Hall 1995

Von Stamm, B., *Managing Innovation, Design and Creativity*, Chichester: John Wiley & Sons 2008

Vroom, V.H., *Work and Motivation*, New York: Wiley 1964

Ward, J.J., 'Marketing Myopia in Industrial Development', *Irish Marketing Review*, Vol. 2, 1987

Weber, M., *Theory of Social and Economic Organizations*, New York: Free Press 1947

Whitaker, T.K., *Economic Development*, Dublin: Stationery Office 1958

Wickham, P.A., *Strategic Entrepreneurship*, London: Financial Times Pitman Publishing 1998

Wild, R., *Production and Operations Management,* London: Continuum 2002

Wilson, P. and Bates, S., *The Essential Guide to Managing Small Business Growth,* Chichester: Wiley 2003

Winkler, J., *Pricing for Results*, Dublin: Irish Management Institute 1983

Wood, F. and Robinson, T., *Business Accounting: Irish Edition*, London: Pitman Publishing 1999

Wood, F. and Sangster, A., *Business Accounting,* Essex: Prentice Hall 2007

Woodward, J., *Industrial Organisation: Theory and Practice*, London: Oxford University Press 1965

Zimmerer, T.W. and Scarborough, N.H., *Essentials of Entrepreneurship and Small Business Management,* Upper Saddle River, NJ: Prentice Hall 2002

Note: Students should refer to the latest edition for all taxation publications. These are updated every year.

References: Legislation

Bills of Exchange Act 1882

Companies Act 1963–2009

Companies (Amendment) Acts 1977, 1982, 1983, 1986, 1990, 1999 and No. 2 Act 1999

Companies (Auditing and Accounting) Act 2003

Company Law Enforcement Act 2001

Consumer Credit Act 1995

Copyright and Related Rights Act 2000

Copyright and Related Rights (Amendment) Act 2007

Employment law (see Chapter 8)

European Communities (Companies) Regulations 1973, 1992, 1993, 1994

European Communities (Single-Member Private Limited Companies) Regulations 1994
    (SI 275 of 1994)

Industrial and Provident Societies Acts 1893–2005

Industrial Designs Act 2001

Industrial Relations Act 1990 (Codes of Practice on Access to Part-time Working)
    Declaration Order

Limited Partnership Act 1907 (as amended)

Partnership Act 1890

Patents Act 1992

Registration of Business Names Act 1963 (with relevant orders and regulations)

Stock Transfer Act 1963

Trade Marks Act 1996

References: Websites

Business Access to State Information and Services	www.basis.ie
Business Angel Partnership	www.businessangels.ie
Central Statistics Office	www.cso.ie/statistics
Chambers of Commerce	www.chambers.ie
Companies Registration Office	www.cro.ie
Custom Research	www.comscore.com
D&B	www.dnb.com
Department of Enterprise, Trade and Innovation	www.entemp.ie
Department of Social and Family Affairs	www.welfare.ie
Director of Corporate Enforcement	www.odce.ie
Employment Appeals Tribunal	www.tribunal.ie
Enterprise Boards	www.enterpriseboards.ie
Enterprise Ireland	www.enterprise-ireland.com
Entrepreneur	www.entrepreneur.com
Equality Authority	www.equality.ie
Equality Tribunal	www.equalitytribunal.ie
EU Public Procurement	http://simap.en.int
Excellence Ireland	www.excellence-ireland.ie
Forfás	www.forfas.ie
Google	www.google.com
Health and Safety Authority	www.hse.ie
Irish Business and Employers Confederation	www.ibec.ie
Irish Congress of Trade Unions	www.ictu.ie
Irish Exports Association	www.irishexporters.ie
Irish Government	www.irgov.ie
Irish Stock Exchange	www.ise.ie
Irish Taxation Institute	www.taxireland.ie
Irish Venture Capital Association	www.ivca.ie
Labour Court	www.labourcourt.ie
Labour Relations Commission	www.lrc.ie
Marketing Institute of Ireland	www.mii.ie

Maternity Benefit Section, Department of Social and Family Affairs	www.maternityben@welfare.ie
MRS	www.marketresearch.org.uk
National Consumer Agency	www.nationalconsumeragency.org
National Disability Authority	www.nda.ie
National Employment Rights Authority	www.employmentrights.ie
National Institute for Transport and Logstics	www.nitl.ie
National Public Procurement	www.etenders.gov.ie
National Standards Authority of Ireland	www.nsai.ie
Nifty Business Ideas	www.niftybusinessideas.com
Office of the Director of Corporate Enforcement	www.odce.ie
Office of the Director of Equality Investigations	www.odei.ie
Patents Office	www.patentsoffice.ie
Pensions Board	www.pensionsboard.ie
Plato Ireland Ltd	www.plato.ie
Proposed National Pensions Framework	www.pensionsgreenpaper.ie
Public Procurement Guidelines	www.etenders.gov.ie
Revenue	www.revenue.ie
Rights Comissioners	www.lrc.ie
Sample business plans	www.bplans.com
Small Business Can	www.smallbusinesscan.com
Starting a Business in Ireland	www.starting a business in Ireland.com
Surveys Online	www.surveys-online.com

Index